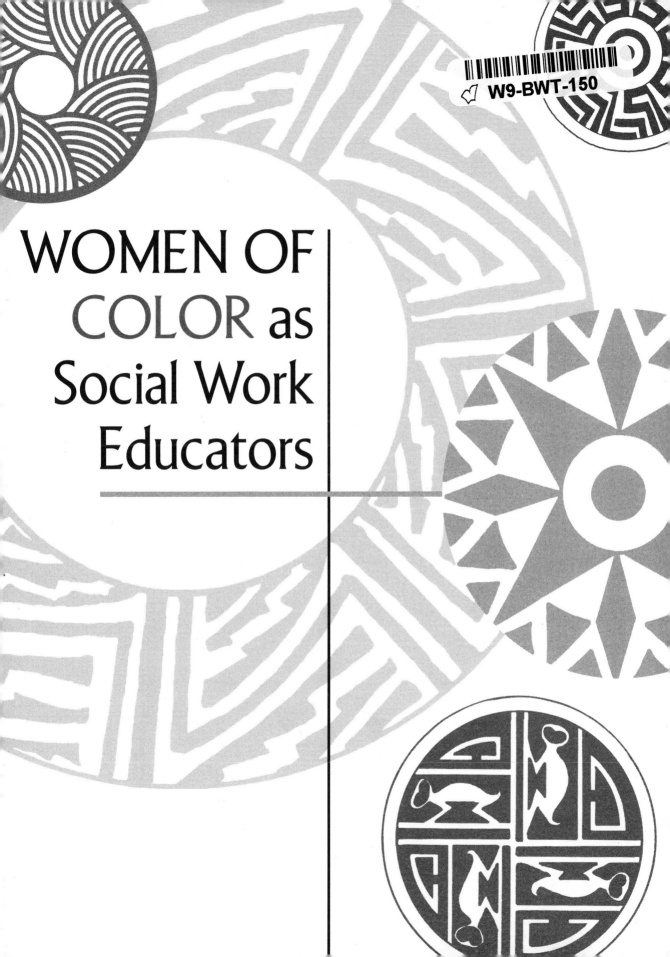

WOMEN OF COLOR as Social Work Educators

WOMEN OF COLOR as Social Work Educators

Strengths and Survival

EDITED BY

Halaevalu F. Ofahengaue Vakalahi

Saundra Hardin Starks

Carmen Ortiz Hendricks

COUNCIL ON
SOCIAL WORK EDUCATION

Alexandria, Virginia

LIBRARY OF CONGRESS CATALOGUING-IN-PUBLICATION DATA

Library of Congress Cataloging-in-Publication Data

Women of color as social work educators : strengths and survival / edited by Halaevalu F. Ofahengaue Vakalahi, Saundra Hardin Starks, Carmen Ortiz Hendricks.

      p. cm.

  Includes bibliographical references and index.

  ISBN 978-0-87293-125-1 (alk. paper)

  1. Social work education--United States. 2. Women social workers-- United States. 3. Minority women educators--United States. 4. African American women college teachers. I. Vakalahi, Halaevalu F. Ofahengaue. II. Starks, Saundra Hardin. III. Hendricks, Carmen Ortiz. IV. Title.

  HV11.7.W66 2006

  361.3092'396073--dc22

2006025319

Printed in the United States of America on acid-free paper that meets the American National Standards Institute Z39-48 Standard.

COUNCIL ON SOCIAL WORK EDUCATION, INC.
1725 Duke Street, Suite 500
Alexandria, VA 22314-3457
www.cswe.org

Contents

HALAEVALU F. OFAHENGAUE VAKALAHI is an associate professor and director of the MSW program at George Mason University, Fairfax, Virginia. Her areas of teaching interests include social policy, human behavior and the social work environment, macro-level practice, and cultural diversity. Her research interests include juvenile delinquency, adolescent substance use and abuse, women's issues, and Pacific Islander communities.

SAUNDRA HARDIN STARKS is an associate professor in the Department of Social Work, Western Kentucky University, Bowling Green, Kentucky. Her teaching interests include social work practice and multicultural diversity. Her research interests include women's issues, spirituality, and cultural diversity.

CARMEN ORTIZ HENDRICKS is associate dean and professor at Yeshiva University Wurzweiler School of Social Work. She was formerly on the faculty of Hunter College School of Social Work-City University of New York. Her areas of teaching and research encompass culturally competent social work practice and education, including field education, working with Latino communities, and culturally competent approaches to child welfare practice.

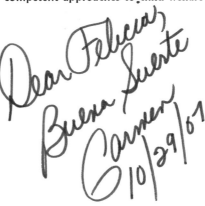

Women of Color as Social Work Educators

About the Authors

AFRICAN AMERICAN AUTHORS

 M. JENISE COMER is a professor of social work at the University of Central Missouri.

 ANITA CURRY-JACKSON is an associate professor of social work and dean of Wright State University–Lake Campus.

 RUBY M. GOURDINE is an associate professor and director of field education at Howard University, School of Social Work.

 DARLENE GRANT is an associate professor of social work and associate dean of graduate studies at the University of Texas, Austin.

 SAUNDRA HARDIN STARKS is an associate professor of social work at Western Kentucky University.

 ANDREA STEWART is a professor of social work and director of the baccalaureate social work program at the University of Arkansas at Pine Bluff (UAPB).

 DIANNE RUSH WOODS is an assistant professor of social work at California State University–East Bay.

ASIAN AMERICAN AUTHORS

 PAULA TOKI TANEMURA MORELLI is an associate professor and chair of the Mental Health Concentration at the University of Hawai`i, School of Social Work.

 RITA TAKAHASHI is a professor of social work at San Francisco State University and director of the Institute for Multicultural Research and Social Work Practice.

LATINA/HISPANIC AMERICAN AUTHORS

 BARBARA A. CANDALES is an associate professor of social work at Central Connecticut State University.

 DEBORA M. ORTEGA is an associate professor at the University of Denver, Graduate School of Social Work.

 CORINA D SEGOVIA-TADEHARA is an assistant professor in the Social Work and Gerontology Department at Weber State University in Ogden, Utah.

NATIVE AMERICAN, AMERICAN INDIAN, AND FIRST NATIONS AUTHORS

ADA E. DEER is a distinguished lecturer of social work and director of the American Indian Studies Program at the University of Wisconsin–Madison.

CHRISTINE LOWERY is an associate professor of social work at the University of Wisconsin–Milwaukee.

HILARY N. WEAVER (Lakota) is an associate professor of social work at the State University of New York, Buffalo.

PACIFIC ISLANDER AUTHORS

HALAEVALU F. OFAHENGAUE VAK-ALAHI is an associate professor and director of the MSW program at George Mason University, Fairfax, Virginia.

DEBBIE HIPPOLITE WRIGHT is a professor of social work and former director of the Department of Social Work at BYU–Hawaii.

SUPPORTIVE AUTHORS

SUZIE CASHWELL is an assistant professor and director of the master's social work program at Western Kentucky University.

DIANA M. DINITTO is a professor of social work at the University of Texas at Austin.

KATHLEEN KIRBY is an associate professor of educational and counseling psychology (emeritus) at the University of Louisville, Kentucky.

CLIFFORD MAYES is an associate professor of education at Brigham Young University–Provo, Utah.

Foreword

Wilma Peebles-Wilkins

In 1925, African American social worker Elise Johnson McDougald described the "double task" associated with the struggle for gender and race emancipation among women of color in the workforce in New York City. She described the working woman of color as follows:

> Through it all, she is courageously standing erect, developing within herself the moral strength to rise above and conquer false attitudes. She is maintaining her natural beauty and charm and improving her mind and opportunity. She is measuring up to the needs

and demands of her family, community and race, and radiating from Harlem a hope that is cherished by her sisters in less propitious circumstances throughout the land. The wind of the race's destiny stirs more briskly because of her striving. (McDougald, 1925, p. 691)

The five groups of exemplars—African American or Black, Asian American, Latina or Hispanic American, Native American, American Indian or First Nations, and Pacific Islander—highlighted in this book on women of color as social work educators have emulated McDougald's poignant turn-of-the-20th-century vision. Halaevalu F. Ofahengaue Vakalahi, Saundra Hardin Starks, and Carmen Ortiz Hendricks have done a masterful job of bringing together the voices of women of color in mainstream social-work educational settings or those social work programs in predominantly White European American institutions of higher learning.

The voices of women of color are heard through "talking stories" that speak to the strengths of those women who have survived and excelled in spite of oppression and discrimination and of women who have excelled in the face of exclusion and lack of acknowledgement—in the face of attempts designed to cause failure. As McDougald so aptly stated 80 years ago, all women of color in social work education are measuring up to the needs and demands of their lives in academia and beyond. Women of color have a double task, complicated by gender dynamics, in their struggle to succeed and contribute in academia. Often, women of color face racial discrimination from White European American women and men and gender discrimination from White European American

men, as well as men of color. This book successfully captures this unique experience by presenting and analyzing the narratives of women of color as social work educators as they relate their strengths, ambitions, and survival.

This book is grounded in feminist theory, the ecological perspective, and the values of the social work profession, which calls attention to academia as a microcosm of the larger society: a microcosm in which oppressive attitudes and societal discrimination are re-enacted—indeed, re-enacted within the broader academic institution and within social work programs, as well as among social work faculty. This reenactment of social inequities is complicated by what Bowser, Auletta, and Jones (1993) have labeled in their classic description as the "unwritten organization." That is, academia comprises cultural practices and barriers that pay lip service to or create the illusion of fair play while sustaining practices that support "White privilege." Both gender and race shape the experience of women of color in academia, an organizational culture guided by unstated and unwritten rules and practices. Analysis of the themes from these narratives of women of color provides an opportunity to alter the "unwritten organization" by informing common academic practices and providing what Bowser, et al. (1993) define as "models of success."

The "talking stories" provide a model for unity, helping women of color reduce their social isolation and understand the need to be connected with one another. It is a model for risk-taking to improve successful outcomes. These stories also sensitize others to the experiences of women of color in institutions of higher learning. The stories have the potential to help reshape the world views of academicians, alter the lens through which women of color are viewed, and more fairly represent women of color in social work education.

This book expands on the Ford Foundation-funded work done in the 1980s by Dr. Yolanda Moses on Black or African American women in the academy by adding all five groups of women of color—African American or Black, Asian American, Latina or Hispanic American, Native American, American Indian or First Nations, and Pacific Islander. This work further broadens understanding of the range of experiences that promotes or thwarts successful experiences for all women of color in academia. In so doing, these authors are helping to formulate a "written" as opposed to an "unwritten" organization and to build a language for communicating about race and gender in the academy.

REFERENCES

Bowser, B. P., Auletta, G .S., & Jones, T. (1993). *Confronting diversity issues on campus.* Newbury Park, CA: Sage Publications.

McDougald, E. J. (1925, March). The double task: The struggle of Negro women for sex and race emancipation. *Survey Graphic, 6,* 689–691.

Women of Color as Social Work Educators

Introduction

This work is inspired by pioneering women of color who have paved the way and established a movement in academia and social work education for present and future generations of women of color. The responsibility to keep the movement alive lies with each woman of color who is a social work educator or who aspires to be one. Furthermore, this work is grounded in the mission and standards of the profession of social work, which iterate respect and appreciation for and knowledge of human diversity in its most inclusive form (CSWE, 2001; NASW, 1999). Such a phenomenon of respect and appreciation for and knowledge of human diversity presents a remarkable opportunity for innovations and persevering advocacy in social work education. It also presents extraordinary opportunities for self-assessment and, perhaps, redirection of personal and professional ambitions, thus contributing to the formation of responsive and effective academic systems.

This edited book represents the first stage of a lifelong commitment to examining the unique experiences of women of color who are social work educators in predominantly White European American systems and institutions. This book focuses on the challenges, struggles, and barriers, as well as the strengths, ambitions, strategies, and successes, of women of color in acquiring opportunities comparable to their White European American female and male counterparts in social work education. It also advocates for and effects positive changes in academia that will benefit upcoming generations of women of color as social work educators. The authors recognize the political implications of this work, but, perhaps more importantly, they understand that one of the core principles of the social work profession is advocacy for change and improvements in systems and personal lives. Such advocacy often requires taking necessary risks.

During the course of this work, in the fall of 2005, the "mother of the Civil Rights movement," Rosa Parks, passed away, leaving a legacy of greatness for all women of color to live by and pass on to succeeding generations. Rosa Parks was a small woman physically, but she projected power and greatness that was felt by the tallest and strongest

person on earth. She is truly a reason that we are able (or allowed) to do this important work of giving voice to the experiences of women of color as social work educators. We are hopeful that the audience for this book will include women from all walks of life, who believe in social justice and elimination of oppression, individuals and groups in the academy such as academicians and students, as well as communities and other systems and institutions external to academia.

PURPOSE OF THIS WORK

The purposes of writing this book are to: (1) bring to life the voices of women of color who are educators and thus contribute to the betterment of social work education; (2) honor these scholar change agents and recognize their strengths and survival as pioneers in a system that has historically been oppressive and discriminatory; (3) enlighten and inspire all educators to work toward collective equality and justice; (4) create opportunities for self-assessment and a spirit of support among those women educators whose voices are heard in this book, those whose voices are yet to be heard, and those leading and managing educational systems and institutions; (5) expand the existing literature on the experiences of women of color who are educators in social work programs and academia in general, contribute to the literature on diversity by ethnicity or race and gender and multicultural and cross-cultural content; therefore informing future research in this area, policy changes in the academy, and strategies for providing proper mentoring and supports; and (6) accentuate and examine the validity of culturally based alternative pedagogical paradigms that has been historically devalued and suppressed in the academy. In other words, the authors hope that the voices within the covers of this book inspire self-assessment and advocacy for change in both the person and surrounding systems.

RATIONALE FOR THIS WORK

The idea for this book grew out of "talking stories" and sharing experiences in educational systems and institutions and people within them among the three coeditors of this book who are women social work educators (one Pacific Islander, one African American, and one of Hispanic American cultural background). Although these women live in three different parts of the nation and come from three different cultural backgrounds, the similarities in and intensity of their stories warrant further examination and comparison. A sense of obligation to advocate for changes in the system, changes that are ethnically, racially, and gender-friendly, grew out of the many hours of interaction among these three women. The "talking stories" time provided opportunities for self-reflection, re-energizing, and reassurance of the responsibilities of these three women to their respective communities of color, educational systems and institutions, and beyond.

The support and encouragement of colleagues were particularly important. The editors wish to thank their colleagues at the universities and CSWE for their endless support, enthusiasm, and belief in the significance of this work. The editors wish to thank Dr. Rowena Fong, in particular, and many other women of color for their guidance, direction, and connection to people and resources necessary to produce this book.

As indicated earlier, this book seeks to help keep the movement of women of color in social work education alive through advocating for social justice by bringing women of color to the forefront of discussion, resolution, and visibility; contributing to communities of color and the educational community; and providing a "connection" for women of color with similar and different experiences in the academy. In addition to filling gaps in the existing literature and emphasizing culturally based paradigms, the authors hope to assist in dispelling myths, misunderstandings, misconceptions, and misrepresentation of the phenomenon of women of color in the academy.

CONCEPTUAL FRAMEWORK

In this book, the experiences of women of color as social work educators are conceptualized by incorporating two major theoretical frameworks, systems or ecological theory and feminist theory, and the core values of the profession of social work as identified in the NASW Code of Ethics. Systems or ecological theory suggests that an interdependent and reciprocal relationship exists between systems (i.e., family, peers) and a person. DiNitto, Martin, and Harrison (1982) further propose that academic systems are social contexts in which societal inequities are reproduced and reinforced, which is particularly reflective of the experiences of women of color in social work education. Furthermore, embedded in the feminist movement, feminist theory advocates for equality among men and women and recognizes patriarchy as the root of women's oppression. In strengthening the relevance of feminist theory to women of color, scholars such as bell hooks (1981, 1989) propose that "To be 'feminist' in any authentic sense of the term is to want for all people, female and male, liberation from sexist role patterns, domination, and oppression" (1981, p. 195). Moreover, advocating for the core values of social work, which include service, social justice, dignity and worth of the person, importance of human relationships, integrity, and competency (NASW, 1999), is the aspiration of the women of color whose voices are heard in this book.

Subsequently, the experiences of women of color as social work educators are discussed from a cross-cultural alternative paradigm—critical, feminist, social, and spiritual perspectives. The authors wish to focus readers' attention on the underlying issues of strengths, survival, ambitions, and successes, as well as institutional racism, oppression, exploitation, and gender discrimination and the personal and professional consequences of such experiences for women of color who are social work educators.

RELEVANT TERMS AND CONCEPTS

Although often not considered by many academic institutions, the identities of women of color are complex and multicultural in relation to race and ethnicity, gender, class, sexual orientation, spirituality, and other factors. Therefore, caution must be exercised in the use or nonuse of certain terms and concepts. The authors refrain from using the term minority as a category because of its link to a deficit model, which is contrary to the deeply embraced strengths perspective of women of color. Nonetheless, this term speaks to the reality that ethnic minorities are

often numerically the majority; however, they remain a minority in positions of power. Throughout this book, the authors will refer to *faculty* or *students of color* as a broad inclusive term.

For style purposes, authors in this book are categorized into five major racial/ethnic groups: *African American* or *Black*; *Asian American*; *Hispanic American* or *Latina*; *Native American, American Indian*, or *First Nations*; and *Pacific Islander*. Women in these groups prefer to be identified by their particular cultures, nations, and national origins. The term *White European American* is used to identify individuals who do not belong to any of the five ethnic and racial groups identified above. The authors recognize the possibility of misidentification, but hope that these terms are sufficiently inclusive to deliver the message of multiculturalism with unity and equity.

METHODOLOGY

The authors recognize the authenticity of allowing the stories of these women educators to be heard in their own voices. Thus, their challenges, strengths, and survival as social work educators are told in their own voices. These voices, in turn, are analyzed for themes and patterns that inform research, policy, and practice in the academy. A selected group of women of color who are social work educators— new, mid career, and seasoned, from different cultural backgrounds and academic settings, but predominantly White European American institutions—are highlighted in this book. The authors provide demographic data on the number of women of color in each level of academic rank, as well as administrators and tenured and untenured faculty who participated in this work.

Research Questions

The research questions guiding this book include: What are the experiences of women of color in social work education? What personal, social, cultural, and systemic-based factors contribute to success or failure among women of color in academia and social work education? (See Appendix: Guiding Questions.

Research Design

Because little has been written about women of color as social work educators, an exploratory research method is essential to examine the experiences of these women in the academy and, particularly, in social work education. Grounded theory, a qualitative research method, is used as the interpretive paradigm for constructing theories about the experiences of women of color as social work educators (Denzin & Lincoln, 1994). As Becker (1993) suggests, the focus is on developing "an account of a phenomenon that identifies the major constructs and categories, their relationships, and the context and process" (p. 254). The inductive nature of grounded theory provides systematic procedures for constructing theories that are grounded in data (Strauss & Corbin, 1990). Such systematic procedures posit that the accuracy of theories about the experiences of women of color as social work educators is inherently related to the process by which it is generated (Glaser & Strauss, 1967). Thus, there is a reciprocal relationship among data collection, data analysis, and theory construction (Godinet, 1998).

Participants

Due to limited knowledge regarding parameter estimates of women of color as social work educators and the sensitive nature of their experiences that is attached to personal reflections of professional self, a networking nonprobability sampling method was used to recruit a convenient sample of participants for the study (Hagan, 1997). The limitation of nonprobability type sampling is the potential for the sample not to be representative of the larger population, thus limiting generalizability of the findings to only the population studied. Although generalizability is a limitation, this study may be replicated in the future to test for consistency and reliability within the larger social work professional and educational community (Godinet, 1998).

Over 40 women of color in social work education across the country were recruited to participate in this work. The contributions of 28 participants are included in this book. The realities of being overworked, devalued, underpaid, having overwhelming family demands, and the political implications of the issues discussed in this book may have influenced the number of participants. Women of color in this book range in age from late 30s to late 60s, with a majority in their 50s. A majority of the women of color who participated in this work are African Americans, which is consistent with their numerical proportion in social work education. Four White European American individuals also collaborated with women of color in writing several of the chapters in this book. The women of color are teaching in universities or employed in states, including Hawaii, California, Nevada, Utah,

Colorado, Missouri, Arkansas, Texas, Kentucky, Wisconsin, Michigan, Ohio, Virginia, Washington, DC, New York, Massachusetts, and Connecticut. Two women of color are teaching in historically Black colleges or universities (BCU). The majority of the women of color have been in academia and social work education between eight and 14 years or more than 22 years. These women are predominantly associate professors and professors with tenure except for two tenure track assistant professors and one tenure track associate professor. There are also four program directors, four deans, two associate deans, and one woman who is working at CSWE. These women currently teach across the BSW, MSW, and PhD programs, but predominantly in combined social work programs (BSW/MSW or MSW/PhD).

Data Collection

Primary data on the women of color were collected through individual reflections and interviews using an interview-guide approach. Each woman of color was asked to submit a chapter of individual reflections using an author's guide or to complete an interview survey. The data collected for this book include 17 chapters of individual reflections and seven interview surveys. (See Appendix for complete list of questions).

Data Analysis

According to Denzin and Lincoln (1994), triangulation of data analysis methods contributes to rigor. As such, specific aspects of several data analysis methods, including inductive analysis, content analysis, and case and cross case analysis, were used as a triangulated way of making sense of the data. Based on immersion in the data and multiple readings over time, the three coeditors identified main themes and categories from the data.

REFERENCES

Becker, P. H. (1993). Common pitfalls in published grounded theory research. *Qualitative Health Research, 3*, 254–260.

Council on Social Work Education. (2001). *Handbook of accreditation standards and procedures*. Alexandria, VA: Author.

Denzin, N. K., & Lincoln, Y. S. (Eds.). (1994). *Handbook of qualitative research*. Thousand Oaks, CA: Sage Publications.

DiNitto, D., Martin, P. Y., & Harrison, D. F. (1982). Sexual discrimination in higher education. *Higher Education Review, 14*(2), 33–54.

Glaser, B. G., & Strauss, A. L. (1967). *The discovery of grounded theory: Strategies for qualitative research*. Chicago: Aldine.

Godinet, M. T. (1998). *Exploring a theoretical model of delinquency with Samoan adolescents*. Unpublished doctoral dissertation, University of Washington, Seattle.

Hagan, J. (1997). Crime and capitalization. Toward a developmental theory of street crime in America. In T. P. Thornberry (Ed.), *Developmental theories of crime and delinquency* (pp. 287–308). New Brunswick, NJ: Transaction.

hooks, b. (1981). *Ain't I a woman: Black women and feminism*. Boston: South End Press.

hooks, b. (1989). *Talking back: Thinking feminist, thinking Black*. Boston: South End Press.

National Association of Social Workers. (1999). *Code of ethics*. Washington, DC: Author.

Strauss, A. L., & Corbin, J. (1990). *Basics of qualitative research: Grounded theory procedures and techniques*. Newbury Park, CA: Sage.

Part I: A Historical Perspective

Chapter 1: Women in Society

Darlene Grant

Diana M. DiNitto

Halaevalu F. Ofahengaue Vakalahi

History, despite its wrenching pain, cannot be unlived, however, if faced with courage, need not be lived again.

—Maya Angelou

This book honors the strengths, ambitions, and successes of women of color who are social work educators. In that context, it also addresses institutional racism, oppression, exploitation, gender discrimination, and the personal and professional consequences of such experiences as women of color strive to survive and flourish in the academy. Women of color have long been portrayed in academic and popular literature as "double minorities"or in "double jeopardy"given their gender and ethnicity or race (e.g., Gonzales, Blanton, & Williams, 2002; Gregory, 2003; McKay, 1983; Petrie & Roman, 2004;

Walls, 2004). Indeed, gender and ethnicity or race are driving forces in one's life; however, this characterization as a "double" minority has become stale–overused and somewhat simplistic. Women in academia and society in general see themselves as more than the sum of gender and ethnicity or race. Social class, culture, sexual orientation, personality characteristics, and a host of factors yet to be identified may play important roles in the decision of women of color to pursue an academic career in social work or other disciplines, as well as to pursue different life options. But characteristics that cast an individual as different from the majority may be used to exclude that person rather than to enrich the environment.

Women of color have also been referred to as "multiply marginalized" (Turner, 2002). Certainly, a variety of factors serve as barriers to the success of women of color in the academy and other job sectors, especially given that success is generally defined in terms of the White European American male majority. However, for social workers, an emphasis on marginalities is reminiscent of the deficit perspective rather than of the strengths perspective in social work practice (Saleebey, 1992). Many faculty members who are women of color have thought themselves unlikely candidates for a career in the academy, yet there was some experience—perhaps a defining moment—when life in the academy became a viable career choice. The stories of women of color portrayed in this book reveal myriad paths and complexities that present challenges for practice, research, advocacy, and policy as the profession works to increase the number of women of color who successfully pursue careers in the academic environment of social work. Most of all, this book celebrates the strengths, ambitions, and successes of women of color who have chosen a career in social work education.

CONCEPTUAL FRAMEWORK

Every individual attempts to make sense of her or his own world. Academicians have been taught to view the world systematically or at least to attempt to do so in terms of theories or explanations of phenomenon. In the "hard"as well as the social sciences, there are often competing theories or multiple explanations for the same event, behavior, or phenomenon. Various explanations have been proffered about why individuals choose an academic career and why they succeed or fail in this pursuit (Alfred, 2001). Often these explanations are unsatisfying, especially when women of color are the ones whose behavior is being explained and those engaged in explaining know little about the realities of women of color.

In alignment with the tradition of *social* work, this book is framed by systems or ecological theory. It is also framed by feminist theories embedded in the feminist movement that helped to shape the lives of many women in the academy and other places of power or prominence in society. Women of color who are social work educators may find systems theory and feminist theories only partially relevant to their life stories. We look to the stories presented later in this book for additional explanations that define the current generations of women of color who are social work educators.

Systems or Ecological Theory

For social workers, perhaps no metatheory or metaframework has been applied more often than general systems theory (also known as systems theory) (see Boulding, 1985; Franklin, DiNitto, & McNeece, 1997; Martin & O'Connor, 1989) or its social work adaptation, known as ecological systems theory, ecological theory, or the life model of social work practice (Germain, 1979; Germain & Gitterman, 1980). From this perspective, all subsystems that form the system of interest are of concern. Given the focus of this book, this includes the individual woman and all her personal attributes (e.g., race, ethnicity, class, sexual orientation, etc.), family of origin, current family as she has created or construes it, social community, work environment, and the broader environments in which her personal and work communities exist. Systems theory also views micro, mezzo, and macro systems as interdependent. The effects of the system levels are reciprocal. Thus, a woman's family and the educational institutions that shape her worldview may have directly fostered and encouraged a desire for a career in academia. Or pursuing a career in academia may have occurred indirectly based on a message that such a career was not a viable option for a woman of color, thus presenting a challenge or obstacle to overcome.

With regard to reciprocal influences of subsystems, we concur with DiNitto, Martin, and Harrison (1982) that colleges and universities are microcosms of society and are generally no better or worse with respect to the treatment of women, people of color, and other disenfranchised groups than most other social institutions. Universities are social contexts in which societal inequities are reproduced and reinforced. With all the references to universities as bastions of progressivism and of liberal professors who populate the academy, colleges are no less sexist, racist, classist, and homophobic than the rest of society (see also Agathangelou & Ling, 2002). Until women, members of historically disenfranchised racial and ethnic groups, and those of different socioeconomic classes and sexual orientations are better represented in national, state, and local elected positions, change in the academy will be slow in coming (DiNitto, Martin, & Harrison, 1982; Newland, 1975; Staudt, 1980). From a systems perspective, the academy can be a preparatory mechanism for women of color to vie for positions that will challenge the status quo in academia and social, economic, and political sectors.

Well-meaning faculty and administrators at all levels in predominantly White European American colleges and universities cannot imagine that they are not doing everything in their power to remedy inequities based on gender, race, or ethnicity (Valian, 2004). Thus, they are genuinely surprised when their efforts to recruit a diverse student body and a diverse faculty do not achieve their expectations or, rather, the expectations of colleagues and students from underrepresented groups who continue to raise charges of gender inequity and structural racism. When a promising African American woman candidate takes a job at less prestigious university B, faculty at more prestigious university A are likely to say, "She was afraid she wouldn't make it here," rather than ask why she did not see their institution as a better option. An American Indian woman senses that her research agenda would not be appreciated, thus she takes a job in an activist organization to help her people rather than in academia. The university's reaction is, "Well, we tried to recruit her," rather than, "What can we do to make this environment more attractive to members of one of the most underrepresented racial groups in academia?" The academy must illustrate to women of color that academia provides a powerful base from which to operate. Just as faculty members encourage students to "think outside the box" to solve problems, the academy must also think more creatively to recruit and retain faculty women of color. Faculties that are more diverse will do a much better job of solving the health, economic, social, and other problems of our times.

The social work profession also struggles with gender, race or ethnicity, class, sexual orientation, disability, and other issues that affect social identity as well as social participation and status. The National Association of Social Workers (NASW) and the Council on Social Work Education (CSWE) have bodies designated to address most of these issues. A 2005 initiative to abolish seats on the CSWE board specifically for members of designated ethnic or racial groups met with grave concern and spirited debate before it was approved in favor of an alternative structure for obtaining diverse representation on the board of directors and other entities of CSWE.

Feminist Theory

For social workers, systems theory complements the profession's biopsychosocial and spiritual approach to solving problems of individuals, families, groups, communities, and other social systems. Systems theory provides a way to at least describe the reciprocal influences of "person in environment." But we can call on more specific theories that are consonant with systems theory to describe and explain the situations of women of color in society. Among them is an array of feminist theories (see Saulnier, 1996). Succinctly defined, feminism is the belief in equality for men and women. Feminist theory views the sources of women's oppression as rooted in patriarchy. This definition identifies gender, but neglects to acknowledge ethnicity, race, culture, sexual orientation, class, and other factors relevant to the experiences of women of color.

The feminist movement has primarily been credited with benefiting White European American women, whose reform efforts focused on gaining social equality within mainstream patriarchy (hooks, 2000). In the academy, for instance, the greatest gains in professorial positions as a result of affirmative action have occurred for White European American women (for a discussion of this, see, for example, hooks, 2003). Feminism has been criticized for its lack of relevance to women of color, but scholars such as bell hooks (1981, 1989) see feminism as inextricably linked with race or ethnicity and culture. Others have distinguished White feminism from Black feminism or rejected White European American women's feminism using a womanist perspective of Black or African American women (Hamlet, 2000; Mikell, 1995; Walker, 1983). The privilege that affluent White European American women hold may lead to a different view of feminism from that of Black or African American women and women of other racial, ethnic, cultural, and class groups. White European American women must protect their own status and may fear diluting the gains that have been made by the women's movement when issues of gender are crossed with those of race or ethnicity. Relationships between White European American women and Black or African American women and other women of color have often been tenuous since, even today, women of color often find themselves in the employ of White European American women and subservient to them (see, for example, Giddings, 1984). Thus, it is not difficult to see why White European American women's brand of feminism may not "fit"or settle well with women of color.

In this book, the term feminism is used according to hooks (1981): "To be 'feminist' in any authentic sense of the term is to want for all people, female and male, liberation from sexist role patterns, domination, and oppression"(p. 195). Even if racism were wiped from the face of social institutions, sexism would remain, including sexism against women of color. Audre Lorde (e.g, 1984) and Gloria Anzaldúa and her colleagues (e.g., Anzaldúa & Keating, 2002; Moraga & Anzaldúa, 1983) emphasize appreciation of diversity and encourage unions to address sexism, racism, classism, and other divisions in society. Older feminists often cringe upon hearing younger women challenge the call to feminism because some younger women claim never to have been subject to gender discrimination. On the other hand, there are groups of young women today who are ardent feminists. Hill (2002) credits the third (current) wave of feminism born in the 1980s and 1990s and composed of Generation X feminists with being much more "inclusive of all races, religions, colors, sexual orientations, and genders" (p. 259).

Whether you are female or male, whether you think of yourself as a feminist or not, and even if you abhor the term feminist, the authors ask you to consider hooks's definition and implore you to keep reading, especially if you are considering a career in academia. The authors of this chapter consider feminist perspectives and analysis to be as valid as antiracist perspectives and analysis in efforts to improve the place of women of color in the academy. The authors are particularly concerned about the place of women of color in social work education. As each woman of color's story unfolds in later chapters, you will be able to evaluate the extent to which these theories are relevant to her experiences and where an understanding of academic career paths can be improved to prompt more women of color to choose this option and succeed.

THE STATUS OF WOMEN AROUND THE WORLD

Women's status varies tremendously around the globe. In some countries, women have attained civil rights protections nearly equal to those of men, and, in other countries, women are still treated as minors or like chattel (Enos, 1995). Illiteracy rates are lowest in developing countries and increase for men and women in the following order: Latin America and the Caribbean, East Asia and Oceania, sub-Saharan African, the Arab States, and South Asia (UNESCO Institute for Statistics, 2002). In East Asia and Oceania, women's illiteracy rates are about 20% compared to nearly 50% in sub-Saharan Africa and more than 50% in the Arab States and South Asia. In terms of upper secondary education, girls are most disadvantaged in Africa and Asia

(UNESCO Institute for Statistics, 2005). In Third World countries such as Bangladesh, Upper Egypt, and Afghanistan, where girls may be forbidden to attend school and women may not be allowed to teach, literacy has lower priority than surviving pregnancy, safety from violence, and finding food (Roudi-Fahimi & Moghadam, 2003; Status of Women in Canada, 2003).

Among the countries in which the wage gap by gender is smallest is Portugal, where women earn 95 cents for every dollar earned by men and Italy, where women earn 91 cents for every dollar earned by men (Social Situation in the European Union: 2003, cited in Information Please, 2005a). Canada has among the best records for gender equity in administrative and managerial positions—68 women to every 100 men, compared to the United States with 67, New Zealand with 48, Cuba with 23, Poland with 18, Japan with 9, and India with 2 women for every 100 men (Neft & Levine, 1997).

Worldwide, women are somewhat less likely than men to have a university degree (Ashford & Clifton, 2005). The gap is closing, but it continues to vary widely across countries. Large gaps that existed two decades ago between women and men in higher education have closed in the United States and other developed countries including, but not limited to, France, Germany, Spain, Australia, Korea, and the United Kingdom (Sundstrom, 2004). In Canada, women are now achieving higher levels of education than men in many cases, with women making up 52% of college students and 55% of university students, including 51% seeking master's degrees and 43% seeking doctorates (Status of Women in Canada, 2003).

Women's political participation is inching up slowly (Ashford & Clifton, 2005). Since the mid-20th century, there have been about sixteen female presidents and more than thirty prime ministers in countries around the world; in 2006, two women became presidents of Chile and Liberia. From 1995 to 2004, the number of women in Africa who held seats in the single or lower chamber of the national parliament increased from 9% to 13%. During the same years, the percentage of women in Latin America and Caribbean countries who held similar parliamentary or legislative seats increased from 13% to 19%. These figures compare with worldwide figures of 12% of women holding such political seats in 1995 and 16% in 2004. Women's representation in parliament was low in Belize, Central America, with three women representatives in both 1995 and 2004. Haiti had no women in office in 1995 and four in 2004 (Ashford, 2005). Women's situation in the world could be compared on many other counts, but the point remains the same: whether it is a Third World or industrialized society, women are disadvantaged in ways that men are not, and they struggle with men to gain equal footing.

STATUS OF WOMEN IN THE UNITED STATES

In the United States, women's activism and service to country are well recorded from colonial times. Since the watershed 19th Amendment to the U.S. Constitution in 1920, which gave women the right to vote, women have made their mark in numerous ways, but many of these achievements took years to realize. For example, the right to choose an abortion did not become legal until 1973. The women's rights movement of the 1960s was critical to continued gains in pay equity and recognition of problems such as sexual harassment and domestic violence. People of color also have a long history of activism, but it was not until 1954 that the Supreme Court ruled in *Brown v. Board of Education of Topeka, Kansas* that "separate educational facilities are inherently unequal." The Civil Rights Act did not become law until 1964. There have been notable gains for other disenfranchised members of society in gay rights and disability rights.

White European American women have made substantial achievements in appointed political positions. Two have been named to the U.S. Supreme Court: Sandra Day O'Connor, who retired in 2005, and Ruth Bader Ginsburg, who continues to serve. Janet Reno was the first woman to serve as U.S. attorney general. Madeleine Albright was the first woman secretary of state. In 2002, Representative Nancy Pelosi (D-California) became the first woman Speaker of the House. African American women have also achieved important appointments. Dr. Jocelyn Elders was U.S. surgeon general. Former National Security Advisor Condoleezza Rice now serves as secretary of state. Dr. Antonia Novello from Puerto Rico was the first woman and the first Hispanic to be appointed U.S. surgeon general. Elaine Chao, head of the U.S. Department of Labor, is the first Asian American woman to hold a Cabinet post. But, from 1999 to 2004, there was only a 5% gain in the number of women serving in the U.S. Senate and only a 1% gain in the U.S. House of Representatives (Center for American Women in Politics, n.d.). The number of women in statewide elected office grew steadily for three decades, from 7% in 1971 to 28% in 2000, but dropped to 25% in 2004 (see also Carroll, 2004).

The number of Blacks or African Americans holding elected federal, state, and local office increased sixfold, from 1,469 in 1970 to 9,061 in 2001, with Black or African American women making the greatest gains (Bositis, 2002). However, very few people of color have ever served in the U.S. Senate. In 1993, Carol Moseley-Braun (D-Illinois) became the first and, to date, the only, African American woman to serve in the U.S. Senate. Among members of the 109th U.S. Congress, 12 representatives were African American women, seven were Latina women, and one was an Asian woman (Center for American Women in Politics, n.d.). In 2005, only two African American women and three Latinas held statewide elective executive offices—1.6% of all 315 statewide elective executive offices. Women of color held 324 or 4.4% of the 7,382 seats in state legislatures. People of color, especially women of color, are grossly underrepresented in appointed and elected public offices and in private sector executive positions.

In 2003, women who worked full time and year-round earned 76 cents for every dollar their male counterparts earned, down from 76.6 cents for every dollar earned by males in 2002 (U.S. Census Bureau, 2005b). While White European American women earned 77 cents per dollar earned by White European American men, Black or African American women earned only 65 cents and Hispanic women only 54 cents for every dollar earned by White European American men. In 2003, women age 15 and older who worked full time and year-round earned a median annual income of about $30,724, compared to $40,668 for men

(U.S. Census Bureau, 2005b). The difference is again more pronounced for women of color. Compared to White European American men, who earned $41,211 annually, White European American women earned $31,169, Black or African American women earned $26,965, and Hispanic women earned $22,363. As a result of women's lower income, their poverty rates are much higher than men's, and African Americans, Hispanics, and Native Americans have significantly higher poverty rates than White European Americans.

The war in Iraq highlights women's growing participation in the U.S. military. In 2003, approximately 215,243 women were on active duty in the military, compared to 1,219,134 men (U.S. Census Bureau, 2005a). In 2003, there were an estimated 1.7 million female military veterans. About 16% of veterans who served in the 1990–1991 Persian Gulf War were women, compared to 5% of veterans from World War II, 3% from the Vietnam era, and 2% from the Korean War.

Progress for women and people of color in the United States has generally been consistent, but too slow. Despite claims that the women's movement and the Civil Rights movement have leveled the playing field, women, African Americans, Hispanics, Native Americans, and other people of color generally lag behind in education, home ownership, health insurance, and other indicators of economic and social well-being.

Women in the United States continue to face stereotypes that are compounded for women of color. Asian women are often stereotyped as exotic, subservient, industrious, and eager to please or demonized as scheming, backstabbing, and oversexualized "dragon ladies" (Haley, n.d.). The cultural stereotype of the "model minority" does mediate more provocative views of Asian women (Media Action Network for Asian Americans, 2004). Many Asian families have very high expectations for academic achievement and career choices for girls as well as boys, but the Asian American population is very diverse. Some Asians come to this country illiterate and with few resources after suffering brutalization by despotic Southeast Asian regimes (U.S. Census Bureau, 2005a). They must often struggle to survive.

More Hispanic females are aspiring to historically male dominated fields and are attempting to break down cultural stereotypes that even their own families and friends may harbor (Gonzalez y Musielak, 2002). In many Latin countries, women are expected to emulate the Virgin Mary, a paragon of purity, chastity, and self-sacrifice. This stereotype carries over to women of Latin origin in the United States, where Hispanic women may be looked upon as subservient to men and poorly educated. They may also be considered sexually aggressive and best suited to be cooks and housekeepers, particularly in the South and Southwest (Haley, n.d.).

The American Indian female is stereotyped either as a strong spiritual earth mother or as the subservient and sometimes vengeful "squaw" or "Cherokee princess," with little or no social or political power unless she is a medicine woman. She is also often stereotyped as powerless in a matriarchal system where men are frequently entangled in the web of substance abuse (Haley, n.d.). Such stereotypes fail to recognize the systemic-based factors that contribute to the poor quality of life for First Nations people living on the reservation.

African American women have been dually stereotyped as "Mammy" and "seductress" (Haley, n.d.). They are seen as either deviant and crafty or nurturing, spiritual, and loyal servants and surrogate mother figures (also see Yarbrough & Bennett, 2000). The Black or African American seductress stereotype has evolved into the stereotype of the lazy, oversexed breeder and welfare mother. In reality, Black or African American women often work hard to raise families in environments where disproportionate numbers of men are imprisoned.

Pacific Islander women have been perceived negatively by the dominant American culture, yet one of the greatest values of Pacific Island cultures is reverence for women and womanhood. For example, in the Tongan culture, the father's eldest sister occupies the role of a *fahu*, symbolic matriarch. A *fahu* has unconditional inherent social status and material and political powers that supersede those of men and other family members. Her powers must be acknowledged whether or not she is present.

White European American women have historically been stereotyped as virtuous, pure, innocent, deserving of protection, and more credible than women of color (Yarborough & Bennett, 2000). Placed on a pedestal, White European American women are seen as submissive and demure (Haley, n.d.) unless they are poor, in which case they are stereotyped much like women of color.

The stereotypes of women and women of color may still serve as the lens through which they are judged as worthy scholars and teachers by students and academic colleagues alike. The attributes within the stereotypes outlined above make it difficult to see women and women of color as competent, responsible, and able to discern and impart knowledge. It also often makes it difficult for these women to see themselves as credible in these important tasks.

REFERENCES

Agathangelou, A. M., & Ling, L. H. M. (2002). An unten(ur)able position: The politics of teaching for women of color in the US. *International Feminist Journal of Politics, 4*(3), 368–398.

Alfred, M. V. (2001). Expanding theories of career development: Adding the voices of African American women in the White academy. *Adult Education Quarterly, 51*(2), 108–127.

Anzaldúa, G. E., & Keating, A. (2002). *This bridge we call home: Radical visions for transformation.* New York: Routledge.

Ashford, L. S. (2005). *Taking stock of women's progress.* Washington, DC: Population Reference Bureau. Retrieved June 14, 2005, from http://www.prb.org/2005women

Ashford, L. S., & Clifton, D. (2005). *2005 Women of our World.* Washington, DC: Population Reference Bureau. Retrieved June 14, 2005, from http://www.prb.org/2005women

Bositis, D. A. (2002). *Black elected officials: A statistical summary 2000.* Washington, DC: Joint Center for Political and Economic Studies.

Boulding, K. E. (1985). *The world as a total system.* Beverly Hills, CA: Sage.

Carroll, S. J. (2004). Women in state government: Historical overview and current trends. In *The Book of the States.* Lexington, KY: Council of State Government.

Center for American Women in Politics. (n.d.). *National infomation bank on women in public office.* New Brunswick, NJ: Eagleton Institute of Politics, Rutgers, The State University of New Jersey.

DiNitto, D., Martin, P. Y., & Harrison, D. F. (1982). Sexual discrimination in higher education. *Higher Education Review, 14*(2), 33–54.

Enos, J. L. (1995). Overall status of women in Africa. In S. Mitter & S. Rowbotham (Eds.), *Women encounter technology: Changing patterns of employment in the Third World.* New York: Routledge.

Franklin, C., DiNitto, D. M., & McNeece, C. A. (1997). In search of social work theory. In D. M. DiNitto & C. A. McNeece, *Social work: Issues and opportunities in a challenging profession* (2nd ed., pp. 45–67). Needham Heights, MA: Allyn and Bacon.

Germain, C. B. (1979). *Social work practice: People and environments, an ecological perspective.* New York: Columbia University Press.

Germain, C. B., & Gitterman, A. (1980). *The life model of social work practice.* New York: Columbia University Press.

Giddings, P. (1984). *When and where I enter: The impact of Black women on race and sex in America.* New York: Morrow.

Gonzales, P. M., Blanton, H., & Williams, K. J. (2002). The effects of stereotype threat and double-minority status on the test performance of Latino women. *Personality & Social Psychology Bulletin, 28*(5), 659–670.

Gonzalez y Musielak, D. E. (2002, July/August). Education: Missing part of the equation. *Hispanic Business Magazine.* Retrieved September 22, 2006, from http://www.hispanic-business.com/news/newsbyid.asp?id=7099

Gregory, A. (2003, June 6). Career network, first person, Black and female in the academy. *Chronicle of Higher Education, 49*(39), C5.

Haley, S. P. (n.d.). Stereotypes: Sexual stereotypes. Houghton Mifflin. Retrieved June 22, 2005, from http://college.hmco.com/history/readerscomp/women/htl/wm_035405_-sexualstereo.htm

Hamlet, J. D. (2000). Assessing womanist thought: The rhetoric of Susan L. Taylor. *Communication Quarterly, 48*(4), 420–436.

Hill, S. J. (2002). 'All I can cook is crack on a spoon': A sign for a new generation of feminists. In G. E. Anzaldúa & A. Keating, (Eds.). *This bridge we call home: Radical visions for transformation* (pp. 258–266). New York: Routledge.

hooks, b. (1981). *Ain't I a woman: Black women and feminism.* Boston: South End Press.

hooks, b. (1989). *Talking back: Thinking feminist, thinking Black.* Boston: South End Press.

hooks, b. (2000). *Feminism is for everybody: Passionate politics.* Cambridge, MA: South End Press.

hooks, b. (2003). *Teaching community: A pedagogy of hope.* New York: Routledge.

Information Please. (2005). *Wage gap, selected countries.* Retrieved June 22, 2005, http://www.infoplease.com/ipa/A0908883.html

Lorde, A. (1984). *Sister outsider: Essays and speeches.* Trumansburg, NY: Crossing Press.

Martin, P. Y., & O'Connor, G. G. (1989). *The social environment: Open systems applications.* New York: Longman.

McKay, N. (1983). Black woman professor–White university. *Women's Studies International Forum, 6*(2), 143–147.

Media Action Network for Asian Americans. (2004). *Restrictive portrayals of Asians in the media and how to balance them.* Retrieved June 20, 2005, from http://www.manaa.org/articles/stereo.html

Mikell, G. (1995). African feminism: Toward a new politics of representation. *Feminist Studies, 21*(2), 405–427.

Moraga, C., & Anzaldúa, G. E. (Eds.). (1983). *This bridge called my back: Writings by radical women of color.* New York: Kitchen Table/Women of Color Press.

Neft, N., & Levine, A. D. (1997). *Where women stand: An interntional report on the status of women in over 140 countries, 1997–1998.* New York: Random House.

Newland, K. (1975). Women in politics: A global view. *Worldwatch Institute No. 3.* Washington, DC: Worldwatch Institute.

Petrie, M., & Roman, P. M. (2004). Race and gender differences in workplace autonomy: A research note. *Sociological Inquiry, 74*(4), 590–603.

Roudi-Fahimi, F., & Moghadam, V. M. (2003). *Empowering women, developing society: Female education in the Middle East and North Africa.* Washington, DC: Population Reference Bureau.

Saleebey, D. (Ed.). (1992). *The strengths perspective in social work practice.* New York: Longman.

Saulnier, C. F. (1996). *Feminist theories and social work: Approaches and applications.* New York: Haworth Press.

Status of Women in Canada. (2003, March 4). *Women and education and training*. Retrieved June 21, 2005, from http://www.swccfc.gc.ca/pubs/b5_factsheets/b5_facsheets_4_e.html

Staudt, K. (1980, February). *Women's organizations in rural development*. Washington, DC: Office of Women in Development, Agency for International Development, International Development Cooperation Agency.

Sundstrom, W. A. (2004, March). *The college gender gap in the United States, 1940–2000: Trends and international comparisons*. Paper presented at the Fifth World Congress of the Cliometrics, Venice, Italy, July 2004. Retrieved September 22, 2006, from http://lsb.scu.edu/~wsundstrom/papers/college.pdf

Turner, C. S. V. (2002). Women of color in academe: Living with multiple marginality. *Journal of Higher Education, 73*(1), 74–93.

UNESCO Institute for Statistics. (2002). *Estimated world illieracy rates, by region and by gender, 2000*. Retrieved June 20, 2005, from http://www.uis.unesco.org/ev.php?ID=5020_201&ID2=DOTOPIC

UNESCO Institute for Statistics. (2005, April). Gender parity in secondary education—Are we there yet? Retrieved June 20, 2005, from http://www.uis.unesco.org/ev.php?ID=6098_201&ID2=DO_PRINTPAGE

U.S. Census Bureau. (2005a). *Facts for features: Women's history month*. Retrieved September 22, 2006, from http://www.census.gov/pressrelease/www/releases/archives/factsfor_features_spcial_editions/006232.html

U.S. Census Bureau. (2005b). *Labor force, employment, and earnings, statistical abstracts of the United States 2004–2005*. Retrieved September 22, 2006, from http://www.census.gov/main/www/citation.html; www.census.gov/prod/www/statistical-abstract 2001_2005.html

Valian, V. (2004). Beyond gender schemas: Improving the advancement of women in academia. *NWSA Journal, 16*(1), 207–220

Walker, A. (1983) *In search of our mothers' gardens: Womanist prose*. San Diego, CA: Harcourt Brace Jovanovich.

Walls, C. M. (2004). You ain't just whistling Dixie: How Carol Moseley Braun used rhetorical status to change Jesse Helms' tune. *Western Journal of Communication, 68*(3), 343–364.

Yarbrough, M., & Bennett, C. (2000). *Common stereotypes of African American women*. Retrieved August 7, 2005, http://academic.udayton.edu/race/05intesection/Gender/AAWomen01.htm

Part I: A Historical Perspective

Chapter 2: Women, Women of Color, and the Academy

Diana M. DiNitto

Darlene Grant

Halaevalu F. Ofahengaue Vakalahi

I do not believe that women are better than men. We have not wrecked railroads, nor corrupted legislature, nor done many unholy things that men have done; but then we must remember that we have not had the chance.

—Jane Addams

In the two decades between 1980 to 2000, college and university participation in the United States "increased by 14 percentage points for Whites [European Americans], 11 percentage points for African Americans, and 5 percentage points for Hispanics" (American Council on Education, 2003). Put another way, enrollment in higher education tripled for Hispanics and Asian Americans and increased by 80% for American Indians and 56%

for African Americans. In the 18 to 24 age group, African American women continued to exceed African American men in college and university enrollment: in 2000, 42% and 37%, respectively. Hispanic women now exceed men in participation rates—in 2000, 37% and 31%, respectively. In the United States, women now account for approximately 56% of college students and "earn about 57% of bachelor's degrees" (Sundstrom, 2004, p. 1). By the early 1980s, women had caught up with men in earning bachelor's and master's degrees, and now women also earn nearly as many professional and doctoral degrees (Sundstrom, 2004). But gender and racially stratified still best describes the status of women and women of color in faculty appointments in the world today. Women's lowest representation is in the "hard" sciences, and their highest concentrations are in the social sciences, including nursing, social work, and education.

For many sociopolitical reasons, it is more difficult for outsiders—women and women of color—to penetrate the inner sanctums of elite institutions like U.S. colleges and universities. The academic system, a historically White, European American, and male-dominant system, generates complex and conflicting processes for women and women of color who aspire to move from new PhDs to entry-level faculty positions. This highly politicized system presents barriers to recruitment, tenure (retention), and promotion (see, for example, Agathangelou & Ling, 2002). The same situation prevails in virtually every society. Nafisi (2003a, 2003b), for example, discusses her experiences as a woman teaching in Iran, where showing "a single strand of hair" has "subversive potential." Nafisi was expelled from the University of Tehran for not wearing a veil, and, at the University of Allameh Tabatabai, her visitors were monitored and her actions controlled. Nafisi's "strand of hair" and going "veil-less" are metaphors for the overt and covert sexism found in institutions of higher education everywhere.

Coser (1981) notes that "academia serves an important—probably the most important—gatekeeper function for the distribution of occupations and positions" (pp. 20–21), and this includes faculty positions. The underrepresentation of women and women of color in academia increases with rank, just as it does in business and the political sector. With few role models in colleges and universities, women and women of color are disadvantaged as they attempt to fulfill their dreams and goals, regardless of how benevolent the White, European American, and male establishment seems to be. On the other hand, as greater numbers of women and women of color enter academia, they are challenging societal formulations of who they should be, negotiating antithetical images of women and women of color, and responding to expectations steeped in stereotypical expectations from both colleagues and students. To see an African American woman teaching an electrical engineering course or a Latina teaching advanced calculus is a social anomaly for students and academics alike. A woman of color as an educator is indeed an alternative paradigm to the traditional White, European American, male educator.

THE NATURE OF THE ACADEMIC SYSTEM

Like other social institutions, universities are highly traditional, bureaucratic structures with a clear pecking order. In the United States, the entry-level position, generally reserved for those who hold a PhD or JD in law school, is assistant professor. After several years, usually five or six, individuals are permitted to apply for tenure and promotion to associate professor, and, if they clear that hurdle successfully, after several or more years, they may apply to be a professor (also called full professor). At one time, promotions in many colleges and universities were based more on longevity than scholarly accomplishments or teaching quality. Today, faculty generally must meet rigorous criteria if they are to move up the ranks. How tenure and promotion criteria are spelled out at colleges and universities varies substantially. Some criteria are carefully or rigidly delineated in terms of the number of articles or chapters published, expectations for classroom and additional teaching activities, and service contributions. Most universities' tenure and promotion guidelines offer decision makers quite a bit of room for subjectivity. This can be a positive experience in terms of reviewing the diverse portfolios that faculty members may present at tenure and promotion time. It can also be a negative experience when extraneous factors influence tenure and promotion decisions. Once tenure is achieved, academia offers far more job security than most other employment sectors. Unless a faculty member engages in serious misconduct or severely neglects his or her work, there are strong protections in most institutions against being fired.

STATUS OF WOMEN AND WOMEN OF COLOR IN ACADEMIA

Study can help clarify issues and identify solutions, but academic institutions, like legislative bodies and their bureaucratic (executive) arms, often use study as a delaying tactic. Virtually every predominantly White European American institution of higher education in the United States has produced some type of report on the status of women and of underrepresented racial and ethnic groups. These reports generally look at gender and race or ethnicity as separate categories, not at the intersection or combination of gender and race or ethnicity as most scholars would do when conducting social science research. These status reports may detail the number of faculty who are African American, American Indian, Asian, and Hispanic, but not tell how many in each ethnic group are men or women. Ethnic group subcategories, such as Mexican American, also are not identified, perhaps because the numbers are often so small that they would be an embarrassment, especially for institutions located in communities with large populations of particular racial or ethnic groups. Agathangelou and Ling (2002) note that this glaring omission "serves only to buttress the academy's existing hierarchy of power and privilege," while still meeting the technical requirements for affirmative action (p. 381).

Chemical and Engineering News boasts that "each year since the turn of the century [the 21st century!], it has surveyed the top 50 chemistry departments to determine how many women are tenured or hold tenure-track faculty position" (Long, 2002). Sadly, in the 2004–2005 academic year, women still accounted for only 12% of faculty in the country's top (defined by research expenditures) chemistry departments (Marasco, 2004). From 1993 to 2002, women earned 31% of all chemistry PhDs, but, in 2002, they accounted for only 66 or 21% of all chemistry assistant professors in the top 50 academic departments (Long, 2002; Nelson, 2005). This is a historical trickle rather than a flow of women into chemistry departments' academic pipeline.

Women are underrepresented throughout academia. A major report, *Diversity in Science and Engineering Faculties at Research Universities*, of the top 50 departments in 15 disciplines shows that "although the student body has diversified considerably, the composition of faculty has remained relatively stagnant" (Nelson, 2005, p. 2). Math is among the biggest offenders. Contrary to the idea that girls do not like math, in 2000, women earned nearly half (48%) of bachelor's degrees in this subject, but only 8% of math faculty are women. In 2002, 60% of assistant professors in math were White European American men, with slightly more than 58% of math PhD degrees awarded to White European American men between 1993 and 2002; 15% of math assistant professors were Asian males, who received 11% of the PhDs during this period; and women received 27% of the PhDs, but represented only 20% of assistant professors. The pipeline leaked for women, though it is unclear whether the discrepancy occurred because women did not seek academic careers or because they were less successful in obtaining faculty positions.

The picture in the social sciences is similarly distressing. In psychology, where 76% of the bachelor's degrees were awarded to women, only 34% of faculty members were women; women earned 66% of the PhDs, but accounted for only 45% of assistant professors. According to Nelson (2005), in the top 50 psychology departments combined, there were only 22 Black or African American female faculty, of whom only three were full professors; 26 Hispanic female faculty, five of whom were full professors; and three Native American female faculty, none of whom was a full professor. There were more Black or African American women faculty in sociology and political science: 32 and 26, respectively. Psychology had the highest number of Hispanic females, but Native American women were abysmally represented. Of the five social or life science disciplines surveyed, psychology was the only discipline that had any Native American female faculty. Of the nine physical science and engineering disciplines surveyed, there was one lone Native American female faculty member in chemistry. The top 50 computer science departments were the only discipline that had not one Black or African American, Hispanic, or Native American female faculty member.

According to the U.S. Department of Education, in colleges and universities, women (U.S. citizens and permanent residents) represent 51% of instructors and 54% of lecturers, equal to or exceeding women's representation of 51% in the U.S. population. Instructors and lecturers are often temporary employees and generally do not have the same voting rights or voice in making decisions in the academy. Thus, it may not be surprising that women are best represented in these positions. Women account for only 34% of all assistant, associate, or full professors in U.S. colleges and universities (see Figure 1).

Figure I: An Approximate Comparison of the Percentage of Women in Academia (Assistant, Associate, and Full Professors) by Race and Ethnicity With Their Representation in the Population, United States, 2001.

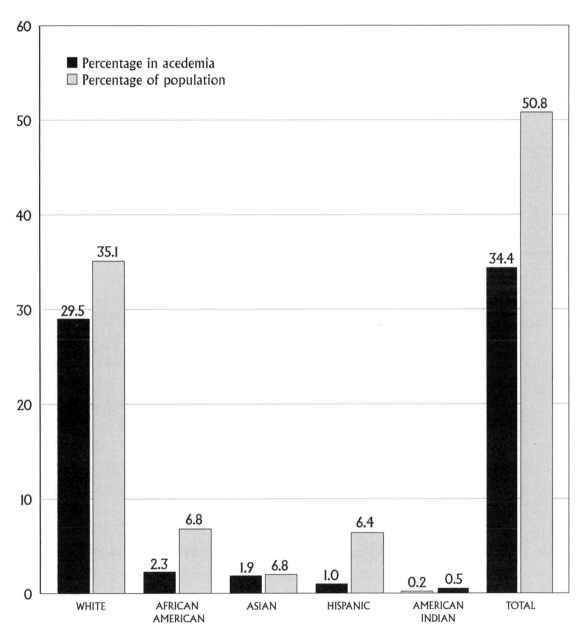

Note: Population figures are based on Census Bureau data for those who reported being of one race and exclude those of two or more races since data reported by the Department of Education for faculty composition are based on single racial/ethnic categories. The Census Bureau reports Hispanic or Latino origin separately from race; since the number of non-White Hispanics is relatively small, the population percentage for White women was calculated by subtracting the figure for Hispanic women in the population. However, Hispanics may be of any race. Percentage of women in academia exclude nonpermanent residents and those whose race or ethnicity was unknown.

Sources: Data for percentage in academia based on U.S. Department of Education as reported in *The Chronicle of Higher Education, The 2004–2005 Almanac.* Data for percentage in population based on U.S. Census Bureau, *Statistical Abstract of the United States: 2004–2005,* Table No. 13.

Table 1: Percentage of Full-Time College and University Faculty by Gender, Race, Ethnicity, and Rank, Fall 2001

	American Indian (%)	Asian (%)	Black (%)	Hispanic (%)	White (%)	Total (%)
Professor (*n*=160,596)						
Male:	.2	4.9	2.0	1.4	68.9	77.4
Female:	.08	.9	1.1	.5	19.9	22.5
Associate Professor (*n*=127,016)						
Male:	.2	4.8	3.0	1.7	53.2	62.9
Female:	.16	1.8	2.4	1.0	31.7	37.1
Assistant Professor (*n*=135,487)						
Male:	.22	5.2	3.0	1.9	43.7	54.0
Female:	.23	3.1	3.6	1.6	37.3	45.8

Note: Totals may not add to 100% due to rounding.

Source: Data from the U.S. Department of Education as reported in *The Chronicle of Higher Education, The 2004–2005 Almanac.* Percentages exclude nonpermanent residents and those whose race or ethnicity was unknown.

The gender gap increases from assistant to full professor, but there has been some progress in women's representation. For example, from 1992 to 2001, the number of women who were full professors increased from 16% to 22% and from 29% to 37% of associate professors; the increase at the assistant-professor rank, where women are better represented, has been smaller, from 42% to 46% (see Table 1 for 2001 figures).

The pipeline leaks at more than one point on the road to full professor. According to Marc Goulden of the University of California, Berkeley, "for each year after securing a tenure-track job, male assistant professors are 23 percent more likely to earn tenure" and "for each year after earning tenure, male professors are 35 percent more likely to be named full professors" (Wilson, 2004). No comparable figures for women of color were available. Apparently, women are dropping out of academia before seeking tenure, moving into non-tenure-track positions, or apply for tenure and are denied.

Table 1 presents the distribution of faculty in the United States by rank, gender, and race or ethnicity, and Figure 1 compares the representation of women faculty by race or ethnicity with their

Table 2: Average Faculty Salaries for Men and Women by Rank, 2004–2005

	Men ($)	Women ($)	Gap in Pay (%)
Professor	94,235	82,874	12.1
Associate Professor	66,941	62,258	7.0
Assistant Professor	56,574	52,261	7.6

Note: Figures include full-time faculty members of the instructional staff except those in medical schools and are based on data from 1,416 institutions representing 1,715 campuses. Salaries are adjusted to a standard nine-month work year.

Source: American Association of University Professors reported in Smallwood (2005). Faculty salaries rose 2.8% but failed to keep pace with inflation for the first time in eight years.

representation in the population. Because Census Bureau figures are not compiled in the same way as Department of Education figures, the comparisons are not exact. But, generally speaking, in 2001, Hispanic women showed the greatest discrepancy in representation in academia; they represented 6.4% of the population, but only 1% of faculty (assistant, associate, and full professors). American Indian women represented 0.5% of the U.S. population, but only 0.2% of faculty. Black or African American women were 6.8% of the population and 2.3% of faculty. White European American women (excluding Hispanics) represented 35% of the population and 29% of faculty. Asian women came closest to matching their representation in the population; they comprised 2% of the population and 1.9% of faculty.

Salaries are difficult to compare because they vary considerably across disciplines and across different types of institutions. Church-affiliated institutions pay the lowest salaries, and private institutions pay the most (Smallwood, 2005). Table 2 shows the average salary and percentage gap in pay for men and women across all types of institutions of higher education by academic rank.

The gap is highest at the full-professor level—12.1%. If there are publications comparing faculty salaries by race and ethnicity or gender and race or ethnicity, they are well hidden.

At Harvard University, the Study of New Scholars is providing considerable information about aspects of faculty life for men, women, and people of color. Among new scholars (the vast majority of whom were assistant professors) at six research universities, Trower and Bleak (2004) found that, compared to men, women were less satisfied with their institutions and their departments, elements of their work ("time available for research" and "resources to support their work" in the form of "assistance for proposal writing and locating outside funds"), relationships (professional interactions with and mentoring from senior colleagues), racial and ethnic diversity in their departments, salary, work-life balance, clarity about tenure requirements, pressure to conform on political views, personal behavior, and attire. Women were also less likely to feel "that their department treats all junior faculty fairly" (pp. 1–2).

Compared to White European American women, women of color felt less clear about tenure processes and criteria and were less likely to feel "that tenure decisions are based on performance rather than on politics, relationships, or demographics." Women of color were also more likely to feel that "assistance to improve teaching," campus childcare, housing assistance, and personal leaves would be beneficial, but they were less likely to feel that "stop-the-clock provisions would be helpful" (Trower & Bleak, 2004, p. 32). The bottom line is that women are less satisfied than men, and women of color are less satisfied than White European American women with the academy as a workplace.

CHALLENGES AND REWARDS FOR WOMEN OF COLOR IN ACADEMIA

"First person" accounts of women of color in academia (see, for example, Gregory, 2003) and analyses of the problems they encounter in traversing and succeeding in academia (see, for example, Agathangelou & Ling, 2002) would scare any sane individual away from such a career. In recent years, women of color in academia have produced a substantial body of literature on the problems they encounter in colleges and universities; however, there is an astonishing lack of attention paid to the benefits of academic careers for women and women of color and their many successes in academic environments. Turner (2002) summarizes the litany of problems that women of color face in academia:

> Being more visible and on display; feeling more pressure to conform, to make fewer mistakes; becoming socially invisible, not to stand out; finding it harder to gain credibility; being more isolated and peripheral; being more likely to be excluded from informal peer networks, having limited sources of power through alliances; having fewer opportunities to be sponsored; facing misperceptions of their identity and role in the organization; being stereotyped; facing more personal stress. (p. 76)

As Boice (1992) describes it, "the literature on minorities and women in academe reminds us of the magnitude of their special problems, of a tragedy in the making" (p. 254). The reader will find that we discuss these problems and challenges, but equally or perhaps more importantly, we discuss the positives of academic careers for women and women of color. We want others to experience the satisfactions we have enjoyed in our careers as faculty members.

Recruitment (Binds That Double)

Due to their scarcity in most fields, women and women of color are often recruited heavily for faculty positions. One author of this chapter roomed with a new PhD recipient, an African American woman, at a conference where faculty recruitment typically is conducted. During the conference, the new PhD recipient received so many recruitment calls from universities that exhaustion finally set in, and the author of this chapter resolved to say that this new PhD recipient was not available. One reaction to this scenario is, how wonderful to be so highly sought. Another is the words that women of color often hear: "It must be nice to be able to write your own ticket *just* because you are a minority." Women and women of color often wonder whether *they* are being recruited or whether the college or university is simply looking for a warm body—a token—to boost affirmative action statistics or demands for more campus diversity. A nagging feeling remains that White European American colleagues will never understand: the work environment disadvantages a woman of color because all others can see is unfair advantage based on race or ethnicity. There is competition for coveted security, wages, and the benefits that accompany scarce academic positions (Morales & Sheafor, 2002). When colleagues or others see the hiring of people of color as reverse discrimination, there may be little hope for a frank discussion of these concerns.

Prospective faculty members of color visiting campuses for job interviews closely scan the environment for signs that diversity is valued and that they will receive the respect and support they deserve. The recruitment phase is a critical point in one's career. This is often the new PhD recipient's main opportunity to garner the highest salary and supports (initial research funding, computer equipment, student assistants, etc.) possible for his or her work. As prospective faculty members are recruited, it is often clear which of them is prepared to negotiate and willing or wants to play hardball in the process. This may be difficult for faculty who come from cultures that value reciprocity, nonconfrontational communication, and trust in fair treatment of people regardless of personal background.

Women of color bring many advantages to the teaching, research, and service missions of the department and the institution, but use of these bargaining chips may put the new faculty member in a "one down position," causing women of color to worry that colleagues will disrespect them for it. Rather than using their bargaining chips, women of color may downplay the demand for them on the market. Downplaying one's assets often comes too naturally for women and women of color and may be reflected at many points along the academic career path—in tenure and promotion statements (where tooting one's horn is critical), interactions with colleagues, and even productivity. Every candidate should figure out how to use his or her most valuable assets and strengths to get the university's best deal.

Our Work Is Significant (and We Won"t Be Discounted)

Women and women of color often express skepticism about traditional research topics and methods. This is hardly surprising since "science" and "research" have been used as tools of repression and discrimination. Blatant examples of this occurred in Nazi Germany. The United States has its own shameful examples, the Tuskegee syphilis experiments being one. Also disturbing is that much research has excluded women entirely or has been conducted "on" women or women of color without including them on the research team or as consultants. As Turner (2002) notes, "as Latina professors, we are newcomers to a world defined and controlled by discourses that do not address our realities, that do not affirm our intellectual contributions, that do not seriously examine our worlds" (p. 75).

Some women and women of color use traditional research methods; others prefer newer, constructivist methodologies. Some study more traditional research subjects; others pursue newer areas of inquiry. Regardless of the research agenda they pursue, women and women of color often bring new perspectives and more culturally grounded approaches to their work. However, they may find that their work is "viewed as insignificant" and they "often receive little or no support for their intellectual pursuits, especially when their work centers on racial, ethnic, and/or gender issues" (Thomas & Hollenshead, 2001, pp. 166–167). Blanchard's (2002) voice on the topic is sharper: "often the academy, despite its objections, is vested in viewing the term *black scholar* as an oxymoron. Insert *woman* and the possibility becomes, in some corners, a sure sign of affirmative action diluting the genius inherent to a white male institution" (p. 256). Blanchard also criticizes "some of our white sisters [who] are so vested in patriarchy that they perpetuate the myth of why we were accepted into graduate school in the first place. They discourage our research efforts, not in any real attempt to helping us focus our scholarship, but rather to safeguard the sanctity of current thought" (p. 256). When a philosophy professor at a "research one" university was asked why his department had only one female faculty member, his response was "we try, but their presentations at national conferences are lacking—their philosophical and theoretical approaches just aren't a good fit for our department." In response to this intellectual hegemony, women of color who are academics speak of the "resistance" strategies they use to cope, such as refusing to conform to what others want

them to research or teach (Thomas & Hollenshead, 2001), and sometimes paying the price for it.

It can be difficult to determine what is constructive, objective, and useful criticism of one's work and what are unconscious racist or sexist reactions. All research and scholarly inquiry can be critiqued, but male or White European American colleagues might be cut slack, while the work of women and women of color may be scrutinized under a microscope and held to a higher standard. Women and women of color are accustomed to working twice as hard to achieve the same recognition for their work as men do. They are also often left in a quandary over how to view or modify their work or whether to modify it at all, especially when they are deeply committed to a particular line of inquiry that meets repeated rejections by refereed journals or funding sources. One way to address this quandary is to increase mentorship to help sort through the issues. Also important to the research that many women and women of color conduct is requiring the inclusion of women and minorities in federally funded research studies. Another boost is the federal emphasis on research on health disparities, which provides new funding opportunities to faculty in many disciplines. Not content to abandon their work or to sulk, women and women of color use these funding options to pursue their research agendas with gusto.

Isolation (One is the Loneliest Number)

The feelings of isolation that faculty women of color often express are palpable. Lee's (2002) example is not uncommon:

I no longer talk to my colleagues about my

frustration and difficulties. Those without my experience would simply assume I was making excuses. As the only Asian faculty [member] in my department, I had to establish a precedent not only for myself but also for other Asian female faculty who may find themselves at southern regional universities. I had to deal with people's preconceptions about Asian women and wear a smiling mask to avoid threatening them, but I had to stand my ground to keep myself against all odds. "What is a woman if she loses herself?" I asked myself every morning. (pp. 401–402)

A lack of empathic understanding increases the isolation of women of color, even among members of groups that are decently represented in a department (see Turner, 2002).

Women of color in academia may describe a process to promotion and tenure that other colleagues would hardly recognize, but such White European Americans hardly ever admit this for fear they will be branded as racist. An author of this chapter was engaged in a dialogue with a White European American male colleague with whom she had spent many hours coauthoring publications during their years as assistant professors in the same department. As they were talking one day, this man was genuinely surprised and saddened that he never considered the realities this female of color experienced given the extra need for advising, university service, and other demands on her time and energy. She did not want him to pity her, and, while they were both anxious about earning tenure, the seat of her anxiety was very different from his. This exchange does give hope for honest dialogue between women and men and among people of different racial and ethnic groups in academia.

Mentorship and Collegiality (They're for Everyone)

Taking one's first faculty position is like taking up residence in a foreign land. Even though assistant professors have "visited" (been graduate students and observed faculty teaching and conducting research and even aided in these efforts), they generally are not fully prepared for their new role. Developmental mentoring occurs naturally for many White European American men. Recognizing that women and women of color often lack natural mentors (other faculty women and faculty of color) in the work environment, more academic departments today appoint mentors to help new faculty traverse the system. Appointed mentors change the nature of the relationship from a voluntary process or mutual collegial attraction to the professional equivalent of an "arranged date" since the senior faculty member and new faculty member may not already know each other. This mandate for mentorship, which may be perceived as paternalistic or maternalistic, may require careful negotiating; however, there is little substitute for purposeful and supportive mentorship.

Having several mentors can be extremely beneficial. Each may bring different strengths or perspectives to the process, and several perspectives can help sort out thorny issues. Though a mentor may be assigned to a new faculty member, new faculty members are often left to approach other potential mentors on their own. This process can provoke anxiety. New faculty often think they are supposed to know how to teach and handle difficult classroom situations when, in fact, many have had no formal preparation for teaching. New PhD recipients often think they are supposed to know how to publish even when they have never submitted an article for review by a refereed journal. Every new faculty member needs guidance in these foreign lands to understand the customs and language of what is a long and arduous journey. Department chairs and deans are also crucial in this process. They can provide sage advice; after all, they are the ones who "take faculty up" for tenure and promotion, and they often have resources to dole out along the route to tenure and promotion. Garnering these resources often requires new faculty to stay on their mentors' good side.

Women and women of color may be very cautious in seeking help and support and aligning themselves with senior faculty. Entrenched patterns may prevail, including taboos against asking White European American men or women for assistance and reenacting subservient relationships. Women faculty and faculty of color have heard stories of doing work for senior colleagues and not receiving appropriate credit or they may feel they will not be viewed as independent, capable academics and will remain in the shadow of a senior faculty member. There are also stories of women and of women of color not helping each other (Blanchard, 2002). The "I made it on my own, and you should, too" view apparently has not disappeared.

Just as new faculty may not approach senior faculty, senior faculty may not reach out to women of color. Senior faculty may perceive that their assistance is not wanted and may be seen as patronizing.

Another issue is that good mentoring can be a rewarding experience, but it is also hard work (e.g., helping new faculty write articles and produce grant applications). Associate professors working toward promotion to full professor and even full professors with heavy workloads may be wary of the time and attention new faculty may need. A stalemate often occurs. No one makes the move, and an important relationship is never realized. On one hand, being approached by a potential mentor can create worry about whether the relationship will be productive, fizzle out, or have negative repercussions. On the other hand, it often brings a sigh of relief to a woman or a woman of color who has learned to expect little from others in the work environment.

Similar dynamics may occur among assistant professors, especially when they are vying for the same resources or when promotion and tenure are viewed as a "zero sum" game, where not everyone can win. Women and women of color should proceed with caution in conducting collaborative work because seemingly collegial and helpful relationships can easily go sour, especially when it is not clear who will do what part of the work and what credit each will receive (e.g., first or second authorship). However, assistant professors are becoming more savvy about joining forces to increase their productivity by including each other on grant applications to improve the chances of getting funding, coauthoring articles to increase the number of manuscripts accepted for publication, and developing and sharing course materials to improve teaching. They are also clarifying in advance with peers and senior faculty work responsibilities and work credits.

The literature is replete with examples of the importance of mentoring and collaboration. As systems theory reminds us, mentorship and collegiality are two-way streets. They require openness on the part of new and senior faculty and among peers. Reciprocity of interaction between mentor and protégé illustrates the classic systems theory concept of interdependence. In social work terms, building trust takes time and evidence that the relationship is safe. Women and women of color seek a balance between dependence and independence (i.e., interdependence) that perceptive mentors and peers can assist them in realizing.

Faculty Women's Organizations
(Tea, Sympathy, and Hard Advice)

In some departments, women can barely be found. One cannot but feel sympathy for the lone woman or the lone woman of color in a "hard" science department. Many colleges and universities have faculty women's organizations or groups that help women learn about the system and develop collegial cross-department relationships (faculty associations for women or people of color seem to be rare, though informal networking may occur). Faculty women's groups often monitor the status of women in the university and encourage reforms. They generally offer seminars on promotion and tenure processes and can provide needed moral and social support to women from all departments. Though very helpful, these groups are generally insufficient to learn about politics in one's own department, how to navigate the department, form productive collegial relationships within it, and learn about the department's expectations and procedures for promotion and tenure.

Not so long ago, a new PhD recipient, especially a woman or person of color, expected little in the way of collegiality. The academy was viewed largely as a system of individual entrepreneurs competing with each other for tenure, promotion, prestige, and departmental resources. Nowadays, faculty members expect much more. The greater influx of women has likely promoted a situation in which greater collegiality and collaboration are expected, not because women necessarily prefer the "warm and fuzzy" approach, but because, consistent with relational theory, collaboration generates enthusiasm and excitement for work, leads to more creative ideas and approaches to scholarship and teaching, makes faculty more productive, and "raises the boat" for everyone in the department. In her work with a team of faculty women (one woman of color and three White European American women; one senior faculty member, one assistant professor, one post-doc, and one research associate; and ranging in age from 30s to 50s), one author of this chapter recalls several times when others have walked by their meetings and, hearing the group's animated conversations and laughter, commented, "You all are having too much fun!" This "fun" may be interpreted as attending to a diversity of perspectives that redresses historical gender, racial, and other inequalities, including different theoretical perspectives. The fun has resulted in more products than any of the members could have accomplished alone.

Informal and Formal Networks
("The Good Ole Boys and the Good Ole Girls")

The structure of academia stipulates formal and informal relationships, behavioral norms, and rules and standards that women and women of color are rarely privy to before entering faculty life. They may also find it difficult to acquire this information once in the academy. Women and women of color must try to decode messages about the rules of conduct and unearth the secrets of academic life. The sometimes dog-eat-dog world of academia lacks resonance for those women who see the world in relational terms and heightens the need for women of color to be on guard in determining who can be trusted in negotiating unfamiliar terrain. Native Americans, for example, often learn communication styles—not correcting or showing up others and maintaining a soft-spoken or low-key demeanor—that are quite different from the debate and discourse in which academics frequently engage. This can make it difficult to access and fit in with informal networks of faculty who are much more individualistic and confrontational.

Women generally don't have access to the "good ole boy" network. One author of this chapter was quite surprised one Friday afternoon to walk into the lounge of a hotel near the university to find the male faculty from her department gathered together. To her knowledge, there was no "good ole girl" network meeting for happy hour. It hadn't even occurred to her that faculty socialized together. In managing their multiple roles, many women rush home to care for children or elderly parents, prepare supper, and do the laundry, and wouldn't have time for that informal socialization. Even if invited, mentioning a childcare conflict and declining the social invitation might be perceived as being less committed to the work environment.

Being associated with the right groups within and outside one's university can be almost as critical to success as a long list of publications, lots of external funding, and stellar teaching evaluations. But one must have an entrée into these groups (DiNitto, Martin & Harrison, 1982). These formal and informal networks are essential because they open many doors to information and resources that one might not learn about otherwise. Faculty women's organizations often try to create such opportunities, sometimes during lunch hours, though we admit that taking time for lunch is a treat for many faculty who are women or people of color. Entrée to national and international committees and work groups within one's own discipline is also critical. Women and women of color must keep their eyes and ears open for opportunities for appointments to prestigious groups and should even advocate for these appointments.

Service (But Not to Exhaustion)

In many departments, faculty members need to be seen as team players. However, faculty are often walked over or used. King, et al. (2002) describe the extent to which women of color in academia "create humanizing change" through university service ("third shift work" as they call it) and the exhaustion it can bring. Thus, one needs to say yes "enough" but not "too much" and to get rid of guilt about not stepping up to the plate or table to be a role model or the expert on "minority" concerns, "cultural diversity," or "multiculturalism" on every committee. A woman of color also gets worn down from being the one who always brings and must explain the "other" viewpoint on the situation (Thomas & Hollenshead, 2001, p. 170).

Increasing service expectations are making academic advancement tougher for all faculty (Fogg, 2003). From the Parking and Traffic Committee to the Faculty Senate, faculty members are called on to serve, and some committees are in particular need of the perspectives of women and women of color. A common refrain of senior faculty at tenure or promotion time is, "We told her not to do that [i.e., so much service]; we told her she needed to publish more." "We" may have told her so and then "invited" her to be a member of far too many committees (see Agathangelou & Ling, 2002). It is difficult for faculty women of color to refuse service requests from those who vote on promotion and tenure. It is also difficult to turn away from or ignore students of color who need support and guidance (Turner, 2002) in colleges and universities where most faculty, staff, and students are White European American; where racist and sexist remarks are heard too often; and where heated debates on gender, race, class, and sexual orientation erupt in the classroom and at other campus venues.

In addition, women and women of color may feel a strong obligation to serve their communities, but this may not be the type of "professional" service that promotion and tenure committees reward, no matter how much it helps the institution's reputation (Agathangelou & Ling, 2002; Turner, 2002). Grounded in a feminist perspective, authors on this topic suggest that women and women of color fight the dominant hegemony and engage in another resistance strategy "to rebelliously identify with community achievement and the approval of kindred colleagues" (Boice, 1992, p. 263).

Constant Comment
(I Thought My Skin Was Thicker)

Most workers, especially in the public sector, are evaluated once a year by their immediate supervisors. Though there may be some higher level scrutiny of these reviews, particularly if the review is negative or the worker challenges it, only a few people usually see them. Not so for academics, who are subjected to constant review and evaluation. In most colleges and universities, students have an opportunity to evaluate every course a faculty member teaches, and students' comments today, particularly to women and faculty of color, can be brutal and graphic. At public institutions, instructor's teaching evaluation scores may be posted on Web sites as public information. Students today are much more aware that their evaluations of instructors' courses count and far less hesitant to see the department chair or dean when they are displeased with a faculty member. At one of the largest universities in the country, there is an annual event referred to as "slam" tables, where students can write comments, good or bad, about an instructor for all passersby to see. Faculty, "junior" faculty in particular, may also be subjected to peer evaluation (observation) of their courses, often by senior faculty whose courses may never have been "observed." This may occur periodically or at the time of major reviews for contract continuation, merit reviews, tenure, and promotion. Even mentoring contains an element of evaluation.

Teaching at a college or university is usually an exhilarating experience. Most faculty look forward to the ongoing exchange with students, but women and women of color often feel especially vulnerable to student and peer review. The teaching styles of women and women of color may differ from those of White European Americans in general and White European American men in particular. Many college and university students have had little exposure to female faculty of color, and White European American students generally do not have close relationships with people of color, especially those in positions of authority. Thus, they may harbor stereotypes about women and women of color, such as they are here because they are women, African American, Hispanic, and so forth, not because they are capable and competent. Even among academics, the power or authority of women of color is undermined or limited (Turner, 2002). Women of color are scrutinized based on their gender and their color. Boice (1992) describes the concerns of faculty of color that mediocre or poor teaching evaluations are often based on immutable characteristics such as gender or race. When students and colleagues encounter a self-assured African American woman whom they perceive as not particularly nurturing, their evaluations of her can be quite negative. African American female faculty sometimes interpret negative student and peer evaluations as having a basis in their refusal to don a nurturing persona in their interactions and work. In addition to keeping abreast of their subject, women of color must decide how to assert their authority, maintain decorum in the classroom, enforce standards, and still receive the positive teaching evaluations needed for promotion and tenure.

Faculty evaluation occurs at many other levels. Every time a faculty member submits an article to a peer-reviewed journal or a grant application for research funding, his or her work is critically reviewed, and sometimes that review is more critical than constructive. Every faculty member must sort out the reasons for these kinds of responses—my work could be improved, my work is being discounted, or the reviewers don't care about or understand my work. Which is it? When is a faculty member being too sensitive, succumbing to the messages of inferiority she has received throughout her life, and when does she need to revise her work?

In many departments or schools, faculty are also reviewed annually by peers as well as their department chair or dean. At the time of tenure or promotion, review occurs at additional levels. External review letters from several senior faculty at other institutions generally are solicited. Following the appropriate departmental and school or college faculty vote on the tenure or promotion application, the department chair or dean makes his or her recommendations. There may also be a review by a university committee composed of faculty, some of whom often have little familiarity with the discipline or the specific area of interest of the individual being reviewed and little familiarity with women of color. In addition, the university's academic officers, including the president (sometimes called chancellor), must consider the application. Last, the university's board of regents or trustees generally must give final approval for tenure and promotion decisions.

All of these processes rest on the good faith of the mostly White European American and male reviewers. After a lifetime of hearing critiques— and worse—of one's racial or ethnic group and constant messages about women's inferiority, women of color cannot be blamed for shutting down. But many do not. In fact, many women take satisfaction in having made it in academia rather than opting for another route (DiNitto, Aguilar, Franklin, & Jordan, 1995).

CONCLUSION

The academic pipeline for women of color often starts leaking at birth due to structural factors such as racial and gender discrimination, high levels of poverty, and low levels of education among too many families in the United States. The leaks continue as young women who are interested in various scientific fields face a variety of societal messages that may dissuade them from these endeavors. Even those women who make it to the faculty ranks drop out more often than men. Harvard's New Scholar study (Trower & Bleak, 2004) indicates that supports that are often unavailable would be helpful to women and women of color. Universities frequently lack even basic policies to stop the tenure clock when the need arises or to provide assistance with childcare.

Though women and people of color in predominantly White European American colleges and universities do not have it easy, there are few places where there is more freedom to be creative and to make work choices (e.g., what to teach, how to teach, what research and scholarship to pursue, and how to pursue it). There are constraints, of course, but the academy allows for deeper thinking than do many other workplaces. The academic freedom of colleges and universities is unparalleled to most other work settings. There are so many opportunities that, some days, the biggest challenge is deciding which ones to pursue. The long hours are offset to some degree by the flexible time during which much work can be accomplished. Expectations for promotion and tenure continue to increase, but so do the resources available to faculty to accomplish these goals. There is more helpful technology, more assistance with grant writing, more journals available for publications, more funds for research, and so forth.

Women of color face challenges in every work setting as they continue to work to make every workplace better for women, men, and their families. Why make the academic workplace an exception? Women and women of color have already begun to humanize the academy by bringing diverse perspectives to their work and attention to issues like mentoring and supportive family policies. The academy provides a tremendous power base from which women can operate. Women of color must seize the opportunity to share their work and deliver their messages in the classroom, the laboratory, the community, and at conferences around the world.

REFERENCES

Agathangelou, A. M., & Ling, L. H. M. (2002). An unten(ur)able position: The politics of teaching for women of color in the US. *International Feminist Journal of Politics,* 4(3), 368–398.

American Council on Education (ACE). (2003, October 8). *Minority college enrollment surges over the past two decades: Students of color still lag behind Whites in college participation.* Washington, DC: Author. Retrieved October 30, 2005, from http://www.acenet.edu

Blanchard, M. L. (2002). Poets, lovers, and the master's tools: A conversation with Audre Lorde. In G. E. Anzaldúa & A. Keating (Eds.), *This bridge we call home: Radical visions for transformation* (pp. 254–257). New York: Routledge.

Boice, R. (1992). *The new faculty member: Supporting and fostering professional development.* San Francisco: Jossey-Bass.

Coser, R. L. (1981). Where have all the women gone? Like the sediment of a good wine, they have sunk to the bottom. In C. F. Epstein & R. L. Coser (Eds.), *Access to power: Cross-national studies of women and elites*. London: Allen and Unwin.

DiNitto, D. M., Aguilar, M. A., Franklin, C., & Jordan, C. (1995). Over the edge? Women and tenure in today's academic environment. *Affilia, 10*(3), 255–279.

DiNitto, D., Martin, P. Y., & Harrison, D. F. (1982). Sexual discrimination in higher education. *Higher Education Review, 14*(2), 33–54.

Fogg, P. (2003). So many committees, so little time. *The Chronicle of Higher Education, 50*(17), A14.

Gregory, A. (2003, June 6). Career network, first person, Black and female in the academy. *Chronicle of Higher Education, 49*(39), C5.

King, T. C., Barnes-Wright, L., Gibson, N. E., Johnson, L. D., Lee, V., Lovelace, B. M., Turner, S., & Wheeler, D. I. (2002). Andrea's third shift: The invisible work of African-American women in higher education. In G. E. Anzaldúa & A. Keating (Eds.), *This bridge we call home: Radical visions for transformation* (pp. 403–415). New York: Routledge.

Lee, J. (2002). The cry-smile mask: A Korean-American woman's system of resistance. In G. E. Anzaldúa & A. Keating (Eds.), *This bridge we call home: Radical visions for transformation* (pp. 397–402). New York: Routledge.

Long, J. R. (2002, September 23). Women still lag in academic ranks. *Chemical and Engineering News, 80*(38), 110–111.

Marasco, C. A. (2004, September 27). No change in numbers of women faculty. *Chemical and Engineering News, 82*(39), 32–33.

Morales, A. T., & Sheafor, B. W. (2002). *The many faces of social workers*. Boston: Allyn & Bacon.

Nafisi, A. (2003a). *Reading Lolita in Tehran: A memoir in books*. New York: Random House.

Nafisi, A. (2003b). Reading 'Lolita' in Tehran. *The Chronicle of Higher Education, 49*(33), B7.

Nelson, D. J. (2005, January 6). *A national analysis of diversity in science and engineering faculties in universities*. Retrieved June 15, 2005, from http://cheminfo.chem.ou.edu/%7Edjn/diversty/briefings/15Jan04Briefings.html

Smallwood, S. (2005). Faculty salaries rose 2.8%, but failed to keep pace with inflation for the first time in 8 years. *The Chronicle of Higher Education, 51*(33), A12.

Sundstrom, W. A. (2004, March). *The college gender gap in the United States, 1940–2000: Trends and international comparisons*. Paper presented at the Fifth World Congress of the Cliometrics, Venice, Italy, July 2004. Retrieved September 22, 2006, from http://lsb.scu.edu/~wsundstrom/papers/college.pdf

Thomas, G. D., & Hollenshead, C. (2001). Resisting from the margins: The coping strategies of Black women and other women of color faculty members at a research university. *Journal of Negro Education, 70*(3), 166–175.

Trower, C. A., & Bleak, J. L. (2004). Study of New Scholars: Tenure-track faculty job satisfaction survey. *Gender: Statistical report* [Universities]. Cambridge, MA: Harvard Graduate School of Education.

Turner, C. S. V. (2002). Women of color in academe: Living with multiple marginality. *Journal of Higher Education, 73*(1), 74–93.

Wilson, R. (2004, December 3). Where the elite teach, it's still a man's world. *The Chronicle of Higher Education, 51*(15), A8.

I AM A WOMAN OF COLOR

Andrea Stewart

September 1, 2005

A mirror reflection of all women, I am uniquely equipped

Beginning with my entrance into a multicultural world

Hosting diverse human beings whose mind sets have clearly shifted

Arbitrary boundaries hindering my progression through life

I will not be stationary, stagnant, or stale as I press forward

You see, I am a woman of color

Red skin, black skin, brown skin, bronze skin, yellow skin,

olive skin, and maybe a little blue skin

Big feet, little feet, flat feet, wide feet, and even narrow feet

Blue eyes, brown eyes, green eyes, hazel eyes, and misty gray eyes

Long hair, short hair, curly hair, kinky hair, straight hair, dreadlocks,

no locks, bald, and maybe some knots

You see, I am a woman of color

Maybe I'm tall, short, petite, medium or large, a figure 8, 9, or 10,

thick or slim, I am in

Just as I am, beauty exemplifies my inner being outward

Refocus your vision and see the real woman that I am

A nurturer, supporter, mediator, believer, motivator, mother, sister,

grandmother, surrogate, and role model

You see, I am a woman of color

I may be an educator, administrator, a counselor, or therapist

It really matters little if I do not change one life

I know now that one becomes many, when each one touches one

Even when I reach out to unify where there are divisions, racism,

ageism, sexism, classism, all the isms surface

Oppression, discrimination, biases, and prejudices bruise my ego

sometimes, but my back will not bend

You see, I am a woman of color

I'll stand tall and boldly voice that I will make a significant difference

and be part of the solution not the source of the problem

Destiny shaped my life and charged me to accomplish my mission as

well as goals

Where failures and defeats seem to stifle my victories,

they will not be champions

My strength embraces my sisters' strength and binds all women's strength

You see, I am a woman of color

Andrea Stewart
Be Blessed!

Women of Color as Social Work Educators

Part I:
A Historical Perspective

Chapter 3: Women of Color in Social Work Education

Saundra Hardin Starks
Suzie Cashwell

In the 21st century, women of color continue to face enormous organizational and systemic, interpersonal, and individual barriers to advancement in the academy. Gender remains an issue and a possible barrier in academia as much as it is in any other institutional setting. The notion of women as educators, particularly in the academy, dates back to the late 1800s and early 1900s. The existence of women of color as educators in social work is an even more recent phenomenon.

Built on the overview provided in the previous chapters and an antecedent to the chapters that follow, the literature on the specific phenomenon of women of color who are social work educators is examined. The existing literature is discussed from a cross-cultural, critical, feminist, social, and spiritual perspective, within the context of the larger academic system. Discussion also focuses on conflicting, as well as complementary, ethics and values between the academic system and social work profession as they relate to and affect the behaviors of women of color as educators. The value placed on the tenure and promotion processes, for whom and how, as well as the struggles and challenges for women of color, are examined. A general overview of the literature on culturally based alternative pedagogical paradigms that have been historically devalued and suppressed in academic systems and institutions is also provided.

A HISTORICAL OVERVIEW

An exploratory examination of the development of female social work educators of color revealed several interesting findings. First, very little is written on women of color as social work educators in the academy, currently or historically. Second, what has been written appears to focus predominantly on African American educators and not on other faculty of color. This finding could be attributed to the social-justice initiatives during and after the Civil Rights movement of the 1960s. It could also be attributed to African Americans being numerically the strongest of the existing groups of color during this time of significant gains, which would directly affect the emergence of opportunities, particularly in the southern states.

Social work education in the academy mimicked education in the United States in general. During the 1800s and through most of the 1900s, education was segregated. Black or African American social workers were educated in "Black" schools while White European Americans were educated in all-"White" schools. As with White European Americans, the education of people of color was heavily influenced by the patriarchal system. Black schools of social work began to form during the early 1900s, and "during the 1920s two social work schools were established for African Americans; the Atlanta School of Social Work and the Bishop Tuttle School in Raleigh, North Carolina" (Carlton-LaNey, 1999, p. 315).

Forerunners and Pioneers

Historically, three African American women stand out as leaders in the early creation of Black universities and colleges. Inabel Burns Lindsay (1900–1983), a pioneer in working with the elderly population and in gerontological studies, was the founding dean of the Howard University School of Social Work and was the university's first female academic dean (Leashore, 2001). Furthermore, Lugenia Burns Hope (1871–1947) assisted in creating the first Black school of social work, recently renamed by Clark Atlanta University as the Whitney M. Young School of Social Work. Similarly, Mary McLeod Bethune was a cofounder and president of Bethune Cookman College, initially created to educate women (Carlton-LaNey, 1999), and a founding member of the National Association of Colored Women. Likewise, women of color such as Diana Wei Ming Chan, Millie Charles, Ada E. Deer, Rosa Gil, Barbara

Solomon, Victoria E. Warner, and many others also contributed extraordinarily to the establishment of women of color as social work educators.

Diana Wei Ming Chan, former instructor of social research methods at San Francisco State University School of Social Work, was a pioneer of contemporary social work education in California. Millie Charles must also be noted for developing the first undergraduate social work program at Southern University in New Orleans (SUNO) in 1965, established at the peak of the Civil Rights movements as an alternative to the all-White European American University of New Orleans. She was instrumental in advocating for the accreditation of baccalaureate social work programs by the Council on Social Work Education (CSWE) and recognizing the baccalaureate degree as qualifying students for advanced standing in master's social work programs.

Ada E. Deer from the Menomonee Nation, director of the American Indian Studies Program at the University of Wisconsin-Madison, has been a steadfast activist and advocate for American Indian issues. Rosa Gil, originally from Cuba, began her social work career in the Spanish-speaking communities of New York City in the early 1960s, focusing on health care issues of children, families, and the homeless. Her academic experiences culminated in serving two terms as dean of health sciences at the City University of New York.

Barbara Solomon contributed to the profession through her work on diversity and Black empowerment issues. Like many other women of color, she began in academia as a practicum supervisor, which led her to a love of teaching and to becoming the first tenured African American at the University of Southern California (USC). At the highest level of her academic career, she became vice provost of USC. Her textbook on Black empowerment, published in the 1970s, remains a classic work.

Victoria E. Warner, instrumental in establishing the baccalaureate and master's social work programs at Florida A&M University, contributed to the transformation of the state-segregated welfare system. She worked with other southern-based social work educators to establish the baccalaureate social work degree as the first-level professional degree. In the late 1960s, she joined others, including Millie Charles, to advocate for CSWE accreditation of baccalaureate social work programs.

Past, present, and future pioneer women in social work education were "multitaskers" before the term was in vogue. They were trailblazers, activists, and advocates for inclusion and equity. However, it remains obvious from this literature review that there continues to be a strong need to identify, develop, and support women of color as social work educators. As we continue to grow the profession, it is imperative that we reflect on what we espouse in cultural competency and multiculturalism.

Professional Responsibility

The Council on Social Work Education (CSWE), in particular, began to address the issues of the need for faculty of color in the 1960s and early 1970s during the Civil Rights era. In June 1968, CSWE added a new standard of accreditation that required schools to provide evidence of efforts to establish racial and cultural diversity in the student body and faculty. Through such accreditation standards, CSWE requires schools of social work to increase the number of students, staff, and faculty of color and to integrate content on people of color into the curriculum (CSWE, 1971). Unfortunately, the literature continues to be lacking regarding the experiences and academic success of social work faculty of color. Furthermore, the lack of faculty qualified to teach in social work programs has been a concern of many social work education administrators. The scarcity of doctoral students of color has further compounded the concerns of administrators in meeting the standards of a diverse faculty. As a result, in 1974, CSWE created a model to increase the number of social work doctoral students of color. Establishment of the CSWE Minority Fellowship Program (MFP) has allowed over 300 social workers of color to receive funding for doctoral-level education (Schiele & Francis, 1996). Furthermore, in 1994, CSWE required that programs "make specific, continuous efforts to ensure equity to faculty and staff in the recruitment, retention, promotion, tenure, assignment and remuneration of program personnel" (CSWE, 1994, Evaluative Standard 3.1).

Currently, CSWE Accreditation Standard 6.0 requires programs to address issues of diversity beyond faculty to the learning context and environment of the academic program. This suggests that not only is it important for faculty to be diverse, but that this also applies to the educational contextual spectrum, which includes the agencies and their clientele as field settings, the program's advisory committees, speakers in special programs, seminars, research, and other initiatives (CSWE, 2003).

In response to CSWE, many universities and colleges have undertaken various methods in attempting to meet this expectation. Unfortunately, as a part of strategic diversity planning, many piecemeal initiatives have added to the distress and lack of value for women of color in academia (Turner & Myers, 2000). One of the initiatives, created in predominantly White European American universities to increase faculty of color with advanced degrees, is termed "grow your own." Administrators of universities and social work programs have responded to the mandate of accrediting bodies such as CSWE to increase the number of educators of color with programs that fund all or part of a doctoral education for students of color.

These "grow your own" programs use a variety of methods, such as paying the salary of a current instructor of color while she or he attends a doctoral program or paying tuition in exchange for payback time. Usually the instructor or student of color is required to remain at the university for a prescribed number of years after obtaining a doctoral degree. The "grow your own" concept ideologically allows people of color to complete a doctoral education without immense financial penalty. While the concept of supporting higher education for people of color as a work incentive is a benefit that should be supported, implementation of the process has been, in part, oppressive and degrading. Such a phenomenon in academia as it relates to women of color as social work educators not only impedes their progress and process, but also has a devaluing and dehumanizing dimension. The term itself implies ownership and often comes with humiliation and loss of respect and dignity.

EXPERIENCES IN CONTEXT

The experiences of women of color as social work educators range from oppression, noncontinuation, and nonpromotion to promotion and positions of deans and directors of social work programs. Educators who are women of color function in a dual culture, where gender and ethnicity or race play a key role in advancement opportunities as well as difficulties. These women educators are subject to overt and covert forms of oppression on many levels. Although not much is written on the specific experiences of women of color as social work educators, it is expected that their experiences are similar to women of color in other disciplines in the academy.

What is this phenomenon of being a female faculty member of color on a predominately White European American campus? To understand the phenomenon and experience, which are discussed in subsequent chapters, one must first understand the context of the social work education environment. This context is created, shaped, and reinforced by various stakeholders in education, including students, faculty, staff, administration, and even regulating bodies of universities. The perspective of each of these stakeholders has shaped the context of today's environment for women of color. Ideally, the context would be one of a culturally competent organization that has "ongoing commitment or institutionalization of appropriate practice and policies for diverse populations" (Brach & Fraser, 2000, p. 181). A culturally competent organization is one that moves beyond giving lip service to affirmative action to embrace diversity. Dreachlin (1996) discusses a

five-stage model for developing culturally competent organizations. Weech-Maldonado, Dreachlin, Dansky, De Souza, and Gatto (2002) summarize Dreachlin's model (1996) as follows:

1. Discovery: Emerging awareness of racial and ethnic diversity as a significant strategic issue.
2. Assessment: Systematic evaluation of organizational climax and culture vis-à-vis racial and ethnic diversity.
3. Exploration: Systematic training initiatives to improve organizations' ability to effectively manage diversity.
4. Transformation: Fundamental change in organization practices result in a culture and climate in which racial and ethnic diversity is valued.
5. Revitalization: Renewal and expansion of racial and ethic diversity initiatives to reward change agents and to include additional identity groups among the organization's diversity initiatives. (p. 113)

Unfortunately, academia with its patriarchal roots, has not progressed beyond discovery as discussed earlier. Expectations placed on women of color in the academy are often a series of paradoxes and contradictions that exist to advance the subtle discrimination inherent in academic systems. Because most programs and schools of social work are multilevel operations within frameworks that are historically oppressive to women and people of color, it is no small stretch to envision the underpinnings and multidimensional aspects of such systems. Regrettably, social work programs and schools are not immune and contain many elements of the larger oppressive system.

This phenomenon is an important aspect for understanding the context of the experiences of women of color within academia. One must remember that a key expectation in schools of social work is teaching for social transformation and the development of social change agents. These are noble tenets and ultimately represent our mission for social work practice. Yet, when students are allowed to maliciously challenge the expertise of faculty, the assignments required, and even the grades awarded, women of color are not supported in accomplishing this integral part of social work education. So how then do we reconcile the notion that our educators do not reflect the changing demographics of this country, nor do their teaching styles reflect the multicultural perspectives that we in the field of social work education so espouse? Are we really preparing our students to negotiate ambiguity with flexibility and to be tolerant of differences in communication and teaching styles? Are the profession's values and ethics conflicting and inconsistent with pedagogical practices?

Pedagogy is critical to dealing with these issues and must be rethought and reconstructed to ensure that, as educators, we are not reinforcing the "pedagogy of the oppressed" (Freire, 1970). Rather, as Guy-Sheftall (1997) suggests, we as social work educators should promote and cultivate pedagogies of transformation and liberation. The attitude that women of color (who choose more nontraditional pedagogies and nontraditional forms of research to create this transformation) are not to be valued impedes the process of transformation and liberation, thus continuing the context in which universities and social work programs only provide lip service to true diversity.

WOMEN AND WOMEN OF COLOR IN SOCIAL WORK EDUCATION

Nationally, women faculty currently comprise approximately 66.2% of the total faculty in CSWE-accredited social work education programs (CSWE, 2005). Of these women, more than 71% are White European American (non-Hispanic), whereas 14.5% are African American women, representing the largest population of color of all female social work educators. White European American women comprise 66% of all White European American faculty, which account for 72% of all social work educators. African Americans, both male and female, comprise 13.4% of all social work faculty; women comprise over 71% of African American social work faculty. Hispanic or Latino faculty (Mexican American, Puerto Rican, and other Latino) represent approximately 4.8% of the faculty in social work education; again, women constitute the majority of Hispanic or Latino faculty (62.1%). Asian American faculty comprise almost 2.5% of social work educators, with over half of the faculty (56.7%) being female. Native American, American Indian, or First Nations educators comprise 1.1% of social work educators, with 64.4% of these educators being women. Pacific Islanders comprise less than 1% of social work educators, with the majority (71.4%) being male.

While it would seem from the above data that women have made their own way into social work education, race and ethnicity only tell part of the story. When examining other factors, women are still lagging behind their male counterparts. For example, 43.6% of male social work educators are tenured, compared to 30% of female social work educators. Regardless of race, men still make higher salaries

Table 1: Number of Women by Rank Across Time

Faculty Rank	1981	1988	2005
Full Professor	762	785	451
Assoc Professor	1,084	888	766
Assist Professor	1,129	1,070	921

Sources: Figures for 1981 and 1988 are from Sowers-Hoag and Harrison (1991); 2005 figures are from CSWE.

than women in social work education. For example, a male full professor makes almost 9% more than his female counterpart, regardless of race. When race is factored in, the salary picture becomes bleaker. Female full professors of color make 19.9% less than female White European American full professors and 29.8% less than male White European American full professors. When examining salaries of professors of color at the assistant-professor level, these radical differences disappear. At the assistant - professor level, female White European Americans earn approximately 2% less than males (regardless of race) and females of color. Males (regardless of race) and females of color are within less than $1,000 of each other, with males of color being paid the most.

A factor that needs further examination is the level of education of women in social work education. Over the last decade, higher education has moved from accepting the MSW as the terminal degree for social work education to requiring a doctorate to teach in a social work program. What is the impact of this issue on women of color as social work educators? Where are women teaching in social work education? Of all women educators in social work, 22.9% are in baccalaureate-only programs, compared to 19.7% of all male social

work educators. Except for African American and Asian American women in social work education, women are approximately equally represented in graduate-only or joint programs compared to baccalaureate programs. On the other hand, Asian American women are more likely to be in a joint or graduate-only program rather than a baccalaureate program, whereas African American women comprise 13.9% of the faculty in graduate or joint programs, compared to 15.1% in baccalaureate-only programs.

Given the emphasis in social work education on moving the terminal degree for teaching to a doctorate degree, one must also ask, what type of degree do women currently hold? An examination of data gathered by CSWE reveals an interesting divide in the educational attainment by women in social work education based on ethnicity (see Table 2). African American, White European American, and Hispanic or Latino American faculty are more likely to have an MSW than a doctorate, while Native American, American Indian, or First Nations and Asian American faculty are more likely to have a doctorate (although not necessarily in social work). As expected, White European American women are more prominent in social work education. They outnumber all other ethnic groups combined. African American women are the second largest group.

Table 2: Educational Attainment by Ethnicity

Level of Education	MSW	Doctorate in Social Work	Doctorate in Other Field
African American	306	223	86
American Indian	19	18	10
Asian American	21	58	14
European American	1,656	989	371
Latina/Hispanic	106	63	18
Pacific Islander	2	2	0

Source: Based on data from CSWE, 2003.

CHALLENGES AND REWARDS FOR WOMEN OF COLOR IN SOCIAL WORK EDUCATION

How successful have women of color been in social work education? According to Schiele and Francis (1996), "by conventional standards, a successful social work academician is viewed as someone who has attained a high academic rank, who is tenured, and who has high publication productivity" (p. 31). Learning how women have fared on these three factors helps explain the challenges and rewards for women of color in the academic setting.

Tenure

Several factors affect tenure beyond publication productivity, including available tenure lines, service, collegiality, and mentoring. The availability of tenure lines is an important factor in understanding women of color's ability to receive tenure. As Di Palma and Topper (2001) suggest, "just as the number of women earning doctorates in social work

rose, the number of tenure-track social work lines decreased" (p. 34). This issue has major implications given that, in some schools of social work, tenure is competitive. A university may hire two or three junior faculty with the knowledge that only one tenure position exists, for which they will compete.

Schiele and Francis (1996) conducted a study among members of the Minority Fellowship Program and found that there was significant difference between men and women who received tenure. In fact, 46.9% of the male fellows received tenure versus only 25.9% of the female fellows. Part of the explanation may be found in the expectation that faculty of color will be available for service and mentoring. Simon, Bowles, King, and Roff (2004) indicated that African Americans are expected to serve on numerous committees to demonstrate diversity. Being the token member of a committee increases the service expectation of faculty of color, which is consistent with other research on academia as a whole. Due to the underrepresentation of faculty of color and the organizational development stage of discovery, faculty of color are often expected to serve on more committees, which leads to heavier service loads (Turner & Myers, 2000). Faculty members of color often have more service responsibilities than their White European American counterparts (Turner & Myers, 2000). Unfortunately, service is not a heavily weighted part of the tenure process.

Another aspect of service is the expectation that faculty of color will mentor other faculty of color in social work education. However, Simon, et al. (2004) indicated that a "senior African American female mentor, may not, in good conscience, be able to take on the responsibility of mentoring more African American women protègès in addition to the other tasks she assumes" (p. 142), thus creating another paradox of choice (too much service or not enough service) for the woman faculty of color as she tries to gain tenure.

According to the study by Schiele and Francis (1996), faculty of color perceived the tenure and promotion process as biased against them and felt it was difficult for them to find colleagues who were willing to allow them to penetrate the "buddy system." Since collegiality is also a part of the tenure process, this finding is a source of consternation. Faculty who have mediocre teaching evaluations, but good publication rates, may be denied tenure on the basis of collegiality. Research is needed in this area to determine how this has affected faculty of color, especially women.

Publication

Administration and university culture continues to devalue women educators of color with its tradi-tional understanding of scholarship within the patriarchal tenure process. Social work education is not exempt from this criticism either. In fact, social work education continues to place more and more emphasis on tier-one journals, which are usually mainstream publications with very low acceptance rates, as a part of tenure and promotion. Thus, "faculty of color find that research on minority issues is not considered legitimate work, particularly if articles are published in journals that are not mainstream" (Turner & Myers, 2000, p. 26). Schiele and Francis (1996) found that, among the partici-pants of the CSWE Minority Fellowship Program, men of color published in social work journals at a higher rate than women (see Table 3). They also found that women faculty of color who received a doctorate when they were older were less likely to be published.

In an earlier study, Hull and Wayne (1994) found that baccalaureate faculty published less than graduate faculty. They also found that relatively few faculty members (graduate or undergraduate) pub-lished. In their research, women accounted for 56% of the publications, but this was not significant given that 55% of the faculty examined were women. They did not examine race, however, their findings may explain Schiele and Francis's conclu-sion that African American women publish less in peer-reviewed journals. As discussed earlier, African American women comprise over 15% of the baccalaureate faculty and are less likely to be in graduate or joint faculty, whereas Asian American women are more likely to be graduate faculty and publish at a higher rate than other female doctoral fellows of color.

Table 3: Average Publication Rate of Minority Fellowship Program by Race/Gender

Race/Gender	Mean Publication
Hispanic/Latino Men	4.5
African American Men	4.25
Asian/Native American Women	2.5
Hispanic/Latina Women	2.36
Asian/Native American Men	1.75
African American Women	1.03

Source: Schiele and Francis (1996).

Another study by Schiele (1991) found that a majority of publications by African American faculty are completed by a few individuals and that African American faculty produce slightly fewer publications than the overall population of social work faculty. He also found that 32.3% of African Americans who responded indicated they had not published; this compares to 20% for academia as a whole. Of those who indicated they had published 21 or more articles, only 5.5% of the African Americans fell into this category, as compared to 11.7% of the overall respondents.

Promotion and Advancement

Given that women comprise more than 60% of all social work academics (see earlier section), one would expect they would make up approximately 60% of each rank. Women appear to be overrepresented in the lower ranks and underrepresented in the highest rank (full professor). Schiele and Francis (1996) found that, among participants of the CSWE Minority Fellowship Program, 9.4% of the men were promoted to full professor compared to only 5.6% of the women. More troublesome was the finding that 64.8% of the women were still at the rank of assistant professor, while only 43.8% of the men were.

An examination of the breakdown of the CSWE 2003 data reveals that 33.8% of the women at full-professor level are White European American, while African American women comprise 5.8%. All other groups of color account for less than 5% of this number. At the associate-professor level, of the 63.4%, the majority of women are White European American (45.2%) and African American (10.8%). Regardless of the professoriate level, Native American, American Indian, or First Nations and Pacific Islander women remain far behind the other groups of color in terms of representation. This may be a function of the limited number of women from these ethnic groups who are in academia. However, one cannot ignore the influence of discrimination on access to social work education for these groups.

Given that "the attainment of higher rank and tenure are necessary prerequisites for the advancement of women to deanships of graduate programs and directorship of undergraduate programs" (Di Palma & Topper, 2001, p. 33), the impact on women

Table 4: Percentage of All Female Faculty by Rank

Faculty Rank	1981	1988	2003
Full Professor	25.8	28.6	46.7
Assoc Professor	42.0	55.4	63.4
Assist Professor	60.0	65.7	70.4

Sources: Figures for 1981 and 1988 are from Sowers-Hoag and Harrison (1991); 2003 figures are from CSWE.

Table 5: Administrative Position (of Women in Social Work Education) by Ethnicity

Ethnicity	Chief Administrator	Associate or Assistant Dean	Director of Programs (PhD, MSW, BSW)
European American	185	44	88
African American	42	11	14
American Indian	1	0	1
Asian American	1	1	5
Latina American	3	2	5
Pacific Islander	0	0	2

of color in directorships needs to be examined. Di Palma and Topper (2001) found a statistically significant increase in the percentage of women moving into social work academic leadership roles, however, this is predominantly at the baccalaureate level, which has less prestige than graduate programs. Unfortunately, ethnicity as a variable was not examined in this study. Simon, et al. (2004) concluded "African American women [in social work] face great organizational, interpersonal, and individual barriers to advancement in academia" (p. 143). They also indicated that "white men are the primary holders of positions of power and leadership in academic institutions and business organization in which social workers are trained and most social workers are employed" (p. 138). However, CSWE (2002) data indicated that women filled 55% of dean or director; associate or assistant dean; and director of PhD, MSW, and BSW programs positions. While women fill 55% of all administrative positions, 78% of those women are classified as White European American. Thus, White European American women are five times more likely to hold a leadership position in social work education than African American women and 31 times more likely than Latina faculty.

CONCLUSION

The literature, which is sparse, indicates that, despite the struggles, barriers, issues with oppressive pedagogy, and lack of mentoring, women of color in social work education have survived and thrived while making significant contributions to the social work profession and the field of education. The remainder of the chapters in this book present the voices of the women who have experienced these issues firsthand. These women are representative of the five major ethnic and racial groups in the United States (African American, Asian American, Hispanic or Latina American, Native American, American Indian, or First Nations, as well as the various levels of academic involvement, from instructors to deans and directors of social work programs. The voices and stories echo each other in similarities and differences. When approached about this project many of the women were excited about the opportunity to share their stories and, in some small way, mentor others who are starting their journeys with the same passion and commitment.

As you read the following stories of women of color as social work educators, you may have more questions than answers. However, the intent of this book is to allow you to ponder the following questions: What are the experiences of women of color in social work education? What personal, social, cultural, and systemic-based factors contribute to success or failure among women of color in academia and social work education? Specifically, how does "functioning" in a dual culture, gender and ethnic or race-based, affect women of color social work educators? What is the "grow your own" phenomenon in academia as it relates to women of color social work educators? What price is paid for institutional support in terms of dignity and respect for women of color educators? Is parity possible in this arena? Why do women of color stay in social work education? What are the patterns of underrepresentation of women of color in social work education? Does social work education practice what it preaches? What are the overt and covert roles, rules, and rituals to which women of color must adhere? What is the responsibility of the profession to women of color?

REFERENCES

Brach, C., & Fraser, I. (2000). Can cultural competency reduce racial and ethnic racial health disparities? *Medicare Care Research and Review, 57*(supplement 1), 181–217.

Carlton-LaNey, I. (1999). African American Social Work pioneers: Response to need. *Social Work, 5,* 311–321.

Council on Social Work Education. (1971). *Manual of accrediting standards for graduate professional schools of social work.* New York, Author.

Council on Social Work Education. (1994). *Handbook of accreditation standards and procedures* (4th ed.). Alexandria, VA: Author.

Council on Social Work Education. (2002). *Statistics on social work education in the United States.* Alexandria, VA: Author.

Council on Social Work Education. (2003). *Handbook of accreitation standards and procedures.* Alexandria, VA: Author.

Council on Social Work Education. (2005). *Statistics on social work education in the United States.* Alexandria, VA: Author.

Di Palma, S. L., & Topper, G. G. (2001). Social work academia: Is the glass ceiling beginning to crack? *Affilia, 16*(1), 31–45.

Dreachlin, J. L. (1996). *Diversity leadership.* Chicago: Health Administration Press.

Freire, P. (1970). *Pedagogy of the oppressed.* New York: Continuum.

Guy-Sheftall, B. (1997). Transforming the academy. In L. Benjamin (Ed.), *Black women in the academy: Promises & perils* (pp. 115–123). Gainsville, FL: University of Florida Press.

Hull, G. H, & Wayne, J. H. (1994). Publication rates of undergraduate social work programs in selected journals. *Journal of Social Work Education, 30,* 54–62.

Leashore, B. (2001). African-Americans' overview. In R. L. Edwards (Ed.), *Encyclopedia of social work* (19th ed.). Washington, DC: NASW Press.

Schiele, J. H. (1991). Publication productivity of African American social work faculty. *Journal of Social Work Education, 27,* 125–134.

Schiele, J., & Francis, E. A. (1996). The status of former CSWE Ethnic Minority Doctoral Fellows in social work academia. *Journal of Social Work Education, 32,* 31–44.

Simon, C. E., Bowles, D. D., King, S. W., & Roff, L. L. (2004). Mentoring in the careers of African American women in social work education. *Affilia, 19,* 134–145.

Turner, C. S. V., & Myers, S. L. (2000). *Faculty of color in Academe: Bittersweet success.* Boston: Allyn & Bacon.

Weech-Maldonado, R., Dreachlin, J. L., Dansky, K. H., De Souza, G., & Gatto, M. (2002). Racial/ethnic diversity management and cultural competency: The case of Pennsylvania hosptals. *Journal of Healthcare Management, 47*(2), 111–124.

Women of Color as Social Work Educators

Part I: A Historical Perspective

Chapter 4: Leaders and Legends in Social Work Education

Carmen Ortiz Hendricks
Saundra Hardin Starks
Halaevalu F. Ofahengaue Vakalahi

This chapter pays homage to all the women of color who have paved the way for so many who follow. These women forerunners represent the finest qualities of hope and courage, commitment and persistence, and the strength and determination that women of color today emulate. Despite the stories of survival in the face of adversity, injustice, and inequality, these pioneers succeeded out of their passion to break through the glass ceiling in academia and establish themselves as academicians of the profession they all love—social work. We recognize a few of these leaders and legends in this chapter.

BARBARA WHITE

Dr. Barbara White is an extraordinary individual and an African American woman in her 60s. In addition to her numberless achievements, she has been professor and Dean of the School of Social Work at the University of Texas at Austin for 12 years. She has thrived and succeeded in academia since 1977 and have become a "household name" in social work education. Before making the career shift to social work, Dr. White taught music education in a public school for several years.

Strengths and Survival

Dr. White's life decisions speak to her strengths and ambitions. As she stated, "I was not supposed to succeed. I was the first college graduate in my family. I grew up with an absent father, segregation, 'ghetto' neighborhoods, and I had dark skin." But Dr. White is a risk-taker as reflected, for example, in her decision to pursue her BSW and MSW degrees while raising her one- and two-year-old daughters. Being a mother was a major life-affirming experience for her. While pursuing her MSW, she met her first mentor. This informal mentor was a White European American woman, which was interesting because Dr. White had never before attended school with White European Americans. This mentor told her, "You have something important to contribute, and I like you for who you are." Indeed, this mentor had a profound impact on Dr. White's future and her ability to take risks and succeed.

Throughout her professional career, Dr. White has had to work around the racism she encountered personally and institutionally. Despite the consequences of racism, she perceived racism as a door opener because it motivated her to succeed and contributed to her high level of resiliency. For instance, there were always Black faculty at Florida State University, but many came and went. The tenure process was never easy, however, Dr. White found people who mentored and coached her as she struggled with her doctoral studies and thereafter as a faculty of color. Consequently, she was the first tenured Black social work professor at Florida State University.

Dr. White survived racism in Florida and later in Texas; however, joining the University of Texas at Austin as a Dean was a major life challenge. She found that Texas reflected more of the characteristics of the South than Florida did. It was a difficult transition, and it was particularly difficult to gain the trust and confidence of the faculty and university administrators. At that point in her career, she needed a strong mentor and professional collegiality. To find this support, Dr. White turned her attention to the greater social work profession and became an integral part of the National Association of Social Workers (NASW) and the Council on Social Work Education (CSWE) in a number of leadership roles, culminating in becoming the president of both professional organizations. Her leadership roles gave her confidence and additional opportunities to grow professionally. "This is why it is so important for me to be a mentor to others and to serve in that capacity," she explains. As an academician and an administrator, she relates to prospective faculty of color that she is there to mentor them and support their success. She states, "I see it as my job, and I have made mentorship part of the culture of our School of Social Work."

Dr. White says that her strong racial and ethnic identity is "omnipresent," which means it is always there. To some people, she is a Black woman first, and she watches their reactions when she is introduced as the Dean. She said, "The social work profession has a responsibility to respect me and others like me in the same way that it respects other members of the profession. The profession should not assume it knows me just because I am a woman of color. It also has a responsibility to grow others like me to take my place and the place of others like me who have contributed something special that this profession needs—diversity."

ROWENA FONG

Dr. Rowena Fong is a Chinese (Asian) American woman in her 50s. She is currently a professor of social work at the University of Texas at Austin. Prior to that, she spent 24 years on the faculty at the University of Hawaii-Manoa. She received her BA from Wellesley College, her MSW from the University of California–Berkeley, and her doctorate in education from the Harvard School of Education. Throughout her career, she has been a strong advocate for immigrant and refugee children and families, Asian American and Chinese children and families, child welfare, and culturally competent social work practice.

Strengths and Survival

It is clear from just a cursory review of her curriculum vitae that Dr. Fong is not only an advocate for many groups, but that she is passionate about her research and publications. She loves research, writing, and teaching and does all three superbly well. She recalls her first years as an assistant professor and her fear of the "publish or perish" dictum. She sought out and found mentors at the University of Hawaii who were available and able to support her work. This mentoring definitely helped since Dr. Fong is the author of seven books, 33 chapters, 19 articles, and monographs and reports too numerous to count. She is currently working on a new textbook, *Culturally Diverse Human Behavior and the Social Environment: Contexts of Cultural Identity*, for Brooks/Cole Publishing. She is also revising her book, *Culturally Competent Practice: Skills, Interventions and Evaluations*, for Allyn and Bacon.

Throughout her academic career, Dr. Fong has worked in environments where there were few women of color in administration or on the faculty, despite living on the diverse islands of Hawaii. Dr. Fong sought out conferences for women of color in higher education as a way to empower herself and others and as forums for networking. She has collected quite an array of colleagues from the U.S. and all parts of the world. She also enjoys mentoring Asian American and Pacific Islander students, who see her as a role model and support for their own struggles and ambitions.

"I have sat on many departmental personnel committees seeking to recruit and retain women of color in the academy, but the incentives for women of color to stay and survive in academia are lacking. We need more resources to support their careers and their families," Dr. Fong exclaims. Her mentors helped her survive the discrimination and biases of the White European American, male-dominated academy. Dr. Fong believes that mentoring of and support for junior faculty of color is of utmost importance if there is to be a diverse academy. She holds CSWE and NASW responsible for supporting women of color in academia; as she states, "Right now we need opportunities to facilitate research and grant writing on issues that reflect the needs of the diverse ethnic communities served by social workers. These opportunities are minimal at best. Getting the backing of CSWE and NASW to support our research on our communities would go a long way towards legitimizing our research initiatives."

E. ARACELIS FRANCIS

 Dr. E. Aracelis Francis is Director of the Council on Social Work Education (CSWE) Office of Social Work Education and Research, and Director of CSWE's Minority Fellowship Program. Dr. Francis is an African American woman in her 60s who was born in the U.S. Virgin Islands. She has taught full and part time in social work education for more than 20 years. Currently, she is an adjunct associate professor at the Howard University Graduate School of Social Work.

Strengths and Survival

Dr. Francis has spent over 25 years at CSWE advocating and successfully securing funding for the Minority Fellowship Program for PhD social work students and collaborating with psychology, nursing, psychiatry, and sociology fellowship programs throughout the U.S. She attributes her long tenure at CSWE to her commitment to minority fellows and the mentorship of Carl Scott.

In her early educational career, Dr. Francis attended Interamericana University in Puerto Rico. In the 1960s, she attended the University of Chicago, where she earned an MSW and then Columbia University for her PhD. Throughout her education, there were very few African American students or faculty with whom she could network; however, in the second year of her MSW program, she met an African American supervisor who became her first mentor. Thereafter, an African American male professor mentored her through her dissertation phase. Upon graduation, an African American woman at Columbia University referred her to Adelphi University, where she taught for four years as an assistant professor. Then she became involved with CSWE in the early 1970s, when she worked with Carl Scott. She sees her current position at CSWE as a tribute to her mentors and to her enjoyment of the work as a minority-fellows mentor. These experiences sensitized her to the diverse and common struggles of African, African American, and Afro-Caribbean people in particular.

Dr. Francis is passionate about mentorship. She says, "If you can find balance, you can get some things done," referring to advocating for and mentoring students of color. She only wishes she had more time to mentor. She observes that students of color who are mentored are assertive, outgoing, and open-minded and will achieve much in their professional careers. Dr. Francis understands the process of doctoral education (the politics, demands, and pressures) and offers students techniques and ideas to facilitate their getting through a PhD program. She emphasizes, "You can have the desire and skill to succeed, but not always the support, particularly if you are a person of color. Never give up and don't let yourself down." On that note, she emphasized the importance of getting and giving mentorship.

In the 1970s, following the advent of the Civil Rights movement, CSWE began to develop task forces to look at issues affecting people of color in social work education. More opportunities became available and more attempts were made to integrate people of color into the academy. For instance, *Black Caucus: Journal of the ABSW* (Association of Black Social Workers) was established in reaction to the exclusion of Black social workers from mainstream social work journals. Dr. Francis also notes that, thus far, CSWE has had only one woman of color as president of the Council and no woman of color as executive director.

Nevertheless, throughout her career, Dr. Francis has been sustained by her safe haven and refuge in the Virgin Islands, a community of families, relatives, and friends, and a home away from home.

ESTHER LANGSTON

Dr. Esther Langston, a professor of social work at the University of Nevada, Las Vegas (UNLV), is an African American woman in her 60s who has spent more than half her life teaching social work at UNLV.

Strengths and Survival

Dr. Langston describes her mother as a natural helper who instilled in her social work values and the importance of good teaching. She was the first African American woman to earn tenure at UNLV. "This was no easy feat," she says, "As I was in a historically White institution, but I submitted my articles to quality journals that were beyond question, and I did not let others define my reality or my value." As an African American female in academia in the 1970s, she was looked upon as an affirmative action hire. This did not prevent her from fighting for pay equity while not yet a tenured faculty member. "I took a stand so no other woman, particularly a woman of color, would have to experience that again," she exclaims. Dr. Langston believes that parity in academia is possible, but, for women of color, parity in academia only comes if you work harder, are smarter, do more, and have the research data to support your positions. For example, early in her teaching career, parents would come to her classes with their children to make sure the African American teacher knew what she was doing. They would show up, ask to sit in on the class, and inquire where she got her degrees. No other faculty member at UNLV had to endure such scrutiny.

Dr. Langston defines duality as having to function within a culture based simultaneously on gender and race. This has added stress to her life, but it has also provided her with a unique opportunity to be a role model to women and African Americans. Both racism and sexism have affected her life as a woman of color in social work education: "I learned to play the political game in the academy because that was the means for my survival." She has stayed in social work education because of the students, and, when students were described as marginal or failing, Dr. Langston believed she could help them graduate and become good social work practitioners; that has kept her going all these years at UNLV.

During her 15-year tenure as program director, the social work program met the university guidelines for affirmative action 100% of the time. Dr. Langston was able to effect cultural diversity in not only the social work program, but in the university as a whole. Dr. Langston believes that social work education should train students to be advocates for social change and economic justice and to provide culturally competent services. She believes in the importance of mentoring and networking to produce effective social work practitioners and educators who are committed to best practice models with diverse communities. She states, "It is important to understand that you are not in this struggle alone. There are other people in the struggle, and you can build on each other's strengths to make a difference!"

CARMEN ORTIZ HENDRICKS

Dr. Carmen Ortiz Hendricks is a Puerto Rican woman in her 50s who began her teaching career as a field instructor in 1975. In 2005, she was appointed Associate Dean and professor at the Yeshiva University Wurzweiler School of Social Work. She spent from 1980 to 2005 on the faculty of the Hunter College School of Social Work of the City University of New York. In 1993, she rose to the rank of tenured associate professor, and, in 2003, she was a candidate for dean at the Hunter College School of Social Work.

Strengths and Survival

Dr. Ortiz Hendricks sums up her academic career as one of "leadership by way of cultural diversity." The social work profession expected her to be an expert on Puerto Rican culture and diversity in general fresh out of her master's program. Her education until then had not taught her very much about her own culture, let alone about diverse cultures. Determined to become an expert, she read everything she could find about Hispanics. In the 1970s, she read articles by pioneer scholars like Emelicia Mizio (1972a, 1972b, 1974), Marta Sotomayor (1977), and Sonia Badillo Ghali (1977). In the 1980s, Dr. Ortiz Hendricks read the writings of Diane de Anda (1984), Maria Queralt (1984), and Lillian Comas-Diaz (1984). And, in the 1990s, the classic article by

Lorraine Gutierrez, "Working with Women of Color: An Empowerment Perspective" (1990) inspired her. Also in the 1990s, she discovered the work of Maria Zuniga (1992) and Rosa Maria Gil and Carmen Vazquez (1996). These Latina authors taught her about the meaning of culture in the lives of Puerto Ricans and Latinos.

Gradually, Dr. Ortiz Hendricks began to develop her own concept of cultural sensitivity and cultural competence. "I taught myself about my culture and the culture of others. I think that is why I am so good at teaching others about culture and diversity. One learns as they teach and teaches as they learn," she explains. It was this emphasis on diversity and cultural competence that pushed Dr. Ortiz Hendricks into leadership positions, first on committees in her local NASW chapter and later as president of the New York City chapter. As a member of NASW's National Committee on Racial and Ethnic Diversity, she chaired one of the subcommittees that developed the NASW Standards on Cultural Competence in Social Work Practice, which was passed by the Board of Directors in 2001. Dr. Ortiz Hendricks is known nationally and internationally for her presentations on culturally competent social work practice and education, and she is a founding member of NASW's Latino Social Work Task Force, which is working to build the Latino social work workforce in New York City. "We need more Latinas/os in our profession as well as more culturally competent practitioners," states Dr. Ortiz Hendricks.

WILMA PEEBLES-WILKINS

Dr. Wilma Peebles-Wilkins, an African American woman in her 60s, has been professor of social work at Boston University for the past 14 years and dean for nine of those years. Currently Dean Emerita, she has been in academia for 28 years. In October 2006, the National Association of Social Workers Foundation inducted Dr. Peebles-Wilkins as a social work pioneer, undoubtedly an award befitting a woman of her caliber.

Strengths and Survival

Dr. Peebles-Wilkins was born in the South in 1945 and spent most of her formative years growing up under legalized segregation. She states, "I grew up in a two-parent household with a religious father who had limited formal education. In my earlier years, I was somewhat embarrassed by this situation, but later I realized all that my parents had given me emotionally. From this experience, I became aware that we learn in many different ways from others regardless of their station in life and level of education." African Americans experienced the worst aspects of segregation—poor service, poor health care, sitting at the back of the bus, and, essentially, having to submit to White privilege. Black women had to contend with male privilege and were commonly viewed as less than equal, sexually promiscuous, and easily exploited. Dr. Peebles-Wilkins grew up in a time when Blacks were openly discriminated against and then blamed for their victimization. She attended a private integrated high school in the 1960s and was one of the "first Blacks" to graduate from a predominantly White university in the South. She explains, "Growing up with these experiences has helped me to succeed and cope with the subtle racism, discrimination, and exclusion that persist today within and outside our profession."

Dr. Peebles-Wilkins insists on self-definition and refuses to be defined by others and treated as a victim: "I present myself as a capable professional who is more than the color of her skin or her gender. I have sought challenging roles in predominantly White European American settings and have been effective at maintaining my self-definition." Above all else, she believes in the resiliency of the human spirit and the Black race.

She also recalls an important encounter in the early 1980s with Dr. John Longres, a Latino social work educator. At its annual program meeting, CSWE held Educational Innovation Exchanges where scholars sat at tables and spoke to interested participants about their projects. Dr. Peebles-Wilkins was completing her doctorate in educational history and philosophy and was doing research that focused on the Progressive Era, John Dewey, and Jane Addams. John Longres visited her table and asked her to develop biographical sketches on selected African Americans for the *Encyclopedia of Social Work*. Developing these biographical sketches helped redirect her research to African Americans and their contribution to social welfare policy and history. She never left the subject again and inspired Black students in her classes to take pride in themselves and those who came before them. She states, "My

ambition is to ensure that positive, self-help content on African Americans continues to be included in the social work curriculum."

In the early 1900s, an African American woman named Elise Johnson McDougal wrote about the double-edged sword of being Black and a woman. As an administrator in a predominantly White European American institution of higher education in New England, Dr. Peebles-Wilkins encountered strong reactions and negative stereotypes as an African American woman. She explains, "If a single Black woman is successful and financially secure, it is not because she worked hard, it is because she has done something wrong." Being able to tune out these negative stereotypes has helped her succeed as a professional in social work education and create an inclusive academic and scholarly community. She strives to develop recruitment and mentoring strategies and policies for other people of color, and fostering a climate that promotes retention is one of her strongest skills as an administrator. She said, "I am not a supporter of insincere lip-service affirmative action, and I am willing to take others on, help translate the contributions people of color bring to higher education, and stand firm behind my conviction that an environment that lacks diversity does not provide a full learning experience."

Dr. Peebles-Wilkins comes from a culture that provided her with self-acceptance and a support network to withstand exclusion and discrimination. For this reason, she is never alone. She comments, "I bring a balanced, realistic interpretation to what is happening, I often do not mince words, and I feel determined to make people hear that which they do not want to hear. And I do all of this without hostility, but with healthy anger."

LORRAINE GUTIERREZ

Dr. Lorraine Gutierrez, a Latina woman of Mexican American heritage in her early 50s, is a professor at the University of Michigan, School of Social Work. She has spent the last 16 years of her life in academia teaching at the master's and doctoral levels.

Strengths and Survival

Dr. Gutierrez recalls attending a predominantly White middle class school in southern California. This middle school placed her in classes for average and below-average students, despite the fact that she excelled in the Iowa Achievement Tests, scoring in the 95th percentile. A teacher questioned why she and other bright students were in lower level classes, but, unfortunately, the school did not support transferring these students to higher level classes. However, this teacher developed and implemented independent study programs to expose these students to a more challenging curriculum. Speaking of this teacher, Dr. Gutierrez said, "I remember him saying to me when I came back from college [Stanford University] during break, 'You made it.' I thanked him for helping to make my success possible. I now know how much teachers can treasure those moments."

Dr. Gutierrez attended the MSW program at the University of Chicago in the late 1970s. During that time, the strong focus on ego psychology resulted in her feeling that the Civil Rights, feminist, and other social movements had never occurred. Perhaps the shock was also due to going from the multicultural milieu of the West Coast to the bifur-cated Black and White perspective of the industrial Midwest. Nonetheless, she learned how to speak up and assert herself. She exclaims, "Up until then I had been very, very shy and unassertive, but I was so concerned about the discourse in my courses about women, Latinos, and poor people that I could not keep my mouth shut all of the time." Dr. Gutierrez became involved with a local coalition for abused women, which developed the first shelters in Chicago. Through interested faculty, she brought these experiences into the classroom. She said, "I think the other students and, quite possibly the faculty, too, were tired of how much I kept bringing up issues of violence against women. Some of them even told me that the whole issue was a fad that would eventually go away." These experiences helped Dr. Gutierrez identify strategies to achieve her professional goals.

Early in her career, Dr. Gutierrez decided she would not be happy in a school where she had to hide who she was in order to fit in or be accepted. Her commitment to practice that is community-based and attentive to privilege, diversity, social justice, and multicultural issues were often unsupported. She received lukewarm or negative performance evaluations because she had chosen this path rather than focusing on securing external funding for more basic research. She said, "It is stressful to feel so out of step with those around me, especially when I think I am doing the right thing." Nevertheless, she persevered and moved up the academic ladder. She pursued promotion to full professor because of the role full professors play in hiring, tenure, and promotion. She explains, "I would have more opportunities to support those who are coming behind me because of my rank." She also continued her research, which has been widely published. She said, "Even though my work may be out of the mainstream, it has often been published, and this has allowed me to get to where I am as a full professor." Dr. Gutierrez was also supported by excellent mentors, including other women in the academy and her brother, a journalism professor in California. She learned from these mentors and others how to negotiate the academy. Nonetheless, she followed her own strict ethics regarding equity, transparency, and integrity. She said, "My work has often been a source of additional stress to me, and I have had to make many more efforts to pace myself, take care of myself, and connect to the spiritual side of my life in order to keep going. Believing that I am helping to make the world a better place to live in also helps."

According to Dr. Gutierrez, the most intense challenge in her life has been being a woman and a woman of color in a male-dominated institution. These challenges especially emerged when she had her two daughters. She explains, "My first daughter was born when I was a PhD student, and I felt very conspicuous attending courses as a pregnant woman. I once overheard a professor I worked for say, 'I don't expect my graduate assistants to get pregnant.' Another faculty member, my primary mentor, doubted my plans to keep on with my studies full-time because he felt the biological demands of taking care of an infant would be too overwhelming for me. When I pointed out that the male PhD students did not get these same questions, they stopped making remarks, but I knew they still had their doubts."

As Dr. Gutierrez climbed the ladder to full professor and to an administrator at the University of Michigan, her gender was an ongoing issue. As the director of a campus-wide center for community service and learning, she was often the only woman or person of color in a room full of administrators. The men appeared to converse only with each other, and it was not easy to be heard. She found herself becoming "unusually assertive." She states, "I have sometimes wondered if they viewed me as being particularly rude for a woman or perhaps just one of the boys."

Dr. Gutierrez believes that her race, ethnicity, gender, and culture play a role in every aspect of her life, every day. It affects the way in which students, staff, and colleagues relate to her and how they expect her to relate to them. She knows that Latina/o students expect more from her than she can possibly give, but she does the best she can. She suspects that majority group students may question her qualifications or capabilities. Research has shown that faculty members who are women and people of color are more likely to receive poor course evaluations. She has been affected by this in some classes, especially when she pushes students to confront their biases and misconceptions. She exclaims, "Certainly knowing where I came from and who I am makes me treat everyone equally and with respect whether it is the person cleaning my office, a student, a clerical staff member, a colleague, or the provost. I hope the social work profession sees me as an ally. I am committed to do all that I can to remain connected with practice and the practice community."

REFERENCES

Badillo-Ghali, S. (1977). Culture sensitivity and the Puerto Rican client. *Social Casework, 58*(8), 459–468.

Comas-Diaz, L. (1984). Content themes in group treatment with Puerto Rican women. *Social Work with Groups, 7*(3), 75–84.

de Anda, D. (1984). Bicultural socialization: Factors affecting the minority experience. *Social Work, 29*, 101–107.

Gil, R. M., & Vazquez, C. (1996). *How Latinas can merge Old World traditions with New World self-esteem.* New York: Putnam.

Gutierrez, L. (1990). Working with women of color: An empowerment perspective. *Social Work, 35*, 149–154.

Mizio, E. (1972a). Puerto Rican social workers and racism. *Social Casework, 53*(5), 267–272.

Mizio, E. (1972b). White worker—minority client. *Social Work, 12*, 82–86.

Mizio, E. (1974). Impact of external systems on the Puerto Rican family. *Social Casework, 55*(2), 76–83.

Queralt, M. (1984). Understanding Cuban immigrants: A cultural perspective. *Social Work, 29*, 115–121.

Sotomayor, M. (1977). Language, culture and ethnicity in developing self concept. *Social Casework, 58*, 195–203.

Zuniga, M. (1992). Using metaphors in therapy: Dichos and Latino clients. *Social Work, 31*, 55–60.

Women of Color as Social Work Educators

Part II: The Voices of Women of Color as Social Work Educators

FOR MEREANA A METAPHOR
VERNICE WINEERA
New York, New York
February 11, 2002

"Come with me," you said,
"I want to show you something."
And from a large kete you pulled another,
and another, and more,
with colors like paua, pounamu,
Papatuanuku.
Taonga beautiful of form.
Colors of puha, Maori potatoes,
pipi from gray–black sand.
Kete, expectant vessels waiting to be filled.
Drawing them forth out of each other,
your fingers caressing each ridge and weave,
you voice a quiet, perplexed thought,

"The kiekie, it feels different here."
It's true. The kiekie, pulled and prepared
in a season of sun,
is rigid, less supple.
Dry, away from homeland air,
life–giving, warm, earth–moist air.
Transported now to winter New York,
your mokopuna grow hard,
toughen in this alien place.
But listen to me, Mere.
Still they glisten,
the inner glow you wove with grace,
with giving hands,
is a felt thing,
and more?
Their mana wills me home
to hill and creek and shore.

GLOSSARY

Papatuanuku	Mother Earth	Pounamu	greenstone (jade)
Taonga	treasure	Pipi	clams
Kete	baskets	Puha	milk-thistle, an edible weed that is a favorite green in the Maori diet
Paua	abalone—its iridescent shell is used to decorate traditional wood carvings; also worn as jewelry	Kiekie	strong vine used in weaving baskets
		Mokopuna	grandchildren, younger generation
		Mana	integrity

Part II: The Voices of Women of Color as Social Work Educators

Chapter 5: ¡SÍ SE PUEDE! (Yes, It Can Be Accomplished!)

Barbara A. Candales

To the memory of my grandmother—Candelaria Candales.
To my mother, Elba Dolores Candales, who continues to provide me with inspiration.

To my husband, Rajeev: destiny brought us together from opposite sides of the world.
To Jai, my son, you were born in my heart. Con mucho amor y cariño!

"[E]ach person carries the seeds for his or her own transformation" (Saleeby, 1992, p. 25). Inside, I carry the seed to my own transformation. My family planted the seed and nurtured it into young adulthood by their examples of struggle and perseverance. The many role models and mentors fertilized the seed with their guidance and support. Likewise, positive experiences gave me the solid roots of strength needed to move through the difficult challenges I faced along the way. The social work profession watered my mind with strong values and ethics, and many clients and students contributed to my development as a social worker and educator. This is my story and my journey.

PERSONAL BIOGRAPHY

I am a 50-year-old, third-generation Puerto Rican and Cuban American, daughter of Arturo and Elba Candales. My cultural identity is strongly connected to my maternal grandmother, Candelaria Hernandez Candales, who left her small coastal town of La Playa de Naguabo, Puerto Rico in 1920 at a young age to seek employment in New York City. She married Andres Candales, a first-generation Cuban from the town of Matanzas, who left the island for political reasons and settled in the United States. My grandmother and her brothers and sisters made a life for themselves in New York City. They all worked hard to improve their life circumstances, each contributing to the neighborhood and community and then achieving the American dream of purchasing a home. My grandmother's siblings returned to Puerto Rico to run their businesses, purchase homes, and eventually retire, but my grandmother remained a lifelong resident of New York City who returned to Puerto Rico yearly.

My parents, both born and raised in New York City, were second-generation Puerto Rican Americans who spoke primarily English; therefore, my first language is English. I was raised in a working-class family mainly in New York City and Connecticut. During the early 1960s, my family moved to Puerto Rico, where my father was stationed. I attended U.S. military schools from ages eight to 12, where all students were required to take Spanish in each grade level. Living in Puerto Rico provided the chance to immerse myself in Puerto Rican culture, to connect with relatives, to hear the language on a regular basis, and to learn about the island. Living in Puerto Rico, although only briefly, was a key factor in solidifying a connection with my ethnic roots and identity later in life. Upon our return to the United States in 1964, my father was stationed in New London, Connecticut. My parents became leaders in the Puerto Rican community, were involved in town politics, and co-founded NUESTRA CASA (Our Home), a nonprofit, grassroots organization established to meet the needs of the local growing Puerto Rican community.

Witnessing my parents' struggles to get ahead in life reinforced my ethnic pride and cultural identity and helped me reach my goal of attaining a college education. I became the only member of my family to receive a college education with one exception: after a 30-year military career, my father retired, enrolled in college, and earned a baccalaureate degree at the age of 51. My parents and extended-family system were my first role models for getting involved in the community and becoming a social worker. Married for 13 years, I have a nine-year-old son. My husband was born and raised in India and immigrated to the United States as a young adult, and our home life reflects our multicultural family history. Like previous generations, my family makes yearly trips to the home built by my parents in the late 1970s in a small barrio in the mountains of Puerto Rico. We also take yearly trips to India to visit my husband's family. Our visits reconnect us with our past and revitalize and nurture our souls.

My career in higher education spans over 25 years. In 1976, after completing my MSW degree, I began my social work practice at the Institute for the Hispanic Family, a program of Catholic Family Services. While at the Institute, I was an adjunct instructor at the community college and Southern Connecticut State University School of Social Work. In 1982, I made a career transition to the University of Connecticut School of Social Work as financial aid director and assistant professor in Puerto Rican Studies. In 1990, I moved again to develop, teach, and serve as program coordinator for a newly approved associate of arts degree in human services at Tunxis Community College. In 1995, I returned to social work education as a field-education coordinator and, in 1997, became the director of the BSW Program at Central Connecticut State University, where I served until 2003. Currently, I am a tenured associate professor with the Department of Social Work. I have been a member of the National Association of Social Workers (NASW) since 1976, serving on the NASW/Connecticut Chapter Board of Directors, co-chaired the Minority Affairs Committee, and served on the Nominating Committee. I am currently a member of the NASW/Connecticut Latino Network. At the national level, I was appointed to the NASW National Committee on Minority Affairs from 1978 to 1980 and the National Committee on Ethnic and Racial Diversity from 2001 to 2003.

Development of the Puerto Rican Community in Connecticut

New York and New Jersey were the primary two states Puerto Ricans migrated to during the first half of the 20th century. As early as the 1940s, the migration shifted to Massachusetts and Connecticut because of the slowing of industrial employment opportunities in the greater New York area and the introduction of contract and non-contract agricultural and other work required to support the manufacturing sector (Morales, 1986; Glasser, 1992). Other trends, such as a U. S. recession during the 1970s, slowed migration. However, in the 1980s, migration increased as a primarily younger cohort of Puerto Ricans (Rivera-Batiz & Santiago, 1995) found themselves unemployed on the island and migrated to family networks established earlier in New England. The migration of island-educated professionals (teachers, social workers, lawyers, and nurses) in the early 1980s was the result of the human-service needs and demands of a growing Puerto Rican community in the United States. When I was completing graduate school, the Puerto Rican population in Connecticut was comprised of older adults, first-generation migrant workers, their children and grandchildren, and new migrants seeking relief from Puerto Rico's high unemployment rate. This population was undereducated, living in poverty, and experiencing multiple and complex problems that were not being addressed by the professional community as it existed in the 1970s.

POSSIBILITY OF A GRADUATE EDUCATION

I never imagined that a graduate education would be possible. Immediately upon completion of my bachelor's degree, an African American adjunct professor encouraged the few students of color in my applied sociology major to continue on with their education. He brought catalogues and applications for us to complete, reviewed our personal statements, and hand-carried them back to the university. My African American roommate and I were admitted. Due to my family's limited financial resources, I received a National Institute of Mental-Health (NIMH) grant (these grants no longer exist), which paid tuition, fees, and a stipend for living expenses. In return, I made a two-year commitment to work with populations of color providing mental health services. This NIMH grant forged an educational and career path in community mental-health. The five other Latino students admitted that fall semester, the first group of Latinos to be admitted to the School of Social Work, gravitated to one another like magnets. Gradually, over the first year of graduate school, a network of support solidified, and we became *como familia* (like family). Together, we organized the first Hispanic Student Organization at the university. We focused our initiatives on three areas: the creation of a course to address the cultural and practice considerations in working with the Puerto Rican community, hiring Puerto Rican faculty, and increasing efforts to recruit more Puerto Rican students to the School of Social Work. More than 30 years later our network of support is still intact.

Both of my graduate field-education internships offered me the opportunity to work with the Puerto Rican community. My first field experience was a placement in a Hispanic clinic in New Haven, Connecticut. I was looking for a connection with the Puerto Rican community, and my field instructor, an important mentor in my life, identified Puerto Rican leaders within social services with whom to collaborate. At this clinic, I realized how isolated the few Puerto Rican inpatients were due to the inadequate number of bilingual and bicultural professional staff available to meet their mental-health treatment needs. During the 1970s, the professional mental-health community was attempting to explore why Puerto Ricans were underutilizing traditional mental-health services and sought to identify new culturally syntonic practice approaches. My field instructor helped pave the way for me to enter the mental-health field and frequently validated the contributions I was making to the Puerto Rican community.

My second internship made a more lasting impression on me as a social worker. From the very beginning of my placement at this neighborhood center, I was immersed in the Puerto Rican community. Identification with this client population is unique because clients look like me, talk like me, and come from cultural backgrounds similar to mine. In addition to providing group-work services, I counseled families living in the predominantly African American and emerging Puerto Rican neighborhood where the agency was located.

EMPEZANDO MI PRACTICA/STARTING MY PRACTICE

Doña Sara Romany, a social worker and director of the newly created Institute for the Hispanic Family, was hired by the School of Social Work to teach the practice course we advocated for the previous year. Doña Sara served as our role model.

By August 1976, I was hired full-time as the first Puerto Rican MSW (in addition to Doña Sara) at the

Institute for the Hispanic Family. The Institute was also at the forefront of grassroots social work practice innovations with Puerto Ricans, as the Hispanic Clinic was in the field of mental health. My new job responsibilities included designing and providing preventive group-work services to diverse groups of Puerto Ricans and providing consultation and education to teachers, nurses, doctors, and social service providers on cultural considerations for practice with the growing Puerto Rican community. This position offered me the opportunity to reinforce my Spanish, as I considered Englishto be my first language.

Over the six years I worked at the Institute, I became responsible for managing the psychiatric clinic, and I taught at community colleges and a school of social work in an adjunct capacity. I began and finished an MPH degree as much of my work was in health and mental health. In addition, a Comprehensive Education and Training Act (CETA)-sponsored Social Service Certificate Training Program, affiliated with a local community college and housed at the Institute, allowed me to teach group work. (The CETA program was a great training model; we recruited and trained indigenous members of the Puerto Rican community as social-service paraprofessionals while helping them access higher education.)

I had many opportunities to form professional relationships over the course of my career, and one such relationship resulted from the search for Puerto Rican faculty at the university, as initiated by the Puerto Rican Student Organization during my student days. Dr. Julio Morales, one of the two faculty hired by the university, established a relationship with the Institute for the Hispanic Family. He came to teach a community practice course for the CETA Social Service Certificate Training Program at the Institute. He was then only the second Puerto Rican faculty member with a PhD I met after six years of undergraduate and graduate education. Many community leaders already saw him as a strong community activist and a highly respected member of the Puerto Rican community. I met Dr. Morales in the spring of 1982, and, the very next day, he invited me to the School of Social Work to explore a joint appointment as financial-aid director and assistant professor in Puerto Rican Studies. Dr. Morales, then the assistant dean of student affairs, was looking to resolve an administrative gap in student financial-aid services and to hire faculty for the Puerto Rican Studies Project. I jumped at the prospect of using my knowledge of the Puerto Rican community and my practice experience to teach at the School of Social Work while continuing to mentor Puerto Rican students. Dr. Morales became my supervisor and mentor.

ESTUDIOS PUERTORRIQUEÑOS/PUERTO RICAN STUDIES

Assuming a dual role—administrator and faculty—was filled with challenges. I came to the university with administrative and practice experience from my six years at the Institute for the Hispanic Family, but I had no specific student financial-aid experience. My primary role included administering more than a million dollars in university financial aid in addition to several large federal-training grants. During my eight years at the university, I implemented a computer-based Student Aid Management

System, increased grant-based financial-aid resources for students, including minority fellowships that supported the recruiting initiatives of the School of Social Work, networked with community agencies to match student work-study funds, and counseled hundreds of incoming and outgoing students on financial aid matters.

Through my involvement in the Puerto Rican Studies Project, I worked closely with Professor Reyes and Dr. Morales. Professor Reyes and I were hired under an NIMH grant. Later, the university secured our salaries when the NIMH grants were cut because of a federal budget crisis. By then, the Puerto Rican Studies Project was praised as a recruitment and retention model within social work education and evolved into the Puerto Rican Studies Substantive Area, a specialization at the School of Social Work and, perhaps, a one-of-a-kind initiative. Professor Reyes was hired to teach the community-practice courses and a course on Puerto Rican women, to serve as an academic advisor to community-organization students, and to recruit students within the United States and from Puerto Rico. My teaching responsibilities included a Puerto Rican history course, a Puerto Rican culture and practice-skills course, and a Puerto Rican studies research course that involved students in action research on salient issues facing the Puerto Rican community.

In 1988, I applied for a tenure-track position within the school, but was denied because I did not have a PhD. Although important, authors have emphasized the limited progress Latinas/os have made in earning PhDs between 1976 and 1996 (Gonzales et al., 2001). Parallels have been drawn between people of color completing baccalaureate degrees and the status of faculty of color positions in U.S colleges and universities (Blackwell, 1996), which was emphasized by Olivas (1996), who states: "I believe that this need [for Latina/o professors] is the single most important key to any hope for increasing Latino access" (p. 376). The Puerto Rican Studies Project was about access to social work education for Latinas/os and responding to the social-service sector's continued demand for graduate–level bilingual and bicultural social workers (Gutiérrez, Yeakley, & Ortega, 2000). Equally important was emphasizing to Latina/o students the possibility of becoming a university professor, researcher, or public intellectual as another step in the educational pipeline.

I was intrigued by the University of Connecticut School of Education's Adult Learning Program. Despite the fact that I had earned an MSW and an MPH, I was intimidated by the prospect of pursuing a PhD. I was apprehensive about taking the Graduate Record Exam (GRE), taking a year-long statistics course, and moving into the unfamiliar territory of adult education and the PhD experience. In their study of Latina/o doctoral student experiences, González et al. (2001) identified my "apprehensiveness" as "entering a new and unfamiliar world" and described the experience as the "strange and unfamiliar world known as the academy [where]... the separation between these two worlds is massive, and the only path from one side to the other is a thin line of wire" (p. 569). So I decided to enter this unfamiliar territory slowly and cautiously.

POQUITO A POQUITO/Little by Little: The PhD Journey

Completing a PhD was not a requirement for remaining at the School of Social Work in my dual position, so, if I made the commitment to a doctoral program, I would be making it to myself. There were no social work doctoral programs in Connecticut at the time; the closest ones were in New York City or Boston, so I began my exploration of the Adult Learning PhD program. I selected course work that blended well with social work and provided the flexibility to focus on a topic I was passionate about—access to higher education for disadvantaged groups, particularly Puerto Rican women. There were no Latino students in my major, which is still a common experience for many Latino doctoral students (González et al., 2001), but, as I progressed through elective course work, there was more diversity in my classes. In the required statistics course, we formed a study group, a small "academy of Latinos" at least for that one course, where we did not feel marginalized, but were empowered by our mutual support and encouragement. As we progressed through our respective programs, it became important to continue checking in with one another as a way of reducing our isolation (González et al., 2001) as doctoral students in a large university.

I was able to progress quickly through the program and complete my comprehensive exams. As I was completing this important portion of my degree program, my major advisor, an expert on the needs of older women returning to school (Lewis, 1988), informed me that she was leaving the university to work in the corporate sector. My advisor had been my role model, providing more than academic guidance. She modeled teaching skills and incorporated an ethic of caring (Gilligan, 1982) similar to the Puerto Rican cultural values of establishing relationships and making a connection on a more personal level. Gutierrez and Lewis (1999) identify "connection" as an important element of the empowerment model. When she left the university, I was assigned a second advisor, who led me in different directions and to a new literature review. Slowly, I began to lose interest in pursuing the PhD, and I took a position heading up a new human-services associate degree program. My doctoral studies took a backseat to developing this new program

At the Institute for the Hispanic Family and the Puerto Rican Studies Project, the approach my Puerto Rican colleagues used centered on Latino cultural values such as *personalismo* (valuing the inner worth of the individual), *respeto* (respect), and mutual trust or *confianza* (Gardella, Candales, & Rivera, 2005; Morris, 1995; Negroni-Rodriguez, Dicks, & Morales, 2003). Sotomayor (1991) expands on the centrality of mutual trust by accurately describing *"confianza* as the glue that holds reciprocal exchange relationships together" (p. xix).

In interviewing for the directorship of the Human Service Degree Program, one of the administrators asked me if I spoke Hispanic! I was stunned and immediately questioned whether I wanted to make this move to a traditional higher education environment with a predominantly White European American student population, faculty, and administrators, and very few faculty or professional staff of color. I knew that, by taking this position, I would be expected to serve as the informal consultant around Latino issues and wear many hats (Torres-Guzmán, 1995; Turner, 2002), a role that people of color are expected to carry out in many work environments. My decision to take the position was based on what I could offer the college. I had experience in student services and social work education and an extensive network of traditional and grassroots agencies that would catalyze the development of the human-services degree program. The community college administration recognized the importance of hiring a faculty member with a social work degree as three of the four state universities and one private college had bachelor of social work (BSW) programs, and transferability of courses was seen as vital to a seamless transition for community college students.

During my five years at the community college, I planned and organized an Anti-Defamation League "Campus of Difference" diversity conference. This statewide conference brought together teams of administrators, faculty, counselors, and students from 15 community colleges. My membership in the Connecticut Association of Latin Americans in Higher Education (CALAHE) facilitated my bringing the 15th Annual CALAHE Conference, "Connecting with the Community: New Directions for Education," to the community college. To recognize my efforts, the president of my college selected me to receive the National Institute of Staff and Organizational Development (NISOD) Excellence Award for my contribution to teaching and learning at the NISOD International Conference on Teaching Excellence in Austin, Texas. I was into my

fifth year and had been promoted to associate professor when I learned of a faculty search at Central Connecticut State University and was urged to apply by the director of the BSW Program.

I was torn about applying for the BSW faculty position because I enjoyed my work in the community college environment as it gave me the chance to work with diverse groups of nontraditional students, including adult learners. For many students, the only access to higher education is through the community college. After much consideration, I decided my goal was to teach in an accredited BSW program and obtain the experience of working in a four-year university setting.

My strong administrative background contributed to my being offered the BSW faculty position. However, one of the university's expectations when I was hired was that I would complete my doctorate degree by the time I was ready for tenure. Therefore, I quickly reconnected with the Educational Leadership Department chair to discuss moving forward with my adult learning program. Because there was a lapse in time from when I started the PhD program, I had to advocate assertively on my own behalf to be allowed to complete my degree and be assigned a new advisor.

This new advisor asked that Dr. Morales from the School of Social Work be replaced with another advisor from the School of Education. This was disappointing because a Puerto Rican person on my committee with an understanding of Puerto Rican culture would be an important aspect of my research. But, because I was under a strict deadline, I gave in to her request after talking it over with Dr. Morales, who said, "Do whatever you need to do to finish the PhD." Second, after updating my literature review and finding little new information on Puerto Ricans in higher education, my advisor sent me to meet with the librarian assigned to the School of Education. I met with the librarian for about an hour with no results. She was so astounded by the lack of research on my dissertation topic that she took it upon herself to continue working on the literature search after I had gone. This approach was unnecessary and a mistake, but my advisor began to recognize and value my strong-background in Puerto Rican Studies. González et al. (2001) highlight the lack of validation as a "recurring and powerful theme" in the narratives of the doctoral students they interviewed. Furthermore, they state, "[a]bsent for many of the students were any authentic indications, either direct or subtle, that validated their work and efforts to make it across their thin line of wire, and toward completion of the PhD" (p. 573).

One year later, my proposal was accepted, and I was ready to start collecting data, but I lost my advisor, who became seriously ill. In addition, two years after starting my new position at Central Connecticut State University, the director of the Social Work Program suddenly faced a health crisis and passed away. The program was at a critical juncture as we had just submitted self-study documents to reaffirm our accreditation status and were expecting a site-team visit by the beginning of the new year. An excerpt from *Reflecting on the Death of a Colleague and Teacher: Lessons Learned* (Phillips & Candales, 2001) describes the circumstances I was facing:

As the semester quickly ended, I realized the magnitude of the responsibility that lay ahead; therefore, I put aside my grief. Meanwhile, I helped the students to grieve as they prepared for their final exams. Then, I put into motion plans for the program accreditation site visit, hired an emergency adjunct and organized and chaired a faculty search committee. In addition to these demands, I faced a deadline to complete the remaining work for my doctorate. Mourning Ilana's death was not an option for me at that time. (p. 25)

I was about to sacrifice some of my own personal goals to maintain the integrity and continuity of the social work program during this crisis and period of transition.

LOOKING FORWARD: LEADERSHIP WITHIN A BSW PROGRAM

In June 1998, CSWE's Commission on Accreditation (COA) voted to reaccredit our program for another eight-year cycle. In its letter, the COA commended the accomplishments of the program and stated, "[t]he Commission particularly acknowledges Barbara Candales's leadership following Dr. S's untimely death." These words were especially meaningful to me, and I would use them later in seeking promotion and tenure. By Fall 1998, I had hired two new faculty members, taken on a mentoring role, and facilitated changing the name of the department to incorporate social work in the title. I was able to obtain more administrative autonomy, increase the budget for the program, and employ a part-time university assistant. Finally, I was following up with CSWE's request for additional information via an interim report, which included securing a new location to house the Social Work Program.

The Struggle for Promotion and Tenure

Promotion and tenure were quickly approaching. In my fifth year in rank I requested a promotion to associate professor. This was supported by the Departmental Evaluation Committee (DEC) and the dean of the School of Arts and Sciences, but not by the Promotion and Tenure Committee (P&T) or the president because I did not have a doctorate. One month later, in May 2000, I defended my dissertation (Candales, 2000) and received my PhD. My department chair retired that same month, and with her retirement came the fight of my academic career. The following fall, my sixth year in rank, I came up for promotion and tenure. The DEC was now comprised of all sociology faculty: one senior faculty in addition to two newly tenured faculty and the newly appointed department chair. I was denied my request, as in previous years, to include a social work faculty as part of the P&T Committee. Around campus, several faculty and staff came to me to express their concern. One staff member had been approached by one of the DEC members (without my being notified, as was the policy) who asked questions about my work in the Puerto Rican community, and another colleague warned me to be cautious. Shortly after, the DEC informed me that it was not recommending promotion or tenure. I quickly wrote a response to clarify inaccuracies, to respond to their comments regarding creativity and productive service, and to add some missing information that should have been included on my evaluation. The dean of the School of Arts and Science, who had supported my request for promotion the previous year, was now only supporting me for tenure. I was clearly angry at the DEC members and puzzled by the dean's decision and, for a brief time, considered filing a discrimination lawsuit. I went before the P&T Committee and clarified the issues the DEC members had brought up. Leaving the meeting, I felt more at ease and confident. The P&T Committee recommended promotion and tenure, but the president supported only tenure. My experience with the DEC the following year was a repeat of my sixth year. I was stunned when two members of the DEC came to my office to tell me "not to take their decision personally." The dean of the School of Arts and Science now had become my advocate and even chastised the committee in her evaluation letter of support. Seven years after starting at the university, I was finally promoted to associate professor. After two years of being weighed down by the demands of moving the Social Work Program forward and completing my PhD, while simultaneously struggling to defend myself, I was finally coming out of the dark tunnel and into the light. I felt that a burden had been lifted off my shoulders.

Latino faculty are "severely underrepresented" in higher education (Antonio, 2003). According to Santiago (2005), only 3% of Latinos earned doctoral degrees in 2001. In 1999, Latinos represented only 3% of the full-time faculty in higher education, with no change in their representation since 1992. Latinos are described as primarily junior-level faculty, with Latino men accounting for about 60% of full-time Latino faculty in 1999. My experience with promotion and tenure parallels the experience of many women of color, Latinos, and, in particular, Latinas (Mindiola, 1995; Montero-Sieburth, 1996; Torres-Guzmán, 1995; Turner, 2002). The narratives of Latina/o faculty include similar themes: personal struggles toward promotion and tenure, being treated as token Latinas/os, feelings of marginality within the academy, and not receiving validation of their scholarly activities that focus on issues of people of color and provide service within the Latino community. Furthermore, since family is central to my cultural life, the issue of balancing family, career, and community is always at the forefront. The issues that Latinas/os face in being promoted and receiving tenure are only one small aspect of what we have already endured to reach the front door of the academy. I am concerned with Latino faculty in small social work programs and wonder if my experience would have been different had I not been Latina. My promotion and tenure struggle, although traumatic, cannot erase the solid connections with my colleagues and the role I have played in social work education in Connecticut.

CONCLUSION

Each person carries the seed for his or her own transformation, but, as I reflect on the steps taken in my journey, mental images of the many role models and mentors who have walked beside me in my journey appear. I remember the day I defended my dissertation, and positioned directly across from me was my Puerto Rican associate advisor smiling at me as I shared and discussed my work with the audience. I felt proud because I knew she, too, had accomplished a great deal and that I was reaping the benefit of her accomplishments by having her as a member of my committee. I am also reminded of my major advisor who said, "You have been transformed just as the [Puerto Rican] women in your study." Yes, I had more than anyone could imagine. Like the women in my study, I revealed a new sense of self and a more passionate sense of identity as a Puerto Rican woman. I had achieved "success" by completing my dissertation and obtaining promotion and tenure, but I also realized there is still much to be done. I remember my grandmother from La Playa de Naguabo, her brothers and sisters, and their struggle to get ahead so that my family would have a better life. I remember a father who, at the age of 51, obtained a baccalaureate degree and a mother who was a homemaker *and* a community leader. These images will always serve as a reminder that, as a Latina, I have a responsibility to give back to my community and to let young Latinas/os know that they must have a *Dream and a Plan* (Gardella & Haynes, 2004). Included in that plan are the role models and mentors who are willing to serve as guides.

Today, giving back includes collaborative projects such as *Comenzamos: Latinas/os in Social Work* (Gardella, Candales, & Rivera, 2005), a model program designed to push back the educational pipeline by reaching out and supporting Latina/o community college students interested in a career in social work, and the Transition Plan between Capital Community College and Central Connecticut State University to enhance the academic preparation of community-college social-service majors for transfer to the baccalaureate degree in social work. Finally, I want to design a weekend program to reach non-traditional learners employed in the social-service field. As social work educators, we must think "out of the box" and explore nonlinear innovative educational tracks that allow traditionally oppressed groups to access higher education and the social work profession. We are a profession with solid roots, and empowerment has been central to our history. Our profession must use the empowerment model to provide Latina/o students access to social work education and to support the recruitment and retention of Latina/o faculty within social work programs. My message is ¡SÍ SE PUEDE! Yes, it can be accomplished—if you create a vision of the possibility that lies ahead.

REFERENCES

Antonio, A. L. (2003). Diverse student bodies, diverse faculties. *Academe, 89*(6), 14–17.

Blackwell, J. E. (1996). Faculty issues: The impact on minorities. In C. Sotello Viernes Turner, M. Garcia, A. Nora, & L. I. Rendon (Eds.), *Racial and ethnic diversity in higher education* (pp. 315–326). Boston: Simon and Schuster.

Candales, B. A. (2000). *Nuestras historias ('Our stories'): Transformative learning process and female, Puerto Rican community college graduates.* Unpublished doctoral dissertation, University of Connecticut, Storrs.

Gardella, L. G., Candales, B. A., & Ricardo-Rivera, J. R. (2005). Doors are not locked, just closed: Latino perspective on college. In M. A. Wolf (Ed.), *Adulthood: New terrain* (pp. 39–51). San Francisco: Jossey-Bass.

Gardella, L. G., & Haynes, K. S. (2004). *A dream and a plan: A woman's path to leadership in human services.* Washington, DC: NASW Press.

Gilligan, C. (1982). *In a different voice.* Cambridge, MA: Harvard University Press.

Glasser, R. (1992). *Aqui me quedo: Puerto Ricans in Connecticut.* Unpublished manuscript.

González, K. P., Marin, P., Pérez, L. X., Figueroa, M. A., Moreno, J. E., & Navia, C. N. (2001). Understanding the nature and context of Latina/o doctoral student experiences. *Journal of College Student Development, 42*(6), 563–580.

Gutiérrez, L., Yeakley, A., & Ortega, R. (2000). Educating students for social work with Latinos: Issues for the new millennium. *Journal of Social Work Education, 36*, 541–557.

Gutiérrez, L. M., & Lewis, E. A. (Eds.). (1999). *Empowering women of color.* New York: Columbia University Press.

Lewis, L. H. (Ed.). (1988). *Addressing the needs of returning women.* San Francisco: Jossey-Bass.

Mindiola, T., Jr. (1995). 'Getting tenure in the U.' In R. V. Padill & R. Chávez Chávez (Eds.), *The leaning ivory tower: Latino professors in American universities* (pp. 29–51). New York: State University of New York Press.

Montero-Sieburth, M. (1996). Beyond affirmative action: An inquiry into the experience of Latinas in academia. *New England Journal of Public Policy, 2*, 65–98.

Morales, J. (1986). *Puerto Rican poverty and migration: We just had to try elsewhere.* New York: Praeger.

Morris, N. (1995). *Puerto Rico: Culture, politics and identity.* Westport, CT: Praeger.

Negroni-Rodriguez, L., Dicks, B., & Morales, J. (2003, February 27). *Cultural considerations in advising Latino/a students.* Presentation at annual program meeting, Council on Social Work Education, Atlanta, GA.

Olivas, M. A. (1996). Latino faculty at the border: Increasing numbers key to more Hispanic access. In C. Sotello Viernes Turner, M. Garcia, A. Nora, & L. I. Rendon (Eds.), *Racial and ethnic diversity in higher education* (pp. 376–380). Boston: Simon and Schuster.

Phillips, E. N., & Candales, B. A. (2001). Reflecting on the death of a colleague and teacher: Lessons learned. *Reflections: Narratives of Professional Helping, 8*(2), 18–28.

Rivera-Batiz, F. L., & Santiago, C. E. (1995). *Puerto Ricans in the United Status: A changing reality.* Washington, DC: The National Puerto Rican Coalition.

Saleebey, D. (Ed.). (1992). *The strengths perspective in social work practice.* New York: Longman.

Santiago, D. (2005, June). *Latinos in graduate education*. Retrieved June 1, 2005, from http://www.EdExcelencia.org/research/facts.asp

Sotomayor, M. (1991). *Empowering Hispanic families: A critical issue for the 90s*. Milwaukee, WI: Family Service America.

Torres-Guzmán, M. E. (1995). Surviving the journey. In R. V. Padilla & R. Chávez Chávez (Eds.), *The leaning ivory tower: Latino professors in American universities* (pp. 53–66). New York: State University of New York Press.

Turner, C. S. V. (2002). Women of color in academe. *The Journal of Higher Education, 73*(1), 74–93.

Women of Color as Social Work Educators

Part II: The Voices of Women of Color as Social Work Educators

To Felicia,
My Sister in
the Struggle
M. Jenise Comer

Chapter 6: The Ditch

M. Jenise Comer

Dedicated to Vern and Daddy; my twin sister, Niecie; my children, Lorin and Wil; and all my sisters and brothers, who shaped me to be who I am.

To my students who taught me to know that I know what I know.

I am compelled to promote the notion that race is a lens that colors our view of and experience in the world. It is important for me to dispel the myth of racial blindness that many students possess. Students believe that the solution to racism, prejudice, and discrimination is to believe that all people are the same and should be treated the same. The notion that this belief system is a fallacy is impossible for some students to fathom, especially when the idea comes from a professor of color. My agenda is to help students to celebrate the notion of *and* as postulated by Kenneth Hardy. We are the same, *and* we are different. It is imperative to see the similarities and understand the differences to demonstrate cultural competence.

To advance this concept, I describe the experience of running the "human race" for members of our society who are diverse by virtue of race, gender, age, religion, sexual orientation, and different physical or mental abilities. When the race starts, the majority members have assumed the posture at the starting line, awaiting the signal for the race to begin. Members of communities of color are awaiting the same signal; however, they are not on the level race track. They are in the ditch. After the starting signal, they must come out of the ditch before they can even begin to run the race. Depending on their circumstances, they have different "privileges," which are tools to help them out of the ditch. For example, those who come from upper-class families have a ladder to climb up out of the ditch and are able to hit the ground running. There are others who have intellectual talent or athletic prowess, which creates a rope for them to pull themselves up out of the ditch. Still others have inherent strengths such as sheer determination or environmental contingencies in the form of a nurturing, supportive mentor. They use these resources to claw their way out of the ditch.

Unfortunately, those who remain have no idea that there is a way out of the ditch. Their view is obscured by poverty, crime, violence, and chemical dependence. Drugs continue to play a major economic and social role in African American life (Gray, 1995). They have become an economic base and a marketable commodity when there is no other viable source of economic self-sufficiency. Drugs also provide a form of self-medication when one's view of the world is shrouded with hopelessness and despair. My access to the academy was promoted by intellectual talent, nurtured by sheer determination, hard work, and the guidance of dedicated mentors.

PERSONAL BIOGRAPHY

I am an African American female with an identical twin sister born in 1950. Our parents never knew they were expecting twins until after I was born first. My mother had been hospitalized because she was gaining too much weight. She was placed on a restricted diet and reprimanded for chewing gum because it was not on her diet. We were born premature; we fit in the palm of the physician's hand, so we remained in the hospital until we gained sufficient weight. Our entrance into the world may have been a reflection of the inequitable health-care services and resources available to people of color

PERSONAL JOURNEY

My family was headed by a U.S. Post Office employee and his stay-at-home wife, a widow with two children. Her first husband was a police officer who was killed in the line of duty. She married my father two years after the tragic death of her first husband. Her devotion to the Catholic faith contributed to the birth of 10 children to my parents, even though my mother was told that she would be unable to have more children after having my older sister and brother by her first husband.

My father was an only child whose mother died during childbirth. My paternal grandfather was an alcoholic who died in a mental institution before I was born. My father's upbringing was very deprived, especially after his father took him away from his maternal grandmother, who raised him in the South. He overcompensated for the loneliness and deprivation by having a large family and developing a penchant for "the best." He would buy what he wanted and pay bills with what he had left. He never learned to manage his money. However, because he had a "good government job," our family never qualified for assistance. Continuous financial difficulties, compounded by the unresolved grief of both of my parents, constituted chronic stressors in my family of origin. My maternal grandfather was an orphan of Black–White parentage. He worked as a porter for the railroad and did odd jobs as a handyman to support his family. When I was only seven, he died of cancer, a mere skeleton of the man I once knew. I am certain that he also suffered from overt and covert institutional racism as a Negro raising a family 50 years after the end of the Civil War.

I am a product of the Civil Rights movement. My twin sister and I started kindergarten in the first integrated public school following the *Brown v. Topeka Board of Education* decision. We were sheltered from experiences of outright segregation. I never saw places marked "Whites only," so my world was extremely narrow from birth until my junior year of high school. We never left town or went out to eat. I will forever remember seeing the *Jet* magazine Picture of the Week with Emmett Till's mutilated body in an open casket during his wake. Watching the news of demonstrations in the South was both frightening and empowering. There was comfort in

being a passive observer of the movement. As slave mothers did, my mother taught us survival skills to protect us from the harsh realities of our society. She always said "smile and be nice." Her strategy kept us safe, but did little to help us develop assertive communication skills or self-esteem. However, the Civil Rights movement provided me with a positive ethnic identity and a heightened sense of racial pride.

A fifth-grade teacher once admitted to my mother that she had never taught "Negro" children before and wanted to know how to do it. My mother's advice was, "You teach them just like you teach the White children." My twin sister received the highest score of all students in the city when she took the high-school entrance examination. As a result, she won a four-year scholarship to Lillis High School. But my sister was never first in our class during elementary school. Thus, it makes one wonder if the teachers ever followed my mother's advice. It was very difficult to feel privileged in that environment.

Hartman and Laird (1983) discuss the importance of "quality relationships and environmental contingencies at developmental transition points" in shaping the persons we become. As members of a parish school, we acquired a church family. When it was time for my sister and me to go to high school, Mrs. Mamie Hughes, my first mentor and an advocate for social justice, arranged for the Catholic Interracial Council to pay for our tuition, books, and uniforms. This environmental contingency allowed us to receive a solid academic foundation and learn good study skills. Unfortunately, the same experience was often marked with prejudice and discrimination. For example, when my sister tried to challenge a grade she received on a freshman history test, the teacher denied he made an error in grading. As she walked away already feeling dejected, I heard him mumble, "I ought to take points off for you wasting my time."

During our sophomore year, a biology teacher was particularly mean and hateful. My twin sister and I were interested in biology and were eager to please her. We would frequently raise our hands to answer questions. She would look at us in the back of the room and say, "Class, let's have some answers from the front of the room." There were few African American students in our graduating class. I was not taught to appreciate African American literature, nor was I taught about the contributions of noted African Americans. Black history was not a part of the curriculum.

A Social Work Student

After high school graduation, my twin sister and I attended a local university, excited about the possibility of becoming physicians, but I am convinced that the services I received from academic advisement were colored by my race and gender. In conversations with advisors and our biology professor, we were asked why we wanted to pursue medicine. A lab professor said, "Why would anyone who couldn't be any better than a beautician want to be a doctor? Why not something more realistic, like teachers?" The same lack of support was evident when I changed my major to psychology. When I declared my new major, I was asked, "What are you going to do with that?" I was told to major in sociology because I could do more with that degree. I never received good academic counseling about either discipline. I was not told that I would need a PhD in psychology, probably because no one ever expected me to complete a BA degree, much less matriculate to complete the PhD. I decided to double major in both disciplines, to follow their advice, and follow a course of study about which I had become passionate. For graduate school, I decided to pursue this *new* field I heard about called social work.

I never experienced positive mentoring from faculty, so I kept my distance out of fear. Distance later became a self-protection mechanism after an experience with a knowledgeable and understanding instructor. During the summer of 1970, he taught an evening class called Contemporary Social Problems. As usual, I was the only person of color in the class. It is significant to emphasize timing, as I took this course after the death of Dr. Martin Luther King, Jr. and the Civil Rights movement. President Lyndon Johnson signed the Voting Rights Act into law in 1965 (Watson, 2005), and, in Kansas City, a Public Accommodations Act passed by a narrow margin (Chasteen, 1968). As a people, I thought we had arrived. But I remember attending a conference in Los Angeles, where Angela Davis admonished us to be careful. According to her, we had been lulled into complacency; we had no leader and no direction, which is an extremely dangerous position.

The controversy in this Contemporary Social Problems course began the very first night of class. The professor asked the following question: "There are more similarities between Blacks and Whites than among members of the White race, true or false?" A traditional-age student sitting next to me answered, "False." The professor's response: "I will give you an A in this class if you can name one difference between Blacks and Whites." She turned and looked directly at me for confirmation and said, "Isn't it true that Blacks have thicker skulls to protect their heads from the sun and larger gluteus muscles so they can run faster?" All I could do was gasp in shock. I always had a flat behind! When the professor asked where she had learned those facts, she said she had learned them from her general biology textbook. For the first time, I was exposed to what members of the majority community really thought of African Americans. It was obvious that they subscribed to the Moynihan perspective of deficits in African Americans.

Over the course of the semester, a single mother stated that she had no sympathy for anyone who just "lays up and breeds." The professor stated that the student's solution would require more of people of color than she would ever be asked to do. I learned firsthand during this class what an anxiety attack feels like. A White European American male student twice my age questioned why the government kept making "us" let "them" move next door because all "they" wanted to do was marry "us." The teacher laughed and assured him that Blacks or African Americans probably did not find his pink skin all that attractive.

At the end of the semester, my classmates invited me to join them at Mike's Bar, which they frequented without me after each class. I made excuses, but they insisted I join them. After they had a few drinks, I learned that the consensus among the class was that the professor had been very supportive of me during the semester because I must have been sleeping with him. It did not matter that their suspicions were unfounded. What I realized was that the slave–master mentality continued to exist. The consensus was that the teacher could have me at will. The nice little Catholic girl, who was not even sexually active, was reduced to a whore in their minds. This was my most painful experience as an African American female. I still feel the pain of that moment every time I tell the story, and I tell the story every semester. Some students understand the message; others do not. One asked, "What did that have to do with you being Black?" I believe that being a person of color always causes you to look over your shoulder to analyze uncomfortable experiences. We are robbed of emotional energy that could be channeled into more productive efforts. As Dr. Bob Jones, my professional mentor used to say, "There is such a thing as healthy paranoia."

PROFESSIONAL JOURNEY

A Social Work Practitioner

My first full-time job as a social worker was at Catholic Charities. After two-and-a-half years, I decided to apply to a residential treatment facility where I had been a member of the Board of Directors. I was hired in the newly created position of deputy director. In addition to my role as an administrator, I provided therapy to emotionally disturbed and abused children in a predominantly African American agency.

Working in an agency with predominantly Black or African American clients created a whole different set of problems than I ever anticipated. While race was no longer a factor, sexism and classism were definite problems. The veteran male staff chose to avoid my direction and communicated directly with the executive director. The female staff decided I needed to be removed. I overheard one of them on the telephone ordering a séance to deal with me. Their agenda became so bizarre that one member of the group got frightened, defected, and confessed.

Despite the lack of support, I was surrounded by a powerful team of African American professionals who nurtured my growth and professional development. I learned about administration and clinical social work from a self-proclaimed benevolent dictator. He provided clinical supervision, guidance, and direction to my work every day from 1977 to August 13, 1984. I was out of the agency on maternity leave when I received a call from the secretary that he had died of a massive heart attack. This was a crisis. My three-year-old daughter asked a million questions as I prepared to take her and my two-month-old son to my mother so I could go to work. Even though I was in shock, her questions forced me to make sense out of the chaos. I told her that he had been put on this earth to do a job; he did a good job, and he was rewarded with a place in heaven.

Stepping back into the agency was a surreal experience. I remember wondering how I was going to lead the agency without my director. I realized that if I would just be still, I could hear his voice and know what he would want me to do. My faith always helped me to survive the most difficult times in my life, and this was certainly one of them. After three months of working as the interim director, the Board chose my former director's widow to be the new executive director. All of the full-time professional staff found other employment over the next year. I was the last to leave.

A Social Work Educator

In the spring of 1985, I supervised two MSW students and a BSW student from three local universities. I believe I impressed the field coordinator from one of the universities because I received a call inviting me to teach a class on campus. I did not believe I could do it, but decided to pursue teaching in the baccalaureate social work program. As an adjunct professor, I taught one class on groups and family theory. I knew the university still needed a full-time teacher, so I applied for the full-time position for the spring semester of 1986. When I was selected for the position, I was encouraged to negotiate for the highest starting salary possible because I would never be able to adjust the beginning salary. When I met with the dean to negotiate the salary, he stated, "You know you have some bargaining chips being African American and female. The only other thing we could want is if you were handicapped." I could not believe someone could say something so ignorant. I was convinced that asking for my current salary was the right thing to do. My department chair balked because he said the amount was too close to his salary.

I had no idea that my starting salary would create such animosity among my colleagues. After teaching one class as an adjunct, the faculty appeared to be friendly on the surface, but they were no longer supportive. I did not know what to expect going into academia from a practice setting. I was teaching three new courses and repeating the course I taught as an adjunct. I later learned that teacher's manuals with standardized test questions were available for three of my four classes. The information was deliberately withheld from me. My program chair admitted to being upset because he also thought I was earning a salary too close to his. I no longer felt safe or that I could trust the people I depended on to mentor me. I often thought there was some protection when discrimination was overt. You knew where you could go and where you could not. In this environment, racism and discrimination were covert, which I think is more difficult to manage. When discrimination is expected, one can plan how to respond. When the incidents are not anticipated, they seem to hurt more deeply. Once again, I just wanted to stay to myself and maintain a safe emotional distance until I knew for sure who was real and genuine and who was not. I recognized that the biggest champions for diversity could also be the most racist.

In the fall semester of 1985, I was the second African American professor at the university. The other was an associate professor of education who later retired, but was never promoted to full professor. I felt isolated and vulnerable. I came to campus knowing about the school's history; my own classmates were expelled during the Civil Rights movement and protests in the early 1970s. Some of the same faculty and administrators were still working when I arrived on campus. The climate supposedly had changed, and there was an effort to hire more African American faculty and staff. One dean placed an article in the school newspaper announcing that he had increased the number of African American faculty in the classroom by 50%: he had hired two new faculty of color.

In 1990, I had an empowering experience quite by accident. As I said earlier, my education left me with no appreciation for my history. I was taught that Black English was embarrassing. I received a notice of a conference from the Menninger Foundation on Unity and Diversity: Empowering Women to Explore Our Differences. A quotation in the brochure caught my attention: "And so I raised my glass among these women, and I said, 'We be's for 'llowin' diffurence, we be's for 'spectin' diffurence, for diffurence don mak no mo diffurence'" (Johnetta B. Cole, President, Spellman College, Atlanta, Georgia). In that moment, I felt a sense of pride and appreciation that I had never known. Dr. Cole's words legitimized a piece of my past that I had not been given permission to honor. I share this quotation with anyone who will listen.

A major struggle occurred shortly after the School of Nursing hired an African American woman with a PhD as the department chair. I was so proud of her. Regal in stature, she had a PhD, and I had hopes that perhaps things were changing at the university. A year later, the dean asked me to participate on an impartial panel and meet with her faculty to resolve numerous conflicts that resulted in a vote of no confidence against the chair. He believed the problems could be resolved and that the chair could continue in her current position. I joined two faculty members who met with the department to hear their complaints. The most egregious complaint was that she promised not to change the curriculum when she was hired, and she in fact was recommending changes. Her defense was that, after a thorough review of the curriculum, she was convinced that the program was in danger of losing its accreditation. Second, faculty members were upset that she painted the walls in the department without consulting them. It was clear to me and other members of the committee that the complaints would never have been issues for a White European American male department chair. However, before meeting with the nursing faculty, one of their faculty members met privately with the chair of the panel and told him that, according to the faculty guide, the impartial panel had no precedence to intervene. He agreed with her, so the panel came to no conclusions and made no recommendations. The report confirmed that we had no power to satisfy the request of the dean. I pressed and finally received a verbal admission of injustice, off the record, for my own personal satisfaction. The panel never offered any support to this department chair.

This incident contributed to my own personal wounding. It is impossible to feel privileged when you do not even feel safe. I saw firsthand how prejudice and discrimination were overlooked at my institution. I had been trained to expect that the organization was responsible for the behavior of its employees. I believed that the president had the power to nip the problem in the bud and hold the nursing faculty to a higher standard of behavior. He could have insisted on zero tolerance for discriminatory behavior. Our president proved to me that he had no commitment to diversity. As a matter of fact, he decided that the term "diversity" was incendiary and divisive, so he changed the name of the Diversity Office to the Office of Community Engagement.

I believe that the experience of Black females is inextricably linked to the experiences of Black males. I was reminded of "my place" in the academy as I observed what happened to three men who brought tremendous talent and expertise to their respective positions. Two of the men replaced the director of multicultural affairs (the original name for the Office of Community Engagement). The first, a dynamic young man recruited from the flagship university, arranged a powerful African American graduation celebration, marked by powerful rituals, symbolism, and affirmation. He was accused of furthering separatism, and his continued employment was threatened. He resigned and moved on to better opportunities. His replacement knocked on our doors without notice to announce himself as the new director of diversity. Even though he was hired by the president, there was no information announcing his position or a welcome reception to celebrate his arrival. I do not believe this was an error or an oversight; it spoke volumes about the president's true value of diversity. The third incident confirmed my belief that the institution was not a safe place. One of my colleagues became chair of the Association of Black Faculty and Staff. He was invited to the president's cabinet meeting, where he voiced genuine concerns regarding the status and treatment of people of color on campus. The president's response was, "What are you doing?" It was clear that his candor was professionally suicidal. That next fall, the same professor put forth his dossier for promotion and tenure. He received recommendations from his department, his department chair, and the College Promotion and Tenure Committee.

When the promotion reached the provost, my colleague was notified that some graduate students had complained about his teaching, and that the university wanted to "reevaluate" his classes. The department chair then withdrew her support for his promotion, which was ultimately denied. At the time, I never knew of any faculty member who was asked to "reevaluate" a class. Once again, I was stunned and wondered how the university could get away with such unfair practices. The incident silenced my voice, and I chose the safety of social isolation. While administrators complained that they could not attract people of color to the campus, I saw a totally different problem. We have lost highly qualified and competent faculty of color because of what happened to them after they were hired. Our most serious problem has always been retention, not recruitment.

When our last president came to the university, he brought a genuine commitment to increase the number of faculty and staff of color on campus. A White European American female was hired to serve as the fourth administrator in the Office of Community Engagement. With the president's support, she was able to generate a different level of involvement to promote diversity on campus. She arranged numerous events to increase knowledge and awareness of issues related to people of color. She was consumed with multiple efforts to make a difference, but she, too, left the university. We now have another African American male, who is determined to exceed the success of his predecessor. It has been interesting to see how much has changed in my 20 years at this school.

Burden, Harrison, and Hodge (2005) studied the perceptions of African American faculty in kinesiology-based programs at predominantly White institutions of higher learning and identified four major recurring themes: resources, opportunities, and power structure; programmatic neglects and faculty-mentoring needs; social isolation, disengagement, and intellectual inferiority issues; and double standards, marginalization, and scholarship bias. Buck (2003) stated:

African American faculty members at majority institutions often feel isolated and overburdened. They feel compelled to perform exceptionally well because they perceive the need to prove their worth in the face of overt or covert accusations that they have achieved their positions simply because of their race. Women faculty of color report even greater pressure than their male counterparts because of the traditional expectation that women will provide service to their students, the department, the institution, and the larger community in greater measure than their male colleagues.

Many of my experiences confirm these observations. I remember my grandmother saying I had to be twice as good to succeed. Consequently, my tendency is to take on too much to prove my worth and value to the university.

A difficult and challenging aspect of my work has been the response to my tutelage from majority students. Johnson-Bailey, Cervero, and Baugh (2004) posits that learners and teachers or facilitators bring with them their "positions in the hierarchies that order the world, including those based on race, gender, class, sexuality orientation, and disability"

(p. 389). In their study of how power relations manifest themselves in a Black or African American woman professor's and White European American male professor's classroom, they found that, in the Black or African American woman's classroom, the following interactions were commonplace: "Challenge to knowledge dissemination, teacher/student confrontations, classroom crosstalk, and reinterpretation or disregard of classroom protocol" (Johnson-Bailey & Cervero, 2004, p. 396). The authors noted succinctly that these occurrences did not take place in the White European American male professor's classroom. This further suggests how race and gender are prime determinants of the classroom experiences of Black or African American women faculty (Ray, 2005).

As a faculty member of color, I have been challenged about the accuracy of lecture content. Bonner (2004) labels this common experience of African American female faculty as "proving yourself over and over." While discussing Black English in a human behavior and the social environment class, one student clearly rejected the notion that there was such a thing and said, "I don't believe that." Another student rejected the position I emphasized during a diversity lecture. I attempted to explain that diversity matters, and I stressed the importance that we are all alike and we are all different, with *and* being the operative word. The students could not believe the concept of difference, demonstrating the safety of cultural blindness. Wouldn't you think that if I know anything, I know something about being Black or African American?

I have always known that my students respond to me in ways that would be considered inappro-priate with White European American male faculty. I spend a considerable amount of time attempting to coach their professional voice and to improve their oral and written communication skills. I am constantly amazed that several students resent all the marks I make on their papers. They never make simple corrections to eliminate conversational tone and phrases such as "a lot of" on subsequent papers, even after I have identified numerous synonyms on their first assignments. Recently, one class challenged me with a concern that they were not learning. We processed the reason for the unfounded allegation, and the issue of race was raised as a contributing factor. The majority group students then became visibly angry. In exploring the cause of the anger, one responded, "I don't like being called a racist." That was an "Aha" moment for me.

I remember sharing another incident with a White European American male colleague. His response was, "They said *that* to you!" with a look of surprise on his face. Most of the time, I believe students are unaware of the racial overtones of their comments and behaviors toward me. Many of my students have never known a person from a different race, much less a person of color in a position of authority. I often encourage them to attend lectures on campus. One advised me that she had never seen a Black or African American man speak professionally.

Teachers and students do not shed their identities and positions upon entering the classroom. Structural issues of race, class, and gender can affect the various dynamics of the higher education classroom (Ray, 2005). My reputation precedes me. Students know that I require a large amount of homework during a demanding semester when other professors also make several assignments. I give specific detail about how I want the work to be completed, but I still hear that they do not understand what I want. I often wonder if I am speaking a foreign language. I had the department chair review the instructions on my syllabus to confirm that I had provided clear and sufficient detail. I sense there is resistance and have learned to recognize the difference between "I don't understand" and "I don't want to do it." I often try to focus on what is happening, paying attention to process rather than content. In most instances, I believe my students miss the opportunity to engage in open, honest cross-cultural dialogue.

I do not allow creative interpretations of the outlines for assignments, and I provide an explanation. My pattern is to return papers for students to rewrite rather than give failing grades if the students have the ability to benefit from corrective guidance. I want to prepare them for the reality of professional practice. I believe that, if the students complete the assignment, I have an obligation to read it and provide feedback to further their professional development. I spend hours grading assignments. I believe that some students interpret my feedback as arrogant and not valuable. Several African American women scholars (Benjamin, 1997; Smith, 1999; Turner, 2002) have posited that African American women who are confident, intelligent, and assertive in their professional responsibilities can be perceived as being a "Sapphire" (Bradley, 2005). I am accused of being intimidating, angry, and having an attitude, which is the meaning of the stereotype of a Sapphire. Students complain about the amount of work, think that I present too much content on African Americans, and that I talk too fast. Is it possible that student evaluations of my teaching suffer because I am a faculty member of color who teaches a rigorous course? On more than one evaluation, the raw numerical scores did not match positive comments made by my students.

As students enter full-time employment or graduate school, they confirm that they did learn "a lot" from me. They thank me for demanding excellence and stressing the importance of following directions. When I asked an alumna what I should do differently, she said, "Nothing, just keep doing what you are doing." She also said that I should just expect that students will be angry, but not change what I do. Unfortunately, these positive reflections come too late for me. While the feedback affirms my philosophy about teaching, it will never improve evaluative scores I receive from current students.

The most significant challenge of my professional career was my personal life. When I started at the university, I was married, with a five-year-old daughter and an 18-month-old son. I lived the experience of role overload, but was scared to death to show any signs of being overwhelmed. Three years later, my marriage ended. I was in a panic over finances after my divorce; my monthly check from the university only covered my house, car payments, and daycare expenses. My large family of origin was an invaluable resource as they watched my children while I worked. God answered my prayers, and consultant work became available for me to make ends meet. My days were long and sometimes exhausting. On several occasions, I worked 12- to 15-hour days. At one point, I thought the pressure was going to kill me, and I said to myself, "I can't keep doing this." In an "Aha!" moment, I thought, "What happens if I don't [keep going]?" The reframe made it crystal clear to me that, instead of being miserable, I needed to be thankful. My mantra became, "God don't put no more on you than you can bear; He has perfect timing, and He don't make no mistakes!" My agenda was survival, and my faith provided me with the stamina to persevere. I had to do this while making room for all the additional work expected of the professoriate: committee assignments, service, and scholarly activities.

My goal was not just to meet, but to exceed all expectations. On one occasion, my supervisor accused me of not contributing to the department. His complaint was that I was not around on Wednesday afternoons. I told him that I advised and met with a Black Greek-letter sorority on campus on Wednesdays. I was confident that my involvement was "legitimate," and I was relieved to be able to defend myself. My supervisor backed off when he realized his complaint was unfounded. I was furious, but shook it off. These were the same people I needed to support my request for promotion and tenure. Remember, I was taught to smile and be nice.

Tenure and Promotion

I was denied promotion the first time I applied. I had no guidance and no idea what was expected. I also did not know that colleagues would share their dossier (tenure and promotion portfolio) to help with the process. I received little inside information to further my career. The response I received from the dean was that I needed more time in rank. I did learn how to produce a more impressive document,

and I was promoted to associate professor and received tenure following my second attempt.

I never thought I would be considered for another promotion, and I knew I had to be responsible for my own professional development. I took on leadership responsibilities in the state chapter of the National Association of Social Workers (NASW) and was elected to the NASW Delegate Assembly; I received a gubernatorial appointment to the state licensing board, chaired the department assessment committee, administered our Title IV-E Child Welfare Grant, presented at national conferences, and published. A male colleague repeatedly teased me that we would never be promoted to full professors in spite of our hard work due to a lack of publications. I realized after a while that I did have sufficient documentation to be considered. I also decided that timing was critical because my department chair had announced his retirement. I sought out colleagues whom I believed were supportive. They shared their dossiers with me for guidance, and I began to collect letters of recommendation from people who thought highly of me.

I experienced a medical setback before I could finish assembling my documents and had to have a section of my colon removed following a routine colonoscopy. I remember working in the hospital bed where I stayed for one week following surgery, writing and e-mailing exams and meeting with people for a project at church. It was clear I did not know how *not* to work. I recovered quickly and met the deadline for submission. My department chair commented with surprise to his secretary, saying, "I think she's got it." I received support from him and the department for promotion to full professor.

The College Promotion Committee presented a

hurdle because I was requesting promotion to full professor without a PhD. In our department, the MSW was identified as the terminal degree. The precedent for promotion to full professor with an MSW was established several years earlier when the director of the social work program, a White European American male, was promoted to full professor. I believe that my colleague who had teased me that we would never get promoted advocated on my behalf. He served on the College Promotion Committee, which recommended promotion, as did the dean. The provost also recommended promotion and sent me an e-mail noting that I had earned his recommendation.

Additional factors related to timing supported my successful promotion. The president was proving that he was sincere in his desire to promote diversity at the university. For the first time in history, the president of the Board of Governors was an African American female. She put into practice the president's desire to increase diversity by creating a task force intended to promote relationships and the university's image in communities of color. I was a member of the task force and supported as many activities as possible. I was confident that I had her support. It was also highly unlikely that the Board would not support a recommendation for promotion from the provost. I was promoted to full professor during the March meeting of the Board of Governors in 2002. Their action made me the first and only African American full professor in the history of the university. I was proud and honored, but the accomplishment is bittersweet. By no means do I claim to be the best. I believe that better faculty than I have come and gone. The best refused to tolerate unfair treatment and moved on.

I started my 21st year at the university in the fall of 2006. I am still the only African American full professor on campus, and we continue to lose outstanding faculty. Retention of faculty of color is a serious, ongoing problem. I currently enjoy affirming relationships with the dean, my department chair, and other faculty in my college and department. I am committed to improving my teaching and technology skills. I am enjoying my involvement as chair of the State Licensing Board and in national professional organizations including the Children's Bureau, NASW, and the Association of Social Work Boards (ASWB). Despite the fact that my parents only talked about work and worry as if the two terms were synonymous, I love my job and am proud to be a social work educator.

CONCLUSION

My personal life has changed significantly. I have raised two wonderful young adults who made my experience as a parent almost easy. My daughter is a college graduate who is establishing herself in a career in the medical field. My son graduated from college and is now in law school. I am honored to be their mother and to have cared for my own mother, who lived with me before she died. The challenges of teaching in a majority White institution are colored by race and gender. The struggles female faculty members face include trust issues, inequitable work demands and evaluations, lack of supportive mentors, negative stereotypes about African American women, the need to prove oneself repeatedly, and the absence of empowerment. My survival strategies included perseverance in the face of adversity, identification of a trusted mentor, a strong achievement orientation, and my faith. My early experiences prepared me to survive challenges consistent with a hostile environment. I know that life is not easy. Anticipation of difficulties and setting clear, safe boundaries can minimize surprises and buffer the effects of unfair treatment. The dilemma is to establish supportive networks while maintaining a level of healthy paranoia. Female faculty of color must give themselves permission to voice the burdens of role overload and other challenges without fear that disclosure will be used to allege that they are not able to handle the task. In my mind, faith in a higher power is both a prerequisite and a coping strategy for managing the challenges, stresses, and strains of success. I know with confidence that God did not bring me out of the ditch to leave me. For this, I feel eternally privileged.

REFERENCES

Benjamin, L. (1997). *Black women in the academy: Promises and perils.* Gainesville, FL: University Press of Florida.

Bonner, F. H. (2004, June 11). Black professors: On the track but out of the loop. *The Chronicle of Higher Education, 50*(40), p. B11.

Bradley, C. (2005). The career experiences of African American women faculty: Implications for counselor education programs. *College Student Journal, 39*(3), 517–527.

Buck, J. (2003). *The state of the African American professoriate: Challenges and responsibilities.* Paper presented at The Ramapo Conference, Mahwah, NJ.

Burden, J. W., Jr., Harrison L., Jr., & Hodge, S. K. (2005). Perceptions of African American faculty in kinesiology based programs at predominantly White American institutions of higher education. *Research Quarterly for Exercise and Sport, 76*(2), 224–237.

Chasteen, E. (1968). Who favors public accommodations: A demographic analysis. *Sociological Quarterly, 9*(3), 309–317.

Gray, M. (1995). African Americans. In J. Philleo and L. Epstein (Eds.), *Cultural competence for social workers: A guide for alcohol and other drug abuse prevention professionals working with ethnic/racial communities* (pp. 70–101). [Special Collaborative NASW/CSAP monograph]. Washington, DC: DHHS Publication No. (SMA) 95-3075.

Hartman, A., & Laird, J. (1983). *Family centered social work practice.* New York: Free Press.

Johnson-Baily, J., Cervero, R. M., & Baugh, S. (2004). Mentoring in black and white: Intricacies of cross cultural mentoring. *Mentoring and Tutoring: Partnership in Learning, 12*(1), 7–21.

Ray, N. (2005). Race and gender in the academy: The experiences of Black female professors in the graduate higher education classroom. *Proceedings of the 3rd International Conference on Researching Lifelong Learning and Teaching.* Stirling, Scotland: University of Stirling.

Smith, P. J. (1999). Teaching the retrenchment generation: When Sapphire meets Socrates at the intersection of race, gender and authority. *William and Mary Journal of Women and the Law, 6*(53), 1–214.

Turner, C. S. V. (2002). Women of color in academe. *Journal of Higher Education, 73,* 74–94.

Watson, E. (2005, August 11). Marching to vote. *New York Amsterdam News, 96*(33), 1.

Part II: The Voices of Women of Color as Social Work Educators

Chapter 7: When and Where I Enter and Exit

Anita Curry-Jackson

I dedicate this chapter to my mother, Mrs. Emma Curry, and other women who inspire women to succeed.

The debate continues on the question of the place of women and men in contemporary America. The debate has become more complex because of the events of the 1960s, mass media, political mobilization, and governmental policies. These events have led to "a flood of information and speculations, government investigations, academic research, the growth of women's studies programs on college campuses, and theoretical debates" about gender arrangements (Lengerman & Wallace, 1985, pp. 1–2). Gender arrangement is based on an assumption of inequality—that the female is subordinate to the male. Likewise, a continuing debate centers on the question of racial and ethnic equality and parity. The race question centers on a similar assumption of subordination and inferiority that is grounded in the notions of both racism and sexism—direct contradictions to the central values of American culture, which include the dignity and worth of the individual human being; the rights of all individuals to equal treatment, equal opportunity, and equal access to achievement; and the democratic rights of individuals to participate fully and equally in society.

An examination of society indicates that these values are submerged by the realities of inequality. The contradictions between "what is" and "what ought to be" become the foci of many American dilemmas. For instance, despite the vastly higher numbers of educated women who are entering the workforce, only a few are able to advance into the higher ranks of their professions, that is, medicine, law, engineering, science, and the academy. Regardless of socioeconomic status or level of education, most women primarily work in female-dominated areas of service jobs, factory work, sales or clerical positions, and professions such as teaching, nursing, and social work. Even those women who "made it" in the professions are relegated to the more "typical" roles of pediatricians, real estate brokers, and instructors or assistant professors without tenure in the academy. The inequality and discrimination women experience is "rooted in the cumulative effects of early childhood socialization in 'appropriate'" sex-role behavior and attitudes for girls and boys by parents, teachers, and peers and differential opportunities for education, training, and career (Beall, Sternberg, & Berscheid, 1993; Bernard, 1971; Goldberg, 1993; Roby, 1972).

The picture for women in the social work profession, particularly in social work higher education, is similar. The social work profession is a microcosm of the wider society. The underrepresentation of women social workers in administration (in proportion to their number in the profession) remains a concern (Chernesky, 1980). Studies confirm that women tend to be in direct-service positions and remain in these positions longer before promotion to the first administrative level, which is likely a lower level administrative position, and that women have limited access to top executive and administrative positions. Thus, women's abilities and potentials are underused, and sex bias in the academy has promoted and reinforced different achievement and aspiration patterns for men and women.

Griffin (2000) summarized the general status of women in the workforce:

> White women have steadily pushed against and at times have broken through the infamous glass ceiling. In this achievement, white women have vaulted far ahead of African Americans of both genders. For example, before the 1970s, white women comprised less than 5 percent of the lawyers, physicians, college and university professors, and business managers in the nation. By 1990, their ranks had surged to more than 33 percent in each of these professional categories. Prior to 1970, African Americans constituted less than 1 percent of all attorneys, 2 percent of

physicians, and 3 percent of college and university professors. By 1990, they represented only 3 percent of attorneys and physicians and 5 percent of professors. Percentages similar to these are found all across the white-collar employment spectrum. White women are the single greatest beneficiaries of affirmative action programs. (p. 106)

In the academy, in 2001, approximately 83% of college faculty members were White European Americans. White European American males comprised 48%, White European American women comprised 35%, and people of color comprised about 15% of faculty in U.S. colleges and universities. In terms of academic ranks, women of color comprised 11.5% of full professors, 14.4% of associate professors, 18% of assistant professors, 17.9% of instructors, and 15.6% of lecturer positions (Digest of Education Statistics, 2003).

Have improvements occurred? Yes, but what accounts for such a different rate of change between White European American women and women of color? The title of Paula Giddings's book (1984), *When and Where I Enter*, frames my approach to my professional journey.

Only the BLACK WOMAN can say "when and where I enter, in the quiet, undisputed dignity of my womanhood, without violence and without suing or special patronage, then and there the whole...race enters with me."

—Anna Julia Cooper, 1892

When one enters the world, as well as *where* one enters, establishes the context for one's life experiences. A nation's formal and informal policies and rules establish parameters for individual success. Thus, it is important to address the social and political environment that influences challenges as well as opportunities for women of color. It seems so appropriate to say, "things have changed, yet they remain the same." Over the past five decades, can one say that opportunities have opened for women of color? What opportunities have opened to me over the past five decades?

I started my tenure as Associate Provost of Wright State University on June 12, 2006. As an associate professor, I have more than 25 years in higher education at Case Western Reserve University, Atlanta University, Clark College, and Wright State University. Since affiliating with Wright State in 1987, I have served as a faculty member, social work field coordinator, department chair, dean, and now associate provost.

I am an active member of professional organizations such as the Council on Social Work Education; the Ohio College Association of Social Work Educators; the Ohio Child Welfare University Partnership (Title IV-E) Organization; and the National Association of Social Workers. I am the immediate past president of the National Association of Baccalaureate Social Work Program Directors, and I belong to several community organizations such as Twentig, Inc., St. Mary's Rotary (Board of Directors), United Way (Board of Directors), and the Chambers of Commerce of Celina, St. Mary's, and New Knoxville/New Bremen/Minster.

PERSONAL JOURNEY

When and Where I Enter This World

Life began for me in 1946 in the segregated South. Because communities were segregated, economic status did not allow people of color to live in communities of their choice. Schools (public and private) were segregated, as were the public libraries, and African Americans could only use the main public library one to two evenings per week. Segregation also applied to public buses, water fountains, and restrooms designated for Colored and Whites. Colored people were addressed orally and in writing by their first names, while Whites expected to be addressed with a title such as Mrs. or Mr. and their last name. Laws sanctioned these behaviors.

When I was 17, in 1954, the U.S. Supreme Court ruled on the *Brown v. Board of Education*. Chief Justice Earl Warren concluded that, "To separate [Black children] from others of similar age and qualifications solely because of their race generates a feeling of inferiority as to their status in the community. We conclude that in the field of public education the doctrine of 'separate but equal' has no place. Separate educational facilities are inherently unequal" (Williams, 1998, pp. 225–226). The Supreme Court did not give a date for implementation, and states were granted discretion regarding implementation of the decision. Consequently, many Southern states closed their public schools and established private schools instead.

During my pre-college years, the country was experiencing a new wave of protests that included sit-in demonstrations. As Williams (1998) writes,

By the end of the 1960, some 1700 students had been arrested throughout the South for disturbing the peace by demanding to be served in segregated restaurants. In 1961 [Thurgood] Marshall filed a brief in the Supreme Court (*Garner v. Louisiana*) that argued that the Fourteenth Amendment gave the students the right to be served in a public restaurant and made the point that the well-dressed, polite young people had never disrupted the peace. The Supreme Court unanimously ruled at the end of the year in a sweeping decision in favor of Marshall and the students. The sit-ins had succeeded. (p. 289)

When and Where I Entered College

After high school, I received a full academic scholarship to a historically Black college and desired to become a social worker. I started college 10 years before the Council on Social Work Education (CSWE) started accrediting undergraduate social work programs, so I majored in sociology with a concentration in social work.

During my matriculation from 1964 to 1968, the Civil Rights movement was gaining momentum with the passage of the Civil Rights Act of 1964 and the Voting Rights Act of 1964. The Civil Rights movement spawned various civil rights organizations and outstanding leaders to champion social and economic justice. In 1968, Dr. Martin Luther King, Jr. came to Memphis, Tennessee, to lead peaceful demonstrations and advocate for the rights of local sanitation workers. Dr. King returned to Memphis in April and was assassinated the night before the march. After his assassination, another march was scheduled in which I also participated. That march was peaceful and demonstrated tremendous support for the striking sanitation workers and their cause.

When and Where I Entered Graduate School

During my undergraduate years, many faculty members strongly encouraged me to attend graduate school; thus, I elected to attend a prominent university in Cleveland, Ohio. Like many urban cities, Cleveland experienced major riots following King's assassination in April 1968. Historically, the School of Social Work at this university had never had more than five African American students enrolled in its first- and second-year classes during any academic year. I entered the program with approximately 20 other African American students, a first for this school. The dean of the school was an African American male, and it had at least five full-time instructional faculty members. It was during my first year of graduate school that the National Association of Black Social Workers (NABSW) was formed. In 1969, with support from Dean John Turner, many African American students attended the first official meeting of NABSW at Howard University. I remained active with NABSW through 1988 as an officer of a local chapter and a member of the National Steering Committee.

The challenges I faced in graduate school did not relate to my academic studies, but to the discrimination I experienced with housing and visiting an area that was not receptive to people of color. I had two encounters related to housing. The first occurred when an African American female classmate and I went to visit a White European American classmate. When we left her apartment, her landlord visited and forbade her from having African Americans in her apartment. She elected to vacate that apartment building. The three of us then set out to find housing in East Cleveland in an Italian community. At least two of the property owners told me that since they planned to live on the first floor, they would not rent to me. However, another Italian family rented the second floor of their house to us. My second encounter occurred in Little Italy, when my roommates and I (two African Americans and one White European American) went to the laundromat. Several youths taunted us and asked the White European American why she was with us. The laundry attendant assisted us with our exit. As we left, the youths threw bottles at our car. We called the police, who said that they could not do anything. The university's only assistance was to instruct students about areas that might not be safe for or tolerant of people of color.

Across the entire university, the number of graduate and undergraduate African American students increased dramatically, which transformed the institution and challenged its culture. Within the School of Social Work, African American students felt supported and were not isolated or segregated; however, tension still existed. One example had to do with an assignment on the Moynihan Report, in which I questioned the paper's conclusions regarding African American families and why the data were aggregated into only two categories—White European American and people of color. I asked why the data did not discuss each group of color separately. The instructor said he did not want the class discussion to be divisive, and he never addressed my question. The instructor seemed to be concerned about the class discussion being divided across racial lines, but my question related to methodology. A second example related to an assignment that required my group to collect data in Little Italy. Based on my two previous racial experiences with Little Italy residents, it was clear that I was not going to be able to collect any survey data. The White European American members of the group collected the data, and I worked on the rest of the assignment. This information, including restrictions on who collected the data, was part of the report. There was no reaction from the instructor. As an aside, about two years later, an African student was harmed in Little Italy, and the university became proactive in making institutional changes with respect to that community. Change was slow even as the country was reeling from King's assassination, the riots, and the Vietnam War.

PROFESSIONAL JOURNEY

When and Where I Entered Social Work Professional Practice

During my last year in graduate school (1970), the dean approached me about a one-year faculty contract on a grant. I joined the school as a faculty field instructor and supervised a unit of students placed at a community agency, a settlement house. The grant was designed to give students a "generic" field experience that included casework, group work, and community organization. My area was group work. This experience appears to align with generalist practice today, where social work graduates are expected to have skills and knowledge needed to work with individuals, families, groups, organizations, and communities.

During the early 1970s, I joined a local neighborhood center where I worked for seven years. I started as a youth outreach director and then became the director of personnel and youth services. The challenge was related to earning a salary comparable to the scope of my work. Although my workload increased, my salary did not. In fact, when I was hired initially, I learned that the previous person, an African American male, earned more than I was offered, even though I had a master's degree and he only had a bachelor's. As the director of personnel, I battled to make sure I was paid at least the same salary as the person who preceded me in the position. My persistence convinced the agency's executive director, albeit with reservations, to increase my salary to the same level as the previous director of personnel, a White European American female. What was the reason behind the salary disparities? Racism? Sexism?

Where and When I Returned to Higher Education

From the eighth grade, social work was my career choice. Working in a setting that assisted individuals, families, and communities to improve their quality of life was my goal. Becoming a social work educator was never on my radar screen. However, once I reentered the world of higher education, I knew I had found my niche. My journey to become a social work educator was unplanned, and I have no regrets.

I returned to higher education in 1978 as a research associate at a university in Atlanta. The following academic year, I joined the faculty at a local college and remained there for nine years. This was an exciting time as I worked with Dr. Will Scott to accredit the social work program. I was the field coordinator from 1979 to 1982, and, in 1983, I became the director of the undergraduate social work program. The previous director did not seem to have faced the same challenges I encountered with respect to resources for the social work program, although I cannot say conclusively that gender was a major factor. I did not have any difficulty meeting with the president and dean; however, the net result was fewer resources available for the program. Fortunately, I was able to secure external grants to assist with special projects compatible with the social work program and its mission and purpose. In 1983, I started the social work doctoral program at the university in Atlanta, and I joined the Association of Baccalaureate Social Work Program Directors (BPD).

In 1987, I earned my doctorate in social work with a cognate in higher education. I believe this degree gave me a competitive edge in interviewing for new positions. Shortly thereafter, I joined the faculty of the Department of Social Work at my current university and experienced an easy transition. Through my professional membership, I knew some of my new department colleagues. I left the responsibilities of department chair at my previous university and became a faculty member only. Difficulties, if any, related more to students' behaviors. They wanted to challenge me. Again, I was not sure if gender or race factored into their questioning. The university did not have many African American faculty members. However, I held firm to important principles of fairness, honesty, and integrity as I interacted with primarily White European American, first-year students enrolled in

sociology courses. At previous institutions of higher education, I did not have such encounters.

In 1992, I received tenure and was promoted to the rank of associate professor. In 1993, I became chairperson of the Department of Social Work, the first African American female chair in the College of Liberal Arts. In 2002, I became the first African American dean in the history of the university. I earned these promotions based on the strengths and competencies I demonstrated at the department, college, and university levels.

Factors Influencing Social Work as My Career Choice

Several factors influenced my choice of a social work career; the settlement house movement was a primary factor. When asked to identify a social worker, most people describe a child protective social worker or welfare worker. That was not my conception of a social worker. Rather, I saw a social worker as aligned with workers at settlement houses. As Trattner (1999) describes, "The settlement house movement began in the 1880s seeking to bridge the gap between the classes and races, to eliminate the sources of distress, and to improve urban living and working conditions" (p. 163). Unfortunately, many of the settlement houses were segregated because they served the populations that settled into a given neighborhood. My experiences with settlement houses (Bethlehem Center), which began at age four, included kindergarten, art classes, music classes (piano and violin), ballet, woodworking shop, drama classes, tennis, and so forth. In addition to being a participant, I was a volunteer and a paid worker. Bethlehem Center set the stage for my pursuit of social work.

A second major factor that influenced my pursuit of social work had to do with opportunities available to women during the 1950s and 1960s. Professional women held positions in elementary and secondary education and nursing. Likewise, Black women professionals were engaged primarily in nursing and teaching.

The educational focus of my college experience was a third major factor. During my matriculation, the college wanted its graduates prepared to teach, so my advisors recommended education courses as electives. My first and only education course confirmed that social work education was the best career choice for me.

The fourth factor to shape my social work career choice was my faculty mentors and other significant persons. Having people believe in you builds your confidence. Throughout my professional journey, people I knew and others I did not shepherded my career. The people who started building my knowledge, skills, abilities, and confidence were my parents and extended family members. My father worked three jobs to keep, at one time, five children in private schools. Even while working three jobs, he seldom missed school programs in which we participated. Many times when I visited his jobs, the employees would say how proud my father was of my high academic record. These accolades put pressure on me to continue to excel. Neighbors supported me as well. This broad range of support was important in the context of the time, when segregation was the order of the day, and racism and discrimination were codified in ordinances and folkways. Having family members and community members validate your importance, intelligence, and talents was important as you encountered overt and covert racism.

All of my teachers (K–12) made me feel special and encouraged me to excel. Several faculty members mentored me, including a White European American female sociology teacher and her husband, a White European American male and economics teacher. All but one of the undergraduate faculty members (White European American and African American) built my confidence. That one instructor was never satisfied with my work, and it amazes me that one faculty member's action still haunts me when 10 others validated my abilities and intellect.

At each place I worked, some of the people wanted me to be successful. Each assisted me in different ways, such as encouraging me to apply for certain grants, directing me to serve on certain committees, or linking me with specific professional organizations. All of these individuals helped me to advance personally and professionally.

Challenges

The challenge is to continue to work toward a society that totally embraces social and economic justice. Without a just society, "the climb to the top" (Harvey, 1999, p. 1) will continue to be difficult for African American women faculty members. According to Harvey (1999):

> There are some immutable characteristics that have been responsible for persons who have the requisite qualifications nevertheless being ruled out of consideration for particular positions in certain types of institutions. The most obvious such characteristic in America's colleges and universities has been race—the history and

legacy of racial discrimination in America has meant that, except in very isolated situations, African Americans have not received equal consideration for positions, especially positions of power and authority, in the predominantly white colleges and universities. (p. 1)

Thus, at the top of the list for challenges are two "isms"—racism and sexism. These two "isms" are difficult to address because our society is in denial about their existence. As Cook (2005) concludes, "Most women will answer no when asked if they have faced discrimination. They see it in the nation, college and department, but they do not think it has happened to them personally. They are wrong" (p. 25).

The "isms" will continue to create challenges for me in terms of my professional journey as well as the professional journey of other women of color. After graduate school and my work at a social service agency, my career plans were not well orchestrated, especially my higher education career plans. As I launched my career in higher education, I knew very little about the structure and dynamics of higher education or about the promotion and tenure process, to which I gave little thought. Naively, I felt a sense of job security. In hindsight, important time was lost; attention to the required activities for tenure must start immediately. I had no mentors during the promotion and tenure process at my third higher education institution. More attention was placed on my preparation for a future administrative position—program director or chair—than on my preparation for the promotion and tenure process. At my fourth institution, I became more aware of the promotion and tenure process, and it took me seven years to obtain tenure. Thus, it is essential to have mentors and a "good network of contacts and associates" (Harvey, 1999, p. 4).

The glass ceiling was another challenge. The glass ceiling allows one to see opportunities for advancement, but not the route to those opportunities. This is where mentors and a network of contacts and associates can be of help. Myers (2002) advises, "Mentors need not be a minority or female; however, regardless of a mentor's gender, race, ethnicity, it is important that [he or she] be aware of the politics of difference [gender and race inequalities]" (p. 10).

I bumped my head twice on the "glass ceiling." One position was a posted opening with specified qualifications. I certainly met and exceeded the written qualifications and felt I had interviewed well for the position, however, I was not offered the position. I was an internal candidate, and an external candidate was hired instead. A second position was a vacancy created by a person moving into an interim, higher administrative position. I met with him and expressed my interest in the position. He stated that his intent was to leave the position vacant because he would do the duties associated with both positions—his new interim position and his previous position. Within three months, the position was filled by a White European American female. To my knowledge, the opening was never posted. There are always plausible explanations for the decisions and choices made, it seems. However, I felt racism was a strong factor with respect to the latter position. I also did not have anyone guiding my career path and championing my advance upward.

Mentors and a strong network can assist with breaking the "glass ceiling," especially when you think you are doing the right thing and in the right way—the formal way. Mentors can assist in negotiating the informal system and making the "net work."

Another challenge is obtaining the necessary experience for future administrative positions. Sometimes the university structure and culture inhibit African Americans' full participation.

> For example, to be considered for a high-level position in academe, such as dean or university president, an applicant must have had previous experience in a similar job setting. African American female faculty members who have not had opportunities to gain previous experience (because of racism, sexism, or any of the other numerous inhibitors of success) find themselves in a cycle that can seem hopelessly difficult to end. (Myers, 2002, p. 8)

CONCLUSION

Dr. Claire Van Ummersen, vice president of the American Council on Education (ACE) and director of the Office of Women in Higher Education presented findings from a report commissioned by ACE's Office of Women in Higher Education. The report, *An Agenda for Excellence: Creating Flexibility in Tenure–Track Faculty Careers*, noted "critical work-life dilemmas that women in higher education experience as well as possible solutions" (Van Ummersen, 2005, p. 7). Dr. Claire Van Ummersen makes a compelling case for immediate action. The future outlook can be positive if, according to Dr. Van Ummersen, we look at the changing demographics and act proactively. As Van Ummersen (2005) notes, "We are soon to have a huge number of retirements, most of them male. We are going to have a massive problem if we do not move women and minorities into those slots. We will run out of faculty." According to the demographics,

> Women now earn 51% of the PhDs awarded to U.S. citizens by American schools but represent only 38% of the full time faculty. And only 15% of full-time faculty are people of color. More women and people of color receive doctoral degrees than receive tenure. [And] disproportionate numbers of women and people of color are found in the lowest-tenure track ranks or in non-tenure track jobs. (Van Ummersen, 2005, p. 7)

An aggressive approach must be taken to develop a pipeline for women of color to pursue terminal degrees in their fields and faculty positions in higher education. Women in the pipeline must have mentors and strong networks to guide their career path in higher education, particularly in social work higher education because, as Myers (2002) writes, "Success in academics depend[s] not only on what you know, but also who[m] you know for support, guidance, and advocacy" (p. 9). Therefore, women of color in the academy must have strong mentors and information links. Mentors must be committed to the success of women of color, particularly African American women, and must embrace diversity, address gender and racial biases, and advocate for their mentees. These mentors must guide women of color through the promotion and tenure process and help assure productivity with respect to scholarship. They must make sure that women faculty of color get support for their scholarship and that the university values their service activities. Many times, African American women faculty are asked to serve on committees dealing with issues of people of color that are not accorded the same importance or value as other university committees in the promotion and tenure process. Thus, mentors must help women faculty members assess the kinds of activities that are valued in the university tenure and promotion process. Additionally, mentors and other associates must educate the university on the significance of scholarship and service related to people of color and multicultural issues. They must assure that African American faculty women are strong, viable candidates for promotion and tenure and for high-ranking academic administrative positions.

Since more women and people of color receive doctoral degrees than receive tenure, more efforts must be directed to identifying these individuals and recruiting them into the academy. The outlook for women of color will be a challenge until there is a serious commitment to diversity and to social and economic justice.

REFERENCES

Beall, A. E., Sternberg, R. J., & Berscheid, E. (Eds.). (1993). *The psychology of gender*. New York: Guilford Press.

Bernard, J. (1971). *Women and the public interest: An essay on policy and protest*. Chicago: Aldine Publishing.

Chernesky, R. H. (1980). Women administrators in social work. In E. Norman & A. Mancuso (Eds.), *Women's issues and social work practice*, (pp. 241–262). Itasca, IL: F. E. Peacock Publishers.

Digest of Education Statistics. (2003). *Full-time instructional faculty in degree-granting institutions, by race/ethnicity, academic rank and sex: Fall 2001*. Washington DC: National Center for Education Statistics.

Giddings, P. (1984). *When and where I enter: The impact of Black women on race in America*. New York: W. Morrow.

Goldberg, S. (1993). *Why men rule: A theory of male dominance*. Chicago: Open Court.

Griffin, P. R. (2000). *Seeds of racism in the soul of America*. Cleveland, OH: Pilgrim Press.

Harvey, W. B. (1999). *Grassroots and glass ceiling: African American administrators in predominantly White colleges and universities*. Albany, NY: State University of New York Press.

Lengerman, P. M., & Wallace, R. A. (1985). *Gender in America: Social control and social change*. Englewood Cliffs, NJ: Prentice-Hall.

Myers, L. W. (2002). *A broken silence: Voices of African American women in the academy*. Westport, CT: Bergin and Garvey.

Roby, P. (1972). Structural and internalized barriers to women in higher education. In C. S. Rothschild (Ed.), *Toward a sociology of women* (pp. 171–193). Lexington, MA: Xerox College Publishing.

Trattner, W. I. (1999). *From poor law to welfare: A history of social welfare in America*. New York: The Free Press.

Van Ummersen, C. (2005). Redefining the academic career path in the 21st century. *Women in Higher Education, 14*(4), 7–8.

Valian V. (2005). Negotiation, gender and power. *Women in Higher Education, 14*(4), 25–26.

Williams, J. (1998). *Thurgood Marshall—American Revolutionary*. New York: Times Books.

Women of Color as Social Work Educators

Part II: The Voices of Women of Color as Social Work Educators

Chapter 8: Ada E. Deer, An Activist for Global Humanity

Saundra Hardin Starks

Kathleen Kirby

I would like everyone across the globe to be a complete human by recognizing each other's humanity. It would mean peace, justice, and equality.
                                                    —Ada Deer

Ada Deer is an American Indian woman who has been at the forefront of political advocacy and the American Indian Movement. She is often referred to as a legend in Madison, Wisconsin, and nationally (S. Jackson, personal communication, February 25, 2005). The story of Ada Deer holds the power to affect, educate, inform, and mentor many. Her story speaks of a journey well-lived and filled with challenges and successes. It speaks of generational vision and regard for the well-being of all people. It speaks of courage to stand on dangerous grounds and to question what too often is left unquestioned and unchallenged.

CONTEXT AND BACKGROUND

The story of Ada Deer began many years ago at a face-to-face committee meeting of a national social work organization focusing on racial and ethnic diversity issues. Finding American Indian or indigenous people to serve on national committees was a difficult task for the staff of this social work organization. Into this meeting walks a very attractive, tall, statuesque woman who identifies herself as an American Indian from the Menomonee Tribe. She had such a presence and energy that one immediately knew that she brought enlightenment and wisdom in the form of knowledge and history, not only to the committee, but to all facets of the social work profession. She provided a wealth of information and experience, not only from the American Indian perspective but from a social justice and culturally competent perspective, that shaped and directed the work of this particular organization's committee.

Initially, the opportunity to work with Ada on a professional level would have been enough by itself; however, she offered much more. On a personal level, there was ever-present informal mentoring, unconditional support, and encouragement. Never would one talk to Ada about any committee issues without feeling her sincere regard and concern for one's personal and professional well-being. As a mentor, she epitomized the strength and empowerment-based orientation of the social work profession by living the real essence of peace and social justice. Also, the significance of history from the American Indian perspective was ever-present in her contributions to this committee. She advocated for linguistic diversity and provided in-depth knowledge, which she enriched with personal vignettes of the American Indian code talkers, supporting the historical perspective for this area of cultural competence.

Cultural competency, feminist theory, and social activism are the backdrop for the presentation of this story. Cultural competency, as defined by the National Association of Social Workers (NASW), is "the process by which individuals and systems respond respectfully and effectively to people of all cultures, languages, classes, races, ethnic backgrounds, religions, and other diversity factors in a manner that recognizes, affirms, and values the worth of these people and their communities as well as protects and preserves the dignity of each" (2001). Furthermore, feminist theory promotes equal rights and equal access for all people. It is also important to note that both of the authors of this chapter have a strong affinity for these particular orientations, thus the authors' connection to Ada and mutual agreement that her voice be presented. One author is a grateful novice who received mentoring from her coauthor and Ada Deer; the other is part American Indian with a strong research background in culture and gender issues.

Over the years, numerous documents have been written about Ada's life and her contributions (Dumez & Sardella, 2003; Skog, 1995). We offer this chapter as an additional tribute to her legacy to enrich and contribute to the lives of future women of color who venture into the academy unarmed and unprepared for the struggles. This is especially relevant for women of color who are American Indian.

ADA'S STORY

Ada Deer never envisioned herself in an academic setting. Yet she is now a Distinguished Lecturer of Social Work at the University of Wisconsin-Madison (UW-Madison), her alma mater, and director of the university's American Indian Studies Program. She has been honored as a fellow at the Kennedy Institute of Politics at Harvard University and has received honorary degrees from five institutions. Ms. Deer's accomplishments include a long list of "firsts," such as the first Menominee to receive undergraduate and honorary degrees from UW–Madison; the first American Indian to receive an MSW from Columbia University School of Social Work; the first woman leader of the Menominee Restoration Committee (Interim Tribal Government); the first woman to serve as assistant secretary of the interior for Indian Affairs (during the Clinton administration); and the first Native American woman to run for Congress from Wisconsin and to serve as secretary of state in Wisconsin. She also initiated the first UW-Madison program to provide social work training on reservations. She attributes much of her success to her mother—the most influential person in her life.

Constance (aka Connie), Ada's mother, was a White European American woman of independent spirit born in 1904. She chose to be a nurse to fulfill her wanderlust and avoid the "gentile" life. After completing her nursing training, she left her family and her identical twin, Adah, for the Rosebud Indian Reservation. Constance was fascinated with American Indian culture and was able to join the tribal people, often visiting her patients in their homes, sharing ceremonies, and learning and respecting natural ways of healing. In Ada's words, her mother did things "out of the box."

Constance was later reassigned to Wisconsin, where she met her husband, the oldest of five children. He lost his mother in the 1918 flu epidemic and was raised in a Catholic boarding school, where he learned to be ashamed of his culture and heritage. He was a well-recognized speaker of the Menominee language, but he did not share it with Ada, often telling her, "Go away—you're just a girl" when she attempted to learn from listening to him and his sister, Theresa. But Constance was accepted by some of her husband's Menominee Pauquot and Pequot family.

The Deer family eked out a living with Ada's father hunting, fishing, doing limited farming, and working in the tribal lumber mill. Although many would see life in a one-room log cabin on the banks of the historic beautiful Wolf River as romantic, the family chopped logs for heat and cooking and carried water daily. Life was hard. Ada, who truly loved the land—especially the nationally noted Wolf River, decided early in life that she would seek something different when she grew up.

When she was about four years old, Ada remembers asking her mother for permission to do something. Her mother asked her why she was asking for permission since she had a good brain and should just use it. From that, Ada learned that she did not need to ask permission—she should just act. She feels that many people are still waiting for permission while she is acting. Later, when Ada was about 12, Connie told her she was put on earth for a purpose. She was an Indian; she should help her people. This was the first of many messages from her mother about the nobility and obligation of helping without imposing her solutions on others. Ada believes that perhaps the most important piece of wisdom from her mother was that she did not have to be an Indian—just be Ada.

Many American Indians or Native Americans have negative views of social workers, who were perceived as removing children from their families when the Child Welfare League of America was extremely active in promoting adoption of Indian children. Ada, however, was exposed to social workers who enriched her experiences during her high school years. These individuals, employed by the state of Wisconsin, organized and planned activities for children identified as current or potential youth leaders.

During her adolescent years, Ada was appointed to planning committees that helped formulate regional and statewide youth conferences. She also attended several camps, including spending four summers at the Christian Leadership Camp Miniwonka in Michigan, where she participated in classes. Ada felt social workers engaging in community organization had enriched and heavily influenced her life. They had expanded her worldview beyond her own community by complementing her experience rather than focusing on problems. For Ada, social workers opened up the world for others and celebrated their strengths and talents.

Ada's mother advocated for her children, insisting they attend the best Milwaukee public schools rather than those on the reservation. This necessitated many sacrifices, including Connie taking the children to school each morning and picking them up after school because the tribal leaders did not allow them to ride the school buses off the reservation. Ada feels she received an excellent education, although the expectations and evaluations of school personnel sometimes were biased by prejudices or lack of exposure to and understanding of American Indian people. For example, Ada chose the college-bound track in high school to the surprise of her school counselor, who expected her to develop a career skill during high school.

Receiving the only tribal scholarship to attend her home university in Wisconsin because of her good grades and high test scores allowed Ada to pursue her dream of becoming a doctor. However, when Ada found that she did not have an aptitude for science, she had to reformulate her career choice. When she asked for her advisor's guidance, he told her that she was good with people, enjoyed new experiences, and was warm and friendly—she should consider social work. Reflecting on this advice and recognizing that she was without a support group in uncharted waters, Ada remembered the positive effect social workers had on her life and decided to attend the best social work school in the country. She was assured by the university's social work faculty that the New York School of Social Work (now the Columbia University School of Social Work) was definitely number one. It seems that Ada Deer gives her all to everything she undertakes and she focuses her entire self on her selected goal.

Ada began her graduate social work education interested in community organization; however, the school she selected did not offer studies in this area—only majors in casework or group work, the school's two tracks. She chose group work since it appeared to be closest to her goal and declined placements in a juvenile detention facility and a state mental-health hospital as not germane to her desire to work in community organizing. She was assigned to the Henry Street Settlement House on New York's Lower East Side, where, even today, immigrants often first settle. There she was fascinated with the variety of cultures, including Hasidic Jews, Puerto Ricans, and African Americans. Ada was also somewhat irked with New York's East Coast attitude of superiority to anyone not from New York. She noted the lack of cultural sensitivity and narrow worldview. It seemed that anyone west of the Hudson River was considered to be from the frontier, and New Yorkers believed was that cowboys and Indians still ruled the prairie.

The three other members of her field placement team, an African American and two White European American males, were older, had advanced academic credentials, and were pursuing the MSW to polish their skills. Ada, of course, was in her first-year placement, but had been exposed to quality social work during her adolescence. Her placement, the LaGuardia Housing Project, was 12 stories high with numerous wings. The team was part of a New York City Housing Authority and Henry Street demonstration project in conjunction with the New York City Youth Board. Each team member was assigned eight floors. They knocked on doors, welcomed the families to the neighborhood, assessed and referred them for family and individual needs, made friends with residents, and promoted community because neighbors often did not know or were unable to understand each other. The program promoted positive social interaction and community organization.

Ada notes that she did not understand the supervision she received. Her supervisor was polite, but Ada had no idea how he perceived her. Ada was young, naïve, and inexperienced and was undoubtedly the first Indian her supervisor had known. He was surprised that Ada was unfamiliar with New York culture and that she asked many questions—some perhaps difficult for the supervisor to comprehend. Ada did not understand how one could be helpful if one did not understand the client's culture. When leading a Puerto Rican girls' group, Ada asked her supervisor how this culture treated sexuality. He replied that the important issue was how Ada felt about sex and told her that she was pretty. Ada was not impressed.

After receiving a negative evaluation from her supervisor, being told that there was no mechanism to modify it, and being asked by her advisor if she really felt qualified to be a social worker, Ada withdrew from school. Afterward, she worked for two years in Brooklyn at an African American church, coordinating prevention projects and after-school activities. As a "girls' worker," she planned and executed projects for six girls' clubs for preschool through high-school-age children. True to form, Ada attempted to empower girls and enhance their social and cultural survival skills. The church members valued her highly and wished her well, regreting the loss of her energy, enthusiasm, and organizational expertise when her tenure ended.

The brightest period in Ada's postsecondary education was a class on social legislation taught by Professor Helen Clarke of UW-Madison. Ada participated in evaluating important legislation, an experience that proved seminal for her. She did not let the problems she encountered during her graduate education bother her; she just pushed through, gathering what she needed for her career. Her eye was on the future; her goal was to learn as much as possible without being overly influenced by the rigidity of thinking that appeared to drive her social work program's lack of multicultural understanding.

Ada reminisces about two of her most important honors. In 1998, when the Columbia School of Social Work celebrated its centennial, Ada was the first person inducted into the Alumni Hall of Fame. She was quite proud of the honor, especially because she was in the company of movers and shakers in the social work field. When she complimented and thanked her former professor, Dr. Alfred Kahn, another inductee and currently a professor of social work at Columbia, for his wonderful, inspiring, and informative history of social work class that she took 40 years earlier, he noted that now he knew why Ada was such a successful politician. Ada received the first honorary PhD at UW-Madison and has received many more since, but she clearly remembers how sweet it was to receive recognition from Columbia.

After graduation, Ada returned to the Midwest and worked in the public-school system for a number of years. After her resignation, she wrote a letter to the superintendent detailing her view on what needed to be done to improve the curriculum and especially noting the importance of emphasizing cultural issues. She said that she was accustomed to being treated with dignity and respect at her undergraduate institution, but she encountered condescending attitudes within the bureaucracy of this institution. Ada smiled to herself after writing her letter, feeling that she surely was her mother's daughter. Later, her colleagues in the school system thanked her for her astute suggestions.

Next, Ada took a job at another University of Wisconsin campus, two hours away from her tribe. It was time for her to work on tribal issues and the concerns brought on by the Menominee Termination Act of 1954 and finalized in 1961. While Ada was completing her undergraduate degree, her mother told her about the problems that could result from this legislation, but Ada did not realize the gravity of the government's actions, having been caught up in her university experience and, quite likely, learning and preparing for the special moment when she would truly help her people. The Menominee Termination Act ended federal supervision of and responsibility for the tribe. This covert form of congressional racism resulted in more oppression of the Indian tribes.

Ada, who had just entered law school, dropped out and used her social work skills to analyze the problem and formulate a plan. She, along with other tribal members, worked to appeal the Termination Act. She went to Washington, where she secured the help of many politicians and influential individuals, including the Kennedy family and former Senator Fred Harris (D-Oklahoma) and his wife, Ladonna, who is a Comanche woman. When it appeared the tide had turned, a Bureau of Indian Affairs (BIA) attorney approached her and suggested an amendment to the Termination Act. She insisted that the act be repealed. It was a historic reversal of American Indian policy. The price Ada paid, however, was separation from her people.

After serving as the chair of her tribal committee, she accepted the job of assistant secretary of the Bureau of Indian Affairs, all the while noting that she might have deferred to a man, but none was able to serve. This position allowed her to further promote the concerns and issues of her people. Ada observes that it takes dedication, devotion, conviction, and commitment to work for the advancement of a cause. The ability to analyze and act is seminal in any process of change. She is now a Distinguished Lecturer in the School of Social Work at UW-Madison, her alma mater, and director of the university's American Indian Studies Program. She has developed field placements on Indian reservations, taught classes in multiculturalism, and contributed greatly to the university's cultural climate. She teaches her students respect for other cultures and the importance of serving the community. With Ada's help and all they have learned from her teaching and presence, students are likely to analyze the situation, formulate a plan for change, and take action. What a legacy! What a legend!

CONCLUSION

So, what does it mean to be a legend and a legacy? How does this story contribute to the mission of women of color in social work education? What is its impact? What does it mean to transform culture, history, and politics as an educator and a social worker?

It means that you are a woman listed among the All National Women's History Month honorees because of your contributions to women's issues. It means that you were chosen to be profiled with 51 others considered elders and exemplars of the social work profession. As part of the development and growth of the profession, it means you have a number of "firsts" in your biography. It means you have made a difference in the lives of others by changing social consciousness and awareness, and, by doing so, you have affected the policies that oppress women in general and, more often, men and women of color. It means you refuse to accept stereotypes of what American Indians do and who they are, particularly in the contemporary significance of a people (Boulard, 2005). When Ada was assistant secretary of Indian affairs, in keeping with her commitment to advocacy and the promotion of American Indian women, she placed several such women in key policy positions. When challenged about this, she asked, "Who notices or says anything when White males staff their operations with other White men?" (Dumez & Sardella, 2003). To date, American Indians continue to be the most disenfranchised ethnic group in the United States. Racial stratification has had a major impact on the ability of this group to move ahead. Consequently, our academic arenas suffer because of the lack of experience of having multiple Ada Deers on our social work faculties.

Beyond all of these accolades, the reality of a sincere spirit dedicated to all human rights is the essence of this woman and the lesson we need to learn from her. Her question to Eleanor Roosevelt about the role of the United Nations and South Africa certainly illustrates this passion for all people. She asked, "How could South Africa be a member of the United Nations and oppress Black people so terribly, and what could the UN do about it? Why didn't they just throw South Africa out?" Ada will tell you that the lesson she learned from this exchange was about patience and education, not violence, as a way to implement change. She has continued this philosophy throughout her academic career as she shares her passion for the rights of all people through her strong social work values, practices, and principles.

REFERENCES

Boulard G. (2005). Setting the record straight. *Diverse Issues in Higher Education, 22*(14), 52.

Dumez, E. W., & Sardella, D. (2003). *Celebrating social work: Faces and voices of the formative years.* Alexandria, VA: Council on Social Work Education.

National Association of Social Workers. (2001). *NASW standards for cultural competence in social work practice.* Washington, DC: Author.

Skog, S. (1995). *Embracing our essence: Spiritual conversations with prominent women.* Deerfield Beach, FL: Health Communications.

Part II: The Voices of Women of Color as Social Work Educators

Chapter 9: I Never Looked Back: Reflections of an African American Social Work Educator

Ruby M. Gourdine

This chapter is dedicated to three special women in my life: my mother, who has the strongest resolve I ever witnessed; my sister, who shares her opinions freely and challenges me continually but is equally protective of me; and my niece, who merely accepts me. Each one contributes uniquely to my development as a woman and scholar. Thanks.

Only the Black woman can say, "When and where I enter, in the quiet, undisputed dignity of my womanhood, without violence and without suing or special patronage, then the whole ... race enters with me" (Anna Julia Copper, 1892, as cited in Giddings, 1984).

The reflective narrative is an effective way to document social work history and contributions. It provides information to practitioners who follow and, therefore, can be instructive to new academics. The narrative in social work literature has gained popularity in recent years. The journal *Reflections: Narratives of Professional Helping* is solely dedicated to personal storytelling as a way to inform helping practices. In 2003, the Council on Social Work Education published Dumez and Sardella's *Celebrating Social Work: Faces and Voices of the Formative Years*, a book containing narratives of 51 social work pioneers. Summing up the narrative experience, the book stated:

> The narrative experience reveals courage to challenge entrenched practice methods along with leadership in bringing about change. The subjects were foresighted enough to foment ideals, try new methods, and translate the basic needs of people into policies, programs, and solutions. Surprising turns of events along with principled decisions significantly affected the direction of these professionals' lives. . . and thus social work's history as a profession. (p. v)

Thus, it is with this understanding of the importance of narratives that I present my story.

PERSONAL JOURNEY

I am an African American woman in my mid-50s currently entering my 14th year at Howard University School of Social Work. I began my journey at Howard University in Fall 1992 as an assistant professor and director of field instruction (education). I achieved tenure and promotion to associate professor in 1997. The school has two programs: a master of social work and a doctoral program. I am actively involved in both of these. Howard University is a historically Black university (HBCU) with high rankings from the *Gorman Report* and *U.S. News & World Report* and is the only HBCU that is designated as research-intensive.

In truth, my ambitions did not include a career in academia. However, I was very sure about social work as a profession even as early as age 12. I envisioned a career as an adoption worker, a goal that I did realize. What I didn't realize is what drove me to sustain such a tenacious commitment to social work at such a young age: a passion for social justice and human rights. Working in both a segregated setting and as the only Black employee (in an intake unit) in an integrated agency setting shaped my passion for my work (Gourdine, 2004). I began to realize the potential for human dignity and felt social work was a venue to pursue social justice and human rights for all, particularly for African Americans.

Personal Biography

I am a descendent of persons who were enslaved. I grew up in both an integrated and segregated society, but it was not until my high school years that society was legally desegregated. Having grown up in multiple locations in the South, Northeast, and Midwest gave me a broad perspective. Furthermore, my family had strong convictions about civil rights. Growing up, I heard and witnessed my family's views and reactions to news reports and achievements of Blacks (they were celebrated), their distain for inequity, and their determination to overcome injustice. As Petrovich

(2004) stated, "[D]uring the formative years of life, persuasion from significant models such as parents has deep and lasting effects on the direction of a person's life, often enabling triumph over severe adversity" (p. 436). Consequently, these influences shaped my worldview, defined by Schiele (2000) as "the overarching mode through which people interpret events and define reality. It is a racial group's psychological orientation toward life" (p. 1).

In my family, education was touted as the way to level the playing field. I heard stories of enslaved relatives, night raids by the Ku Klux Klan, and injustices experienced at jobs and other places, but I knew I was expected to achieve in spite of these injustices. Obstacles could not be blamed for my lack of success. There was a pride in being Black and having the potential to overcome adversity. A former field instructor described me as having "an intense sense of human rights and dignity" (Gourdine, 2004, p. 74). I never thought about myself in that way, but I did revere the notion that, to God, all people were equal, and I could not be dissuaded from this belief. My challenges were to achieve when society expected me not to; to uphold standards when it was not always popular to do so; and to challenge myself when I thought I had given all I had to give.

Following is a review of reflections from some African American social work pioneers that mirror some of my experiences and are instructive to me personally as I continue my academic career:

- Will Braxton Scott—"I largely avoided administrative appointments beyond department chairmanships because a higher level of responsibility could have overtaken my ability to do substantive developmental work within the social work program" (Dumez & Sardella, 2003, p. 17).

- Ronald V. Dellums—"When the poverty program was evaluated, it was said not to have worked, but I think the philosophical bases and the constructs that went into the Great Society were brilliant ideas. What brought them crashing down had nothing to do with the fundamental merit of the ideas. I think politicians came to realize that they were funding a revolution" (Dumez & Sardella, 2003, p. 21).

- Barbara W. White—"I consider myself a shy person, one who doesn't exude power. I try to bring people and ideas together and mediate among the elements of a system in order to make it productive" (Dumez & Sardella, 2003, p. 23).

- Majorie B. Hammock—"In examining the criminal justice system, one can gain understanding of the legacy of slavery and oppression and the exploitation of particular groups in this country" (Dumez & Sardella, 2003, p. 91).

- Douglas Glasgow—"I returned to the East Coast to serve as dean at Howard University School of Social Work following in the footsteps of the giant Inabel Lindsay. My immediate task was to realign the curriculum to build research capacity for studying significant changes in the African American community" (Dumez & Sardella, 2003, p. 55).

It is the knowledge that African Americans are making a difference in society and particularly in social work that strengthens my resolve to continue in the profession.

PROFESSIONAL JOURNEY

Student Experiences

My journey toward academia started before I was accepted into the doctoral program at Howard University School of Social Work. The dean at that time encouraged me to apply to the program and was relentless in his conviction that I could earn a doctorate. I avoided him for about two years before deciding that I would take a chance and apply to Howard University School of Social Work's doctoral program. I was very reluctant as I was not sure it was what I wanted.

I hit an impasse when I experienced much political maneuvering with social services within Washington, DC. This was a time when Washington first elected an African American mayor. His election was seen as an opportunity for many African Americans in the city. Each group positioned itself for changes, and, at times, these changes were fraught with political challenges. A number of my colleagues were very upset and dissatisfied with plans emerging for people of color in social services that made it difficult for them to be hired at higher levels and receive promotions. It was as if the majority was making decisions for people of color without their involvement. Workers of color often were expected to carry out dictates and plans in which they had no real voice, thus causing cognitive dissonance. We all sought ways to fortify our-

selves—some through changing jobs, some through leaving the profession and some by going back to school. I chose the latter.

Just before I entered the doctoral program, I experienced a personal setback. My favorite aunt died of cancer (I am her namesake.). After this happened, I questioned whether the decisions I was making were the best ones. Yet, I persevered and continued my course of study. Mine was a competitive yet cohesive class of doctoral students. I think we all had to prove that we could, indeed, meet the requirements for a doctorate. Most of my colleagues from that class maintain close relationships, and we work on projects together. Several of us have supported each other through personal milestones as well and professional triumphs and challenges.

During the doctoral program, my classmates and professors challenged me. The program focused on the strengths of people of color, on promoting research, and writing from that perspective. This approach allowed us to debate social issues as we did not all agree on leadership, cultural practices, and the best way to combat social ills. These discussions led to some very interesting classes. It was also very enlightening to read the research and writings of people of color who were also professors at the school or university including Drs. Douglas Glasgow, Harriette and John McAdoo, Joyce Ladner, and others. Their achievements, knowledge, and commitment energized me.

At this time, people of color were beginning to have an impact on the social-science literature and were providing different perspectives on research directed toward the needs of people of color. During my graduate-school experience, we studied Dr.

Andrew Billingsley's seminal work, *Black Families in White America* (1968). In the aftermath of the Civil Rights movement, this particularly riveting statement in his book stood out to me: "To say that a people have no culture is to say that they have no common history which shaped them. And to deny the history of a people is to deny their humanity" (p. 37). This statement was a response to Nathan Glazer and Daniel Moynihan's work (1963), *Beyond the Melting Pot*, which suggested that Blacks had no culture. I was encouraged by Dr. Billingsley, having had the opportunity to meet him and read most of his writings validating the Black experience. Furthermore, he was the architect of Howard University's School of Social Work's reorganization in the aftermath of the 1960s' Civil Rights and student movements.

Having the opportunity to affirm myself through seeing models of what I hoped to become was liberating. As Bandura (1982) and others (Schunk, Hanson, & Cox, as cited in Bandura, 1997; Petrovich, 2004) noted, "Seeing these role models perform successfully typically raises the efficacy beliefs of the observer" (p. 433). I also had excellent mentors, who encouraged me and provided me with many opportunities. I knew I was fortunate, so I made sure I was prepared so as not to disappoint them. I am a highly motivated person who has taken the opportunities available to advance my career and, having done so, I am aware that now I am expected to be a mentor.

My mentors during my doctoral education were Dr. Joyce Ladner (noted sociologist and former acting president of Howard University) and Mark Battle (well-known social worker, entrepreneur, and former executive director of the National Association of Social Workers)—two legends in the field of social science. As a student of Dr. Ladner's, I read with much enthusiasm her work, *Tomorrow's Tomorrow: The Black Woman* (1971). The comment on the back cover sums up her work in this book, which has intensely influenced me:

> Ms. Ladner, a young Black sociologist, succeeds in challenging many "established" theories about the Black family in general. For she concludes that the Black community has a distinct, autonomous social system which regulates much of its own behavior; that the dominant society itself should be examined for the pathological behavior it attributes to certain minority groups; and that the Black girl and her family have made incredibly healthy adjustments to conditions not intended to promote their well-being.

Social Work Educator

Becoming a social work educator was not my goal when I completed my doctorate degree. I saw myself as an administrator in a program area, not working at a university. I started my postdoctoral work as a consultant evaluating a teenage pregnancy prevention program and was hired to administer a social work program at the state office of special education. After I had worked for a number of years in this position, my interest in academia was piqued, and I was encouraged to apply for a faculty position. My first application was rejected, as I had published only once. I was encouraged and assisted in publishing more of my work, so my second application was successful. My mentor helped me enter the publication world, and, for that support, I am eternally grateful.

My position as an assistant professor and director of field instruction (education) at Howard University was on the tenure track and required me to meet the criteria for promotion and tenure to remain at the university. Seeking tenure is an arduous process. I had support from administration and faculty to meet my goals. Even so, academia presents many challenges on a number of levels. It is a process during which the individual must be motivated and tenacious to succeed, even with support. I also administered the field-education program and, initially, was the only person assigned to recruit agencies, place students, and handle problems. I designated a specific day each week, during which I was to research and write. I tried to set aside this day religiously because it helped me keep focused on completing my projects. This was difficult to do at times as there were so many competing projects and, of course, the academic challenges of teaching, committee work, and political alliances. Fortunately, I was successful in getting articles published, obtaining grants, and conducting community service. I had established a broad base of colleagues during my years as a social worker, and these relationships offered the opportunity for collaboration.

Professional Challenges

Being at Howard University School of Social Work has benefits and challenges. My colleagues and I often are sought out to participate in projects and offer our expertise, and, at other times, there seems to be the notion that we do not possess the same skills as other academics. Juxtaposed with the inter-

nal stress to achieve are the external strains on our academic progress. This environment at Howard University motivates me to meet higher standards. In addition, it is important to note that Howard University could be viewed in the wider community as different from White-majority schools. The prejudices that exist in society against African Americans and their achievements have not faded.

My personal struggle is balancing the competitive academic environment and my commitment to building the institution. Holding an administrative position necessitates substantive work with students, other administrators, and faculty and requires the establishment and maintenance of standards, the creation of resources, and sensitivity to encourage students to achieve advanced degrees. Developing administrative policies, writing manuals, and other procedures are not counted as academic writing even though they require a substantial amount of time and effort to complete. Larger and publicly funded White-majority institutions typically have more financial resources. Thus, the old adage is probably true for us: We do more with less. Typically, persons who work at Howard University are highly committed to maintaining the institution and giving what they can to maintain it. Sometimes this means sacrificing academic publishing. It is a real challenge to do both, but the importance of having an institution like Howard cannot be diminished.

Mentoring in Academic Settings

Mentoring is a natural way to assist new faculty in achieving tenure and promotion. The mentorship relationship is a way to help new faculty get acclimated to the institution and its culture and help them understand the politics and requirements for promotion and tenure. Mentors can assist in publication opportunities as well. My publishing experience started with the help of my mentor and allowed me to understand publishing requirements and opportunities. I have since worked with a couple of my mentees (former and current doctoral students) to do the same. These former students now work at White-majority institutions, and, from time to time, they seek my counsel about their academic experiences, especially regarding political issues. Collegial relationships, which can be within or outside the institution, also provide the opportunity for publishing. In recent years, higher education institutions have placed more emphasis on interdisciplinary work.

The Black Perspective

There are differing opinions about the use of theories and their applications in teaching, but, at Howard University, there is a clear understanding that more than mainstream theories should be used to discuss interventions. In addition, faculty use their own research and publications to inform students about social work practice with people of color. Students are asked to include information about people of color through our philosophical "Black perspective," as described below.

Six principles summarize the Black perspective that serves to both frame the social work curriculum and is a guiding philosophy, reaffirming the richness, productivity, and vigor of the lives of African Americans and Blacks in other parts of the world. The Black perspective is an affirmation of

strength that delineates ways the strengths of African Americans can be used to respond to oppressive and discriminatory systems. The Black perspective guides the school of social work in generating knowledge that is not monolithic and does not make global characterizations designed as one-dimensional concepts and theories that reduce the common experiences of African Americans to simplistic characterizations. The Black perspective requires capturing the rich diversity that flavors the African American experience. The Black perspective gives primacy to African American content; the perspective is positive, not exclusionary. Finally, the Black perspective emphasizes the importance of the cultural, political, social, and historical links of African Americans with Africa and the Caribbean since schools of social work have a mission to educate African Americans and foreign students for positions of leadership (from Howard University, School of Social Work, 2003). (For further information see Howard University School of Social Work's student manual and field education manual.)

The Cultural Context

My perception of my contribution to social work education as a woman of color is positive. African American women do not necessarily accept the feminist perspective as the feminist movement was not seen as including African American needs (Martin & Martin, 1985). Black women in slavery were already doing much of, if not all, that Black men were doing. The womanist perspective is viewed as more inclusive than the feminist perspective. I envision the women in the Civil Rights movement as having been more womanist than feminist.

Women and women of color live in a sexist society and experience it at most institutions. Women are often placed in caretaker roles. Men may have higher paying positions and assume leadership roles in greater numbers than do women. For instance, only recently women have become presidents of universities or held deanships or other high-level university positions. It seems that these barriers are now breaking down, but these issues still warrant attention, particularly from women of color. In addition, women and women of color have become more aggressive in competing for various roles at the university.

A teaching tactic I use is to ask new students about the contributions to social work made by African Americans or other people of color; sadly, many of my students have not heard of a lot of exemplars, but they are receptive to and hungry for more of this knowledge. Last year, as a result of a class discussion, a student recommended that I share my story with the AARP Voices of Civil Rights project. This was extremely rewarding for me. I introduced a new teaching strategy in terms of learning about the impact of social issues on a person's worldview. I now ask students to tell me about the decades from 1960 to the present. It is interesting that many know about civil rights and Martin Luther King, Jr. Some are not familiar with other leaders, however. For instance, many were not aware of Stokely Carmichael (Kwame Ture), and if they have heard of him, they view him as a mystical figure. They were in absolute awe when they found out he attended Howard. Clearly, the messages of African American contributors are neglected in high school and undergraduate programs. The Black and womanist

perspectives help me to contextualize the work of African Americans and other people of color. I have heard that people of color at White-majority institutions are not as comfortable with including racial content in their classes and that, in fact, they may be critically evaluated for interpreting these perspectives (personal stories, CSWE conference at Fordham University, February 2005).

Benefits of Social Work Education

I have stayed in social work education because I find it stimulating, invigorating, and satisfying. There are some frustrations, but they can be overcome. I also have a strong commitment to leave some mark at the university through the students I teach. Often, students whom I hold to a certain standard and who initially see my holding them to that standard as a deterrent to their success later thank me for providing them the guidance they needed to acclimate to the profession. Upholding standards and supporting students can be frustrating and tiring, but it does have its rewards. The sense of accomplishment is empowering to students and often moves them to levels they did not think they could reach.

Women of Color and Society

Women of color are ever mindful that they represent the race whenever they present publicly. When I present at national conferences, I am often approached by someone who says something like, "Oh, you're from Howard. That was a wonderful presentation. . . but I met a Howard graduate who didn't seem to know. . . " The individual looks to me to explain every Howard University graduate's behavior and knowledge as if all "Howardites" are alike and perform at the same level. We have exemplary students, and we have students who require more assistance. Our difference may be that we have committed to educate both because we know the issues that accompany persons who are not afforded the opportunity to develop. Sometimes it is not the academically stellar student who makes the best practitioner. Knowledge and behavior are different qualities. People have to prepare themselves and believe in their ability to achieve. One must not minimize the art of preparation (although Black women may be seen as overachievers). Jones and Shorter-Gooden's work, *Shifting: The Double Lives of Black Women in America* (2003), documents this phenomenon:

> And shifting is often an internal, invisible. It's the chipping away at her sense of self, at her feelings of wholeness and centeredness—often a consequence of living amidst racial and gender bias. To shift is to work overtime when you are exhausted to prove that you are not lazy. It is the art of learning how to ignore a comment you believe is racist or to address it in such a way that the person who said it doesn't label you [as] threatening or aggressive. It is overpreparing for an honors class to prove you are capable, intelligent, and hardworking or trying to convince yourself that you are really okay no matter what the broader society says about you. It is feeling embarrassed by another African American who seems to lend a stereotype truth, and then feeling ashamed that you are ashamed. And sometimes shifting is fighting back. (pp. 7–8)

Impacts of Policies, Practices, and Theories

The policies, practices, and theories that regulate social services have a tremendous impact on clients, educators, and students. Often, policies and practices are implemented without input from those most affected by them. Our former dean and current provost invited me, along with a colleague, to participate in advising a former congressman on the welfare reform bill. After attending several hearings, we noted that welfare recipients were not included in the hearings we witnessed, which caused us to ask about their participation in the process. I believe this happens all too often—that policies and practices are not necessarily sensitive to the people they are supposed to help. In *The Diverse Society: Implications for Policies*, Cafferty and Chestang (1976) sought to achieve two goals: to show diversity in America and to show how a social policy can respond to the diversity. We are still struggling to make this a reality. For example, welfare reform was driven by the perception that people receiving benefits were undeserving. Our faculty noted that we needed to refocus on advocacy in social work education precisely because of what we witnessed in poor underserved communities, in which many people of color often live.

CONCLUSION

Being a female faculty member at a historically Black institution is probably significantly different from being a woman of color at a White majority institution. As a Black person at a historically Black college, you typically do not have to explain your existence or assume the weight of all the sins of the

Black community. As Petrovich (2004) notes, "Similarity in attributes such as gender, ethnicity, race, age, education and socioeconomic level tends to increase the power of modeling influences, even when these personal characteristics are unrelated to performance capabilities" (p. 433). That, however, is not to say that there aren't prejudices against Blacks in terms of perception of accomplishments and achievements.

Nonetheless, being at an HBCU has buoyed my personal achievement. The camaraderie is refreshing, the sense of history is empowering, the sense of mission is energizing, and the sense of achievement is rewarding. We validate each other without explanation, and we can challenge each other without feeling that racism affected the critique. It allows an academic freedom that assumes if you research issues related to Black people, it is okay and helpful in understanding Black people. There are times when our sense of scholarship is assailed, and we may need to reevaluate our research and teaching strategies. This is a positive event as it helps keeps us on our toes.

At Howard University, we participate in national and international adventures; we are not about isolation or exclusion. The principles of the Black perspective speak directly to this nonexclusionary practice. We are encouraged to look at oppression where it occurs. During the Rwandan massacres, students volunteered to work with the aftermath of this tragedy in Rwanda. Howard has a powerful history, and being a part of this legacy is a gift. However, as a woman, I recognize that there continue to be issues of salary equality, opportunities for promotion, and acceptance of women in all parts of academia. Far too often, women may be seen as the caretakers of the institution. Oppression is oppression, and women must seek to remedy it. Recently, the university started a certificate program in women's studies, and the School of Social Work offers a course on women, power, and change. Therefore, there is a clear recognition that all is not achieved in terms of women in academia or society. All women of color will not be able to get positions in institutions of color, so there certainly need to be ways to incorporate women of color into White-majority institutions. These situations should represent what the profession of social work cites as a part of its mission—including diversity.

Lecroy and Stinson (2004), in their article on social work's image, correctly noted that, as "the public's approval of social work wanes recruitment in the profession suffers" (p. 165). Social work has suffered from the same problems existing in society. It has been slow to recruit minorities and lobby for the rights of people of color. The better it does at meeting its mission, the better it may be at recruiting women of color to the profession and academia. These problems are noted in the preface of Barbara White's book, *Color in a White Society* (1982). White stated, "[T]he articles here confirm that people of color still face problems in the United States—problems that are manifold and diverse. . . Also significant and challenging are the color-related problems that apply to social workers in their own practice and in their own national organization" (p. v).

I have committed myself to writing and researching issues pertinent to the Black and African American community. I believe this is a valuable contribution. It does not mean I am unable to contribute to other aspects of social work. I am; I'm not monolithic. I teach and prepare students to enter any academic setting. I am convinced that I have much to learn and much to share. As I reflect on my decisions and commitment to my profession, I can honestly say that once I chose social work as a profession, I never looked back.

REFERENCES

Bandura, A. (1982). Self-efficacy mechanism in human agency. *American Psychologist, 37,* 122–147.

Bandura, A. (1997). *Self–efficacy: The exercise of control.* New York: W. H. Freeman.

Billingsley, A. (1968). *Black families in White America.* Englewood Clifts, NJ: Prentice-Hall.

Cafferty, P. S. J., & Chestang, L. (Eds.). (1976). *The diverse society: Implications for social policy.* Washington, DC: National Association of Social Workers.

Dumez, E. W., & Sardella, D. (2003). *Celebrating social work: Faces and voices of the formative years.* Alexandria, VA: CSWE Press.

Giddings, P. (1984). *When and where I enter: The impact of Black women on race and sex in America.* New York: W. Morrow.

Glazer, N., & Moynihan, D. P. (1963). *Beyond the melting pot: The Negroes, Puerto Ricans, Jews, Italians, and Irish of New York City.* Cambridge, MA: MIT Press.

Gourdine, R. M. (2004). A beginning professional's journey towards understanding equality and social justice in the field of social work. [Special issue]. *Reflections: Narratives of Professional Helping. 10*(1), 73–81.

Howard University, School of Social Work. (2003). *Reaffirmation self-study report.* Washington, DC: Author.

Jones, C., & Shorter-Gooden, K. (2003). *Shifting: The double lives of Black women in America.* New York: HarperCollins.

Ladner, J. A. (1971). *Tomorrow's tomorrow: The Black woman.* New York: Doubleday.

Lecroy, C. W., & Stinson, E. (2004). The public's perception of social work: Is it what we think it is? *Social Work, 49,* 164–174.

Martin, J. M., & Martin, E. P. (1985). *The helping tradition in the Black family and community.* Silver Spring, MD: National Association of Social Workers.

Petrovich, A. (2004). Using self-efficacy theory in social work teaching. *Journal of Social Work Education, 40,* 429–443.

Schiele, J. H. (2000). *Human services and the Afrocentric paradigm.* New York: Haworth Press.

White, B. (Ed.). (1982). *Color in a White society.* Silver Spring, MD: National Association of Social Workers.

Part II: The Voices of Women of Color as Social Work Educators

Chapter 10: My Path and My Dance: Professional Social Work Practice

Saundra Hardin Starks

This chapter is dedicated to my daughter, Shannon, who has chosen the profession of social work for herself and has her own path, her own dance, and her own rhythm. She is the most precious woman in my life. It is also dedicated to all the powerful women who have influenced my life and continue to keep my spirit healthy. They are many and are considered as my mothers, my spirit sisters, and my friends. Last, I pay tribute to my mother-in-law, Ruby Starks, who passed away two years ago but left her loving spirit and memories with me and our family. She always affirmed me in my many roles and taught me so much about being a loving and strong woman.

I am an African American woman in my 50s and am very proud of my heritage, which also includes American Indian and White European American ancestry. I am a tenured associate professor of social work at Western Kentucky University (WKU). I have also served as interim director for the Baccalaureate Social Work program at WKU. Both my master's in social work and doctorate in counseling psychology were earned at the University of Louisville. As a Licensed Clinical Social Worker, I have over 25 years of social work practice. I have been a Board Member of the National Association of Social Workers (NASW), Chair of the National Committee on Racial and Ethnic Diversity (NCORED), and am currently serving on the NASW International Committee and the National Board of the Association of Social Work Boards (ASWB). My research, publications, and presentations have been national and international in the areas of cultural competency, women's issues, mental health, and spirituality.

PERSONAL JOURNEY

May the strength of my story lend encouragement and enlightenment to all who follow my journey. . . my daughter, my goddaughters, my students. I preface this monologue with an often unpopular view that teaching is social work practice and social work practice involves teaching. Various other practice roles within the profession have also been a part of my journey and, I believe, are critical to the overall effectiveness of an integrated social work practitioner. Whether I function as a regulator of professional standards by serving on the state or national licensure board or I consult or provide clinical supervision, I am constantly aware of the impact and responsibility that is inherent in ethical social work practice.

A dance begins with the first step, and so my story begins and ends with the first step of reflection, ongoing self-inventory, self-actualization, and challenge. Had I not learned to dance and appreciate the music and the dance of life early in my career, I probably would not have survived in the academy. The metaphor of music and dance has always provided a sense of rhythm and rhyme to my life. It is said that only through chaos do we really get ready for the dance. And what a dance it has been for me and all who have participated in my journey. Often surrounded by chaos and confusion, I have learned humility, flexibility, and to navigate through ambiguity.

This chapter is reflective; it is spiritual; it is happy; it is angry; and it laughs and talks back, as does my life story. The messages contained in this chapter express who I am and how I like to think I have become a wiser woman who is a social work educator, practitioner, supervisor, regulator, business woman, wife, mother, daughter, sister, friend, and mentor to many. Because African American women have historically been socialized to embrace multiple roles, they often create various dances (postures) to enjoy their many roles. I certainly believe this is a part of my culture and my experience.

The Sharing

Oral histories are such an important part of the traditions of ethnic people. When no one else would listen or could hear the injurious postures of the administration, my other "sisters" could. Both my ethnic sisters and some of my White European American sisters who value diversity and embrace differences played significant roles. They also teach using culturally relevant alternative paradigms. It is a frightening awareness for those who teach social work to be faced with the reality that not everyone in social work education is capable of real inclusion and the acceptance of difference.

My story, while critically important to share, also carries a risk as it reveals the element of distrust so common for people of color. Allowing others to have such intimate knowledge of my life and my process is not comfortable. But what do we tell our social work students? How can you ask others (clients) to do what you are unwilling to do yourself? I believe disclosure in any of its various forms represents something different for African American women. What it means to us is often different from what it means for those in the dominant culture. It often means "airing our dirty laundry" in a way that makes us vulnerable to those waiting for opportunities to discount and dismiss us. Perhaps this learned distrust will permeate the telling of all the stories of ethnic women. I am not sure that the residual of cultural paranoia ever leaves individuals of color or that it would be wise to let it go.

Spiritual Beginnings

Faith is the substance of things hoped for and the evidence of things not seen.

—*Hebrews* 11:1

As my story unfolds, I must first stop and give thanks and reverence for the Divine Spirit who is the creator of all things and who guides my life in a way that keeps me safe and focused. I grew up calling this force God, Jesus, and the Holy Spirit. I have since accepted a broader understanding and use many references to this Divine Spirit. In the same

manner, I am grateful for my early religious roots, which planted the faith I needed to survive. My only regret is failing to find the needed balance of social work practice and spirituality in my teaching sooner. My omission possibly came as a reaction to the staunch fundamentalist attitudes and values brought to the classroom by the majority of the students in my geographical region. I found this fundamentalist religiosity to be such a misuse of religion and spirituality. It is so often also consistent with the perpetuation of oppression and cultural exclusion. In spite of this concern, my research and scholarly contributions do reflect my strong connection to a sense of spirituality (Starks & Hughey, 2003).

I am grateful for the three other major dynamics in my life that shaped my resilience and my ability to advocate for others. First, I was born Black. Second, I am female. Both of these characteristics are used as elements of oppression. Third, I chose the profession of social work even though it is also a profession that is often oppressed in terms of credibility, job security, and salary equity.

Origins and Roots

I started life as a blessed and fortunate child of many mothers and grandmothers. My maternal great-great-grandmother was born a slave. My maternal and paternal greats and grandmothers were all of mixed heritage—African American, American Indian, and White European American.

I am the oldest of five children and was raised primarily by my grandparents, along with many mothers and many strong female role models. I always prided myself on being my mother's oldest child and my grandmother's youngest child, which I thought was the best of both worlds. From my mother, I get my attraction to fashion and flair for engaging people and seeing their goodness. However, I never liked hats or the color pink as a child due to my mother's insistence that my two sisters and I wear both. My mother had what Cunningham and Marbery (2000) called "hattitude." She loved hats and could have been listed in the book, *Crowns*, which profiles the significance of African American church women and their hats. It was part of her style, her confidence, and her symbol of that powerful mix of faith and fashion.

On reflection, I was much older before I could really appreciate my mother's value and role in shaping my social work destiny. My maternal grandmother was a much more powerful and influential woman, who also had a career as an educator (long before that vocation required a college degree to teach in the colored schools). She had gone to Lincoln Institute for teachers' training, but my memories of her were as a manager and businesswoman. She managed the family grocery store and rental properties while my grandfather managed the farm. This certainly inspired my love for learning and entrepreneurship.

Long before I entered formal education in the first grade, I was reading, writing, and curious about many life issues. My grandmother instilled in me a love of learning and my uncle a love of debate. Although I am the first generation to be college-educated in my immediate family, there was a college professor on my dad's side of the family and aunts and uncles on both sides of my family who had attended postsecondary education institutions.

My elementary school, a "colored" school in rural America during the 1960s, was a two-room schoolhouse, with first to fourth grades in one room and fifth to eighth in another. This was the next level of inspiration for my belief that I could excel. While my academic and religious beginnings were very segregated because it was the early 1960s, my social and some of my family life was very integrated. My grandparents, with whom I lived, owned the neighborhood grocery store on a main highway where most of the customers were White European American. This was the early beginnings of informal integration for me.

Formal integration in rural Kentucky did not begin for most of us until much later. I was in 10th grade and had been bused for one year to an all-Black high school in a neighboring county. So, in spite of the used hand-me-down, outdated textbooks and lack of educational equipment, something much more important came out of the experience of being with all Black teachers in a two-room school house. Those teachers instilled in me a sense of pride, courage, encouragement, discipline, and a belief in my importance and my ability to accomplish anything.

I learned early in life that women like my grandmother were opinionated, courageous, and commanded respect while being very much in control of their families, lives, and destiny. This was probably the beginning of my belief that Black women were awesome, large, and in charge. It was later that I heard and understood the phrase: *If you educate a woman, you educate a nation.*

Leaving Home: The World Beyond

College and the university experience brought me much awareness of the broader world that was both rewarding and oppressive. Racism? Oppression? Of course; it was the 1960s, and we had just discovered the real meaning of "I'm Black and I'm Proud." After changing my major several times (from teaching to secretarial science to party queen), I arrived at sociology with a concentration in social welfare. It was the closest thing to social work my university offered at that time.

My undergraduate experience was one of many firsts. We were the largest class of African American students ever to be enrolled and graduate from this south-central Kentucky university. With this came racist professors and racist student peers, some of whom were unintentionally oppressive. This was balanced with the discovery of a group of understanding and helpful White European Americans who were totally accepting and grateful for the experience of multiple cultures. We braved the journey and, for the most part, demonstrated amazing resilience. In hindsight, this was great preparation for the real world. My undergraduate experience provided the foundation for a deeper understanding of the impact of social injustice and the need for advocacy and activism. I discovered social work and began the preparation for beginning-level practice.

PROFESSIONAL JOURNEY

Professionalism Has a Color and a Culture

My first job as a social worker with a community mental-health center was a result of continued contact with one of my first mentors, a White European American female who was a school social worker and the field instructor for my undergraduate field placement. She epitomized everything in a social worker I desired to become. She was highly ethical, genuine, courageous, outspoken, and a voice for the oppressed. Future mentors were equally valuable in sharing their many gifts. What they all had in common was that they really believed in me and thought that, as a young African American woman, I had a great deal to offer to the world of social work. They persuaded me that I, too, could be an effective social worker. It is interesting to note that all of my early mentors in social work were White European American females; there were no local African American professional social work role models for me to emulate.

These early professional beginnings increased my desire for advanced knowledge and further reinforced my fit for the profession. Next was graduate school. By this time, I was married with two children, but I had also developed a deeper passion for community mental-health practice. I further expanded into professional voluntary service by becoming a member of the National Association of Social Workers (NASW). This was in response to a comment I made about the lack of Black social workers in the association, at least at the local and state level in Kentucky. A friend (who was White European American, quite the advocate and one of the most ethical social workers I know) suggested that I join NASW, become active, and make a difference. So, 30-plus years later, I am still involved, active, and trying to make a difference. From my service on the

National Board of NASW to my tenure as chair of the National Committee on Racial and Ethnic Diversity (NCORED) that developed the standards for cultural competency, I have tried to make a difference and work for inclusion of the issues of people of color.

Bends in the Road

My shift in primary focus from being a full-time social worker in a university counseling center and teaching part-time to being a full-time social work educator came rather suddenly. Ready to broaden my experiences, I surprised myself and applied for a full-time teaching position. I became the second African American female to teach in the social work program at this university. Although 15 years later I continue to hold this position, it does sadden me to know that not only in the social work department, but in the entire university, there are so few African American professors. I submit that this has to do with the paradigms used for recruitment and retention. In fact, our program has had only two African American females, one African American male teaching, and usually only one or two of us at a time. The other two faculty members were wonderful mentors to me and made sure that I understood the overt and covert roles, rules, and rituals necessary for survival.

It is important not to forget that racism and oppression are deeply ingrained in the fabric of institutions and the political system in the United States (Freire, 1970; Kivel, 2002). Even social work has allowed cultural biases to have subtle inroads into its theoretical and pedagogical bases that create cognitive dissonance (Solomon, 2004).

The "Grow Your Own" Process in Academia: A Double-Edged Sword

The opportunity came to advance my education and have the university support and pay for it. It sounds great and wonderful in theory; however, in practice, it is much more complicated. It came under the cloak of a program called "Junior Black Faculty," developed to increase recruitment and retention of African American instructors. It was also designed to encourage pursuit of terminal degrees. What a wonderful alternative and creative model when taken at face value! The doctoral degree certainly provided energy and credibility to my dance in academia.

I initially chose a doctorate in social work and was accepted at a major university in a neighboring state. Admission had to be delayed because of departmental circumstances in my university of employment. A major transitional crisis was occurring, and the social work program was being transferred to another college. The program's accreditation status was being challenged, so I was asked to delay my admission and assume the position of interim program director to help maintain stability and some sense of continuity. This was particularly important because most of the other faculty had left the program. My dedication and commitment to the program and the profession helped me decide to stay.

Are loyalty, commitment, and dedication rewarded? I think not always, and it is not always appreciated by the administration. The more you do for little or nothing, with little or nothing, the more is expected of you. From the people who later ask, "Haven't we done enough for you already," to the new players on the scene who had no sense of history of the program nor cared to be informed about the history, I learned the lesson of distrust.

In spite of the setbacks and challenges, this venture of the "grow your own" process has many benefits. While the concept of supporting minority higher education as a work incentive needs to be supported, implementation of the process has the potential to be oppressive and degrading. My experience had a devaluing and dehumanizing dimension. Comments were made and postures taken that suggested a lack of respect and questioned my integrity.

Although others were hired into the program at the assistant-professor level with the MSW as the terminal degree, I was required to choose between having academic rank or institutional support to pursue a doctorate degree. This was a no-brainer. I chose the institutional support with instructor rank and a promise that I would return at a salary appropriate to my experience and training. The administrative players changed over the three years, and I earned the doctorate degree and reentered with assistant-professor rank without the salary appropriate to my experience and training. Someone commented that I should have negotiated a higher salary before I left to do my doctoral work. Again, this is consistent with many other experiences in academia—a mixed bag.

Most of us know that doctoral programs are tenacious and treacherous, but being African American, female, and nontraditional with an established career and professional life is a formula for chaotic process and disconnect. My friends and family thought I had abandoned them, but I am so grateful

they did not give up on me. The African American tradition of nurturing and reaching out created a safety net that would not let me fall through. The positive developments from these experiences were that my research shifted to an area that was relevant to my personal experience at the time. I changed dissertation chairs from a male professor who wanted me to conduct deficit-based research on African American males to a woman of mixed ancestry who shared my philosophy of cultural pluralism and feminism. My new research focused on collecting qualitative data from the voices of African American women, and my new dissertation title became *African American Women at Midlife: The Dance Between Spirituality and Life Satisfaction* (Starks, 1999).

In spite of these challenges, I gathered the right music, enhanced the dance, performed, and succeeded on the path to a completed dissertation and a doctorate, which I guess finally allowed me to be a "qualified minority" for the academy. Most people of color know this to be code for "safe," "exceptional," or acceptable.

Assistant Professor: Still Carrying the Load

My experiences teaching in academia range from negative incidents, such as those mentioned above, to positive moments, such as being awarded professional faculty mentor of the year by a recent MSW graduating class. This award was such a meaningful and totally unexpected honor for me. It is difficult to realize what impact you have on students when you spend so much energy on being the best teacher you can be without compromising style, passion, commitment, and culture.

My first experience with blatant student defiance was when a student walked out of my class after I challenged another student's continued use of the phrase "colored people." As discussed in Chapters 2 and 3, there is a different level of social acceptability with faculty members of color by students. According to Daufin (1995), students seem to feel they have more right to complain about the professor when the professor is a woman of color, challenging grades, assignments, and so forth. Students challenge the authority of women educators of color in a variety of ways, including tardiness, class absenteeism, and direct verbal insults. Departmental administration all too often unintentionally supports or reinforces this behavior by choosing not to address it.

While all of this contributed to making me a more rounded and effective professor, this perspective was not necessarily shared by those who were in administrative positions. The real-world policy-making and advocacy experiences I could bring to the classroom were exactly what students needed, but these rarely strengthened my annual teaching evaluations. There seemed to be a double standard regarding the expectations of and allowances for White European American professors and women-of-color professors. I doubt White European American professors experience an administrator writing a devaluing comment on their annual evaluations such as "Her student evaluation scores were higher on this particular class; however, it was an elective," meaning somehow this course was not considered to have the same value as a required course. Interestingly, the course was on women and social work.

Another example of how this double standard was perpetuated played out when a female student was allowed to drop my class and remain in a corequisite class because she was not ready to give up her racist attitudes, values, and beliefs. She explained that these attitudes, values, and beliefs were ingrained in her from her family, and she did not want to stay in my course and do the "ism" project. She declined when I offered this project as a vehicle to work through this type of socialization. The project included an immersion experience that could have given her a different perspective and, perhaps, move her toward freedom from racist and oppressive attitudes and behavior. The student's decision to drop my class and stay in the corequisite course was approved initially by the faculty and the program director. As a result of this incident, a written report about my "attitude" was placed in my personnel file. This report mentioned my outspoken defiance in suggesting that the social work program might not want to adjust curriculum policy to accommodate a student's racism.

Students use opportunities such as this to further devalue professors of color on their student evaluations. Students have made comments such as "You need to understand how we are used to being taught," "You are pro Black," or "Dr. Starks is racist" on evaluations. This is particularly true when the concept of White privilege is addressed. In addition, students stereotype women of color as "Miss," while giving male faculty the title of Doctor, even after faculty women of color have corrected this mistake on numerous times.

Student evaluations rarely give an accurate appraisal or reflect the complexities of teaching.

One might use the analogy of asking teenagers or adolescents to evaluate their parents during those difficult years of oppositional immaturity that constitute a natural phase of growing up. Students often make faulty assumptions and misinterpret classroom events. It should be unconscionable to use these as a primary measurement for quality of teaching and as a basis for merit and promotion. Both the research and the literature on African Americans teaching in predominantly White undergraduate programs support this argument (Benjamin, 1997; Turner & Myers, 2000). In spite of this, however, these are continually used to help evaluate a professor's teaching capabilities.

Administrators have also used the "divide and conquer" strategy by making such comments as "Other faculty of color who teach the content of diversity and racism do not have these negative evaluations." In one particular incident, the comparison was with another African American female professor who taught in a graduate-level counseling program. This is an entirely different cohort of students from undergraduate social work students with, most often a different maturity level and more open and inclusive worldviews.

Processes such as tenure, which place little emphasis on service, also disenfranchise women of color in higher education. Service is such an important element for women of color and especially for women of color in social work. Such service also includes important informal participation in voluntary groups such as churches, civic, sorority, university minority programs, and other community humanitarian initiatives. In addition to these informal service projects, there is tremendous pressure to participate in various university committees.

Many times over the years I have been asked to participate in just one more departmental search committee that needed minority representation. Because departments other than social work also required representation—due to a lack of faculty of color to fill the "role"—many times women of color are asked to attend meetings for their mere presence, not necessarily for their ideas (Turner & Myers, 2000). Framing these expectations is the reality that success in academia is measured by the attainment of a high academic rank, tenure, and publication productivity. But who in administration takes into account the additional committees and responsibility one has as an educator of color in a predominantly White European American university? These committees, particularly the search committees, seemingly are designed to insure sensitivity to the need to increase diversity of faculty, yet it does not seem to happen. Nobody talks much about the "We Need a Black" committee responsibilities of African American faculty members. The cumulative effect of these experiences often results in the three Bs—burnout, bitterness, and benign-ness.

Themes of Oppression in the Academy

"Haven't we done enough for you already?" became a theme or unspoken attitude from a certain administrator. It was one example of a statement made in response to my request for salary adjustment during the annual evaluation process. There are many painful and humiliating covert parts to this story. Even though unintentional oppressive and offensive statements are not directly meant to harm, the research and the literature support my contention that these statements damage a person's spirit in subtle ways that even the recipient is not always aware of the damage initially (hooks, 2003; Kivel, 2002).

My salary levels were proportionally lower, my student evaluations were used to deflate my annual teaching evaluations, and I often felt punished for my outspokenness and willingness to question program and professional integrity issues. Sometimes this created a struggle not to succumb to discouragement and the temptation to give up on academia. I stayed through the numerous subtle demoralizing and patronizing nuances. My stay further strengthened my resolve to survive, and I cultivated the most amazing sense of humor in the process. Many times I pondered leaving. I remained in academia and social work because I knew my contribution and my ability to serve as a role model for those who were not even aware of my influence on their attitudes and behavior was needed. I stay in academia and social work because life is supposed to be full of challenges; that is how we grow. I stay in academia and social work because that is who I am. As a young social worker, I had no idea of the journey ahead. But, afterward, like Maya Angelou says, "I wouldn't take nothing for my journey now" (1994).

One of my former administrators and I have both grown tremendously from our disagreements and program conflicts. I would like to believe that, because of these experiences, which were sometimes painful, this person will forever be a better administrator of women of color. He will be a better administrator because he is now less defensive and more open to listening and learning. He is also much more sensitive and culturally responsive. As I,

too, have grown and matured, my personal social work mission is to enhance the awareness of all social workers to raise their standards and level of accountability in cultural competency and social justice.

The Politics of Cultural and Ethnic Representation Versus Adaptation and Authenticity

This catch-22 proposition represents the disparities of expectation and the discounting of cultural elements. It has been with me all my professional life. Must I always explain that I do not speak for my racial group or battle with that internal voice that says I do represent my people? How tiring it is to struggle constantly with this form of duality. How tiring it is to constantly be educating adult White European American people to look beyond their own experiences.

Survival: She Who Laughs Lasts

Women of color use multiple strategies for survival. For years, I had a poster on my office door with a phrase I directly credit with maintaining my sanity during the most difficult of times. It simply said, "She who laughs lasts." Since historically I have a penchant for needing to learn things the hardest way possible, this mantra about humor became vital to my survival in the academy. Humor is often used in the African American community to relieve stress and to minimize the sense of powerlessness. In many instances, I was living a dichotomous experience, having to balance the politics of cultural and ethnic representation with trying to maintain a sense of adaptation and authenticity.

We all need others to participate in our dance in various ways. We all need people who take on multiple roles of helper and adversary to grow and fully appreciate the products of our hard work. As mentioned before, many guides, supporters, coaches, and mentors have participated in my venture. On reflection I can say I always learned as much as or more than from my adversaries as I did from my supporters.

The Learning and Growing

There is an old saying that goes, "That which does not kill us makes us stronger." I am a believer. Many were the times I thought it might be better not to try to continue to function in a place where I felt devalued, unappreciated, misunderstood, and in which always needed to raise the consciousness of others to consider a different paradigm. From almost always being the major department voice speaking out against oppressive actions to being the one in the department to serve on the committee nobody talks about or considers the "We need a Black committee," I was pleasing no one and jeopardizing my physical, mental, and spiritual health.

As a result, I became skilled during my doctoral studies in identifying the dominant culture paradigm that controlled what was considered acceptable, safe, and appropriate pedagogy. I thought I could still be creative and individual in my teaching style. It quickly became apparent that this is not always a good idea if an individual wants decent teaching evaluations that lead to early tenure and promotion, appropriate salaries, and administrative support.

How much we learn depends on how open we are to the process and how we embrace constructive criticism, as well as how well-grounded we are in our own identity and rooted in a sense of purpose. I have often had to remember a quote by bell hooks (1994): "The university is basically a politically conservative framework which often inhibits the production of diverse perspectives, new ideas, and different styles of thinking and writing." It is such a paradox when one believes that many grow up mystically thinking a university setting always encourages and supports diversity.

CONCLUSION

We do not always recognize when we make the move from victim to survivor again and how many times we reflect or reject the notion that we are victims. In fact, I did not feel much the victim because that took energy I could not afford to expend. So many times my dance was offbeat and the rhythm would not come until I learned how to adjust the music, step back, reflect, and come up with a different strategy.

When I began thinking about writing my story, I thought it would be long and negative because there were so many painful experiences I did not want to relive. Long-term ruminations are not healthy, nor are they my style. My philosophy of life has always been to let go and move on. In my practice of assertiveness and directness, I have left few things unsaid to the people I felt needed to hear what I had to say. As a result, I have always felt purged and able to move forward. Taking the lessons learned and harnessing newfound energy for the next adventure or battle is a critical component of survival.

Participating in the crafting of a path that provides for success for others is rewarding and so much a part of what is expected of women of color in general. Reflecting on the many oppressive and abusive elements in academia in general, writing this story and putting my voice in print in such a personal way enrich the catharsis and healing. It also challenges me to maintain memories of the positives, such as students who had new insights and new passion for the profession and those whom you knew you had contributed to shaping into ethical advocates for human rights. I treasure the opportunities I have had to assist in carving this path for others so they would experience less strife and more opportunities to enjoy their journeys and their dances. I am strengthened by my experiences in academia as both a role model for students of color and for students who have never had exposure to a woman of color in a role of authority.

Insights about the female focus of my life are relevant to this discussion, too. Are we not here because we stand on the backs of those who have gone on before us. . . the pioneers? Those mentors and supporters were role models who, by example, encouragement, and demonstration, gave vision and faith to my process. These women are represented in my family, friends, sorority sisters, and colleagues, as well as nationally renowned social workers like Dorothy Height, Millie Charles, and other women with whom I had only a chance meeting. Many others were my contemporaries and significant to my personal professional journey. Their stories, for various reasons, were not available for this project, but they definitely deserve recognition. Among these women of color are Ruth Mayden, Josephine Allen,

Gladys Hall, Marjorie Hammock, Sharlene Furuto, Patricia Lockett, and so many others. In the African American culture, it is thought that we show gratitude for those who have pioneered the way for us by helping to make a way for those who follow us. That is what this story is about.

Therefore, I continue to survive, thrive, and consider myself a success, although I am not without battle scars, trials, and errors. At the same time, I continue to experience many joys, positive adventures, and opportunities for celebration. My greatest tribute to my commitment and dedication as a professional social work educator is that my daughter has chosen to follow in my path. Also, many students who were so upset with me during my classes have later come back to thank me and tell me how they appreciate now what they then did not have the knowledge, values, or skills to appreciate. They now understand what I meant by the "real world" experiences of social work.

When did I stop allowing others to define my reality as a social work educator of color in a predominantly white university? When did I master the balance between professional identity and cultural integrity? I am not sure I know the answers, but I think Maya Angelou says it best in her poem, "And Still I Rise:"

> You may write me down in history with your bitter, twisted lies,
>
> You may trod me in the very dirt, but still, like dust, I'll rise
>
> Does my sassiness upset you? Why are you beset with gloom?
>
> Cause I walk like I've got oil wells pumping in

my living room.

Just like moons and like suns, with the certainty of tides,

Just like hopes springing high,

Still I'll rise.

Did you want to see me broken? Bowed head and lowered eyes?

Shoulders falling down like teardrops, weakened by my soulful cries?

Does my haughtiness offend you? Don't you take it awful hard 'cause I laugh like I've got gold mines diggin' in my own backyard?

You may shoot me with your words, you may cut me with your eyes, you may kill me with your hatefulness, but still, like air, I'll rise.

Out of the huts of history's shame. . . I rise

Up from a past that's rooted in pain. . . I rise

I'm a black ocean, leaping and wide, welling and swelling I bear in the tide.

Leaving behind nights of terror and fear. . . I rise

Into a daybreak that's wondrously clear. . . I rise

Bringing the gifts that my ancestors gave, I am the dream and the hope of the slave.

I rise. . . I rise. . . I rise.

In the final analysis we must all assume responsibility for shaping our own professional identity and sense of purpose. So, as long as I can rise and laugh, I will dance. By continuing to raise my voice to challenge social inequities, I will contribute to the development of the profession of social work and to students not only at Western Kentucky University, but throughout the United States and the world.

REFERENCES

Angelou, M. (1994). *The complete collected poems of Maya Angelou.* New York: Random House.

Benjamin, L. (Ed.). (1997). *Black women in the academy: Promises and perils.* Gainesville, FL: University of Florida Press.

Cunningham, M., & Marberry, C. (2000). *Crowns: Portraits of Black women in church hats.* New York: Doubleday.

Daufin, E. K. (1995). Confessions of a womanist professor. *Black Issues in Higher Education, 12,* 34–35.

Freire, P. (1970). *Pedagogy of the oppressed.* New York: Herder and Herder.

hooks, b. (1994). *Teaching to transgress: Education as the practice of freedom.* New York: Routledge.

hooks, b. (2003). *Teaching community: A pedagogy of hope.* New York: Routledge.

Kivel, P. (2002). *Uprooting racism: How White people can work for racial justice.* British Columbia, Canada: New Society Publishers.

Solomon, B. (2004). Beyond cultural insensitivity and institutional racism: An equipoise approach to the delivery of health and human services. In K. E. Davis & T. B. Bent-Goodley (Eds.), *The color of social policy* (pp. 205–218). Alexandria, VA: Council on Social Work Education.

Starks, S. H. (1999). *African American women at midlife: The dance between spirituality and life satisfaction.* Unpublished doctoral disertation, University of Louisville, Louisville.

Starks, S. H., & Hughey, A. W. (2003). African American women at midlife: The dance between spirituality and life satisfaction. *Affilia: Journal of Women and Social Work, 18,* 133–147.

Turner, C. S. V., & Myers, S. L., Jr. (2000). *Faculty of color in academe: Bittersweet success.* Boston: Allyn and Bacon.

Part II: The Voices of Women of Color as Social Work Educators

Chapter 11: Archetype, Culture, and Gender: A Maori Social Worker Reflects on Her Academic Career

Debbie Hippolite Wright

Clifford Mayes

For my daughters, Morgan and Karamea.

In the last two decades, there has been increasing research conducted on what Schön (1987) called "reflective practice." This concept refers to the process whereby people who are (or who are preparing to become) doctors, lawyers, social workers, teachers, and other professionals who deal with people daily reflect deeply on the psychological dynamics, political purposes, and spiritual commitments that have led them to their profession and shaped their experiences as professionals. The primary goal of the quasi-therapeutic process of reflectivity is to help practitioners become professionally effective, emotionally and politically sensitive, and ethically fulfilled in their work. Over the last decade, such reflectivity has become especially salient in graduate schools of psychology, social work, and education (Cornett, 1998; Mayes, 2004, 2005; Richards & Bergin, 1998).

In this chapter, a professor of social work (Debbie) and a professor of education (Cliff)—both of whom teach and maintain small counseling practices—reflect on Debbie's experience as a Maori psychotherapist, social worker, and academician in largely White European American patriarchal institutional environments. Cliff facilitated Debbie in her "therapeutic" reflective processes. Cliff, who has researched and written about reflectivity over the last decade, has found that reflective processes often progress deeply and unfold most smoothly when the facilitator and reflecting practitioner share a "common vocabulary" with which to frame and pursue the processes (Mayes, 2001, 2002). Such "epistemological anchoring" can prevent reflectivity sessions from becoming mere exercises in free association or self-absorbed rambling. In reflectivity (as in psychotherapeutic processes), psychic energy must ultimately be "contained" by models and images that enable one to make sense out of one's inner and outer experiences, thereby enabling those experiences to promote the transformation of self, setting, and other.

Since both of these educators often use a Jungian approach in research and practice, it seemed sensible to use Jungian terms and models to frame and direct Debbie's reflectivity. This "anchored reflectivity" led to a host of compelling and trans-formative insights into Debbie's history, present situation, and future prospects as a female psychotherapist and academician of color. First, however, it is necessary to review certain basic concepts of Jungian psychology before exploring Debbie's reflective processes, which, extending over several hour-long sessions, resulted in almost 200 pages of transcribed text, the highlights of which are examined. In doing so, the aims of this work are to: (1) provide an "exemplar case-study" (Yin, 2003) that other researchers and practitioners may use as a methodological and conceptual starting point in their own work; (2) offer a rich description of the struggle of one woman of color academic to be heard and to make a difference in White European American patriarchal institutional environments; and (3) suggest a few ways in which Debbie's individual struggle may shed some light on similar struggles faced by other female academics of color.

JUNG: A CONCEPTUAL FRAMEWORK

Jung (1953/1972) suggested that "there was a very deep psychosocial well from which individuals of all sorts, and cultures and religions of all times and all places, drew in order to produce the images, themes and stories that expressed their ways of seeing and being in the world" (p. 66). Jung's approach to the psyche focuses on those inherent structures and pre-dispositions at the deepest level of our psyches that prompt us—despite personal and historical variations in language and imagery—to interpret and engage the world in much the same way from epoch to epoch and from culture to culture. Jung called these structures and dispositions *archetypes*. He suggests that we all have our psychic being largely because of our archetypes, which, because they are shared and "objective," reside in and emanate from what Jung called the universal *collective unconscious*. According to Jung, what vary are the *archetypal images* that are used to flesh out the archetype, which depend on personal and cultural factors.

The innumerable archetypes at the core of the psyche manifest themselves in such imagistic forms as the trickster, the lover, the divine child, the shadow, the magical animal, the nurturing mother, the witch, the law-giving father, the prince of darkness, ritual sacrifice, initiation, holy matrimony, mandalas, trinities and quaternities, judgment, heaven, hell, atonement, and many others. These archetypes are activated or, to use the Jungian term, "constellated," by typical life situations that are relatively constant across cultures such as birth, a child's relationship to his or her parents, puberty, courtship, marriage, vocation, aging, and death. The constellated archetype is a psychological lens through which an individual and a culture see, interpret, value, and act on the world. Jung believed that this, in many cases, explained the striking similarity among the world's myths, rituals, and religions. Such belief explains many of his patients' dreams, fantasies, fears, and hopes that paralleled with such precision the narratives and imagery of the world's greatest mytho-cultural systems—religions. Archetypes link the personal realm to the transpersonal realm and the transitory to the timeless.

One of the first archetypes the individual encounters in dream or fantasy on moving from the personal to the transpersonal level is the *anima* (for the male) and the *animus* (for the woman). These are the female and male forms, respectively, of the Latin word for "soul." Woman is always the primary mysterious "other" for man, just as man plays the same role for woman. The oldest story in the world is the mutual attraction of the sexes—and their mutual puzzlement at each other. Whenever a contrasexual figure stirs a profound emotional response in a person, whether in a dream or waking life, there is probably some degree of archetypal activity brewing within that person, in addition to whatever else may be happening sexually.

Learning how to integrate one's contrasexual elements without forfeiting one's primary gender identity is a major requirement of individuation in Jung's view for two reasons. First, if we do not acknowledge the contrasexual elements in our individual psyches, we will tend to project them onto someone else. Many marital problems result from the husband inappropriately projecting his mythical *anima* figure onto his all-too-mortal wife and by the woman doing the same with her very fallible husband. Second, if we do not consciously face and incorporate our contrasexual energies into our complete psychic economy, then those energies will "rebel" and assert themselves in overbearing and unhealthy ways. Men, *anima possessed*, begin to personify a caricature of the archetypally feminine principle—snappy, sloppily sentimental, and given to erratic moods. Conversely, *animus–possessed* women begin to personify caricatures of the archetypally masculine principle—opinionated, stubborn, and caught in twisted webs of ambition and pseudologic.

Jungian Ego Psychology

Although Jung deeply focused on the transpersonal dimension of psychic functioning, he never lost sight of its *personal* nature—its strictly biographical dimension. For instance, Jung coined the psychological term *persona* to refer to the ego-invented and ego-protecting façade that we don for others to see. Having *personas* is not in itself a negative factor. In fact, it is very necessary because the *persona* "mediates between the ego and the outer world" (Samuels, 1997, p. 215). Problems regarding the *persona* arise when it no longer functions as the ego's servant, but becomes its master, resulting in a false personality (Jung, 1971, p. 425). Another Jungian contribution to ego-psychology is the idea of the *shadow*. As Jung (1953/1972) wrote, "By *shadow* I mean the negative side of the personality—the sum of all those unpleasant qualities we like to hide, together with the insufficiently developed functions, *and the contents of the personal unconscious*" (p. 66, note 5; emphasis added). Many people incorrectly take Jung's idea of the shadow to mean that it is simply the cavernous repository of all that is evil in us. To be sure, the Jungian shadow contains much that is evil, for we do not like to see evil in ourselves. But evil is not banished to the shadow because it is evil so much as because it is something *we prefer not to acknowledge as belonging to us*. Hence, repressed memories are also in the shadow. So are "qualities we like to hide." These qualities may actually be quite positive—talents, virtues, or potentials that we have hidden not only from others, but from ourselves because openly acknowledging them could place us in emotional or social peril. Also residing in the shadow are certain "insufficiently developed functions."

It is important to confront the shadow because many things that one has repressed can, if consciously acknowledged and carefully nurtured, emerge from the shadow and help one become a more complete and powerful person and more *whole*. There is yet another reason that we must confront our own shadows that relates to the Jungian concept of *projection*. If we refuse to consciously and healthily face our own shadows, we will unconsciously and unhealthily project them onto others. In dreams, the shadow is usually the same gender as the dreamer and often associates with a dark element. The dream character might have a dark complexion and dark hair, a fact that generally seems to be as true for analysands of color as for White analysands; the figure may be wearing dark clothes, and sometimes he or she is literally standing in or peeking out of a shadow. The fact that the shadow has been "despised" by consciousness can also be symbolized in either dream- or waking-consciousness by aliens, citizens of an opposing country, members of a minority group, criminals, beggars, or by characters who seem unethical, sick, or menacing. Some racism may be a form of shadow projecting (Adams, 1996).

Cultural Aspects of Jungian Psychology

Jungian psychology has been accused of being apolitical, but this is untrue, as demonstrated by recent research that extends and applies Jungian ideas to political and cultural issues (Adams, 1996; Gray, 1996). Jung's own social vision was a mix of politico-cultural conservatism and radicalism. On the conservative side, Jung warned that members of a society should be aware of and duly honor the sacred narratives and normative values that underlie their culture: "Anything new should always be questioned and tested with caution, for it may very easily turn out to be only a new disease" (Jung, 1954, p. 145). He detested "the present tendency to destroy all tradition or render it unconscious" (Jung, 1959, p. 181). Besides, our personal identities are so interwoven with our individual and collective histories that we cannot know *ourselves* if we do not know *them*. We can know ourselves deeply and resist attempts at political domination only by a solid appreciation of our past. This is the reason that "loss of roots and lack of tradition neuroticize the masses and prepare them for collective hysteria" (Jung, 1959, p. 181). Unlike many people who argue culturally conservative points, Jung did not do so due to a sense of cultural superiority. A great student of culture, from the nearest to the most distant in space and time, Jung traveled from the jungles of Africa to the deserts of New Mexico to gain firsthand experience of first-world peoples, about whom he wrote with great admiration and love. Hence, there is a lifetime of personal and intellectual experience in Jung's pithy observation, "the white race is not a species of *homo sapiens* specially favored by God" (Jung, 1967, p. 82). Another political implication of Jungian psychology is Jung's belief that the idea of the shadow and projection could help members of a culture examine their culture's darker side. As individuals have shadows they tend to project onto others, so do societies (Odajnyk, 1976).

Debbie's Reflective Processes

A presentation and analysis of major Jungian themes that emerged during the interviews between Cliff and Debbie is offered here. Debbie's reflectivity is framed in Jungian terms that were personally, professionally and culturally empowering for her.

Theme 1: The Midlife Transition

Everyone knows the phrase "midlife crisis." The idea of a difficult transition from the first to the second half of life is part of the popular repertoire of psychological concepts. Carl Jung, the first 20th-century psychologist to focus on this phenomenon, was the first great modern psychologist of the developmental time from midlife to death. He laid the groundwork for succeeding researchers of later life such as Erik Erikson (1997) and Lawrence Wrightsman (1994).

Debbie, now in her mid-40s, certainly evidenced one of the prime psychological markers of this period—uncertainty about her next major professional step in life. Indeed, it was not clear that her next step *would* be professional or if it would instead entail dramatically reducing the scope of her academic career to spend more time with her teenage children. Because Debbie's career has been in the service of helping students of color find intellectual and professional empowerment—a calling that she feels has deeply spiritual dimensions—she indicated the need to seek "the Lord's confirmation and assurance" that moving from academia into a more domestic setting "would be where I would be of most value." This push and pull between her sense of mission as a social worker and woman academic of color on the one hand and a mother on the other hand was a theme throughout much of the interview.

Debbie: I think that now is the time of my life that I want to be more of a mother.

Cliff: More of a mother. What would that mean?

Debbie: I want to do something feminine. More womanly. I've only got a short time left before my children move on!

In the classical Jungian developmental model, the second half of life is the time when one begins to connect strongly with the contrasexual inner-other—the man with his *anima* and the woman with her *animus*. For instance, the businessman who has worked tirelessly establishing a company, at age 50 may want to spend more time nurturing his grandchildren, relaxing in nature, or working on his garden. At the same time of life, a woman who has dedicated herself to hearth and home may decide to return to school to pursue a graduate degree, start a business, or run for public office. In terms of Debbie, whose life has been largely spent in the political fray of cultural and academic battle, the classical Jungian picture has been reversed: It is in the second half of life that she is now processing, with increasing urgency, how she has had to sacrifice something from her "feminine" side to steel herself for the work of breaking down the institutional bastions of White European American male privilege. Because of her role as a cultural activist, Debbie had to access her animus quite early in life. It is in the second half of life that Debbie—reversing the usual pattern—is more involved with issues of her "femininity."

Theme 2: The Persona and the Animus

Another characteristic of the midlife transition is that the *persona* often becomes more problematic. The social masks that one has worn to succeed or merely survive in public contexts become less and less relevant to the increasingly pressing existential issue of one's own mortality and of what to do with one's remaining years as those years become much fewer than those that have already passed. What the poet T. S. Eliot called "the overwhelming questions" of one's ultimate purpose in having lived and the legacy one will leave behind become the governing themes of the second half of life.

The fact that Debbie has been a female academic of color has made this ethical and developmental issue extremely complex. Throughout this reflective process, she often identified how she had shaped her *persona*, sometimes consciously and sometimes not, to best fill her role as a powerful agent of cultural change. The question with which she struggled throughout the reflective process was how much she had adopted White European American male postures and perspectives to be allowed to play in the White European American male arena of academia.

Certainly, the idea and practice of being a powerful woman has never been a difficult one for Debbie, given her own innate strength and the Maori reverence of the woman as the *wharetangata*— that is, the child-bearer and life-giver, whose womb is "the house of humanity." In the Maori view, a woman's *mana* (power) is inextricably tied to her connection with the primal, eternal reality of Mother Earth, *papatuanuku*. In Debbie's experience growing up as a Maori girl, she had abundant evidence that the woman's *mana* is not merely a charming cultural relic, but a very real psychosocial force. When a Maori woman has her mind fixed on something important and good, Debbie laughed, a man is well advised not to try to impede her, but rather to "get out of her way!"

Cliff: As you were growing up, did you see many examples of people "getting out of the way" of feminine power?

Debbie: Oh, lots and lots of examples—lots and lots of times. My great-grandmothers, grandmothers, and aunties all had tremendous mana. *They were key to the welfare of their families,* hapu *(subtribe), and broader community, which included* Pakeha *(Europeans). So I'm talking about them having this deep sense of their own* mana.

Cliff: And do you feel that mana *within yourself as well?*

*Debbie (laughing): Oh, yes! I have that power. I have tapped into and used that power—*mana wahine *[woman's power].*

In Jungian terms, Debbie was deeply in touch with both the *cultural* archetype of the *mana wahine*, the powerful woman warrior, and with the *universal* archetype of the female as Amazon (de Castillejo, 1973). Indeed, anyone who has known Debbie for only five minutes cannot possibly miss the fact of her power!

Jung postulated that the second half of life is when it is most natural for one to access and express the contrasexual inner–other. Maori culture and Debbie's experiences clearly evidence profound developmental wisdom in this regard.

Cliff: Deb, it seems to me that most of the examples you've given of powerful women in your life are of older women. This is so different from standard American culture— you know, where a woman is only interesting if she's young and sexually desirable and gets increasingly neglected as she gets older.

Debbie: That's so true, Cliff. But a Maori woman only really comes into contact with her power after the childbearing years. So I'm more fully coming into my mana *because I'm a middle–aged woman now. And that's the most powerful time.*

Indeed, it is because of the potency and wisdom of the woman in the second half of life that, in the Maori ritual of approaching members of another tribe for the first time, the woman stands at the head of her tribe's combined forces.

Cliff: Debbie, a couple of times you've alluded to the Maori ritual of encountering another tribe, and you've said that women play an especially important role in that. Could you say more about that?

Debbie: Well, you see, Cliff, it's the older woman who is out there, full-on, as the approaching visitors or enemies come. She's standing at the very head of the group—everyone else is behind her. And she does the call to say, "Advance so we can see you. Come a little closer."

Cliff: Sounds a tad on the dangerous side!

Debbie: Oh, yeah, most definitely. And not only that, but it's also that woman who can say, if necessary, "We're ready! We're ready to battle now!"

Clearly, Debbie has very little trouble accessing the power of her contrasexual inner–other—her *animus!* Nevertheless, Debbie struggled mightily throughout the interviews with the question of how much of her power was an authentic expression of the gender wisdom of Maori culture and how much of it was an aggressive White European American male *persona* that she had adopted to succeed in White European American patriarchal institutions. How much of her power came from her Maori roots and how much from "playing White?"

Cliff: What do you mean by that phrase, "playing White," Deb?

Debbie: Well, in order to, you know, overcome the road-blocks in the formal setting of academia and to deal effectively with my White, male, and middle–age and older colleagues, I had to cultivate that formal academic identity.

Cliff: I know that routine alright—the traditional credentials and tenure game.

Debbie: That's it. You know, "I have a PhD, I'm a professor, I even have full professorial rank"—just to be heard at all!

Cliff: And did this get you "heard?"

Debbie: Oh, yeah. I was heard that way alright. And I have to admit that it was kind of exhilarating because I was, finally, being heard.

Cliff: And that was both good and bad.

Debbie: Yep. Both good and bad. Because what was happening to me, to my mana *as a Maori person, as a Maori woman? And it just hit like a brick, and then I said to myself, "Wait a second! I'm running around, playing White, you know, with White ways of doing things, White management styles, and I'm leaving behind my Maori-ness, my true strength."*

Cliff: And what kind of personal, emotional cost did that entail?

Debbie: A big cost, I can tell you! I was becoming depleted as a person. I had really gobbled up the "White perspective" of doing things, and I had moved so far away from my Maori culture. I was mimicking. I was "playing White."

Again, it is clear that Debbie's movement into middle age with its attendant *persona* and *animus* and *anima* issues, has been rendered even more complex by the fact that this transition is overlaid with issues of cultural struggle. Not only does she wrestle with the strictly personal questions involved when critically examining one's own *persona*—which is difficult enough in any circumstances—but she must also wrestle with the paradox of how that *persona* may represent both a betrayal of her fundamental cultural *identity* and a strategy to further her culture's *political cause*.

Theme 3: The Shadow

As indicated earlier, the shadow is comprised of those parts of oneself that, for whatever reason, one would rather not acknowledge as one's own. Hence, we tend to project our shadows onto others as a way of *externalizing* and disowning what is really unfinished *internal* business. Those elements of Debbie's power that stem from having adopted an inauthentic White European American male identity are the unpleasant shadow of those bright elements of her power that are truly *mana wahine*—that genuinely emerge from her identity as a Maori woman. The internalized oppressor, in short, is part of Debbie's shadow.

As a very self-aware psychotherapist, Debbie recalls times when she has projected that shadow onto colleagues. She recalled a time when she was working at another institution and not the one at which she presently teaches.

Debbie: I had a colleague there who was a small, Southeast Asian woman—very details-oriented and sort of disconnected from her own emotions. And sometimes I felt that she was my shadow in some ways.

Cliff: You felt that at the time or you see it now in retrospect?

Debbie: Well, I think I sensed it at the time, but it's only now that I'm able to put it into words—you know, because of the kind of process you and I are engaged in right now.

Cliff: Let's go back to how you felt about her at that time, alright?

Debbie: Sure. OK. Well, let's see. I guess I was often very critical of her. But I also felt for her, too, because I think she was trapped. She was stuck. But that was just a feeling I had, really—nothing I particularly put into words.

Cliff: And now?

Debbie: Well, now, as you and I discuss it, I suspect that many of my negative feelings about her at the time came from the fact that she was me, too—being trapped, being a kind of performing puppy for the institution over and over. Yeah, she was my shadow. That's really it!

In Jungian dream analysis, it is felt that the shadow often appears as a person of color or an ill or dwarfed person of some sort, and that this is true even in the dreams of people of color (Mattoon, 1985). Debbie's experience lends some credibility to this claim. She reported, "[I]n my dreams, my shadow figures are usually small, dark, and very materialistic women." This is not a surprising form for the shadow to take for Debbie, who, in fact, is tall, powerfully built, and deeply devoted to the spiritual values affirmed by her church. Debbie's shadow (in both her waking, professional life and in her sleeping, unconscious life) is often a diminutive woman of color who is susceptible to the lure of worldly rewards. This mirrors the threat to Debbie of being culturally and ethically diminished as a Maori woman by the seductive appeal of institutional power and largesse. Fortunately, Debbie's ability to reflect deeply on this subconscious dynamic and the images in which it expresses itself allows her to believe that she could now be better able to handle this shadow element in herself and avoid projecting it onto others.

Theme 4: The Cultural Politics of Sexual Domination

As noted previously, in some neo-Jungian theory, racism is seen as a projection of the racist's own personal and cultural shadow onto another group. The multicultural Jungian psychotherapist, Michael Vanoy Adams (1996), has speculated that this idea helps explain why males from supraordinate groups often seem to feel so free to psychologically and physically violate women from subordinate groups: such men, projecting their psychosocial shadow onto subordinate women, attempt to dominate (and thereby purge) their own shadows by violating the oppressed female. This act is rendered permissible in the mind of the "master" because he "sees" the slave woman only in terms of the shadow he casts over her—that is, as a lusty sexual animal. The physical and psychological violation of women of color by their White European American overlords thus emerges as a psychosocial act of not only sexual, but also (and perhaps even *primarily*) cultural and political violence.

Cliff: I know this is sort of hard, Deb, but could you tell me more about that sexual harassment you experienced when you were working at that state hospital?

Debbie: I was working as a social worker there. And a psychiatrist, during a case review, said out loud to everyone that was there—because I was presenting a report and I think he was wanting to diminish my mana—but he said, kind of offhanded, while I was talking about something serious, "Haha! I just had this fantasy of mud-wrestling nude with you on the floor of a grass shack!"

Cliff: Have you often gotten that kind of harassment from White male bosses?

Debbie: Often enough. . .

Certainly, Debbie is an attractive woman, however, what was going on in this instance was more complex than just a male sexual fantasy. Note, for instance, that this psychiatrist—probably a product of the White European American male discourse of conventional medical models of the psyche—is "upstaging" Debbie in her more intuitive, relational and archetypally feminine analysis of a patient's case. He thereby makes it clear that his White European American patriarchal view of the psyche is the only institutionally acceptable one and that Debbie's view—which is a rich product of her experiences as a female of color from a first-world culture—will not be tolerated. Indeed, if necessary, Debbie's views will be ridiculed, symbolically "wrestled," and forced into "the mud." In this sense, then, the sexually degrading comments that constitute the interruption merely encode and reinforce the power that the head psychiatrist has already exercised by inappropriately and smugly interrupting (i.e., violating) Debbie's presentation and dismissing it with a vulgar, irrelevant comment.

Oppressive gender politics certainly exist in this situation, but even more salient perhaps is the culminating image in the psychiatrist's fantasy about Debbie. He is wrestling her not only in the mud (which symbolizes his own sexual shadow), but also in a "grass shack"—clearly an allusion to a Polynesian architectural structure, which now comes to symbolize the structure of the culture itself. It is not only Debbie the *woman* whom he is raping, but Debbie the *Polynesian woman*. He enters and dominates the shack before going on to enter and dominate her. His salacious imagery betrays the fact that his fantasy is not only a personal psychosexual one, but is also an archetypally cultural one. Maori culture is reduced to the stereotypical image of a "grass shack." In short, sexual oppression and cultural domination so intermingle in this man's discourse and fantasy that it is impossible to tell where one

starts and the other leaves off. Nonetheless, that is how Debbie made sense of this experience in both political and cultural terms and reflecting on it in political, cultural, and archetypal terms.

Debbie: It's a White patriarchal view of powerful women of color.

Cliff: That seems right to me—"right," I mean, in the sense that that interpretation uncovers a lot of what was going on that was a whole lot more than just sexual.

Debbie: Yeah. And now that I think of it in those terms, I think that memory of that psychiatrist sort of stayed with me because it was about more than sexual harassment— although it was certainly about that, too! But, in general, I guess I see now how that incident explains so much about how White men in power have often treated me.

Reflecting on this experience in terms of both colonial politics and archetypal psychodynamics helped Debbie make sense of the experience—and thereby grow from it both psychologically and politically.

Theme 5: The Archetype of the Great Mother

One of the most powerful archetypes identified by Jung—and one that is prominent in many cultural narratives and practices—is what Neumann (1954) called "The Great Mother." Although this archetypal energy is probably more active in female than in male teachers and therapists (Chodorow, 1978; Gilligan, 1982), a connection with the nurturing Great Mother can sustain both men and women practitioners in their difficult jobs. It can also invest their classrooms or consulting rooms with compassion.

Nevertheless, overidentification with the Great Mother, as with any archetype, leads to psychological imbalance. Every archetype has its shadow, which, in the case of the life-sustaining archetype of the *nurturing* Great Mother, is the archetype of the *enmeshed* Great Mother (Jacoby, 1984). A common problem for practitioners who are inflated by the Mother archetype is that they are ultimately exhausted by trying to fill that role. Nurturing— even appropriate nurturing—is hard. Excessive nurturing depletes. Care, however praiseworthy, must also recognize its limits—beyond which nurturing becomes enmeshment.

Throughout the interviews, it was clear that Debbie was trying to come to terms with this powerful archetypal energy in herself—an existential task made more poignant and complex by the fact that the energy and imagery of the Great Mother is so important in Maori culture. Debbie identified with the transgenerational archetype of the Maori Great Mother.

Cliff: I can see how all of the incidents that you recall and all the stories that you tell of older women in your life are deeply, deeply important to you. Seeing them has been pivotal in defining yourself. Would that be a fair way of putting it?

Debbie: Yes, it would. In fact, you could go so far as to say that my mother and grandmother and aunties—well, they are me!

Debbie's challenge is to make this powerful archetypal energy operate in her life in ways that are appropriate to where she presently finds herself in her personal and professional development. On one hand, of course, Debbie naturally embodies that archetype in her role as the mother of four children. Yet, she often wondered aloud throughout the interviews if she had performed that role adequately or whether she had sacrificed it somewhat to pursue her career as a cultural worker and activist. Recall the section in the interviews when Debbie said, "I think I want to be more of a mother! I want to be involved more with my children. I actually just feel like I want to do something feminine. More womanly. I mean, I've got just a short time left before my children move on." The irony in all of this, Debbie noted, is that her "maternal" commitment to her students, clients, and their psychosocial struggles—a commitment that also draws upon archetypal energy of the Great Mother—is precisely what may have been interfering with expressing the same kind of archetypal energy in her family life.

Debbie spoke of the program she had created at her present university as something to which she had, in her words, *given birth*. This tender ethos of care was also evident in her description of her teaching style, which she rendered in imagery that was both highly feminine and highly Maori. For instance, she described how she uses elements of the female-led ritual of encounter (discussed above) to create more of a "family" environment in her classroom one in which her students could access their own Polynesian roots.

Cliff: Deb, as you know, one of my major research interests is how a person's cultural assumptions and practices affect how one sees oneself as a teacher—affects how one actually teaches. Can you think of any examples of this in your own classroom practices?

Debbie: Oh, sure. Lots of them.

Cliff: What's one that just comes to mind?

Debbie: OK. Well, I could begin with what we actually do to begin with at the beginning of each term. See, what I try to do is establish a Pacific Islander perspective. I have all the students stand up together and move together as a whole, very organically interrelating—and then I call out the beginning of a chant, "Hiki mai i na pua i ka Laie."

As the teacher, I model this. And then they—even if they're not Pacific Islanders, but are even Asian or White— well, they then call back to me, "Hiki mai i na pua i ka Laie." If they don't get it, if it's not sounding right, I go again, "Hiki mai i na pua i ka Laie!" And, in this way, they start relying less and less on the paper and books and more and more on each other, on these beautiful words they're hearing and repeating. They have to stand closer together and hear from each other. Well, that's a metaphor for what happens in the classroom—for how the classroom becomes a family, a community, in a Maori way! I'm starting them off, from day one, with this is what it is. You have to listen. You have to form a group, you have to help each other, you have to get in sync. And pretty soon the students really start getting it, and they start singing back, "Hiki mai i na pua i ka Laie!"

CONCLUSION

Reflecting on the archetype of the Great Mother— indeed, the Great *Maori* Mother—Debbie was able to better understand that a major challenge for her at this stage of her life and career was to draw on the psychospiritual energy available in this archetype and to find a balance between her domestic and academic venues.

Debbie stated: "I'm drawn to that—to the 'Great Mother archetype,' to mothering, to putting my energies of birthing and mothering and assisting where, you know, I can see that it's of value. And I think it's of most value if I'm not putting it solely in one place or the other—but am striking a balance

between both places. And, yes, I think that's possible. I'm coming to see that's possible!"

Reflecting on the cultural aspects of her personal and professional life framed by the theories of Jung was clearly of great value to Debbie. The reflective processes provided her with understanding as a therapist, social worker, professor, cultural activist, mother, and wife regarding where she has been, where she is presently, and where she plans to go. Armed with such knowledge, Debbie concluded the interviews feeling that she would now be able to better balance all of those different, yet interrelated parts of herself—and thus be of greater service to her family, students, and culture.

One hopes this example of reflectivity will inspire other female social work educators of color to engage in similar reflective processes. In doing so, they may find, as Debbie has, that such reflectivity is a useful tool in their struggle to find personal balance, pedagogical effectiveness, and political power.

REFERENCES

Adams, M. V. (1996). *The multicultural imagination: Race, color, and the unconscious.* London: Routledge.

Chodorow, N. (1978). *The reproduction of mothering: Psychoanalysis and the sociology of gender.* Berkeley, CA: University of California Press.

Cornett, C. (1998). *The soul of psychotherapy: Recapturing the spiritual dimension in the therapeutic encounter.* New York: Free Press.

de Castillejo, I. (1973). *Knowing woman: A feminine psychology.* New York: Putnam.

Erikson, E. H. (1997). *The life cycle completed.* New York: W. W. Norton.

Gilligan, C. (1982). *In a different voice: Psychological theory and women's development.* Cambridge, MA: Harvard University Press.

Gray, R. M. (1996). *Archetypal explorations: An integrative approach to human behavior.* London: Routledge.

Jacoby, M. (1984). *The analytic encounter: Transference and human relationship.* Toronto, Canada: Inner City Books.

Jung, C. G. (1953/1972). *Two essays on analytical psychology* (R. F. C. Hull, Trans.). Princeton, NJ: Princeton University Press.

Jung, C. G. (1954). *The development of personality: Collected works* (Vol. 17, R. F. C. Hull, Trans.). Bollingen Series XX. Princeton, NJ: Princeton University Press.

Jung, C. G. (1959). *Aion: Collected works* (Vol. 9.2, R. F. C. Hull, Trans.). Bollingen Series XX. Princeton, NJ: Princeton University Press.

Jung, C. G. (1967). *The practice of psychotherapy:* (R. F. C. Hull, Trans.). Princeton, NJ: Princeton University Press.

Jung, C. G. (1971). *Psychological types:* (R. F. C. Hull, Trans.). Princeton, NJ: Princeton University Press.

Mattoon, M. A. (1985). *Jungian psychology in perspective.* New York: Free Press.

Mayes, C. (2001). Cultivating spiritual reflectivity in teachers. *Teacher Education Quarterly, 28*(2), 5–22.

Mayes, C. (2002). The teacher as an archetype of spirit. *Journal of Curriculum Studies, 34, 699–718.*

Mayes, C. (2004). *Teaching mysteries: Foundations of spiritual pedagogy.* Lanham, MD: University Press of America.

Mayes, C. (2005). *Jung and education: Elements of an archetypal pedagogy.* Lanham, MD: Rowman and Littlefield.

Neumann, E. (1954). *The origins and history of consciousness.* New York: Pantheon Books.

Odajnyk, V. (1976). *Jung and politics: The political and social ideas of C. G. Jung.* New York: Harper and Row.

Richards, P. S., & Bergin, A. E. (1998). *A spiritual strategy for counseling and psychotherapy.* Washington, DC: American Psychological Association.

Samuels, A. (1997). *Jung and the post-Jungians.* London: Routledge.

Schön, D. A. (1987). *Educating the reflective practitioner: Toward a new design for teaching and learning in the profession.* San Francisco: Jossey-Bass.

Wrightsman, L. (1994). *Adult personality development: Theories and concepts.* Thousand Oaks, CA: Sage Publications.

Yin, R. K. (2003). *Case study research: Design and methods.* Thousand Oaks, CA: Sage Publications.

Women of Color as Social Work Educators

Part II: The Voices of Women of Color as Social Work Educators

Chapter 12: "Untitled, Until Further Notice"

Christine Lowery

To my mother, grandmother, and generations of Laguna and Hopi women who have continued to pave the way for me and other women of my tribes.

My name is Christine Lowery. I am an American Indian woman, 57 years of age, from the Laguna and Hopi tribes. I am an associate professor at the University of Wisconsin–Milwaukee, where I have been teaching since Fall 1994 in the BSW/MSW combined program. I am currently the undergraduate program coordinator and my current research focuses on ethnographic study of aging and cultural change on the Laguna Pueblo in New Mexico. Between 1971 and 1974, I served as a journalist in the U.S. Navy. I received my BSW in 1976, MSW in 1978, and PhD in 1994. My dissertation title was

"Addiction and Recovery in the Lives of Six American Indian women." I spent 12 years in social work practice with American Indian people in Nevada, Arizona, and Washington, including medical social work and child welfare and foster care. I was also involved in organizational urban practice in Portland and Phoenix. (Please note: editorial changes have added politically correct language.)

PERSONAL JOURNEY

The Association for Behavior Analysis International (ABA) held its 31st annual meeting during the Memorial Day weekend of 2005. Listed in the program was a theoretical paper that posed the question: "Are women of color, Asians, and Southern Europeans inherently inferior to the rest of us?" There is no information in the program about what the paper might cover, so the title stands alone. The author is a White European American male professor, one of many who dominates these meetings and who enjoy prestige and privilege. Granted, this author—a full professor with a loyal student following—desires to be seen as controversial; however, he does not have to consider the confirming behaviors reinforced by such a title. In a large conference that lists only one or two titles that reference cultural diversity, Asians and women of color, with a couple of notable exceptions, are invisible. I am changed in subtle ways by this listing, and my disappointment is reinforced more often than I care to admit.

Retrospectively, the challenge of racism has been critical in my journey. Because I come from a culture of caring and was raised by strong and suc-cessful Hopi women, I adopted the axiom that one could do anything one wanted if one worked hard enough. Three generations have had some painful challenges. Still, the axiom has not been reframed within a racial context, nor revised with our realities until now.

During the 1940s, six days a week, my grand-mother, Hilda, walked two miles from the village of Moencopi to the employees' club in Tuba City, Arizona. At the club, she baked bread, cookies, cakes, and pies from scratch, in addition to serving three meals a day for the predominantly White staff who taught in the boarding schools and manned the government services. In the winter, she would leave the village by lantern light before the sun came up. She would return after sundown. In the summers, after preparing food for her children, she would work in her garden in the lower village until dark and work her way home by lantern light. Hilda capitalized on the cooking skills she learned as a Hopi woman. During her young adult years, from 1918 to 1923, the government took the Hopis ages 18–20 to Sherman Indian School in Riverside, California. In the summers, between school years, she worked as a housemaid for a German family, where she also learned cooking skills.

One morning, the employees' club manager confronted Hilda and, based on hearsay, charged her with stealing fruit and food from the club. Hilda, after all, did have six children to feed. Her Hopi husband abandoned the family to start a second family with a Navajo woman, which sent Hilda out to work for a living. When confronted by the club manager, my grandmother explained that she took no fruit, but she did take leftovers. She explained that she warmed and set leftovers out twice daily for the employees. When no one ate the leftovers, she packed them carefully in tin cans and carried them home to her children. On the morning of the confrontation, Hilda promptly left the club and walked home, probably anxious about how she would support her family. That same evening, the club manager came to the village, admitted her accusations were unfounded, and apologized. Hilda returned to work for three more years before she could leave, but those relationships and that environment were never the same for her. It is this type of treatment and the residual emotions that linger for years.

Many of the Wisconsin students with "White privilege" come from predominantly White European American communities. While many White European Americans feel they are the victims of reverse discrimination in the workplace, there is still little consciousness about daily prejudice or continued racism. I see this in the classroom every semester. In their course evaluations, a few students consistently write, "Everything is about race for Lowery!" Even a few budding social workers in a course I teach cannot seriously consider that life for many people of color in a predominantly White European American environment is qualitatively different. Here is the challenge and opportunity to revamp the social work courses to help them see differently.

So, Here We Go...

Although the sun was bright in Toronto, the wind pushed the clouds into hide-and-seek patterns with the morning light. My husband (a White European American male, culturally similar in social work academia) and I were waiting for breakfast. A three-day conference on empowerment processes had just ended. Our recent marriage was pushing us to find compatible work sites in academia; I was on leave from my current university, and he was ending his time at his university. The dean of the school where I had earned my PhD four years earlier had asked me to consider applying for a position in the program.

"I think we should probably look at Seattle," my husband said thoughtfully. The waitress rounded the corner to our section, plates of food steaming. By the time she set our plates in front of us, tears were streaming down my face. She was caught off guard, as was my husband, and I sat watching the butter melt into the squares of my waffle. I was melting, too, right into a post-traumatic stress disorder-like moment and overwhelming sadness. "I honestly don't think I can go back," I said softly, now watching a shaft of sunlight appear, disappear, and reappear on the carpet. The waitress retreated, probably knowing this was not about the food. I could not even name the reasons why I could not go back. My tears evacuated the conscious hurt. My partner, now practiced in hearing stories of racism, listened as I tried to regain some balance. I later called a former classmate and asked, "What happened to us?" She was far more aware than I, named the racism, and reminded me of some of the events.

PROFESSIONAL JOURNEY

A Culture of Racism

There is something about a culture of racism that is felt deeply by people of color. It is in the air we breathe. It is not the slights—like being cut off by White European American males in favor of their own voices in the classroom or one's instant invisibility when two White European American people talk, even if you are all friends. It is the attitudes, the denial of patterns even when pointed out, the ignorance, the unconscious racism in the classroom, and the real inability to see. It is the daily treatment, both inside the department and outside the school, on the university campus, in the city in which the school is located, and even in the state of the nation at the time.

Geography and diversity do make a difference in the type of racial experience one will have, and that depends on the level of threat perceived by the dominant society or provoked and maintained by the corporate media. For example, September 11, 2001, unleashed racist behaviors that might have been otherwise limited to verbal insults. On September 12, 2001, on the way to the university, I dodged a can of pop hurled by someone in a car full of angry teens. Someone yelled that I should get back on the boat. On campus, Hmong students and students from Iran and Palestine fared far worse for a much longer period.

Looking back, I cannot force myself to recall the many small and big moments or micro and macro aggressions, as named in the current literature. It would be harmful to do so and, thus, repression serves a purpose. But we—students of color, so-called "junior" faculty of color, and staff of color—were all confronted by racism during our time in Seattle. In my second or third year in the PhD program, the MSW students of color forced the racism issue out into the open. They called for a forum, which was quickly organized. The social work image calls for openness, multiculturalism, and providing a "forum for voices not previously heard." The collaborative solutions called for by social work are much harder to construct and maintain.

The first person to speak at the forum was a White European American male, an adjunct professor. He told us what we should be doing and how to do it. He was fed up with or fearful of us. This demonstrates conscious or unconscious facets of a culture of racism: don't lose control of the situation and reinforce the hierarchy. Students of color talked about their experiences in the classrooms and in the school. One undergraduate faculty member, who was Jewish, voiced her dismay privately. I remember a flash of anger when she said, "I didn't know." As the undergraduate coordinator, how did her lack of understanding of racism and the school environment affect the undergraduate experience? Everything is *not* just fine for everyone in schools of social work.

BJ Bryson, a sister-student, and I organized a series of discussions on racism, "Three Sundays in May," with an emphasis on the power differentials in the school. One afternoon, we talked to only one student. Another afternoon, we had a "preaching to the choir" experience with about six faculty and the dean. All in all, about a dozen people participated. This was our honest contribution to the situation—education, telling our stories, and listening to theirs.

Afterward, I went back to my basement apartment, where, no matter the Seattle rain, the lighting inside was bright and healthy. There was no follow-up—although there was some talk—no organizing the allies, no confronting the most racist professors, and no discussion of the power structure that cemented the decision-making hierarchy.

This academic milieu was not without its shining moments, however. For two years, three American Indian MSW candidates—two practiced social workers and a tribal court judge—joined two American Indian PhD students to form a critical mass. Emily Salois (Blackfoot) had her young grandson with her to help her negotiate the urban jungle, and Agnes Sweetsir (Alaska native) had a new foster baby. Together, we created a psychological, social, and cultural comfort zone for one another and with other Indian students across campus. To address a visible knowledge gap for the school, the MSW candidates held a small conference on Indian issues. With presentations, they extended their generosity to students and faculty.

Two faculty of color provided opportunities for me to demonstrate my research knowledge through presentations of my dissertation in progress. Six American Indian women allowed me to interview them for 12 hours each over a period of three months and helped me complete my dissertation on addiction and recovery issues. I received one of the first Magnuson Dissertation Awards, which allowed me to totally concentrate on my dissertation for one year. And, as an option, I would teach an elective course on American Indian social work issues to students predisposed to the topic.

Four people in the PhD cohort were important for support: two lesbian women, Sue Steiner and Lynn Keenan; Serge Lee, who is Hmong; and Reiko Hiyashi, a Japanese woman. The research team I worked with was made up of all White European American women, each of whom was supportive one-to-one. My role in the research was crucial, and my skills were appreciated. Looking back, were it not for the racism, this could have been an intensively supportive environment.

For a short period, the school made an extraordinary effort to recruit faculty of color, but did so without confronting the racism. The faculty of color generously welcomed me into their meetings for a year before I completed my dissertation. They were the first to hear my colloquium and critiqued it for public presentation. These people were leaders and role models; they were mature and practiced in social work; some were published, and all were research-trained. By the time I completed the PhD, the faculty of color had dwindled. It was the attitudes and behavior: White European American was right, and color was inferior, making tenure an emotional rollercoaster. Several faculty of color left to invest their research agendas, talents for service, and multiple intelligences in other places in other states.

To leave and not return is often the healthy thing to do. One cannot change a culture of racism without investing heavy spiritual power. A PhD in most schools of social work renders you bereft of spirit at the end, even if you have some level of consciousness. Spiritual power must be rebuilt in other settings, if at all. In academia, I sometimes cannot remember what spiritual power feels like; there are so many competing contingencies.

Finding a Place

In searching for a place to teach and do research, I interviewed at three sites where American Indian students were welcomed and supported. I also looked for a potential mentor who would provide guidance with the tenure process and, perhaps, some personal support. I chose the sites with care, but I didn't consciously consider racism. The first program in Montana had a strong BSW program with a good number of American Indian students over the years. The faculty was welcoming and supportive, but the campus atmosphere would be decidedly uncomfortable if racial animosities—always simmering—bubbled to the surface. Although invisible when walking among the young, White European American Montana males, I understand why American Indians in Montana (and elsewhere) have to pay attention to feelings of racial oppression, discomfort, and safety. At the second campus, I needed a Black or African American woman to translate what I was saying to her White European American, male colleagues, who misinterpreted my statements. This did not seem out of place in her experience, and all I could think of was the enormous energy it would take to work in such a place.

The University of Wisconsin was unique since women faculty conducted their recruitment at the Council on Social Work Education (CSWE) meetings and talked with me in a group. At the time of my campus visit, social work and criminal justice shared one executive committee. The White European American males in the criminal justice program—former police officers—were part of the executive committee. During my interview, one man—dressed in sweats—exited, then returned with a basket of popcorn for himself. When he entered, he interrupted my comments and diverted the group with a short discussion about popcorn. Ten years later, he is the dean of the program and now wears suits instead of sweats.

During that visit, three female faculty members heard my qualitative research presentation and had the foresight to invite the three women from American Indian Student Services. But, at the end of the day, I let the program director know that I would not be coming to the university. I could not see enough faculty interest in the contributions I could make. (A senior faculty member actually told me that when I started doing "real research," he supposed he would "have to mentor" me.)

The next day was rescheduled because the program director heard and believed me. At the end of the day, the dean made an offer, which I accepted within a week. Sharon Keigher became the chair of my tenure committee, my in-house faculty mentor, and my friend. Ironically, during my first year, a female faculty member advised me to abandon this friendship because this association would not serve me well in the department. "How can I?" I answered. "Sharon is the *only* faculty member who has extended me a close friendship. How isolated do you want me to be?" I received no response.

Dr. Keigher set up two critical appointments. First, there were women in sociology and history who were doing impressive research, and I had a chance to talk with Margo Anderson from the history department, who became my formal campus mentor. Second, I had lunch with the four Indian faculty—two assistants and two associates—

across campus. The promise of a continued relationship with others like me was compelling. The Indian humor and friendship helped to support me through my first three years.

Now there are new American Indian faculty on campus. Within 10 years, intergenerational differences in our experiences in the academy are quite evident, and they value other ways of participation. Still, there are three American Indians (two associates and one program director) who meet for coffee with laughter once a semester. For two of us, independence from our departments is a common characteristic of our survival in academia. There are multiple Indian student activities and potlucks each year, including a powwow during "Indian Week." And, for the first time, I have a stellar American Indian female student to mentor, who has chosen the University of Washington for her master's program.

Departmental Matters

There are a number of stories to tell, and I have selected a few to share. In my first two years of teaching, a female faculty member used our undergraduate students to relay messages to me. The pattern of message-sending is not new. During the 1980s, in the only non-Indian environment I have ever worked as a social work practitioner, the White European American male supervisor actually asked a White European American male student intern to "monitor and report" my behavior in the group we coled. The student intern felt awkward about this situation and responded by telling me. Incidentally, the intern—who was 20 years older than I—was also my tennis partner. I addressed the situation

quickly and face-to-face. I invited the supervisor to attend the group at any time with the group's permission. The oppression at the Veterans Administration was real for women. In spite of the support of the psychologist next door, with whom I shared a couple of clients, I was able to stay in that environment for just six months.

The next situation was different. This was not just a job, but the development of an academic career. The faculty member was critical of my preparation of students in human behavior. She appropriately used Human Behavior and the Social Environment (HBSE) committee meetings to outline what should be taught, but never visited any of my classes for review as she was entitled to. Instead, she surveyed the students and criticized my teaching. When I first came to the university, she took me out to lunch. At this first meeting, she was adamant about her stand on equality and race—a red flag—since this is not a topic usually discussed in a first meeting. She explained that one of the servants, a person of color, in her childhood home was one of the best people she had ever known. When I was ready to step out of her car, she explained that she did not see color. I asked that she see mine. My color, I explained, reflected the context of my life experiences in this country. My color told a story that was different from hers. Because of the hierarchy and values structure in this society, my color held meaning for many people, which determined how I have been treated. She took me literally.

My way of teaching undergraduates was different from her way. As a woman of color from a pueblo culture, I do not pay homage to the psychoanalytical format in the introduction to psychology course.

The content of the HBSE course was additive, and I want students to have deeper knowledge of fewer topics demonstrated through different methods of learning. In the mid-'90s, we read and debated Carol Gilligan's concepts of the "ethic of care" and "ethic of justice" and the development of young girls and women and Mary Pipher's *Reviving Ophelia*. We compared the "ethic of care" with Kohlberg's moral development. We studied the development of Black males in a racist environment using Nathan McCall's *Makes Me Wanna Holler*, along with the theories of Erikson and Vygotsky. The students wrote and presented group papers as part of the teaching and learning structure on assigned topics from an analysis of Bowlby's attachment theory across cultures to aging across cultures.

"I'm angry to find out that I'm not being taught what I should know," wrote one White European American male in an e-mail. (I recently discarded this e-mail. I'm amazed that I keep evidence of harassment for years, perhaps to remind me of how I have dealt with past issues.) During this period, I usually responded to students who expressed a lack of confidence in my teaching methods by using the CSWE standards and academic freedom to choose materials that meet solid criteria for creating interest in reading, exploring, and dialogue at the undergraduate level. Eventually, I quit teaching human behavior and began teaching cultural diversity courses. I actively addressed workload issues with the program director. I had teaching assignments that took some energy to change: two classes on the same day, two classes back-to-back with a 10-minute break in between, night classes only, and being assigned a new graduate course

three weeks before the semester started (I had to teach this one and played catch-up the whole semester). Others received a one-course release to prepare their tenure materials; I was assigned a second course during the semester I was up for tenure.

In a more recent example, under a different program director, I evaluated a female adjunct faculty who was teaching the entry-level practice methods course. She had been evaluated previously by two other faculty members. When my evaluations as a woman of color differed from those of my White European American colleagues, I realized my burden of proof was higher. I had to be prepared to present far more evidence; thus, I observed two classes and documented my concerns with multiple examples. My written evaluation was greeted by the current program director with an angry, "Why now? She's been evaluated by [others], and they had no concerns." Student evaluations were also good. "Have you read the report?" I asked. I usually like to express the elements of racism quickly. "I know that, as a woman of color, I have to document more carefully than my White colleagues. I honestly have real concerns about the teaching based on my observations." My report had not been read thoroughly, just skimmed. My concerns included the faculty member's inability to make the connection to theory; isolated examples not connected to the lesson; evidence based only on personal examples; and an inability to connect student examples to course content. A lack of understanding of cultural diversity was a glaring concern. There was more, but these will suffice.

I had the adjunct faculty coordinator sit in on my meeting with this adjunct faculty to review the evaluation. This is not required, but I knew I needed evidence, and another set of eyes is useful. The adjunct faculty did not answer clarification questions knowledgeably, and the coordinator appeared to validate my concerns. This particular adjunct faculty no longer teaches in the bachelor's program. But "validation" is tricky, and this adjunct faculty now teaches in the graduate program; complaints about this person come only from women of color. Like most students, they recognize that the semester is short-lived, and it is not worth their energy to attempt change.

Unexpected Racisms

When people of color work with other people of color, we often let rest the shields we hold up in the "world." Consequently, we are "hit" harder because we think we are safe, do not see it coming, and are unprotected. Paulo Friere talks about "horizontal violence." If we cannot do it to the "man," we do it to each other. For me, these incidents are even more painful than the usual racism from the usual suspects. I understand the rage and the demeaning, abusive behavior. I do not like the threats.

As a pueblo woman, I frequently talk about the influence of my grandmothers. This was ridiculed in a memo written by a faculty member of color as "hearing voices" and "contact through the psychic hotline." There was a time when I had to leave the campus for a year without pay to escape the real threat of continued harassment. For those who think this should have been a faculty matter, faculty power varies from school to school and vacillates week to week. On the other hand, I took the year and completed a journal article, researched and

wrote three chapters, and coedited a graduate textbook, now in its fourth edition. I also married my coeditor.

Tenure and promotion, like the dissertation process, was a useful exercise. These processes provide review of our work with discussion and feedback. What is significant in my tenure-and-promotion process is that I was able to call on two American Indian social work scholars, John Redhorse and Herb Granbois, to review my work.

The Undergraduate Program

Lack of funding, lack of staff, and lack of appreciation for small undergraduate programs seemed to be the norm, but I saw a different opportunity in this experience. I waited 10 years for the coordinator's position to open, pending a retirement. The retirement also opened up the introductory social work courses leading to the three-course practice methods sequence.

Early in my academic career, my focus was on teaching at the undergraduate level. Redesigning courses (human behavior, cultural diversity, and research methods) to reflect a level of intellectual challenge suitable for the critical development of social work practice has been one of my strengths. From my cultural perspective, "intergenerational" teaching, seeing the whole because one can understand the interrelated parts, is a useful way to establish a grounded perspective of social work. Undergraduate education is critical since most of our students probably will not return for a master's degree. This is a good opportunity to create a thirst for social work knowledge, prepare students for professional service, and provide an introduction to tools for lifelong learning. At the undergraduate level, I want to insure an understanding of how students can weave experience, knowledge, practice, professional values, and evaluation into solid social work practice, beginning with the course Social Work 100.

Building the undergraduate program requires "intergenerational" relationships with adjunct faculty and mentoring new faculty as they learn to teach. Small-group work, communication about university requirements, exchanging teaching resources, and a communal understanding about CSWE standards are practiced. Students benefit from our work as they advance from one course to another. One significant challenge is to elevate course content across the curriculum. Coaching adjunct faculty willing to take on previously designed courses, and heavy assignments, grading burden and all, has been one strategy that works.

My priorities in social work education have always been to strengthen the quality of students we prepare for the profession. I continue in social work education for this purpose. Contributing to this movement is the group of men and women of color who work to introduce specific content into cultural diversity texts for our profession, particularly the works edited by Doman Lum and his collaborators. The caliber of scholars of color in social work, many of whom wrote for this book, is encouraging.

CONCLUSION

Academia is driven by its relationship with government-funded research entities and the development of products for the market. The goal of university leadership in schools with more than 27,000 students is to achieve Research-I status. The chancellor at my university has a three-prong program to encourage biomedical research in southeastern Wisconsin and has done good work in this area. (Graduating students of color is another goal.) When he talked to the social work and criminal justice faculty, he emphasized the large government research grants. I challenged him:

> What about people of color who do not fit into the large research center environment? What about those of us who became PhDs to do work with our people—work that does not readily garner large grants? Where do we fit in your vision of this university?

Realistically, scholars of color create our own fit, often based on our own research agenda; we create our own place in academia. I recognize that I will probably not make full professor in this setting. Although I actively selected a Research-II university with minimal requirements for tenure and promotion, the standards still emphasize major research grants.

I am one of those who earned the PhD in an effort to work with my own people. The work of my lifetime is ethnography on the Laguna Pueblo, the home of my father and the place to which I will return when I leave academia. I always wanted to know my great-grandparents at Laguna. I have so little information about who they were as people in their Laguna community. My Hopi mother, as a young wife who did not know the Keresan language, knew my grandparents in their 90s and loved them dearly. When I was four, we left the village of Paguate and, as a young family, followed the railroad work to Barstow, California, and later to the uranium mines in nearby Grants, New Mexico.

At age 50, I returned to Paguate, and I am finishing this manuscript in the restored pueblo-style home my grandparents built in the 1940s. My research plan for the next few years is to observe, learn the customs and the people I left at age four, and write about the elders who are here. Clearly, I am writing for their descendents 20, 50, and 100 years from now. I may not reach a full professorship in academia, but I am the only researcher doing ethnographic work with the elders at Laguna. As women of color, we may find the work we need to do far from the university setting and in a place where we may feed our needy spirits. And this is a good thing because it has everything to do with survival, living a good life (health), and contributing to our people.

Women of Color as Social Work Educators

Part II: The Voices of Women of Color as Social Work Educators

Chapter 13: East–West Convergence, An Uneasy Balance

Paula Toki Tanemura Morelli

These recollections and evolving thoughts are dedicated to women unknown to us, who, over multiple generations, made our lives possible.

> *Angry in the ultimate dimension*
> *I close my eyes and look deeply.*
> *Three hundred years from now*
> *Where will you be and where shall I be?*

(Nhat Hanh, 2002, p. 43)

By the time I was seven years old, my life was affected by experiences that caused me to yearn for human dignity and social justice. I understood injustice from my immigrant grandparents' stories of mistreatment, my parents' and maternal grandfather's incarceration and confinement during World War II, and the discrimination I experienced. Despite these early influences, even as a child, I believed justice was possible.

I grew up in the confluence of Asian, Pacific, and Western cultures and attempted to develop within myself valued Asian characteristics of inter-generational responsibility, humility, and sensitivity to another's welfare before my own, as well as the Western-Eurocentric characteristics of independence, egalitarianism, and success-minded competitiveness. Simultaneously living the values of an individualistic Western culture and that of collectively oriented Asian and Pacific-basin cultures is a challenging, uneasy balance, which can translate into feelings of confusion, fear, unworthiness, oppression, marginalization, hope, pride, and empowerment. My narrative of survival is directly connected to the generations before me, whose values, love, hopes, dreams, and sheer persistence now permit me to speak. The implicit obligation of this gift is a responsibility to contribute to the betterment of generations to come.

While my decision to become a social worker was rooted in childhood experiences and observations of situations begging for social justice, it was also related to my personal search for meaning and identity. Anger about injustice and oppression remains an enduring part of who I am; however, in this phase of my journey, developing knowledge to advocate for the disenfranchised and mentoring the next generation are the focus of my energy. I share the narrative that follows with the hope that it will serve as a footstone upon which others may stand and move forward.

BIOGRAPHY: ORIGINS OF THE UNEASY BALANCE

My life experiences are made meaningful within the context of my family history. While this history is important to me, this account targets particular portions of remembered history, which formed the basis of my evolving worldview. I called upon the narratives, past and present, of my parents, grandparents, aunts, uncles, and other relatives in this effort to examine what contributed to my evolution as a social worker.

In 1943, I was born Paula Toki Tanemura in Chicago, Illinois. My known ethnic ancestry links me with the people of southern Japan, the Philippines, and Spain. My birth and birthplace were largely the result of World War II and Executive Order 9066[1]. My parents, Richard Masuo Tanemura and Beverly Fusako Yamamoto, were both born and raised in Hawai`i, however, they had never met before the war, and it was highly unlikely that their paths would have crossed as they were in different parts of the world when Pearl Harbor was bombed on December 7, 1941. Richard was an American Merchant Marine in Asia, and Beverly was a student at the University of California–Berkeley. Richard's ship was bombed by the Japanese off the coast of Australia, and he was transported to San Francisco for reassignment.

---

[1]The primary rationale for internment was "military necessity" for reasons of national security. EO9066 was a blatant denial of Japanese American citizens' civil rights, but mainstream Americans made no significant protest against it. In four separate cases (*Hirabayashi v. United States; Korematsu v. United States; Endo v. United States; Yasui v. United States*) young Japanese Americans challenged Executive Order 9066 and the race-based curfew all the way to the U.S. Supreme Court, where their basic civil rights were denied because they were not White (Hata & Hata, 1995).

On February 10, 1942, two months after the declaration of war, President Franklin D. Roosevelt issued Executive Order 9066, denying Japanese Americans their civil rights and initiating their evacuation and incarceration. It was during this period of roundup and evacuation that my parents met, married, and were interned at Heart Mountain, Wyoming, in one of 16 concentration and isolation camps in the United States.

The origins of my uneasy balance began well before my parents' meeting and well before each of their parents' meetings. This account is limited to a segment of our remembered history, and, while my family may appear idealized, like most families, we have internal conflicts, good times, and bad, but the values and characteristics described are at the heart of our resilience.

McCully Grandpa and Grandma

My mother's parents, Toki Muramoto and Hirouemon Yamamoto, were from Yamaguchi-ken and Hiroshima-ken, Japan, respectively. They both came to the United States at separate times during the early 1900s seeking a better life. Entering the country via Ellis Island, Toki and Hirouemon met at an English-language class in Hawai`i. They married and had four children. Theirs was a caring, practical alliance; they were different in character, equally hardworking and devoted to their children's well-being. My mother, Beverly Fusako, was their only daughter, the second of four children. Grandpa Hirouemon was a contractor and property manager. He built their home on reclaimed swampland in an area now known as McCully on Oahu, Hawai`i. My grandparents lived a rural lifestyle much like what they would have lived in Japan, only they were in a residential area of Honolulu; they raised chickens, grew a vegetable garden and fruit trees, and made their own medicinal teas, which they shared with their neighbors.

A man of few words, Grandpa Hirouemon led a frugal, disciplined life, invested well, and seemed peaceful throughout his life. Grandma Toki, the youngest of eight girls, was like a boulder: bold, and talkative, yet generous. My grandfather became a Christian while my grandmother remained Buddhist; he studied English diligently while she spoke only a smattering of English. My grandmother often mixed Japanese and Hawaiian in her daily speech, which caused me to confuse Hawaiian words for Japanese.

During the war, my grandfather was among 400 men taken from Hawai`i to Angels Island, and he was incarcerated at Santa Fe, New Mexico, for four years because he owned property in Japan. However, my grandparents did not appear bitter, rarely spoke of misfortune, and lived by *shikataganai* (there is nothing we can do about it); that is, one must make the best of difficult situations and carry on with life.

McCully Grandma and Grandpa represented Japanese tradition, a formal family structure, predictability, and expectations of achievement. They were pioneers, able to adapt to a new life in Hawai`i, to a diverse culture and the modern age. I thought their ways were old-fashioned and tried to disassociate myself from what I perceived to be the shackles of Japanese tradition. What I did not realize then was how their modeling had already affected my sense of self and ability to survive.

Molokai Grandma and Grandpa

My father's mother, Kikue Tanemura, was born in 1898 in Yatsushiro-gun, Kumamoto, Japan. She lost her mother at an early age and was raised by her grandaunt, a Buddhist priestess, on the grounds of a small Buddhist temple. In 1918, at the age of 19, Kikue came to Hawai'i *yobiyosei* (called) to be with her father, Jukichi Tanemura, a blacksmith by trade. Kikue married Mariano B. Araullo from Manila, Philippines, an educated Ilocano employed as a bookkeeper for the Libbey-McNeil sugar company in Kahalu'u, Oahu. They had two children, my father, Richard Masuo, and my aunt, Marie. In 1924, Grandpa Mariano left Hawai'i and subsequently died in California, and Grandma Kikue became a single parent.

Determined to support her family, Grandma trained in Japan as a tailor and opened a dress shop in Waikiki. She remarried, and the family continued to work hard and live modestly. In her late 40s, she and Grandpa Shikada moved to Molokai because of job opportunities and the fact that her daughter, Marie, married and moved there. Between the ages of 5 and 14, I spent most of my summers in Molokai, where the slow pace of rural life provided space and time to reflect. Grandpa Shikada was a contractor working in Kaunakakai and Kalaupapa. His hobby was landscape painting. I would tag along with him and try to paint. Though often a quiet man, Grandpa was also a humorous fellow and would paint faces on us while we slept. Patience and the value of quiet observation were part of what I learned from him.

I always had a special connection with my Grandma Kikue. She would often recount that, upon seeing my grandmother for the first time when I was three years of age, I went straight into her arms without hesitation, as if we had always known each other. Perhaps more than any other, her influence lives in me. By example, she taught me that attitude is 90% of doing things well and that, through creativity and resourcefulness, answers can be found and skills are transferable. She taught me the value of loyalty and the many meanings of love. I enjoyed being with her. She taught me how to cook, sew, fish, garden, clean, find food in the forests of Molokai, and to do each of these well and with care. In retrospect, the discipline involved in her teachings became the foundation for other things I was able to do.

My Father: Rebel With a Cause

When my father's family lived on Oahu, Hawai'i, they struggled economically. There was literally no sleeping space in their home for him. Therefore, at age 15, Richard lived on his own or with various Hawaiian families. According to Aunt Marie, her brother was popular, socialized easily, was very resourceful, and was able to live in such circumstances without becoming a problem. Being on the move was an exciting way of life, so, at the age of 17, he became an American Merchant Marine. By the age of 22, my father had been around the world as an American Merchant Marine, experienced the devastation of war, and, along with thousands of other Japanese Americans, was rounded up by the U.S. military and imprisoned. Clearly, he had a right to be angry and vocal about being deprived of his rights as an American citizen of mixed ancestry[2].

---

[2] Japanese-Filipinos were also interned by Executive Order 9066.

My father taught me to be critical of "truth" and to look beyond the surface for deeper understandings. When he returned from voyages to other countries, he talked about how U.S. aid never reached the people it was intended to reach. For example, U.S. shipments of food and supplies meant for delivery to India would be diverted right on the docks to Russian ships. He told me long before the Vietnam War started that we would be involved in such a war. In my youth, I thought these were strange notions since no one else ever spoke of such events, and I regarded his tales with skepticism. However, when these events became publicly recognized realities, I realized not only was my reality very limited, but that complex factors beyond our control could affect my life. My father's raw messages about life in other countries awakened me to how historical and geopolitical factors on the other side of the world could have volatile effects on everyone's life.

My Mother: Hope for the Future

My mother, Beverly, came from a background that enabled her to be an independent thinker. She graduated from high school in Hawai`i and was sent to "finishing" school in Japan. At Doshisha University, she learned Japanese ways and arts. Her Western upbringing made her stand out; she was different and often was the object of ridicule from fellow students. However, as a bilingual student, she was valuable and had many unique opportunities to interact with foreigners and provide translation services.

When World War II was declared, my mother was beginning winter break at the University of California–Berkeley, but, in the midst of the chaos, she could not secure transportation back to Hawai`i. Executive Order 9066 confined Japanese Americans to the Japan town area of San Francisco for eventual dispersal to the concentration camps. She met my father at the San Francisco evacuation area and married him at the second triage area, the Pomona race track in California. From Pomona they were sent to Heart Mountain, Wyoming[3], along with thousands of others.

Life in the concentration camp was degrading, depressing, and oppressive, and my parents were determined to find a way out. My parents took jobs picking sugar beets on the outside on a sugar-beet farm. Once there, however, the severe cold made beet-pulling conditions unbearable; my father objected to being used as slave labor and returned to camp.

During the summer of 1942, my parents both secured work outside the camp and were released to go to Chicago. There, my mother's work involved finding employment for other interned Japanese Americans so they could be released as well. My father worked as a bartender and ukulele player until the summer of 1944, when they left Chicago for New York City so he could resume work on merchant ships. However, when he tried to get work, the mayor of New York stated that "Japs" should not be on American ships. Seeking justice, my father went to *The New York Times* and, with the help of a reporter, had an article published in the *Times*[4] about

---

[3]The physical and social conditions at the internment camps are well documented, but are not discussed in this account.

[4]In 1944, a photo of me as an infant appeared in *The New York Times* accompanying the article, "Good Enough for Sea Duty But Not LaGuardia."

race-based employment discrimination. This event effectively enabled his reinstatement into the American Merchant Marines in New York City.

GROWING UP IN HAWAI`I: WHY ARE WE INVISIBLE?

In 1958, I became acutely conscious of racism. Although I knew the horrible feelings that accompanied discrimination, I did not know the brutality of racism in our country or how pervasive it was until I went to the Southern part of the United States. My mother's brother, Shigeo, was graduating from the Emory University School of Dentistry. In celebration, my parents, sister, and I went to Georgia for his graduation; it was a trip I shall always remember. We flew to Detroit, Michigan, where we picked up a car my parents purchased and drove to New York and then to Georgia. For the first time in my life, I witnessed segregation. I saw bathrooms marked "Colored" and "White," places where they would only serve Whites, and living areas that appeared poverty-stricken and were solidly Black or African American. I felt the stares of people when we went to my uncle's graduation, when we entered restaurants, and when we tried to find a place to stay. On May 31, 1955, the U.S. Supreme Court banned segregation in public schools, and, a month earlier, on April 4, 1955, Rosa Parks was arrested in Montgomery, Alabama, for refusing to give a seat to a White European American man, yet, in 1958, de facto segregation was still part of daily life in the South.

My childhood beliefs about *the land of the free and the home of the brave* were turned into broken illusions. My belief in American equality was shaken; I wasn't safe from racism nor was there safety in the fact that my Uncle Shigeo served in the 442nd U.S. Army infantry or that my Uncle Joe served in the Korean War. Loyalty, hard work, and being a productive citizen would not prevent me from being discriminated against in this country.

In school, we were taught that White European American histories represented the origin and center of modern civilization. Little or nothing was taught about American Indians, Native Americans, or First Nation people, Africans, Asians, Southeast Asians, Pacific-Basin people, or Hawaiians. It seemed strange that we did not learn the history of non-European immigrants: Chinese, Japanese, Koreans, and Filipinos. I wondered why nothing was taught about people like us; didn't we contribute to the United States? Why did I have to go to college to learn about the history of my culture? Not surprisingly, the primary source of information about my own cultural background came from family, Japanese language school, and movies. Mainstream society rarely acknowledged the achievements or positive qualities of minority people; in movies, for example, Asians were portrayed as sneaky, evil, or comical.

All of this notwithstanding, throughout my adolescence, I held American cultural ideals above those of my ancestry. I felt at odds with time-honored traditional ways of Japanese culture, which did not appear to have meaning in the context of American life. What was the value of sitting through a Buddhist funeral for hours, listening to prayers? Why should I have to behave in an unassuming, accommodating, other-oriented, and selfless manner?

Why did I have to anticipate everyone's needs and not my own? Why can't I express my contrary opinions or be negative if I feel that way? Why does being female in either cultural context have so many disadvantages? These and myriad other conflicts were negotiated on a daily basis alone and without consultation. Negotiating a balance among the expectations of the dominant culture, my family's cultural expectations, and my own needs was expected without question or complaint: as the Japanese say, *gambatte* (persevere)!

It was obvious the *haole*[5] had power and privilege by virtue of historic and colonial imperialism. This dominance elevated the status of their physical appearance, language, social characteristics, and culture to a more desirable level than cultures of people of color. This notion of White European American superiority was constantly reinforced by the media. Asians and Pacific Islanders wanted to receive recognition, but the unspoken reality was that one had to be White European American to be valued. I could try to be White European American, but, since that was impossible, the resulting internalized oppression often caused me to hate myself. If I took on the characteristics of the dominant culture, it was distasteful to my family, but if I did not, I would not be successful by Western standards. In either case, I risked disapproval or low social status.

The next best thing was to combine dominant "ideals" with my own cultural heritage. This is easier said than done, however; it took years to work

---

[5]White person, American, Englishman, Caucasian; formerly, any foreigner (Pukui & Elbert, 1986).

through and back to myself. I had to learn how to be engaging and conversational without feeling like I was bragging, bold, or aggressive. I had to learn how to be assertive, ask for help, not feel obliged to anticipate another person's needs, and not personalize another person's insensitive behavior. At my core, I continue to respect all beings, to strive to be selfless, loyal to family and friends, and to act swiftly and decisively when it is important to do so.

Internalized Oppression

My first experiences with racism were painful and frightening. At the age of seven, I remember being screamed at by my grandmother's *haole* employer because my sister and I were not allowed to be on certain parts of his property. The kitchen where my grandmother worked was the only place we could be, and we were definitely not allowed to play with his grandchildren. It was difficult to understand why so much anger was being directed at us. At times, I assumed that my fear was a result of my own failing and my own weakness and inability to stand up for myself. Being female and non-White European American was a serious disadvantage. Females were vulnerable to abuse and not taken seriously. I often wondered, "Why do I have to feel bad about myself? What did I do?" I also remember my grandfather sharing how, as a young boy, he was chased away when looking through the gates of Punahou School, a school for White European American children. Again, I ask, "Why did it have to be that way?"

The overt racism of sugar plantations had subsided by the 1950s, but discrimination continued in many ways and was evident by the way Native

Hawaiians and immigrants were treated by employers and the deference with which people of color responded to White European Americans. This was especially true on the neighboring islands, where pineapple and sugar plantations were still operating. The old colonial families continued to use White privilege and de facto racism to control the economy, governance, and state educational policies.

MOVING ON: THE IRONY OF IDENTITY

The Civil Rights era brought change, but living with de facto racism and my personal struggle for identity motivated me to leave the islands. At the time, I could only describe my discomfort as a "love-hate" relationship with Hawai`i. In reality, these feelings were the manifestation of my internal struggle with the contradictions of life in Hawai`i. It seemed as though there was no way to be myself. I felt like nobody trying to be somebody and *somebody trying to be nobody* at the same time.

I left Hawai`i in 1963 to attend a university in Oregon. I wanted to be free of the conflict I experienced in Hawai'i, but I found that I continued confronting the contradictions even more squarely. I lived, schooled, and developed solid relationships with mainland White European Americans. I had fun away from home. Like most teenagers who leave home, the values and strengths my family had given me were the sources of my emotional survival. In 1964, I transferred to the University of Southern California (USC), graduated in 1965 with a BA in sociology, and became an Aid to Families with Dependent Children (AFDC) worker in Compton, California. In California, too, I learned about racism and saw its effects in the first Watts riots.

Living away from Hawai'i, I learned that stereotyping could be used to my advantage when it was positive, but the image of *model minority* was also a form of oppression that kept one trapped in another's image of what you should be. In either case, people did not truly see me. I have slowly come to recognize and reconcile my various identities and the external factors that affect my sense of self, feelings of acceptance, and sense of belonging. These factors are negotiated in various ways depending on the setting, geographic location, and whose numbers dominate. I have learned to be cautious in situations where people have no experience with Asian Pacific Americans or are unwilling to deal with diversity. The combination of being female, minority, and multicultural presented challenges I lived through because I fully expected myself to do so. It was the path to my survival. I had no other choice.

Looking back, a large part of what sustained me through adverse times came from the way of life my parents and grandparents lived and shared with me, the stories of their struggles, and the care with which they taught me not only traditions, but to value and honor all beings. Their stories instilled pride, a sense of belonging to an ongoing history passed down over centuries, and knowledge that their strengths were the heritage that would guide me. My grandparents are gone now, and my father is as well, but it is the essence of their strength that I cling to when difficulties arise, in times of confusion, when I have disheartening experiences or am just plain tired. Perhaps strength comes from simply knowing that, if any one of them were missing, I would not be here and that as they did for my sake, I must do for others' sake as well. From the collective of my past experiences as well as the experiences of others, I came to value and view the development of a positive ethnic identity as a potential source of resilience and strength in dealing with oppression and maintaining psychosocial well-being.

Ironically, it took leaving home for me to become aware of and recognize the importance of identity development and how the lack of positive recognition of ethnic and racial identities or *racism by neglect* within the context of daily life affects well-being. The relationship of ethnic-identity development to psychosocial adjustment is supported in research with African Americans, Asian Americans, and Latinos (Bond, 1928; Brown, 1931, as cited in Spencer, 1987; Ethier & Deaux, 1990; Kitano, 1982; Parham & Helms, 1985, as cited in Phinney, 1993; Phinney, 1988, 1991; Phinney & Chavira, 1992; Phinney, Alipuria, & Rosenberg, 1979, as cited in Phinney, 1993).

SOCIAL WORK AND SOCIAL JUSTICE

In 1965, after receiving a bachelor's degree in sociology, I had no strongly developed intention of becoming a social worker. It simply happened because I needed a job and had notions about some kind of social change. The Civil Rights movement was part of the context of the times. As I said earlier, I was an AFDC worker in Compton, California, during the first Watts riots. My deeper consciousness about social justice took shape during this period. In the following year, I entered the social work master's program at USC. In 1968, Dr. Martin Luther King, Jr. spoke to our class. For me, it was a defining moment that crystallized the meaning of justice and the purpose of my childhood experi-

ences with oppression and discrimination. His unshakable faith that justice would prevail was so alive and clear. Even when his talk was disrupted by a bomb threat, Dr. King continued to share his thoughts with confidence and strength.

In the years between 1968 and 1993, I worked with youth incarcerated in the Los Angeles County juvenile justice system; children with mental illness in psychiatric hospitals; families involved with Child Protective Services; and individuals in need of group and individual therapy. I also developed and implemented drug-intervention programs for children in the Kauai, Hawai`i, public education system; assessed Vietnam veterans for services; conducted forensic evaluations; provided training for employee-assistance programs; provided mediation services; and taught parenting. What emerged out of these years of providing direct services was my need for research and program evaluation skills. Interventions required funding, and funding required knowledge about the efficacy of interventions and how to conduct evaluation research.

The PhD

Consequently, in 1993, I returned to the continental United States to attend the University of Washington (UW) in Seattle. Naively, I expected to find social work engaged in new paradigms of knowledge development and education. The fantasy dissolved quickly; UW was as traditional as they come. In fact, most social work researchers emulated the hard sciences by using the scientific paradigm as the end-all to receive federal funding. Clearly, past survival skills would be critical: observe each situation carefully, seek allies, and do more than is expected. It was important to be careful about of whom one asked questions that challenged accepted paradigms. Simple questions about why context is not considered in research, why or how an intervention found effective with middle-class White European Americans could be applied to a culturally different group with similar results, or why methodologies, outside the scientific paradigm could not be created to understand human phenomena were all considered provocative, depending on whom you asked. I remember a colleague asking why the PhD education required quantitative research methodologies but not qualitative research methodologies. The answer given was, "If that's what you wanted, then you should have gone somewhere else."

In the same breath, I must emphasize that my success in the academy must be credited to the progressive, collectively oriented faculty who silently continue to fight for the cause of social justice within the UW School of Social Work. Their tireless support was about making sure I received the type of training and education that fostered critical inquiry and creative approaches to research. These individuals helped me to position myself in community research and produce scholarship that enabled me to graduate in four years. Their mentorship was priceless, and I shall always be grateful to Anthony Ishisaka, Sue Sohng, Edwina Uehara, David Allen, and many others, who pushed past the accepted boundaries. I am honored and privileged to be among them and, therefore, to be committed to social justice.

What was this mentorship like? It facilitated my potential, noticed my strengths, and honored my being. The mentoring I received had these important characteristics:

- My mentors cared about understanding who I am and my historic, geopolitical context.
- My mentors experienced oppression and marginalization themselves.
- My mentors provided outreach and direct, consistent, practical guidance, which was selfless and without ego involvement.
- Meetings with them cultivated my critical thinking, socialization, and laughter.
- My mentors understood and appreciated differences in ways of seeing, knowing, and being.

Surviving Tenure: Whom Do You Want Tenured and Why?

In 1996, armed with a degree, a modicum of knowledge, community-research experience, and previous work and life experience, I accepted an assistant professorship at the University of Hawai`i, Manoa. We considered many factors important to our family situation and decided, rather than seeking international work or a position on the continent, we would return to contribute to the `aina[6] that nurtured us.

---

[6]Aina refers to the land or earth (Pukui & Elbert, 1986); in addition to its unique physical properties, I use the word to include the people and cultural properties of Hawai`i.

Would I be able to make a solid contribution and attain tenure? This appeared to be a true test of the education, mentoring, and modeling I received. Over time, I came to realize that assistant professorship is a type of hazing. My survival in the academy depended on figuring out how to be collegial, fitting in, being accepted, and demonstrating value as a teacher, scholar, researcher, and contributor to the community, university, and profession without annoying those with seniority or saying things that were contrary to their beliefs and values. Thus, not only did my teaching, scholarship, and relationships with students, colleagues, and community need to demonstrate competence before I would be deemed worth retaining, I had to be careful not to *rock the boat*. If I could not accomplish and accommodate within four years, I would be out.

In the academy, experienced faculty are well aware of both explicit and implicit expectations within the tenure process. They know that competence and academic excellence are necessary, but often insufficient to receive tenure. Narrowly defined standards of excellence can be a double-edged sword: working effectively to retain those who meet criteria, but excluding excellence within diversity. In my experience, part of the tenure process is demonstrating excellence, but it is also about surviving the tyranny of individuals within a school who believe their ontological, epistemological, and methodological ideologies represent "correct thinking."

Having survived such a tenure process, I believe social work schools must critically examine potential for bias in all their processes. Faculty need to recognize and value paradigmatic diversity and the limitations of their perspectives. Furthermore, tenure committees must explore and acknowledge new definitions of excellence beyond the traditional narrowly defined dimensions. What are the range of ways in which faculty contribute to special populations, communities, or others within the state or in relation to the school's mission? Why aren't these contributions given full recognition in the tenure process? How does the school insure workload equity between women and men? How does faculty composition within a personnel committee affect the tenure process for particular individuals? How do biases or differences in philosophy affect the tenure process? How can bias or imbalance be guarded against and eliminated from the process?

In June 2001, battle weary but energized, I emerged from an arduous process tenured. Taking a stand and making my politics known contributed to the male-dominated vote against me. I do not regret the path I took. The core of my resolve came from the *kiai*[7] of those who stood with me and my mentors who were with me through it all; my partner, Tom; my son, Tommy Tora; my nuclear and extended family; a support-network of friends and colleagues; and especially the unbroken connection to the values and strength of my heritage.

In many ways, the academy remains antediluvian in its refusal to develop a more progressive tenure process. The system often turns a blind eye to faculty who bully and intimidate junior faculty over ideological differences. These bullies openly

---

[7] Japanese for spiritual strength, life force.

maintain their power by denying tenure to faculty who are not of their persuasion and by maintaining the status quo. When ideological and personal conflicts become a part of a tenure-review process, it ceases to serve its purpose. The following are recommendations:

- Tenure-review committee members as policy should openly discuss any serious conflict a potential member may have regarding a candidate.
- Individuals with a clear conflict of interest must be removed from the committee[8].
- Open, safe discussion of philosophical and ideological differences should be encouraged.
- Culturally mediated differences in ontological, epistemological, and methodological approaches should be recognized, honored, and utilized when appropriate.
- Relevant community contributions and productivity should be recognized at a commensurate level as other achievements in the tenure process.

These are but a few ideas regarding how the academy can commit to pluralism and become more relevant to the communities and people it serves.

---

[8] Our 2003–2009 faculty union agreement now includes a provision allowing "an individual candidate to exclude participation by other department members where the candidate believes that a conflict exists that would prevent the Faculty Member's fair evaluation of tenure or promotion application."

Balance and Mind-Blowing: Pluralistic Social Justice

I tell my students we need to have our minds blown regularly. That is, optimal learning occurs when we work through uncomfortable situations. When we are caught off guard in that way, there are opportunities to discover humility and our strengths. We can reframe every unlikely situation as an opportunity to learn. Here, again, what my family and especially my mother and grandmother, Kikue, taught me holds true: *Anything is possible, if one is patient, taking time to observe and learn.*

In light of such possibilities, my socialization and life experience in both Eastern and Western[9] a cultural perspectives enabled me to continually engage the challenge of balancing many ways of perceiving, understanding, and behaving in the world. Time has not diminished nor eliminated my awareness of the distinctions between the worldviews with which I struggled. I still negotiate conflicts between my relational values and my individualistic, equality, and independence-based values. I am continually negotiating and creating my path between competing paradigms.

CONCLUSION

The essence of what I have learned in the academy is that, if we are truly committed to transformation and social change that targets social justice, multi-

---

[9] I acknowledge the oversimplification in the use of Eastern and Western in describing the essence of collective and individualistic cognitive perspectives. Nisbett (2003) provides a detailed examination of this topic.

culturalism, and empowerment, our schools of social work need:

- Conscious development of paradigmatic diversity within schools;
- The freedom and safety to discuss a range of ontological, epistemological, and methodological ideologies that come from within and outside the academy;
- The creation and intentional support of a normative working environment in which constructive self-criticism and the acknowledgment of limitations enhances a search and resources for new avenues of development and growth in one's perspectives;
- Definitions of excellence that are broader and inclusive of other paradigms of knowledge; and
- Ongoing, open discussion about philosophical, political, and power issues from diverse perspectives.

A large part of my mission in the academy is to develop and deliver social work education that reveals the cultural bias embedded within systems intended to serve the public; to advance the understanding that we are no different from those we serve; to work together with our consumers in developing more effective services; to diminish the separation between the academy and our communities; and to increase the number of faculty whose actions support culturally diverse perspectives in all aspects of our lives.

Where will we be in 300 years? What will we leave as a legacy for the generations to come? Will we continue the struggle between Eastern and Western perspectives to our ultimate destruction? Or will we transform this destructive path by practicing social justice that respects and honors our pluralism? In my humble opinion, such a transformation will require continual examination of our penchant for dualities and imperialist habits and continual practice of deep insight into our real fears about being.

> There is no birth, no death; no this no that; no high no low; no more beautiful. The wave does not have to die in order to become water. The wave is water in this very moment. (Nhat Hanh, 2002, pp. 170–171)

REFERENCES

Ethier, K., & Deaux, K. (1990). Hispanics in ivy: Assessing identity and perceived threat. *Sex Roles, 22*(7/8), 427–440.

Hata, T. H., Hills, D., & Hata, N. I. (1995). *Japanese Americans and World War II: Exclusion, internment, and redress.* Wheeling, IL: Harlan Davidson.

Kitano, H. (1982). Mental health in the Japanese-American community. In E. E. Jones & S. J. Korchin (Eds.), *Minority mental health.* New York: Praeger.

Nhat Hanh, T. N. (2002). *No death, no fear.* New York: Riverhead Books.

Nisbett, R. E. (2003). *The geography of thought: How Asians and Westerners think differently and why.* New York: Free Press.

Phinney, J. S. (1988). *The development of ethnic identity in adolescents.* Presentation at Utah State University Workshop on Identity Formation, Utah State University, Logan.

Phinney, J. S. (1991). Ethnic identity and self-esteem: A review and integration. *Hispanic Journal of Behavioral Sciences, 13*(2), 193–208.

Phinney, J. S. (1993). A three-stage model of ethnic identity development in adolescence. In M. E. Bernal & G. P. Knight (Eds.), *Ethnic identity: Formation and transformation among Hispanics and other minorities* (pp. 61–79). Albany, NY: State University of New York Press.

Phinney, J. S., & Chavira, V. (1992). Ethnic identity and self-esteem: An exploratory longitudinal study. *Journal of Adolescence, 15*, 271–282.

Pukui, M. K., & Elbert, S. H. (1986). *Hawaiian dictionary.* Honolulu, HI: University of Hawai`i Press.

Spencer, M. B. (1987). Black children's ethnic identity formation: Risk and resilience of caste-like minorities. In J. S. Phinney & M. J. Rotheram (Eds.), *Children's ethnic socialization: Pluralism and development.* (pp. 103–116). Newbury Park, CA: Sage Publications.

HEROINE
Renuka Sooknanan

It is in understanding
the depths of this struggle,
to approach the crossroads
and not know the boundaries
because for us there are none.
It is to caress a flickering lamp
glowing a beautiful hope
because darkness is sure to follow.
In this struggle,
we,
I understand
my heroine
is today, was yesterday
will be tomorrow.
Marching somewhere
chanting loudly
writing feverishly
sleeping seldomly
between resisting and battle
never knowing
what strength is needed
to rise out of bed
to congregate amongst the hungry
        masses
fighting for the revolution.
My heroine is someone
I don't know.
(Renuka Sooknanan, 1995, p. 98)

Part II: The Voices of Women of Color as Social Work Educators

Chapter 14: Demons and Bunnies With Red Wings: A Tale About Navigating Academic Life Through the Lens of Ethnicity, Class, Gender, Sexual Orientation, and Luck

Debora M. Ortega

This chapter is dedicated to my first dean at the University of Kansas, Ann Weick. While she may not have always seen the demons or understood the bunnies, she always managed to recognize my gifts and talents. Her strength, integrity, and the respect she bestowed on all her faculty and staff will forever be a model of "deaning" at its best. Thank you, Ann, for the lessons learned.

Not surprisingly, I have started the chapter about my experience in academia with a title that reflects the end of the story rather then the beginning. I am, of course, supposed to communicate like that—all the researchers tell me it is so—that Latinos tell a story in a nonlinear fashion. The telling of the story has many twists and turns, and the journey that occurs for the listener as the story unfolds is as valuable as the story itself (Elliot, Adams, & Sockalingam, 1999). Of course, each listener judges the actual value of the story.

The characters in the title of this chapter, demons and bunnies with red wings, became significant to me in the year after I was awarded tenure. The demons and the bunnies have always been more or less present. Well, perhaps the truth is that, while they are always present, at times, I have been less aware of their presence. It has been since I obtained tenure that I have had the luxury or maybe felt compelled to reflect equally on my career as it has been and what it might be destined to become. It is in the thinking of "who I am" and "who I will become" that the demons and bunnies become animated.

THE DEMONS

The distinct features of my demons are personal, but they originated in my encounters with injustice, discrimination, and prejudice. At their core, the demons are made up of those insecurities experienced by all people regardless of race, ethnicity, class, gender, and sexual orientation: the small insecurities that find their way into your mind, that question your competence, abilities, and judgments that grow to large proportions after being fed by the societal, institutional, or collegial demons. Oppression breathed life into the demons, but the exact form they take is of my own creation.

Even after so many years of living with demons, I still find myself taken aback by their presence. Currently, the most active demon is the "Counter-Affirmative Action" demon. I remember the day he appeared like an apparition. It was after I received my MSW degree, and I was serving on an ad-hoc admissions advisory board. It was the first time I had heard a discussion about an affirmative-action criteria for applicants of color. As I revisit the meeting in my memory, the discussion or at least the way the demon remembers the discussion is one that resonates with subtle messages of incompetence or substandard performance by students of color because they were of color. Students of color were reduced to a check mark in the box declaring their minority status. My reaction was not to engage in critical thinking about the messages I was hearing, but to immediately travel back in time to my own graduate-program admission. Had a reviewer, years earlier, decided to admit me only because of my color? I doubted my educational legitimacy despite high academic performance, awards, and successful completion of the program. I also questioned the very reason I was selected as a member of the ad hoc committee. Was I picked for my special talent, gift, or strength or because they needed a brown person? Like the emperor without clothes who discovers his nakedness, I wondered how many people asked and answered the same question about me. Alas, I fed the demon, and it grew.

Of course, I am not the only one who feeds the demon. I remember sharing the exciting news that I was admitted to the doctoral program at the University of Washington with a friend and fellow social work colleague. Her response was that I must have gotten in because of my "diversity." I found her comment so surprising given that we knew I had taught several courses as an adjunct faculty member, presented at national conferences, organized a statewide conference, participated in a research project, and served on numerous committees at the university. I consciously worked to create the strongest vitae to increase the chances I would be admitted to a doctoral program. I tried to beat the demon down with this awareness, but still it grew.

Demons do not necessarily become weaker as you advance in your career. I am reminded of an experience when I was an assistant professor. A senior faculty member, whose focus is prisons and jails, approached me about working with her on a large community meeting. The intent of the meeting was to have a forum for the community to discuss issues related to the reentry of incarcerated people into the community after completing their sentences. I was surprised by the request since the topic was far from my area of expertise. She assured me that her request was based on her experience with me as a remarkable facilitator of large and small groups. Of course, this was a proud moment. Someone I respected, a feminist and a senior faculty member, asked me to help her because of my exceptional skill. Ah, the demon was shrinking or at least asleep. Soon after, in a meeting with a White European American senior faculty member, when he asked why I was a key member of the planning group with a strong public presence, her response was about not being able to have one more White European American face on the stage in a community of predominantly people of color who were angry about the issue. After he left the meeting, she confessed that she was unsure why she had said that, and the real reason was because of my excep-

tional facilitation skills. She fed the demon a seven-course meal, and I added dessert as I tried to sort truth from fiction.

Demons are complex entities. Their presence is always uncomfortable. However, my response to the demons can be very productive. For instance, the Counter-Affirmative Action demon drives me into overachievement. I work hardest at exceeding the standard (in every category), not because of personal gratification, but to prove that *I am not the faculty candidate of color who was hired just because of her color even if she underachieves.* Thus speaks the demon voice that cracks the whip and judges the worth of my contributions.

The Antidemon

The bunny with the red wings is perhaps the antidemon. I learned about bunnies with red wings from a (famous) senior Latina social work scholar. She offered the story below in response to my request for advice about how my contribution and work could or should look like after receiving tenure.

The story is actually a children's tale about a young rabbit who is always wishing to be something he is not (Bailey, 1945). For example, while he is out one day he sees a duck and wishes for webbed feet. Another time he sees a puppy dog and wishes he had a puppy dog tail, and so on and so on. His mother reminds him that those characteristics are not about who he is, but are associated with "others." As often happens with these types of stories, our hero, after some sage advice from a hedgehog, stumbles across a wishing well. In the middle of the process of wishing, he sees a little red cardinal and, as he is apt to do, wishes spontaneously... for red wings. The not-surprising consequence is that the red wings emerge. Finding himself ordinary, or even lacking, the bunny sets his sights on being more like the "other."

The bunny is thrilled with his new acquisition although he is not sure exactly how to use them, resulting in one or two flying mishaps. Excited by his new wings, he hurries home to share his news with his biggest supporter, his mother. Of course, since her little son was an ordinary rabbit at the beginning of the day, his mother does not recognize him with his red wings and chases him out of the rabbit hole. Our hero is very confused and upset by his mother's actions. Not to be dissuaded, he sets out to see his other friends, duck and puppy dog. They, too, do not recognize the bunny and are troubled by this unnatural animal. As the bunny struggles with his new self, he also seeks home and friends and finds himself apart or in exile from his cultural connection and support.

Eventually, the bunny with the red wings makes his way back to hedgehog, who, being wise, recognizes the bunny's true self. Our miserable little hero struggles with being alone and having a gift that has become a great burden. Hedgehog sagely suggests a return trip to the wishing well as a remedy for the bunny's distress. Fortunately for our hero, the wishing well has one more wish to give, and so the red wings disappear. The bunny, excited and apprehensive, returns home to his mother. Immediately upon seeing her son, whom she fretted about all night, she not only recognizes, but welcomes him with all her love back to the bunny hole. Her response upon hearing of his adventure is to remind him that the gifts, talents, and strengths he possess-

es as part of his true nature are not only the essence of who he is, but how he is loved and identified by his family and friends. The taking on of someone else's valued characteristic not only made him unrecognizable, but burdened and isolated. The bunny's outward journey was the catalyst for the introspection he needed to recognize his unique contribution as a bunny.

The Moral

It has been seven months since I first heard the story of the bunny with the red wings. I have thought about the story and its tale of marginalization and reacceptance. The first time I heard it, I was reminded of old struggles that began long before my road to academia. I have always been successful in negotiating the school environment, and education is probably the most effective acculturation tool. Unbeknownst to my family, who encouraged me and hoped I would have educational success and receive an undergraduate degree, the process of acquiring that degree would change me in a way that would begin to make me seem like a different animal. I, of course, was not aware of any difference. Just like the bunny in the story, I was confused about my family's response.

As I acquired more degrees, the distance and difference between who I was in the *cuna* (cradle) of the family and who I was becoming as a social worker widened. Education gave me a different vocabulary, and social work education gave me a completely new set of tools with which to understand human interaction, permission to speak secrets out loud, and a demand for introspection that made the red wings beginning to emerge obviously painful. I was unprepared for this consequence of the metamorphosis.

It is still ironic to me that as a Chicana lesbian in a Catholic family, my educational experience alienated me more from my family than my coming-out experience. This could be because, although my awareness of my sexual identity was new, it did not alter who I was. It in fact reinforced all that I was. It was through education that I became a creature to whom they did not know how to relate, a part of them and apart from them.

THE BEGINNING OF THE STORY

One of the gifts of master's level social work education is the focus on a self-reflective process. It is one thing to be a bunny walking around with red wings and quite another not to know you have red wings or not know that you are a bunny. It was in my MSW program that I became aware of the degree to which I had morphed into something that was not quite bunny and not quite cardinal. Despite this realization, I was sure that my true self was (and is) a social worker, a Latina social worker. The true gift of social work to me was its history, values, and ethics, which acted like a compass pointing north to the rabbit hole.

The Journey

Like most journeys, the journey down the road of academia did not begin with my being empty-handed (or empty-headed). I brought with me a confidence in who I was/am as a social worker, a belief about the purpose of the profession, well-developed practice skills, a keen sense of group development and dynamics, and the feeling that completing a PhD was not for my personal edification, but was a responsibility to my family and to *la Raza* (technically, the definition is "the Race;" in this context, it is more like "the People").

While I understand that the sense of responsibility is a strong cultural value for Latino people, I am confused about how this cultural tenet could be so strong in a second-generation American. Cultural responsibility—family responsibility—cultural responsibility—family responsibility. . . these two aspects of my life melt into one responsibility. This hybrid responsibility can feel like *una carga* (a burdensome load). It compelled me to stop doing social work with child-welfare families, a job I loved, and begin my doctoral program in the hope that I could have a greater impact on the lives of vulnerable children and families. Responsibility has also been the *bestia de la carga* (beast of burden), carrying me past barriers and over hurdles that I felt certain would derail me from my lofty goals (i.e., finishing the PhD and being awarded tenure). I find myself at the same time stronger for being part of a collective identity and paradoxically marginalized for not being Mejicana or Xicana. Yet, the beast of burden carries me, even today, on my journey despite my feelings of being an "internal exile," as described by Judy Baca (Neumaier, 1990).

CONCLUSION

As a woman of color and a lesbian social work academic who is connected yet disconnected, *comadres* (women who are connected to me because we live in solidarity)[1] and mentors have helped me find my way through the academic system. *Comadres* are those rare women who share most of the characteristics that make me not quite bunny and not quite cardinal. Their stories of their journey to and

---

[1] A union of interest and purpose and sympathies among group members (adapted from http://www.wordreference.com/definition/solidarity).

through the world of academia validate my own experience. Those moments, which usually take place at some social work conference, remind me that social work has its own bunnies-with-red-wings culture. *Comadres* offer comfort by wiping away the illusion that one is standing alone on the margins. I always attend our major social work conferences because they allow me to strengthen and feed my relationships with my *comadres* over time. These connections, which might happen over an hour or two, sustain me for a year. It is not so much the content of the conversation, but the feeling that I am standing together with another like-minded, like-experienced bunny. My relationships with *comadres* strengthen and gain depth and texture as we learn life lessons that exceed the boundaries of academia.

Mentors are the second most important tool for the academic journey. Mentors are much different from *comadres*. Mentors can be women of color or lesbian, but, in my life, they are seldom both (being both is such a rarity that they often end up being *comadres*). In my case, the longest-lasting mentoring relationships have been with mentors who emerged naturally rather than those who have been assigned by an institution. The value of mentors is in their ability to interpret the academic system. They bring an understanding of the workings of the school or department that allows for the maximum benefit. For a new faculty member, deciphering governance documents, merit reviews, negotiations about work-load, and promotion-and-tenure committee information was not always straightforward. Learning to balance or to pay attention to the most valued components of our work as academics is the professional lesson my mentors have taught me.

Mentors are not quite hedgehogs; they are more like mother bunnies who can wrap an experience, no matter how painful, in words of wisdom. Advice-giving and wisdom emerge from their desire for your success.

So, in the end, I have yet to find the sage hedgehog to guide me to the ever elusive wishing well. I have, however, found other bunnies with red wings, blue wings, and purple wings. The generosity with which they have shared their stories, strengths, and accomplishments makes being not quite bunny and not quite cardinal less painful, and, in times of need, more than makes up for the mysterious wishing well. It is also possible that I am discovering the sage hedgehog everyday within myself and in the people who love, respect, and challenge me.

REFERENCES

Bailey, C. S. (1945). *The little rabbit who wanted red wings.* New York: Platt and Monk.

Elliot, C., Adams, T., & Sockalingam, S. (1999, September 31). *Tool kit for cross–cultural communication.* Retrieved March 8, 2005, from http://www.awesomelibrary.org/multiculturaltoolkit patterns.html

Neumaier, D. (1990). Judy Baca: Our people are the internal exiles. In G. Anzaldúa (Ed.), *Making face, making soul: Haciendo Caras: Creative and critical perspectives by feminists of color* (pp. 256–270). San Francisco: Aunt Lute Foundation Books.

Part II: The Voices of Women of Color as Social Work Educators

Chapter 15: Constructing a Bicultural Professional Identity

Carmen Ortiz Hendricks

I dedicate this chapter to Carmen Roman Velez, my grandmother and one of the smartest women I have known despite her third-grade education, and to Haydee Velez Ortiz, my mother and the hardest-working and most dedicated of mothers. I also want to acknowledge my two aunts, Lucy Velez and Rosaida Velez Santos. Without the love, support, and sacrifice of these four women, I would not be the woman I am today.

As earlier chapters demonstrate, Latinas who achieve some measure of professional status and success undergo a self-examination process throughout their careers as they struggle to bridge their personal identities with their publicly constructed selves. This chapter is a narrative about my experiences in constructing a professional identity without entirely sacrificing my Latina cultural identity. I wish to speak from personal experience and as a part of the sample under investigation in this book. I do not claim to speak for other Latina professionals, nor do I speak for other New York, Puerto Rican, social work educators. However, *mi esperanza*, or my hope is that other Latina professionals involved in similar struggles will realize that the contradictory and ambivalent feelings they experience are not simply a result of personal inadequacies, nor are they solely attributable to external, oppressive forces that seek to maintain the status quo. Rather, Latinas are members of distinct ethnic minority groups that pose a threat to the dominant, majority, White professional establishment simply by striving to realize personal ambitions and professional objectives and by demanding their share of the power and privilege associated with the academy.

Personal Biography

I am a light-skinned, Puerto Rican, New York, professional woman in my mid-50s. I was born in Puerto Rico, but raised in New York City since the age of three. I am 100% Puerto Rican dating back to my great-great-grandparents, which is a rare occurrence in this era of the Puerto Rican diaspora all over the world and Puerto Ricans' predisposition to intercultural marriage. My family raised me to believe that education was everything, and they sacrificed to provide me with 16 years of private Catholic schooling, piano lessons, and ballet classes. I was expected to be a genteel woman who would attract the right kind of husband. I only dated Irish Catholic boys, and naturally I married one 33 years ago. Since then, I earned my master's of social work

and my doctorate in social welfare. Following 25 years at Hunter College School of Social Work, where I rose from the rank of lecturer and field coordinator to tenured associate professor, I moved to Yeshiva University Wurzweiler School of Social Work, my doctoral alma mater, as associate dean and professor. I have worked in MSW programs for most of my 30-year career in academia.

Before proceeding, it may be useful to explain the difference in meaning between *Latino* and *Hispanic*. The Hispanic community in the United States is creating a new culture that is not exclusively the culture of its countries of origin, nor is it the assimilated, mainstream U.S. culture. The Hispanic culture is a unique blend of both. What to call this multiethnic and multiracial population is often debated. The label *Hispanic* was coined in the mid-1970s by federal bureaucrats in response to a concern that the government was misidentifying segments of the population by classifying those with ancestral ties to the Spanish culture as Chicano, Cuban, or Puerto Rican (Schmidt, 2003). Hispanic is used by those interested in advancing social and cultural goals, and this term generally refers to persons of Spanish origin who are Spanish speaking and often have Spanish surnames. *Latino* is a term used by those primarily concerned with equality and activism. It generally refers to persons who are of Caribbean and Central and South American ancestry and includes indigenous peoples who lived in these countries before the settlement of European and African peoples. Most Hispanics prefer to be identified by their national origins, which may have several variations, including Mexican, Mexican American, or Chicano (an indigenous and activist name), or a Puerto Rican may refer to herself as Borinqueña after the original island name, Boríqua. Most institutions of higher education "have not considered that the members of many racial and ethnic groups have complex identities based on class, generational status, gender, sexual orientation, ethnic identification, abilities, spirituality, etc. Some Hispanics are biracial or multiracial and resist being labeled as belonging to one single ethnic or racial group" (Schmidt, 2003, p. 2). Many Hispanics are a blend of European, African, and indigenous peoples, and it is difficult to categorize them, especially on census data, as belonging to any one racial group. For stylistic purposes, I use the terms interchangeably.

PROFESSIONAL JOURNEY

Growing Up Bicultural

Latina professionals confront many dilemmas growing up in a bicultural world. As members of a heterogeneous ethnic group where inter- and intragroup diversity is highly complex, Latinas struggle growing up in a world that ascribes to them a homogeneous identity. Latinas have very distinctive bicultural experiences depending on country of origin, birth in or outside the United States, skin color, social and economic class, sexual orientation, age at migration or immigration, mental and physical abilities, or religious training and education. Likewise, to survive, Latino families may strongly encourage acculturation to mainstream U.S. values by emphasizing Whiteness, nonaccented English, education as the road to success, intergroup marriage, and other assimilation techniques. But, as acculturated women, Latinas are also expected to adhere to Hispanic cultural norms and values (*respeto* or

respect, *familismo* or the importance of family, *personalismo* or intimately knowing another, and *dignidad* or the dignity of all living beings, *patria,* to maintain ethnic pride, and above all, *marianismo,* to be good and virtuous Latina women.

For Hispanics seeking a place in the mainstream, professional world of academia, biculturalism has a whole new meaning, with a host of attendant challenges. Latinas in the academy must adjust and survive in three cultures—the personal, the mainstream, and the professional—while fighting a sense of marginality in all three. A few of my personal experiences can best illustrate these points.

- Throughout my educational experiences in the 1950s, 1960s, 1970s, and later in the 1990s, I was the only Latina in my classes and the only student who was constantly asked questions about where I came from and whether I spoke Spanish. This uniqueness was a two-edged sword that made me feel "special," but that contributed to my sense of strangeness or difference.

- Hispanic people were rarely mentioned in classroom discussions and never as scientists, poets, scholars, teachers, philosophers, artists, or as leaders or positive role models. Desi Arnaz, Carmen Miranda, and Xavier Cugat were the popular role models of my childhood.

- In college, as a Spanish literature major, I studied the historical, as well as literary contributions of Hispanics. Yet, in four years of study, not one Puerto Rican novelist, playwright, or poet was ever part of the curriculum.

- In graduate school, instructors mostly talked about the impoverished nature of Hispanic families because they primarily spoke Spanish at home, and being bilingual was looked upon as a form of cultural deprivation. I was systematically taught about the perceptual, cognitive, and linguistic problems of poor, minority children. I learned that cultural and linguistic deprivation were, in part, a result of maladaptive mother–child interactional styles that, in turn, contributed to poor school performance and low IQ scores.
- And, in the 1990s, I was the only Latina in my social work doctoral program.

These experiences failed to affirm the values of my culture and contributed to some measure of alienation and marginalization from my own culture of origin.

As a social work professional working primarily with African American and Latino families from diverse backgrounds and economically deprived communities, I began to question many of the assumptions or misconceptions I learned in graduate school. My practice did not always fit with the scientific, theoretical paradigms or skills learned in the classroom, agency, or in professional journals. I became keenly sensitive to and mistrustful of the political nature of social-science inquiry and began to question how social research could reflect the reality of Latinos, especially Puerto Ricans in the United States, more adequately.

When one grows up hearing denigrating remarks about one's race or culture, it makes it very difficult to maintain ethnic pride and avoid internalized oppression. One learns to listen selectively and question everything, including praise for one's accomplishments. Take, for example, the first time I read *La Vida* by Oscar Lewis (1966) and became aware of the influence of social-science theories on public opinion. Lewis introduced the notion of a "culture of poverty" in his study of a poor Puerto Rican family from the slums of San Juan and provided a sociological explanation for why its members remained poor. Lewis asserted that the poor develop a unique configuration of shared understanding in adapting to their common circumstances. In other words, the poor raise their young to accept circumstances they are familiar with, thus creating a vicious cycle of poverty. Culture based on socioeconomic status rather than common history became a popular factor in the explanation of racial and ethnic differences.

Similarly, Glazer and Moynihan's *Beyond the Melting Pot* (1970) asserted that "the Negro is only an American and nothing else. He has no values and culture to guard and protect" (p. 53). Such research stigmatized the Black family as promoting and perpetuating a "tangle of pathology," which was the "principal source of the aberrant, inadequate, or antisocial behavior that. . . serves to perpetuate the cycle of poverty and deprivation" (p. 76). This orientation blamed children's low IQ on the lack of intellectual stimulation in their homes. Family structures were blamed for most inadequacies among family members. Although considered passé, these concepts, grounded in "blaming the victim" (Ryan, 1971) ideology and a vision of "another America" (Harrington, 1962), remain in the thinking and practices of many American social workers in the 21st century.

The New Latina Professional

When I listen to non-Latino colleagues discuss Hispanic clients, I often become angered by the attitudes and misconceptions of professionals who implicitly or explicitly denigrate the Latino culture. Social workers have a duty to promote an underlying respect for culture and its inherent strengths (NASW, 2001), but it is an occupational hazard to focus on the harsh realities, vulnerabilities, and pathology of Latinos living in this society. Social workers tend to emphasize statistics of poverty, mental illness, illiteracy, child abuse, and chemical addictions among Latinos, but rarely explore the strengths and resiliency in Latino families that help them overcome barriers and achieve satisfaction in education, employment, and family life.

The social work profession also does not prepare White European American social workers adequately to work in communities of color. Many colleagues expressed fears about walking through "minority" neighborhoods, and these same colleagues assumed it was easier for African American or Latino social workers to "blend in" with the community. But, in reality, social workers do not easily blend in, be it in communities where they do understand culturally appropriate behaviors or in strikingly different environments. For example, I am completely fluent in both English and Spanish, but my non-Hispanic married name, speech, and light skin color set me up as a prime candidate for suspicion and mistrust. While my colleagues saw me as blending in, I had to deal with estrangement from my own culture. As an educated Latina professional, I attracted more attention in diverse neighborhoods. My professional clothes identified me as a middle-class, "high-tone" or "uppity" person who has somehow made her way out of the "hood" and is now returning to help those less fortunate than herself. One client properly characterized me as eager to leave her home to return to my nice suburban residence before it got too dark. To win her trust, I felt compelled at every opportunity to clarify and reaffirm my cultural identity. I would let her know where I was born in Puerto Rico; I would use Spanish slang or "Spanglish," a combination of English and Spanish words; and I would let people tell me things *en confianza* or in confidence, setting up powerful ethical conflicts and dilemmas. Sometimes in my zealousness to overcome class differences, I would be as patronizing as my White European American colleagues in my attempts to overcome differences and demonstrate my cultural competence.

I believe that class differences are more pronounced between women. When interactions between different social classes is minimal and when contacts are channeled only through social institutions such as schools or social service agencies, a great gulf opens up between Hispanic women. The professional, middle-class Latina social worker is first perceived by her Latina clients as an angel who speaks their language, knows what it is like to be a migrant or immigrant, and can really help with their problems. This positive transference can quickly give way to a negative transference in which the Latina worker becomes like all other social workers: an agent of the system, unhelpful, or ineffective.

I had to work hard to forestall these attitudes, establish rapport with families, and understand how clients perceived their realities. Gradually, Latina clients began to confide in me, disclosing their fears and misgivings about the world around them. They wanted their children to have a better start in life than they had, and they astutely recognized that opportunity brings hope as well as danger. The hope was that hard work and a little luck can make success a possibility for their children. The danger lurked in the form of too much "Americanization" and all the other bad things America can produce—disrespect for parents, denigration of the culture, and social problems like drug abuse, unwanted pregnancies, gangs, and racial profiling. They feared for their children. Success means having access to economic resources that have been denied to these Latina women no matter how hard they worked, but success also means that their children may "grow away" from them in very profound ways. I was particularly sensitive to this cultural alienation, having experienced painful estrangement from my own family as I became more educated, Americanized, and professional.

Latina mothers reinforced for me the true meaning of biculturalism. They socialized their children to be bicultural, which meant teaching them to interact competently within their own cultural and familial environment as well as outside in mainstream society, while simultaneously exhorting their children not to give up their culture of origin. If these mothers were successful in their parenting, their children would be able to draw from the experiences and values of both, but maintaining a healthy bicultural perspective is hard work. How exactly do Latinas prepare themselves to move effectively into mainstream society while still maintaining

the home-culture identity? How can educational institutions be more effective settings for the intellectual and emotional development of bilingual and bicultural identities? How can research more adequately reflect and account for the reality of the bicultural experience?

Latinas may be trained to be bicultural in their homes and outside in the broader community, but a college education is yet another cultural experience that challenges their bicultural identities. There is a prescribed way to talk as an educated person and within a professional community. Professional jargon or the language of "academese" is difficult to master, and it serves both to define group membership and to obscure meaning. Latinas and other bicultural people have to develop a third set of interactional styles, becoming, in effect, tricultural or transcultural. These tricultural interactional skills are especially useful when Latinas need to "switch hats" when speaking to different people in different contexts—professor to student, client to worker, and worker to worker. This is an added burden of or major strength in maintaining a tricultural identity.

Affirmative Action

A great deal of legislation designed to reduce social inequality was passed during the 1960s and 1970s, and some Latinos were notably influenced by increased employment and education opportunities. I am one of the lucky beneficiaries of this "enlightened" legislation. While most Latino clients remained below the national income average or continued to live in highly stressful environmental conditions, some of us earned scholarships, graduated from college, and succeeded in gaining status through employment in certain professions. If one was a hard worker and spoke Spanish, one was in demand, especially in most social agencies. In the 70s and 80s, speaking Spanish seemed more important than the initials after my name. I was often the only Latina on a social work staff and felt exploited and misunderstood. My status reinforced feelings of tokenism, and of being the exception to the rule and the one Latina permitted to make it into the mainstream. These feelings are not unlike survivor guilt, which produces an intense cultural consciousness and a passionate yearning for equality and autonomy for myself and others like me.

Latinas who are successful professionals encounter yet another jeopard: that their success is not their own. Success, failure, or even the smallest acts reflect on all Latinos. Educational institutions, for the most part, have supported affirmative action. Latinos and other students of color are the visible evidence of a university's reparations for society's past injustices. Implicitly stated in affirmative-action initiatives is the belief that academic or job-performance standards are lowered to grant admission to students or workers of color, and they, in turn, are held responsible for lowering standards. Furthermore, if a Latina succeeds, she is seen as the exception to the rule and a credit to her race or ethnic group. But, by their very success, Latinas cease to be members of the group they supposedly represent and risk jeopardizing their membership in the Latino community.

I can attest to my struggles with this double-bind situation, and I have generally struggled in isolation. Often I thought, "If I fail, all Latinas fail, but if I succeed, I am an exception and bring attention to other Latinas who are unable to achieve in similar fashion." Successful Latinas are expected to be both representative of and exceptional for their culture or find some way to neither succeed nor fail. This double-bind might account for the fact that many Latina social work students are reticent to share their work or to ask for help. Perhaps this is out of fear of confirming White European American student or faculty beliefs that they are unprepared or not up to par. As a teacher, I have noted that Latinas are often reluctant to speak in the classroom, to ask for clarification, or to offer an opinion. Latinas may also hide their intellectual uncertainty from each other rather than admit openly that they have internalized a great deal of insecurity that is very real on a daily basis. I work to encourage all students to speak their minds and express their personal and professional opinions. Avoidance is partly due to the recognition that questions and opinions are seldom heard without awareness of the racial and ethnic characteristics of the speaker. Sometimes, the very presence of a Latina professor in the classroom frees students of color to speak more openly.

Another dilemma is that when a Latina takes a stand on an issue related to race or ethnicity, it is generally assumed that all Latinos share the same opinion. As a result, an awesome burden is placed on vocal Latinas, who feel compelled to serve as unofficial spokespersons for the Hispanic culture and community. Many Latinas resent this onus of responsibility, while, at the same time, recognizing a social responsibility to pursue and explain relevant racial and ethnic issues. Evidently, the repetitive negative messages in the university environment or the professional community have a serious impact on Latinas as students, researchers, scholars, and practitioners.

The Experienced Latina Professional

There are no easy answers to ease the impact of these crosscultural dilemmas. However, experienced Latina professionals may easily be overwhelmed by the sheer numbers of less experienced Latinas seeking their help and advice. Latino faculty cannot afford to overextend themselves when their attention needs to be directed toward university politics and playing the tenure and promotion game for their own survival—activities that take precedence, but are less enjoyable than mentoring young Latino professionals. Latina faculty do not want students to see how their careers are totally determined by White European American academic standards or how powerless they really are in the academy. Student ethnic organizations can offer some support and a comfortable environment in which Latinas can discuss the issues and frustrations unique to their experience. However, there exists the need to maintain or save face by appearing competent and strong to one's Latino peers. A negative sanction from one's own ethnic group is far more devastating than one from White European American colleagues. Nonetheless, Latinas need to seek out mentors and friends who can help ease the stresses encountered in academia. Mentors can encourage Latinas to explore nontraditional approaches to research, to safely challenge ideas, and to force Latinas to clarify subjective and unsubstantiated concerns about their teaching or research endeavors.

Based on my personal experiences, these dilemmas do not disappear, but follow Latinas beyond graduate school and into places of employment, postdoctoral work, and in all academic and professional environments. In fact, sometimes the problems seem to intensify rather than diminish with time and progress. For example, it is well documented that women of color experience multiple role and identity conflicts (Babcock, Burpee, & Steward, 2001; Home, 1997a, 1997b). As a Latina professional, I am expected to be an objective teacher and scholar and yet hold on to my subjective Latino perspective both within and outside the academy. This contradiction creates anxiety and a feeling of futility, emotions that can inhibit creativity and productivity. One's minority status and visibility are ever present and always apparent to students and other colleagues. In paraphrasing Becker's 1963 work, *Outsiders*, "whether one is a physician or middle-class or female will not protect them from being a [Latina] first and any other of these things second" (p. 33).

In fulfilling their professional roles, Latinas interact increasingly more with the White European American power structure and significantly less with members of their own ethnic community. Many Latinas fear losing distinctive cultural qualities and identities completely. Coping with conflicts between different belief systems is not a new experience for Latinas; however, they are often unprepared for the personal transformations they must undergo. Extended interactions with White European American colleagues and exposure to different ways of thinking can alter worldviews and change Latinas' ways of thinking. It is painful to return to one's roots or homeland only to discover that one has changed and is now a stranger, a marginal member within one's own ethnic community. I have suffered deep, emotional turmoil when I have found myself detached from my own ethnic community and alienated in the mainstream professional world.

This leads to "double marginality," defined as belonging to and feeling a part of two worlds, yet never at home in either. This is similar to "double consciousness," which W. E. B. DuBois (1961) described as "a peculiar sensation . . . this sense of always looking at one's self through the eyes of others, of measuring one's soul by the tape of a world that looks on in amused contempt and pity. One always feels his two-ness. . . An American, a Negro, two souls, two thoughts, the unreconciled striving. . . two warring ideals in one dark body whose dogged strength alone keeps it from being torn asunder" (pp. 16–17). It is of little consequence to a Latina to be recognized and respected for her contributions, scholarship, or leadership if she is not accepted as a complete woman by her family and peers. As Mitchell (1982) advised, "What is required is a summation and integration of our personal and professional experiences into a meaningful synthesis both for self and the profession" (p. 39).

Problems and stresses already inherent in being a minority woman and a professional are compounded when the ideologies of the two reference groups contradict and conflict. In an attempt to sustain a feasible balance between cultural and social identities, I often find myself in a no-win situation:

1. If I sell out and totally embrace the Western, White European American system, I might enjoy some of its benefits and rewards, yet negate valued parts of myself as a Latina woman. Selling out or denying one's culture is the ultimate compromise a Latina can make.

2. If I completely reject the White European American power structure, I may not be any better off as I forfeit the opportunity to influence it in ways that will create a more receptive and responsive atmosphere for my cultural input and for those who follow me.

3. Therefore, I have to "buy in" by strategizing to gain power within the system and to ultimately influence social, political, and educational policies and to offer alternative theories and interpretations of research data and findings.

I believe that ethnic integrity is compromised less by buying into the system and negotiating for power from within than from the outside looking in. There is a fine line between "selling out" and "buying in." Fear of going too far distinguishes the concerned professional from the "sellout." As professional social workers—practitioners, educators, researchers, and administrators—Latinas are at risk, vulnerable to charges from either side of selling out or of being written off as nothing more than an agitator rather than a serious practitioner or scholar. Perhaps this is why Latinas are overly cautious before speaking or writing about the Latino experience, hoping that their statements and opinions accurately and fairly reflect the Latino experience in general and not merely their subjective experiences. Since research is a vehicle for effecting social change, Latinas need to carefully consider the possible consequences their work might have on other Latinos or the Latino community in general.

A healthy paranoia emerges for Latinas as they deal with being co-opted by the system. It is a fear that evolves from hearsay or from having one's words or work used for purposes of "surveillance" aimed at Latinos. It is a fear that one's scholarship may unwittingly be used against Latinos or for purposes other than those intended. It is a mistrust of any research that investigates the Latino experience. The central dilemma in my scholarship and research is that Latinos are embedded in the same environment that denies the complexity of their experiences. The social sciences are based on the premises and methods of the very systems Latinos need to question. It is a fundamental fear of exploitation and co-option.

Low-income Latinos have been subjected to countless research studies on diabetes, substance abuse, smoking, school dropout, teenage pregnancies, bilingual education and learning disabilities, illiteracy, child abuse, poverty, and mental illness. Puerto Rico was the "natural laboratory" for early research into the effects of contraceptive pills. The negative consequences of past research do not make Latina scholars receptive to research as a positive change agent. Latinos should be mistrustful of Latino or non-Latino researchers seeking entry into their communities. Latina researchers must not only criticize standard research on their communities, but they must also propose viable alternatives and promote socially responsible research.

Objectivity is critical. As a Latina, I am often in the position of conducting research on my own racial and ethnic group. Being a member of the ethnic group under study has advantages and disadvantages. As a Latina, I can bring a two-prong analysis to data by applying an objective interpretation as well as a sociocultural perspective. It is difficult to remain objective about research issues when they affect one directly. Research cannot be completely value-free, and ethical neutrality is something to strive for, but hard to achieve. Latina scholars are compelled to strive for true objectivity, even when the values, beliefs, and priorities of Latinos are violated by existing research methods. I cannot violate the standards of those methods if I am to be considered a respectable researcher. How does one objectively study a population that is considered "deviant" when the researcher is a member of the "deviant" group? Does empathy for the population under study enhance or distort the nature of research? Latino scholars, a growing constituency within the social work profession, have a great deal to contribute to social work research and scholarship if they are free to pursue their perception of social reality. For example, we need to encourage crosscultural interdisciplinary approaches that use inductive methods of ethnographic research to describe behaviors in natural situations and to investigate behaviors in terms of experiences and practices that are culturally relevant. Ethnographic data can enable scholars to understand how context affects and guides particular behaviors.

There is a dearth of research on successful Latinas or their educational and occupational aspirations. Little is available that distinguishes the experiences of majority and minority women as professionals or scholars. Research has identified major stressors for female minority students, including fear of success; sex-role attitudes and stereotyping; and role strain and conflicts (Babcock, Burpee, & Stewart, 2001; Baruch & Barnett, 1987; Egan, 2004; Fortune, 1987; Gibbs, 1984; Greenberger & O'Neil,

1993; Ortiz Hendricks, 1993; Home, 1997a, 1997b; Reeser, MacDonald, & Wertkin, 1992). To a large extent, professional education and practice ignore Latina strategies to survive with their professional and personal selves intact. Schools of social work and professional organizations can make a significant contribution by recognizing that Latino perceptions of social reality can contribute to rather than detract from all fields of practice.

CONCLUSION

Skeptical, frustrated, and yet optimistic, I know I have made a valuable contribution to the profession, and, as a middle-aged I still have a great deal to contribute to social work scholarship and to leadership within the profession. I am recognized for scholarship on culturally competent social work practice and education, including field education, Latino issues, and child-welfare practice. I was president of the New York City chapter of the National Association of Social Workers (NASW) and president of the Association of Latino Social Work Educators. I have sat on the boards of NASW and the Council on Social Work Education (CSWE). I am a founding member of a New York City Latino Task Force that is currently strategizing to develop the Latino social work workforce and to increase the number of culturally competent social work graduates who can effectively meet the needs of the growing Hispanic community. And I am the first Latina to become associate dean at a prominent New York City School of Social Work, which positions me to influence social work education in a very fundamental way.

The contradictions that I and many other Latina professionals experience are still an organizing force in my life. I work hard to insure that my scholarship adequately reflects the reality of Latino lives, and I strive to make a difference in Latino communities. I want all social workers to become culturally competent practitioners and teachers. I am hopeful that this book can help to ease the stress on the next generation of Hispanic scholars and inspire them to deal with the contradictions in constructive ways. We all need to reconstruct our multiple cultural identities. *Siempre hay esperanza!* There is always hope!

REFERENCES

Babcock, M. D., Burpee, M. R., & Stewart, R. G. (2001). Sources of stress and coping strategies of full-time MSW students. *Arete, 25*(2), 87–95.

Baruch, G., & Barnett, R. (1987). Role quality and psychological well-being. In F. J. Crosby (Ed.), *Spouse, parent, worker: On gender and multiple roles* (pp. 63–73). New Haven, CT: Yale University Press.

Becker, H. S. (1963). *Outsiders: Studies in the sociology of deviance.* London: The Free Press of Glencoe.

DuBois, W. E. B. (1961). *The souls of Black folk.* Greenwich, CT: Fawcett.

Egan, S. (2004). *Multiple roles of female graduate students, role strain, and culturally competent organizational practice.* Unpublished doctoral dissertation, Fordham University, New York.

Fortune, A. E. (1987). Multiple roles, stress and well-being among MSW students. *Journal of Social Work Education, 23,* 81–90.

Gibbs, J. T. (1984). Conflicts and coping strategies of minority female graduate students. In B. W. White (Ed.), *Color in a White society* (pp. 22–36). Silver Spring, MD: NASW Press.

Glazer, N., & Moynihan, D. P. (1970). *Beyond the melting pot: The Negroes, Puerto Ricans, Jews, Italians, and Irish of New York City* (2nd ed.). Cambridge, MA: MIT Press.

Greenberger, E., & O'Neil, R. (1993). Spouse, parent, worker: Role commitments and role-related experiences in the construction of adults' well-being. *Developmental Psychology, 29*, 181–197.

Harrington, M. (1962). *The other America: Poverty in the United States.* New York: Macmillan.

Hendricks, C. O. (1993). *Cross cultural conflicts in social work education: The Latino experience.* Unpublished doctoral dissertation, Yeshiva University, New York.

Home, A. M. (1997a). Learning the hard way: Role strain, stress, role demands and support in multiple-role women students. *Journal of Social Work Education, 33*, 335–346.

Home, A. (1997b). The delicate balance: Demand, support, role strain and stress in multiple role women. *Social Work and Social Sciences Review, 7*(3), 131–143.

Lewis, O. (1966). *La vida: A Puerto Rican family in the culture of poverty–San Juan and New York.* New York: Random House.

Mitchell, J. (1982). Reflections of a black social scientist: Some struggles, some doubts, some hopes. *Harvard Educational Review, 52*(1), 27–44.

National Association of Social Workers (NASW). (2001). *Code of ethics and standards for cultural competence in social work practice.* Washington, DC: Author.

Reeser, L. C., MacDonald, F., & Wertkin, R. A. (1992). Enhancing student coping and modifying the stressful academic environment: Advice from students and faculty. *Journal of Teaching in Social Work, 6*(2), 87–97.

Ryan, W. (1971). *Blaming the victim.* New York: Pantheon Books.

Schmidt, P. (2003, November 28). Academe's Hispanic future. *Chronicle of Higher Education,* A8.

Part II: The Voices of Women of Color as Social Work Educators

Chapter 16: Working From Can't See to Can't See

Dianne Rush Woods

I'd like to dedicate this chapter to my sons, who have shared my life and my relationship with the academy for the past nine years. I appreciate their sacrifice and their contribution to the richness of my life.

My name is Dianne Rush Woods. I am an African American woman in my 50s. A long-time resident of San Francisco/Bay Area, I have two sons, three sisters, two brothers, and a large extended and fictive kin network. I believe in myself and my ability to accomplish much in life (academically, spiritually, and socially). I returned to school to complete my PhD following a 20-year absence. However, the University of California–Berkeley (UC–Berkeley) has always been my home school. I am a 1960s Special Opportunity Services (SOS)/Upward Bound Program graduate. I spent all of my summers from eighth

Felicea!
I hope that you enjoy my story!
Diane

grade through 12th on the UC–Berkeley campus in supportive classes and tutorials. In addition, the staff of this program helped me apply to a number of prestigious colleges and universities. I attended Scripps College, received my BA in sociology from UC–Berkeley, my MSW from University of California–Los Angeles (UCLA), and finally returned to complete my studies in social welfare (PhD) and public health (MPH) at UC–Berkeley.

My life in academia has been wonderfully transformative and challenging. I am a tenure-track assistant professor (up for tenure and promotion this year) and have taught at California State University–East Bay (CSU East Bay), formerly known as California State–Hayward, for six years. The social work MSW program at California State University–East Bay is two years old as of 2005. I helped to develop the program from the ground up. I served alongside the chair of the department as one of the two original faculty members. The first class of 50 students graduated in Spring 2005. I was a faculty marshal during our first graduation ceremony. I was also on the field organizing our students, making sure they lined up to receive recognition as our first graduating class, and hugging them as they came off the stage after their names were called. It was a humbling and wonderful moment.

Before teaching in the MSW program, I taught in the social-services portion of an undergraduate sociology department at the same university. I coordinated the field-placement component of that program and taught policy, human behavior and the social environment, and introduction to social welfare courses.

PERTINENT PAST HISTORY

When I was in seventh grade, I walked into my first junior-high-school class, English, and my teacher, Mrs. Jones, an African American female, looked at me and said, "Dear, you must be in the wrong classroom." The class was printed on my schedule, but, not believing I was assigned to her class because her students typically were White European American and Asian American students, she sent me to the office to correct my schedule.

Forty years later, I still remember this comment, along with the comment from my so-called academic advisor, who advised me to take typing because, "Dear, you won't be going to college." Consequently, it is my desire not to stand in the way of or make assumptions about my students. I want to be of service to them, providing them with a caring, supportive educational experience. I also want to assist them in divesting themselves of or examining closely their own personal biases concerning race, gender, socioeconomic status (SES) and class, culture and language, disability, and oppression.

Student Experience

Academic environments have always felt like home to me. My mother, Alice Rush, supported my love of education and of school. She allowed me to spend long summer days at the main library in Oakland reading everything I could get my hands on. She valued education, but, as a sharecropper's daughter, she was never able to complete high school. However, she returned to school during my adolescence, and we graduated from high school and received our degree and certificate in the same year. She pushed me to go further in education.

Like my mother, I always worked. I have never just attended school, so academic life was always accompanied by the need to survive financially. My mother could help only so much. I qualified for scholarships and actively sought employment, but the obligation to work and support myself changed the college experience. I became a combination student and emancipated working young person. I completed six years of school and graduated with an MSW from UCLA. Two years later, I was awarded my license by the California Board of Behavioral Sciences. I worked as a therapist and clinician and manager for 20 years. The world was pretty wide open for young social workers. I specialized in working in hospital-based programs and then moved to employee-assistance work and managed care. As director of two national provider-relations networks, I began to feel the need to do something different and to do something more.

Completing the PhD program was that something more, and it proved to be both a transformative and demanding process. As a single mother, I struggled to raise two young African American boys successfully while pursuing my degree. The challenges were tremendous. Simple issues like conflicts between the times of mandatory classes, school, and childcare schedules drove me crazy. We moved to a university-sponsored family housing unit, the Village, which probably saved my life. In this rather tranquil environment, I was able to focus on the task of completing my PhD and MPH.

The Village was heavenly for a single mom. Childcare was available, and schools were excellent and nearby. The courtyard in which I lived offered the opportunity to develop friendships with many who were traveling the same road and struggling with the dual roles of parenting and academia. Clearly, if I had been a young, single, or married woman with no children, the journey would have been a different experience.

As I grew accustomed to the school schedule, I learned to rise very early (5:00 or 6:00 a.m.), study, exercise, and then launch my children's day. I then rushed to campus and, with the help of a circle of friends I developed in my program, completed coursework, my papers, oral examinations, and the dissertation. My cohort was small, but it included some incredible individuals who were collectively oriented. I was the only woman of color in our group, so friendships and support were, by default, crosscultural. We developed study groups, met in dyads and triads to master difficult subjects, experimented with courses outside the department, and eventually formed a dissertation group to ensure the success of individuals in our cohort.

One activity I did forgo was participation in the research centers at UC–Berkeley. This may have been to my disadvantage because I was not connected closely to any particular academic mentor and I did not coauthor publications while in the PhD program. But I was able to publish a book on managed care early in my academic career. I worked with a colleague and friend, Gayle Tuttle, on *The Managed Care Answer Book for Mental Health Professionals*, which was published by Brunner/Mazel in 1997.

My job as an employee-assistance therapist at the university health center helped me keep my work activity separate from school. The job gave me a sense of autonomy since I was very concerned with the infantilization that occurred in class and the dependence on faculty for obtaining a graduate-student researcher position. Since I was and am interested in teaching, I was more interested in the opportunity to serve as a graduate-student instructor. These opportunities were rare, but, over time, I was able to present and build up my confidence in teaching.

Completing the dissertation and walking in the Black graduation ceremony at UC–Berkeley were two of the high points of my life. My sons both graduated around this time (one from high school, the other from elementary school). It was a wonderful time of transition for all of us.

PROFESSIONAL JOURNEY

Challenges and Struggles

I was raised in a rich oral tradition that sometimes conflicts with the flow required for academic writing and presentation. I struggled to master linear forms of communication (scholarly writing) during my PhD program following 20 years of absence from the university. Academic writing and understanding the shape and rationale of statistics were essentially language-acquisition issues for me. Orally and visually oriented, I was able to work in a community of peers to acquire the necessary mastery.

This struggle makes it easier for me to understand the difficulty certain students have with the academic environment. As a first-generation student from a very poor family, I can often spot those students who feel that maybe the challenge is too much and that they have possibly made a mistake by returning to college. I am willing to assist them and guide them to resources that helped me in my struggle to excel in the academy. Students are often inspired when they learn that being born and raised in poverty, being a first-generation student, and struggling with writing need not prohibit them from succeeding academically.

There is another side to the coin; because it is clearly possible to succeed academically, my students are pushed to go the extra step. One student who recently graduated said:

> Professor Woods, I know that you do not remember this. However, when I was first in your class, I handed in a paper. You read it and gave it back to me without a grade. You said, "I know that you can do better than this. This is what I want you to do. Take the extra time and make the corrections." You do not know what a difference this made to me. No one had ever stopped and taken the time and said, "I know that you can do better than that." Not only did you take the time, but you also told me what and how.

My own challenges in terms of academic writing and the linear process have made me keenly aware of the need to support, encourage, and push students to excel. The assistance I received at UC–Berkeley when I needed it made it clear that academic excellence has as much to do with the support you receive as with what you produce, especially for students of color, who often feel like "strangers in a strange land." Since faculty of color are still a rarity in the academy, we can journey together and create a meaningful environment for students from lower socioeconomic backgrounds and first-generation college attendees.

My Professional Needs

At this point, the most urgent challenge is that of tenure, but I do have the support of my chair and dean. Each year thus far, I have been granted retention; however, I am still concerned by my intense involvement in the work of the department and the accreditation process. The accreditation process, preparation for classes, administrative requirements, and other university-related work make it difficult, if not impossible, to focus on this important piece of work, as well as other writing projects. I have been able to complete several journal articles and continue to work on a textbook. It became important to verbalize my concerns to my chair in order to be able to prioritize this academic time.

In the midst of all this, I need to find time to work on issues other than academic matters. Rather than having more time with my family, I have less. There is a strong expectation that we be present on campus even on the days we are not teaching. This was not my initial understanding, but it is an unspoken understanding in our department. Carving out family time when I need to be at work at all times is extremely difficult. I definitely need mentoring to assist with this issue. In all, the most daunting challenge is having too many priorities, far too little time, and too few supports to manage them all.

Dealing With Resistance and Racism Amongst the Student Population

I think my assertiveness and grounding in African American culture can be off-putting. Sticking to my guns about class conduct and the quality of the work expected of my students is very important to me. Expecting students to be respectful is also of great importance. On the other hand, according to Bradley (2005), the "most jutting theme in the literature on African American women faculty is their unappreciated presence in the classroom." It is generally recognized that women faculty often receive unequal treatment from students. However, recent studies and writings have documented that some White European American college students perceive African American women professors to be incompetent and feel at liberty to challenge their authority. I have been amazed at the unprofessional, White-privilege-based behavior of some students. One of them challenged the decision-making process for a scholarship. Once I explained the process, he continued to quiz me concerning reasons for the decision. His inability to get what he desired concerning a scholarship turned into a campaign to have me identified as either incompetent or unethical. Unfortunately, he was able to partner with a faculty colleague to further some of his actions. From time to time, it felt like a spiritual lynching.

Another struggle I have to deal with is the strong Black woman stereotype. I have to be careful not to allow myself to be sucked into the "work-horse" role. Being strong at work helped with the task of creating a new social work department with an African American chair and later a Vietnamese male peer. I found that, by the third year, I began to burn out. I took on too many tasks, and it became the expectation that I do so. I found that I just was not able to work from "can't see to can't see" without giving up my life, my family, my research agenda, and my writing. Further, there were those who depended on my hard work and who also wanted to take credit for it. I couldn't allow this, so I pulled back from working so hard. Wilma Kin, professor of history, discusses juggling family and the requirements of the academy. She chooses, from time to time, to step back from professional development and to support family (King, 1996). I want to balance the two, but it is quite difficult.

Strengths and Ambitions

As a strong, assertive African American woman, I am proud of my heritage and am pleased to operate in a multicultural and culturally respectful context. Grounded in the oral tradition, teaching, talking, and sharing words with students is a joy for me. Grounding students in theory and then exposing them to the real deal and what happens in the real world of social work is important to me. My family was very poor, which meant we dealt with both eligibility and social workers during my childhood. The experience was often not pleasant, but understanding it from the client perspective gives me a perspective that is helpful to students who want to "help" others.

Being a faculty member of color means that I have to deal with individuals who have yet to face their own racism and sexism. As an individual who lived before the era of integration and assimilation, I understand racism. As a woman who grew up in the 1950s and 1960s, I also understand sexism. Addressing racism, sexism, and other biases as they manifest in the classroom provides a vital wake-up call for students, especially White European American students, who believe these biases have been addressed and vanquished.

In terms of ambition, if the opportunity to chair the department became available, I would consider it. But, for now, I am focused on obtaining tenure. This struggle is the quintessential one that will ensure a more stable life. As Dr. Melvin Ramsey (2002) wrote in response to Dr. Cornel West's scholarship being challenged by then-Harvard President, Dr. Lawrence Summers:

> It is imperative for African American faculty to do the important scholarship in their field that produces recognition of their insightful creative work. These efforts lead to earned tenure and a protection from the political forces, often arising from local campus sources, which could stifle their contributions. Faculty members can confront unwarranted political challenges when their academic credentials are strong and validated. However, as with any political struggle, one must make careful strategic moves that befit the local environment. (p. 39)

Bradley (2005) writes about the career experiences of African American female faculty. She explains that women and faculty of color are over-represented at the assistant-professor level (Alfred, 2001). Singh, Robinson, and Williams-Green (1995) also identified some of the risk associated with being an African American faculty member. They contend that African American women faculty are far more disadvantaged at universities than are White European American women and other faculty of color. Specifically, African American female faculty members are promoted and tenured at a lower rate than either African American men or White European American women. It is important for me, as an African American faculty member, to keep my eye on the prize and to work as hard as possible to obtain tenure.

Once that part of my academic process is completed, I would like to find time to conduct more research on nontraditional students. My secret love is blues and jazz singing. The perfect combination would be teaching, developing myself as a jazz singer, and completing one research project and one article each year. Balancing life with research, creativity, writing, and teaching as meaningful parts of the equation is my dream.

Social Work Educator

The experience of being a social work educator is much different from what I had expected. Because I was the first person in my family to graduate from college, the position of professor was exalted in my mind. The position is important, but one of the problems is that I am an older person who has lived a life and who feels quite competent. Yet, entering the ranks of junior faculty, I experienced infantilization and disempowerment at many turns. It is difficult to reconcile the position that one assumes as junior faculty with one's self-image. If one's self-esteem is not strong, one can be broken down rather easily. Senior faculty know best, or they believe that to be the case. I am constantly scrutinized to make sure that I address things the way they should be in the opinion of administration and senior faculty.

It is important to stay centered. I have enjoyed my time as a faculty member at my university even though I have difficulty from time to time with my junior status and all the work that is heaped on junior faculty. It is difficult. I also resent the level of pay, which has not kept up with the cost of living. There is a statewide crisis regarding the deteriorating level of pay for state university professors, so I am not alone. The status of the professorate far exceeds the pay. Thus, being a member of the union is an essential part of my professional role.

Contradictions in My Role

On the one hand, I am a junior faculty member, and I really do need to learn the ins and outs of the professorate. On the other hand, I am given so many administrative tasks that I get caught up in those tasks and find teaching, which is my passion, coming in second place. Often I feel second-guessed and like I am on call all the time, which can be a wearying, discouraging experience. On the one hand, I am doing a lot of work that I learned to do in the field at the MSW level (administration, budgeting, and supervision), and I enjoy feeling competent in an area of professional expertise. On the other hand, I want to become a better teacher, conduct my research, and grow into newer roles. It is difficult not to become the department workhorse when I insist on hanging onto old, more comfortable roles such as administration and supervision. It is almost a self-fulfilling prophecy where I assist in setting myself up as the department workhorse. My chair keeps telling me that we (African Americans) are a people who have been known to work from "can't see (before sunrise) til' can't see (after sundown)." He and I have done this and succeeded with the help of many in getting the department accredited. But the workhorse role is a dangerous one.

The underside of the process is that, in being this strong, I fail to take care of myself very well. I need more time to prepare for teaching and to work on developing curriculum and community-based empowerment-related research. I need to re-establish certain boundaries. For example, I have never had a summer off in the entire time I have worked as a tenure-track professor. I volunteer to teach for additional pay, but I inevitably receive calls to participate administratively. This is because we are understaffed; our administrative staff could be larger, among other reasons. It does not truly matter because, like a workhorse, I continue to pull the plow even though I really need to be put out to pasture for a while. I am working on this and must accept responsibility for allowing it to happen. In my opinion, this is the downside of functioning as a woman of color in academia.

The Divine Side of the Professoriate

I am in a unique and wonderful situation as the majority of the faculty in the department are people of color, as are a number of our students. This environment is empowering in that all faculty have dealt with racism, gender bias, or homophobia. This gives us a common ground in dealing with issues of oppression, discrimination, and multiculturalism. Fears and concerns related to racism within the department are minimized, and our students receive a consistent message about addressing oppression and discrimination. Our Latino/a, Asian, and African American students see that they are mirrored in the faces and experiences of many of the faculty and staff. I believe this adds to the credibility of the social work department's mission, which is to produce urban professionals who are multiculturally competent and who understand oppression and discrimination.

Additionally, working in a new department with other faculty and staff who are passionate about building a program is fulfilling. Our chair often says, "We are building this airplane as we fly it." I had the unique experience of acting as second-in-charge of a program that grew from 60 to 140 people by the second year. I have had to struggle with giving up some of the unofficial authority I formerly had to allow new faculty to enter the process. Over time, I will back away from these responsibilities and dive into my qualitative research and the mental-health sequence, which I also chair. There are too many demands right now, but help is on the way. We are hiring new faculty, and the demands should subside. As Jesse Jackson says, "Keep hope alive."

The Academic System

I chose to focus on local teaching universities because of my passion for teaching and my desire for family stability, which necessitates remaining close to our primary and extended family. When I accepted a position at a local university, I received a salary that was comparable to the employment contract offers that others in my dissertation group received, except that I was at the mercy of old machinery and cramped office space. I had two peers in the department (junior faculty) who were marvelous. They were collegial, supportive, and ready to help in any way possible. Their support (writing group participation and mentoring on my dossier) made my entrance into the department as a tenure-track professor palatable. Unfortunately, I had a run-in with a colleague who decided that she could shift all of her work to me and who acted in what I perceived to be a haughty, abrupt, and unprofessional manner. This surprised me, and the rift never healed, nor was she ever supportive. She was not a faculty of color, and we were never able to mesh our styles.

Nonetheless, I was assigned a mentor outside of my department in the fall of my first year at the university. My first meeting with her was one of my most meaningful experiences at the university. She helped me focus on my writing, research, and teaching agenda and advised me on how to meld the two so I could accomplish all three at the same time. Since I am in the process of writing a textbook that examines the history of people of color and their relationship to the developing U.S. social welfare state, I chose to teach the social policy course and integrated coursework focused on my area of interest. It has been extremely beneficial. She has been a wonderful mentor. Although we do not meet often, she keeps track of me and my progress through the academy. Recently, we saw each other, and she noted that it was time to meet since I would soon be reviewed for tenure. This is what I want—someone who watches out for me and my well-being, someone who does not need me to do work for him or her, or who judges me within my own department—an external mentor.

I believe that many people of color are bicultural, and I fall into this category. Operating in the multicultural environment of the university works well for me. Navigating the course between my culture, my own matriarchal environment (I was also raised by a single mother), and the patriarchal university environment can become frustrating. It is frustrating to have my decisions questioned or dismissed, but I know this is very similar to the cor-porate world. On the one hand, I have great power vis-à-vis the students. On the other hand, as a junior faculty member, I have more power than most because of my role of director of field and the informal assistant-chair role I hold. Yet, at the end of the day, I feel relatively powerless in the system. My level of tension and stress, secondary to the feeling of powerlessness, builds up over time. Typically, I spend time with the department chair discussing these issues.

Price for Institutional Support

I guess working hard and long is the price that is paid for institutional support. I have been able to get assigned time on a regular basis. This has allowed me to focus on administrative work in lieu of teaching a full course load. But I tend to teach and work during the summer based on loyalty to the department and college and the desire to ensure accreditation success. So overworking is part of the price for institutional support. However, the payoff is that I have been able to serve on committees such as the Executive Committee of the Academic Senate based on loyalty from the institution. Release time and grants opportunities have been given to me because of my persistent participation in faculty activity and governance (Academic Senate, all departmental committees, research committee, search committees, curriculum revision, and accreditation activities).

Gender Issues

I regularly deal with gender issues. They seem subtle, and they rarely alarm me. But, from time to time, the power imbalance that allows me to do more than my fair share of the work (always attempting to prove my worth), the pay disparity between other faculty with my experience and me, and the second-guessing add up to a rather significant feeling of anxiety and a sense of futility.

Why Social Work Education?

I stay in social work education because I love to teach. I love it when I have the time to prepare and deliver an effective lecture. I know it does not happen with every lecture, but it happens enough to make it worthwhile. I believe the world needs helpers and individuals who understand practice and solid intervention techniques. I am a seasoned practitioner with the ability to disseminate clinically sound information. In addition, I can ensure that students are exposed to the cultures represented in our area (Mexican, Central American, Vietnamese, Chinese, Korean, African American, European American, and Afghan). My eye is focused on understanding these populations better and their generativity or ability to care for each other, using the Eriksonian model of understanding adult development. I want to ensure that the next generation of social workers receives culturally competent and culturally effective training. I feel responsible for providing some of this training.

I am also aware that the struggle will be less difficult once I receive tenure. It is difficult to stay the course when I am feeling overworked, but I know the demands on my time will change and the financial rewards will be greater. The payoff is wonderful and competent students, and I hope at some point to have more time to think and write about the work I do with them.

Responsibility of Social Work Profession

The profession needs to support more women of color in attaining the PhD. This can be done through continued support for programs such as the Council on Social Work Education's Minority Fellowship Program, which provides financial and moral support, advice about employment, education, and so forth. In addition, the university needs to provide support for research, writing, and collaborative work; offer a formal mentoring program; support faculty in dealing with inappropriate and racist behavior; and support time off for administrative work and work toward completion of research and writing.

CONCLUSION

Among the many lessons I learned, I concur with Alexander-Floyd (2004) in recommending the following seven habits of highly successful Black junior faculty:

1. Learn the expectations for promotion and tenure.
2. Learn to say no early and often to protect time for research.
3. Actively work to improve teaching.
4. Hunt down good advice.
5. Develop a pattern of research productivity.
6. Negotiate your contract well.
7. Refuse to give up your faith, stop exercising, or eating right.

REFERENCES

Alexander-Floyd, N. G. (2004). The seven habits of highly successful Black junior faculty. *Black Issues in Higher Education, 21*(10), 66.

Alfred, M. (2001). Reconceptualizing marginality from the margins: Perspectives of African American tenured female faculty at a White research university. *Western Journal of Black Studies, 25,* 1–11.

Bradley, C. (2005). The career experiences of African American women faculty: Implications for counselor education programs. *College Student Journal, 39,* 518–527.

King, W. (1996). The road taken, twice. *Black Issues in Higher Education, 13*(2), 33–34.

Ramsey, M. R. (2002). Dear BI career consultants. *Black Issues in Higher Education, 19*(7), 39.

Singh, K., Robinson, A., & Williams-Green, J. (1995). Differences in perceptions of African American women and men faculty and administrators. *Journal of Negro Education, 64,* 401–408.

Women of Color as Social Work Educators

Part II: The Voices of Women of Color as Social Work Educators

Chapter 17: ATREVERSE A SOÑAR COMO UNA MUJER DE COLOR:
Dare to Dream as a Woman of Color

Corina D Segovia-Tadehara

First and foremost, I would like to thank my family, each of whom played a significant role in my decision to continue and further my education, as well to venture into the world of academia. My parents, Jesús and Estella, instilled in me the importance of acquiring a higher education, and were willing to help me however they could. Without their strength and determination, I would not have been able to follow their lead. My sisters, DiAnna and Odett, and brother, Jesse, provided the encouragement, stability, and grounding that only siblings can. My children, Eric and Niki, have always been such good sports and great supports while I worked toward attaining this or that goal. I would further like to thank my many friends for "hanging in there" with me throughout my struggles, in particular, Tomi, and my dearest friend and colleague, Mark, for helping me find the path to Weber State University (WSU).

No hay limites para nuestras abilidades, metas, y sueños. Si puedes soñar, puedes poner tus metas para obtenerlas y puedes sobrellevarlas aunque otros piensen diferente (filosofìa educacional y profecional de Dr. Corina D Segovia-Tadehara, 2005). There are no limits to one's abilities, goals, and dreams. If you can dream, you can set goals for attaining them. Then you can certainly achieve them, in spite of what others might think (Educational and professional philosophy of Dr. Corina D Segovia-Tadehara, 2005).

As a faculty member of the Social Work and Gerontology Department at Weber State University in Ogden, Utah, I have the opportunity to teach a variety of courses. One of my favorites is teaching the first sequence of human behavior in the social environment. This class involves helping students take an in-depth look into their own developmental life process from birth to present time. They are required to write an "identity formation" paper, which examines their personal histories, memories, decision to choose social work as a career, and many other aspects of their lives. Because this is a project about the student, I make it an assignment that allows them to be creative, sharing only that which they feel comfortable sharing and including both positive and negative experiences. This project has evolved into a book—a "Me Book" experience that helps students gain an understanding of themselves with the ability to connect the dots, so to speak, and see the bigger picture, from past to present, looking ahead to countless possibilities.

When I was invited to write this chapter, I found myself looking at it in terms of working on my own Me Book. I am reminded of the comments students make in their concluding chapters, in which they are asked to provide a summary of their experiences and reactions to this assignment. Many note their ambivalence at the thought of having to write about themselves. The majority expresses gratitude for having been given such an assignment, and others share their desire for more time to refine their final product. I can honestly say that I understand their ambivalence, and, like my students, I am grateful for the opportunity to share my story.

PERSONAL BIOGRAPHY

As long as I can remember, my parents have strongly emphasized the importance of education. They have been the driving force in helping me realize the need to reach for and attain my educational goals despite frequent obstacles. It is because of their support, the support of my siblings, and the support of others I have met along the way that I have been able to overcome the struggles of life, education, and those imposed upon me not only as a woman, but as a woman of color. To provide the reader with a better understanding of me, Dr. Corina D Segovia-Tadehara, I believe it is necessary to share some vital characteristics of my parents and my siblings. You see, it is because of my parents' perseverance and tenacity that I have managed to come this far in my life. Likewise, each of my siblings has played an invaluable role in my development.

My Parents

Over the years, I have watched as my parents, Jesús and Estella, worked long, hard hours to ensure that my sisters, brother, and I would have a better life and more opportunities than they did while growing up. One of my earliest memories was when we moved to California from Texas in 1961, just after my brother was born. During the drive, Dad told us that we could no longer speak Spanish, our native language. We would have to speak only English if we were going to "fit in," be accepted, or succeed in life. At the age of three, I could not possibly know the ramifications this directive would have in my later years. I also did not give much thought to it since I was too young to understand what he meant. I do remember, however, that I spoke and understood both Spanish and English, at least as much as any three-year-old could. From that moment on, Spanish was no longer the main language spoken in our home. I eventually began to understand, a little at a time, why Dad was so adamant, as I observed the struggles each of my parents had to endure throughout their lives.

My Father, Jesús

Dad worked for the federal government at the Veterans Administration (VA) for 29 years, from 1961 to 1990. Before that, he had served in the U.S. Air Force for four years. He worked his way through the federal system despite his lack of a high school education or support from his supervisors. Dad's first position with the VA was as an admissions clerk with a General Service 3 ranking (GS-3), and it was five years before he received his first promotion to a GS-6. Throughout those years, as others received promotions, Dad would train them in their new positions, despite the fact that he, too, should have been promoted. It seemed as if Dad had to prove himself over and over again before he would finally receive that initial promotion. After that, he applied and received a promotion every few years until he became chief of Medical Administrative Services at Boston's VA Medical Center, with a ranking of general manager 14 (GM-14), the first Hispanic GM-14 at the Boston Veterans Administration Medical Center.

Even after retirement, Dad was actively recruited by the University of Massachusetts to become its director of veterans' affairs. He was to begin work on a Monday and was discussing his responsibilities with his would-be administrator when the topic of education arose: "So, where did you get your college education?" To which my dad replied, "I have no college education. I dropped out of school in the 11th grade to help support my family, but I did earn my GED." Needless to say, Dad was hired and "unhired" on the same day. He understood the situation, however, and harbors no ill feelings toward the university or administrator: "It's a university, *mija*! They can't have someone working as a director who only has an 11th-grade education. That wouldn't be right." The irony of this situation is that Dad's education stood in the way of his promotions while at the VA: "It was used as an excuse to not promote me, but I believe it was more of who and what I was [Mexican] than what I didn't have." My dad made a name for himself despite all of his setbacks. It didn't matter what kind of obstacle was placed before him; he always looked ahead and fought for what he believed he deserved.

My Mother, Estella

Mom worked for the housing authority in Fresno, California, from 1963 to 1969, when she decided to quit and attend the University of San Diego, where she completed her four years of college. During this time, Mom was offered a full scholarship to Harvard University's Medical School in Cambridge, Massachusetts; she would have been the first Hispanic female ever to attend. She was also offered a full-time teaching appointment at a junior-high school in the San Diego area. However, due to familial responsibilities, she had to turn both opportunities down. I often wonder how things would have turned out had she received a Harvard education. The fact is, she placed her family ahead of her own educational goals and dreams.

In 1974, Mom began her work with the federal government as a GS-4 civilian worker in the U.S. Navy in Washington, D.C. Within 12 years, she advanced to a U.S. Air Force Logistician GS-13 rank, unheard of for women, let alone a Hispanic woman. Although her four years of college helped in her promotions, such promotions did not come easily, and my parents had to hire attorneys on two separate occasions to help in that process. Mom had been surpassed by many other civilian workers for promotion—some with less seniority or education—but because they were White European American, middle-class men and women, they received promotions ahead of my mom. As was the case with my dad, Mom had to train many of those who were promoted. In one instance, her direct supervisor, who was from the Middle East, believed women had no right to be in the workforce. He claimed that Mom had not met her obligations for promotion when indeed she had and denied her advancement. When an attorney was enlisted to help my mom's case, the supervisor immediately promoted her.

My mom had to work extra hard to establish herself with each promotion, and she received many awards while working for both the Navy and Air Force. Sadly, though, she had to deal with constant sexual harassment from military officials. In any case, her strength as a woman, a Hispanic Aztec Indian woman, helped her stand firm and not walk away. She fought for her rights and won. Mom retired in 1988 as a Logistician Grade 13 from the U.S. Air Force.

As I reflect on the experiences of my parents, I am impressed by their strength and their determination to get ahead in life and succeed, regardless of the obstacles placed before them because of their ethnic background, and, in Mom's case, her gender. They set their goals, held on to their dreams, and never looked back at what was supposed to be or what was expected of a young Mexican American family in the 1960s and 1970s. This is the foundation laid by my parents: the very foundation from which I have learned, succeeded, and continue to attain my goals no matter the obstacles.

My Siblings

While our parents always emphasized education, they also encouraged us to pursue and excel in that which we were interested, even if it did not include a college education. It did not matter what we wanted to be in life; we knew we could and would achieve our goals as long as we had the support of our parents. The example our parents set for us, especially with regard to education, was paramount.

My sister, DiAnna, received her bachelor of science in organizational behavior from the University of San Francisco and is currently an engineer with Pacific Bell Telecommunication Systems. My sister, Odett, briefly attended Brigham Young University and is currently employed at a major hospital in Salt Lake City, Utah, as the lead medical secretary over surgery. My brother, Jesús Jr., graduated with a bachelor in business administration from Northeastern University in Boston, Massachusetts, worked for Lotus Corporation as a systems engineer, and founded Elanza, an interactive business solutions consulting firm; he sets up computer systems all around the world.

My siblings' experiences illustrate that the examples set by my parents contributed to the success of their children. With or without a college education, each set and attained his or her career goals, in spite of challenges. I believe that it was my parents' courage, strength, and determination to improve their lives and the lives of their children that guided us toward our life goals. Their encouragement and support along the way continues to provide direction.

My Journey Toward Academia

My given name was Corina, after the 1950s song, "Corrina Corrina." I am a Mexican American, Spanish, Aztec Indian woman in my 40s. I have been a tenure-track assistant professor in the social work program at Weber State University (WSU) since July 2002. While the tenure-and-promotion process was somewhat intimidating, I managed to receive "good" to "excellent" ratings in teaching, scholarship, and service, and I am making sufficient progress toward tenure.

Education was my dream, and becoming an academician was my ambition. However, it was not always easy for me to maintain my vision toward attaining my goal. In looking back, I discovered that I was only one of a handful of Hispanics in the schools I attended during my early years. It wasn't until we moved to San Diego that I began to notice an increase in the number of children of color around me. When I first started school in San Diego, I was only one of two girls in a photography class. The boys teased us, and the teacher simply ignored them. The other girl dropped the class; I stayed.

I was also enrolled in a Spanish class, but the teacher assumed that, because I was Hispanic, I should be able to speak the language, so he transferred me to Spanish for the Spanish-speaking. I could not speak Spanish, and the students in the class all laughed at me because I could not pronounce the words clearly enough for them to understand. I was angry and hurt that my dad would allow such a thing to happen to me by telling me to stop speaking my native language that summer day in 1961. I continued trying and actually became friends with some of the students in the class. They would try speaking with me in English, and I would speak to them in Spanish; it was a give-and-take experience. In the end, I believe we all learned from one another.

When we moved to Virginia because Mom and Dad had been transferred to Washington, DC, I worked really hard at improving my grades and graduated in 1976 from Annandale High School. Graduation ceremonies were held at Constitution Hall that year. This was to be one of the greatest days in my life, and it would be the first of several educational successes.

I had not formally applied to any college or university, but I had taken my ACT and SAT exams. Because I had listed Utah's Snow College on my exams, the scores were automatically sent to the school's admissions office; during the summer, I received an acceptance letter to attend. I was so excited because I was going to college, but I only attended Snow College for one semester. I met a young man who was half Japanese American, Tomi Tadehara, and he and I were married July 12, 1977. After we were married, I made several unsuccessful attempts to go back to school. Finally, in 1988, at the age of 30, I began my full-time bachelor's education at Westminster College of Salt Lake City and graduated in the summer of 1991 with a BS in psychology and a minor in Spanish.

As long as I can remember, I always wanted to be a psychologist. My friends always confided in me; many said it was because I was a good listener. When I spoke with my advisor at Westminster, he asked me what I wanted to do with my degree. When I told him, he asked, "What if I told you there was a profession out there that you could do everything you just described to me, and more, but with much less education?" He talked about social work, the education involved, and the ability to become a therapist with a master's degree. He opened the door to a new opportunity and helped me apply and become accepted to the University of Utah Graduate School of Social Work master's program in fall 1991. I graduated in 1993.

Upon graduation, I was offered a full-time position as a case manager and therapist at the Utah AIDS Foundation. I worked with many individuals affected by HIV/AIDS, from infants to the elderly,

gay and straight, men, women, and children. After about three and a half years in this position, I began to realize that I was burning out. I could no longer provide services to my clients with the passion and energy I once had because people were dying almost daily. I had been counting the number of clients who had died as a result of AIDS complications and stopped when the number reached 40—that was just during my first year. I had no time to grieve the losses and knew I could not continue and maintain my own health. My parents knew I was struggling and decided to make me an offer I could not refuse. They offered me the opportunity to go back to school, helping me financially to earn my PhD.

I enrolled at the University of Utah Graduate School of Social Work again in 1995, completed my coursework in 1998, conducted my research study, and defended my dissertation in April 2000. I was nominated to be the doctoral student graduation speaker for commencement ceremonies in May 2000 and officially earned my PhD in May 2001. During the 2000–2001 academic year, 20,176 doctoral degrees were awarded to women in the United States; of these, 4.1% (n=829) were awarded to Hispanic women, of which I was one (Chronicle of Higher Education Almanac, 2000).

I can honestly say that the years spent earning my doctorate were the longest of my life, but, in the end, they were also some of the most gratifying and rewarding. I had finally attained another of my educational goals. I finished a rigorous program in spite of the many obstacles. Ultimately, I earned my degree for myself; however, one of the greatest lessons I learned while completing my education is that no single person can stand alone. Moreover, no one should have to withstand the struggles, frustrations, and emotions or relish in the accomplishments all by herself or himself. Throughout my academic experiences, numerous individuals have stood by me and provided extensive guidance and support; to them, I am eternally grateful.

PROFESSIONAL JOURNEY

Challenges

It would be easy to say that my journey as a doctoral student was without incident, but that would not be true. A few individuals believed I was "not doctoral material." After having dropped below the required or recommended grade point average of 3.0 one semester, I was told that I would have to leave the program. I was devastated and determined to find out what I could do to remain in the program. In a meeting with one of my professors, I was told that I should reconsider whether a doctoral education was right for me: "Maybe you should take some time off, take care of your babies, and then decide if you really want your PhD." Another said, after learning of my struggles in one of my research courses, "You clearly don't understand and will never get research, so why not just quit now?" In both instances I responded that I would not quit and asked what they were willing to do to help me succeed. To improve my GPA and remain in good standing within the program, I was told I could rewrite my final paper for the research course and re-present my oral presentation over the summer. I managed to get through the process, and my grade improved to an A-. My professor later told me she knew I would make it through the program because of my "tenacious attitude." I smiled and thought of my parents.

The qualifying exam each student must take to progress into the next and final stage of the PhD program was also a challenge. The exam consisted of both quantitative and qualitative research portions. Although I felt good about my exam and believed I had passed, when the results arrived in the mail, I discovered that I had failed both exams and was asked to meet with the doctoral director. I was given an opportunity to retake the exams, but would have to spend an extra year in classes, including additional research and statistical courses.

I was determined to pass and enlisted the help of a classmate as a tutor on quantitative methods; he was an excellent teacher. With tutoring and an additional qualitative research course, I believed I was more than ready for the exam. I was given one day to complete it, and I finished with only minutes to spare. Once again, I believed I had passed my exams and could begin my dissertation. Within a few days, I received the results. I passed the quantitative portion, but once again failed the qualitative. I was told that the professor believed I had not "put forth as much of an effort on the qualitative portion as the quantitative" and that I "clearly do not understand research." I was given an ultimatum: I could take the qualitative portion again, but this time I would have to analyze all five articles and complete them in a designated period of time or I could quit. I wanted to quit! I was in my office at home trying to decide how to proceed when I received a call from my then-qualitative research professor. She could tell I was upset and asked if I was okay. I asked her if she believed that I understood qualitative research. She seemed surprised by my question and simply replied, "Of course you do! Based on all your assignments, exams, and final paper, you definitely know what you are talking about with regard to qualitative research." With that, I wrote 42 pages of analysis. Within a week's time, I received a letter telling me I had passed.

Strengths

I have managed to overcome many obstacles in my life, both personal and professional, but I believe each has been made easier by the fact that my family's support was always readily available. Had it not been for the words of encouragement from my then young children, Eric, 9, and Niki, 4, telling me, "It's okay, Mom, everything will be alright," I might have succumbed to the pressures of my education. As it stands, both of my children have impressed me to no end with their mature level of understanding and compassion toward me. It was because of their patience, love, and understanding that I was able to continue. It was also because of them that I knew my journey toward academia would be justified because, in the end, we would have more time together as a family, more time to enjoy one another's company, to travel, and to play.

The completion of my educational journey and the beginning of my professional one has certainly paid off. My children have not only developed a clear understanding of what education means to and for them, they also have experienced firsthand the struggles associated with reaching for and attaining such a dream. Yet each is adamant about securing his or her rightful place within the realm of education.

Eric is now 20 years old, attends Weber State University, and is interested in medical social work. Eric's one true passion in life is baseball. His dream in life would be to play on a major league team. At the age of 16, Niki has developed into a very strong, independent, and mature young woman. She is in 11th grade and is hoping to achieve her associate's degree while in high school. Niki aspires to become a writer, psychologist (or social worker), and interior designer. She is fully aware of the fact that she can become anything on which she sets her mind. Like her brother, Niki dreams of college and would love to attend Stanford University.

As I have watched my children develop into young adults, I am constantly reminded of their individuality, as well as their similarities. Both are strong and determined. Both have learned to deal with and overcome obstacles. Both understand the importance of education and know that it will play a significant role in their adult lives. I am further reminded through observing my children that the foundation my parents built for my siblings and me will continue to stand firm for future generations to come.

A Social Work Educator

My teaching experience began while I was employed at the Utah AIDS Foundation. Part of my responsibilities included going to various agencies to educate individuals about HIV. I was invited to public and private schools, including elementary, junior high, and high schools; universities and colleges; drug- and alcohol-treatment programs, for residents as well as staff; health and mental-health facilities; corporations; and hospitals throughout the state of Utah. Discussions centered on the intricacies of working with and treating persons infected with or affected by HIV, as well as disease transmission and progression. Occasionally, I was called on to present material on behalf of clients to educate their coworkers on universal precautions while working with someone infected with HIV. These experiences led me to create a graduate-level *HIV/AIDS in Social Work* course, which was submitted to the Social Work Curriculum Committee and accepted as an elective course. I can honestly say that these and other experiences added to my desire to teach full-time.

Before taking my position at Weber State University, I taught bachelor's level social work courses as an adjunct instructor at the University of Utah and was recruited by the Spanish department at Westminster College to teach first- and second-level Spanish classes. With this added teaching experience, I was ready to look into securing a job within a university setting, thus, I attended the Council of Social Work Education Annual Program Meeting (APM) in Orlando, Florida. While there, I had an opportunity to interview for potential jobs at a couple of universities, but I did not enjoy the experience. It seemed as if the only reason I was asked to interview was because of my ethnic background. When the interviewers learned I was Hispanic, they immediately asked me how I would feel about working with a large Hispanic community in their area. On one interview, I was told, "We have a large Latino population and are searching for someone who will be able to bring [recruit] these individuals in." My responsibilities would include recruiting students and maintaining community relations by con-

ducting community-service projects in the area. I was also promised that a strong mentoring program would be available for me as a faculty member. These responsibilities, as well as teaching a full course load, seemed overwhelming, especially for someone just beginning a career. I questioned whether I would have the mentoring support I would need to help me through the first few years and soon discovered that I would be mentoring and advising all already-enrolled and incoming Hispanic students.

When I returned from the conference, I decided I would complete my education before taking on teaching responsibilities. I was not about to accept a faculty position before I had defended my dissertation. I continued teaching as an adjunct instructor and conducting HIV-related research and program evaluations for the University of Utah Social Research Institute and the Utah AIDS Foundation. I thoroughly enjoyed research and definitely understood both quantitative and qualitative research methods. The position at Weber State University (WSU) became available two years after graduation. Dr. Mark O. Bigler, a former colleague from the Utah AIDS Foundation, has been a great mentor to me throughout my academic experiences, and the opportunity to work with him once again was an added bonus. I applied for the position and began as an assistant professor in July 2002.

Ever since my hire, the department has seemingly been in a state of transition. For example, until July 2005, the department chair position was filled with a member of the Criminal Justice Department, and only recently has someone from within our department been appointed to serve as chair, beginning in the new academic year. Additionally, a member of our faculty retired last year, and, at the end of this year, our director of field placement also retired. So, as we look toward the upcoming academic year, we will begin with not only a new department chair, but two new faculty members as well—three major changes at once. However, my experience within the department has been that we, as a faculty, are highly capable of forward motion, even in the face of change. I, for one, welcome the changes and challenges that may follow because each member of the faculty seems to have a vision with regard to the future of the department.

One of the most important attributes associated with becoming a faculty member is collegiality. In the four years since I joined the university, I have had the opportunity to collaborate with faculty members within and outside the department. This promotes cohesion and growth for faculty, staff, students, and the university as a whole. The ability to become involved in department, college, and university committees provides a "behind-the-scenes" look at academia. Collegiality has manifested itself in a variety of ways: for example, faculty members from various departments offering to help me through the tenure-review process, collaborating on research projects with social work and other faculty, advising student club officers, and mentoring new faculty and students to ensure their success within the department and university. Each of these examples has added to my positive experiences as a faculty member and enhanced my desire to continue working to ensure that collegiality remains an important part of my faculty experience.

My experience as a social work educator has been fairly consistent with regard to course evalua-tions and student feedback. However, at the end of each semester, I attempt to gather feedback from my students over and above the university evalua-tions, both positive and negative. I believe the only way I can improve my teaching is by incorporating the feedback of those I have taught. While I have been complimented on my teaching style, I have also discovered that it is not conducive to every student's way of learning. I have been told that I should provide more structure and detail and pay more attention to certain issues and less to others. Ultimately, I must cover the course content and attempt to find a balance with how it is presented. I have also come to realize that, as long as I teach, I will never please every student who comes into my classroom 100% of the time.

There have been many times when students of color have approached me and expressed their grat-itude to the university and department for having hired me, a Hispanic woman. When asked why, some have elaborated and said they believe I can under-stand their struggles better than other professors and that I take time to listen. They add that they believe other professors care, but it is sometimes easier to express themselves to me because I am not only a woman, but a woman of color. One Native American student said it best: "Sometimes you just have to see that there is someone like yourself who has accomplished something. Then you can say, she did it, so can I!"

CONCLUSION

As I have had time to reflect on my life's experi-ences through writing this chapter, I am amazed at how my career decisions, while not predestined, were highly influenced by my parents' career paths.

Their careers were not just about promotions or working for the government. Rather, their careers were about values and ethics and ensuring their clients were cared for professionally and effectively. My parents were advocates, brokers, researchers, educators, mediators (Zastrow, 2004), and every other social work role. I followed in their footsteps. While I am not a government employee, I do work for the people. I work for my clients, students, department, college, university, and the academy, and I try to ensure that the services I provide are services they will need to survive. I further strive to adhere to the standards, values, and ethics of the profession.

Throughout this process, I have also struggled; struggled to identify how my experiences, both positive and negative, have been influenced by my gender and ethnic background; struggled to find the meaning behind the life I have experienced as a woman of color; and struggled to find the words with which to share these experiences and help others like me come to understand that it is acceptable to go after your dreams in spite of the many times you are told not to or that "you won't make it" or "you will never understand research." I have also struggled to share with other young women of color who aspire to become something in life, that goes against their family systems and society and that it does not matter who you are, where you come from, or what you have, you can and will succeed because you are strong, you are determined, and you are a woman of color.

Suddenly, the obstructions that clouded my vision have disappeared. The lessons I have learned throughout my life are many. While I have not had to struggle in the same manner as my parents, grandparents, or great-grandparents, I have been able to benefit from their struggles. I have witnessed their determination, perseverance, and unwavering strength to improve their own lives and the lives of others. The foundation my parents laid was built for anyone within the entire family system to build upon if she or he so chooses. It just so happens that my parents were the ones who dared to take the first step, placing in motion not only their lives and the lives of their children, but the lives of future generations.

My parents were the first in both of their families to do many things. They were the first to venture out away from the comfort and support of their own families; first to go beyond what was expected of them, becoming migrant workers traveling from farm site to farm site; first to stand firm and fight back when faced with overt acts of discrimination; first to believe no one had the right to take away their dreams; and first to believe they could have anything they wanted out of life, that they were just as deserving, capable, and able to achieve the American dream and live it to its fullest. They were the "door openers" for their family.

REFERENCES

The Chronicle of Higher Eduction Almanac. (2000). *The 2000–2001 almanac.* Retrieved April 16, 2007, from http://chronicle.com/free/almanac/2000/almanac.htm

Zastrow, C. (2004). *Introduction to social work and social welfare: Empowering people* (8th ed.). Belmont, CA: Brooks/Cole-Thomson Learning.

Women of Color as Social Work Educators

Part II: The Voices of Women of Color as Social Work Educators

Chapter 18: Truth and Consequences: My Personal Journey as a Woman of Color

Andrea Stewart

I would like to dedicate this chapter to my oldest sister, Deborah McDaniel, who provided support, guidance, and nurturance during my early years as a student, young mother, and educator. She is currently a renal patient and demonstrates the same willpower to survive, conquer, and live life to its fullest as my mother did while she was a renal patient.

I have always been inquisitive and committed to excellence. The sixth child of nine brothers and sisters and the "baby" girl, I always felt I had to achieve at the same or higher academic level as my older siblings. There are certain inherent, God-given traits and characteristics such as resilience, tenacity, commitment, dedication, and steadfastness that build upon my strengths. As a single parent and the mother of one son, I have seen my goals and aspirations shift from "I believe I can achieve excellence" to "excellence without excuses." From an early stage in my young adult life, a dedication to the profession of social work education was first and foremost on my agenda, as was becoming a role model for young women of color pursuing a professional career in academia.

My pathway to academia was not clearly delineated or defined, yet it was predestined. Through reflection on my past, I recall the plight of my mother, who lost her hearing at the age of 30 as a result of a heparin overdose. Heparin was used to thin her blood as she had kidney dialysis two days a week; however, it also impeded and stunted her overall well-being. Because I felt overwhelmed by my lack of interest in the medical field, I was of little help with my mother's kidney dialysis. My three older sisters provided the medical assistance necessary as two of them were pursuing nursing degrees. At times, it appeared that my mother failed to understand my hesitation to assist. Blood flowing through tubes and needles and sometimes my mother fainting while on dialysis pushed me to assist in another direction. This led me to discuss the ways I could assist with my high-school sociology instructor. She shared information about available social services and disability services. When she asked me about my educational goals, she encouraged me to consider a career in psychology, sociology, or social work. In my desire to enhance my mother's quality of life, social work seemed the obvious career path to pursue.

Divinely knowing that she would not reach her 50th birthday, my mother always encouraged me to pursue higher learning opportunities. My mother, an only child, did not have the opportunity to see her vision for me become a reality; she died at age 41, early in my sophomore year in college. It was not enough to experience and grieve the loss of my mother during a critical period of my life; I also experienced the loss of my grandmother, who had recently turned 57. She died eight months later. When I moved in with my grandmother shortly after the death of my mother, I had hoped to ease her pain through serving her unselfishly; however, she was hospitalized within one month. Although she remained hospitalized until her death three months later, she found the strength to encourage me to pursue higher education. Her exact words to me were, "Baby, never give up on your dreams, and don't quit school, regardless of the circumstances. You will be successful."

Devastated and emotionally drained, I faced the difficult challenge of whether to complete and further my education. In the still of the night, I felt compelled to look through my high school memories book. My eyes froze when I turned to a page and recognized my mother's handwriting: "Honey, out of all of my children, you will be the one to reach your dreams and fullest potential. Pursue your dreams because you will be successful." I recall tears trickling down my face as the fond memories of my mother smothered all the pain. As heartfelt memories are stored in each chamber of my heart, my mother's vision for my life has served as a guiding light reflecting my present status as a woman of color in academia.

DIVINE DESTINY: IN THE PURSUIT OF SOCIAL WORK EDUCATION

One day, as I was walking down my hallway at home preparing to retire for the night, I heard a still small voice whispering, "You will have your PhD by the time you are 28 years of age." I looked around to see if one of my family members was speaking. To my surprise, I was alone. The next day, I shared this experience with my mother, who only completed high school. She suggested that I speak with my father, a nontraditional student who was enrolled in a college with a predominantly Black student population. My father's response was a nonchalant "Interesting." Thus, I still did not have a clue about what a PhD was or what it entailed. However, I remembered my high school mentors, my sociology instructor and counselor, whom I was certain had an answer. Both of these mentors were White European American, but we had established trusting relationships that endured through my senior year. Also, my high school counselor, as well as other counselors, voluntarily provided me with scholarship applications to various colleges, universities, and private donors. These counselors were aware of my parents' limited funding capability for higher education. When my mentors explained the PhD and its requirements, I immediately decided to pursue my undergraduate degree and to consider other degrees, including a PhD.

Furthermore, I was determined not to be a teenage mother like both my mother and older sister. According to research, critical factors such as poor school performance, school dropout, unemployment, poverty, divorce, and single parenting can impede educational success and financial security (Franklin, 1992; Freeman, Logan, & Gowdy, 1992; Hyde & Kling, 2001; Julia, 2000; Tebb & Schmitz, 1999; Zhan & Pandey, 2004). Thus, the internal drive to break the cycle of teenage pregnancy was fueled by my desire to pursue higher education and become financially stable. Also, to dispel the myths and stigma associated with African American single families, such as long-term dependency on government assistance, pursuing my education would be my primary focus. Pandey, Zhan, Neely-Barnes, and Menon (2002) indicate that "postsecondary education is the key to exiting from poverty permanently" (p. 109), and most of the women with children who have gone to college while on welfare have exited from poverty for the rest of their lives (p. 110). I have constantly heard the phrases "Knowledge is power" and "Education is the key to success." These phrases became a reality for me.

My mother and grandmother instilled within me the assurance that there was a spiritual being and higher power that would lead and guide me through life's hurdles, pitfalls, and challenges. Since childhood, I have embraced spirituality and the supernatural experiences that served as a firm foundation throughout my adult years. My spiritual beliefs, practices, and rituals influenced my lifestyle. Although research reflects odds that were not in my favor, I did not consider it too strange when I was foretold my divine destiny to complete my PhD by my 28th birthday. Divine destiny, combined with my personal ambition to improve my mother's and grandmother's quality of life, resulted in social work education as my career choice.

PURSUING EXCELLENCE: LIFE AS A STUDENT

The unwarranted confrontations with university faculty and administrators who "prejudged" and seemed opposed to human and cultural diversity were quite challenging within itself. Often, it appeared that it was not one's academic and intellectual abilities that would result in completing curriculum requirements leading to degrees, but the stamina, endurance, and perseverance to succeed individually. Pitfalls, personal crises, and life-changing events steered my career path to social work education and administration. It was in spite of these experiences as a student that I realized academic and professional success.

Master's Education

The challenges, pitfalls, and hurdles that confronted me during my graduate education made me aware of the reality of racism, sexism, and ageism. I developed a greater appreciation for individuals who have experienced discrimination, bias, prejudice, and economic and social oppression. My graduate education experience was quite stressful and traumatic from day one. It was obvious that some of the instructors had preconceived notions about and prejudices against a select group of students accepted into my class. One White European American male instructor did not hesitate to tell me during a meeting that some Black students who were accepted into the program from a certain historically Black college (HBCU) could not read or write well. He indicated that they all should start out with a third-grade textbook. Insulted and unprepared for this statement, I was immediately forced into a "fight-or-flight" mode.

Out of approximately 35 full-time students, only five African Americans were accepted into the graduate social work program including me. Only one African American male was accepted, but he did not return after the first semester. Nonetheless, I refused to accept failure, excuses, defeat, or self-pity. Only success, nonexcuses, victory, self-confidence, self-assurance, God-confidence, God-assurance, and future successes affected my psyche.

I recall a traumatic experience I encountered with two professors, a White European American female and male. I met with the White European American female instructor to review my final examination. In our meeting, I pointed out the two different colors of ink used to mark my examination and asked why. Actually, my academic advisor, who was an African American female, reviewed the examination earlier and had noticed the two inks used. She also noticed that my score had been changed with a second color of ink by four points, which was just enough to drop my grade to a "B" instead of an "A." My instructor replied, "Did it ever occur to you that I ran out of ink? Anyway, you do not look like an "A" student. You come from the wrong side of the tracks." I was absolutely furious and insulted by her remarks. Angrily, I kicked her door to avoid retaliatory action that would result in my expulsion from the program. Fortunately, my academic advisor was in her office across the hall from this instructor. She came out and invited me into her office to console me. We discussed the possibility of an appeal; however, the decision rested with me.

The graduate school of social work did not have an appeals or grievance procedure in place, so I had to use the university's student appeals procedure external to the graduate school. First, I met with my academic advisor, the dean, and my two instructors to discuss my grade and review my examination. During this meeting, I experienced a painful betrayal of trust and confidence. My academic advisor blurted out, "I told her not to appeal. I told her that a grade of "B" would never change to an "A." I felt like someone had stabbed me in the heart. Every part of my body ached as a result of fighting to hold back the tears that threatened to pour out of my eyes.

When the meeting was over, I quietly walked down the hallway with my academic advisor. When we found ourselves alone in the hallway, I said, "If this is what being Black is all about while teaching at a majority White institution, I will never teach at such a place. I will never do a student, Black or White, the way you just did me in that meeting with all of those White faculty members." I did not wait for a response because she could not possibly provide me with one I would accept.

The reality of my coping and functioning effectively in a dual culture as a young woman of color matriculating at a predominantly White European American university set the stage for my future preparation to teach diverse student populations. Nothing in my earlier experiences in the school systems I attended had prepared me for an African American instructor's compromise to appease her White European American colleagues rather than to stand up for an African American student who was portrayed wrongfully and discriminated against. Of

course, I failed to discuss the issue further with this advisor. I only know that her response to the political and social pressures presented by her colleagues was too high a price to pay to "belong" and "be accepted" in a predominantly White European American institution.

After much deliberation with other faculty members, my classmates, and family members, I chose to appeal the grade. I met with the Student Government Association president, who was a White European American male. He was quite supportive, unbiased, and informative about the appeals procedures. After reviewing my examination and supporting documents, he decided to select an appeals committee and set a date for the appeal. I informed my academic advisor of the appeal, but she was not invited to attend.

The day before the appeals hearing, I spoke with several of my classmates to request copies of their final examinations, which included scores and comments. I convinced them I would not reveal their names or copy the section that included their names. To my surprise, the White European American students had been given more points for the same question and incomplete responses. For example, my response to one of the questions was verbatim from the required textbook. Instead of receiving 20 total points, I received 16 points. A copy of the textbook's answer was provided for the committee members' review. They agreed I should have received the total points for the response; however, one White European American student only provided one correct response, and she received 10 points out of 20. Written on her examination was, "I gave you 10 points for effort." Another White

European American student received 18 out of 20 total points for three out of four correct responses. Again, the instructors' commented, "I gave you points for effort."

Although the appeals committee members were all White European American, including the student representative, they recommended that my grade be changed from a "B" to an "A" and commented that the instructors were biased and their grading was arbitrary and capricious. My grade was changed, and I received a 4.0 grade point average, which reflected my goal for year one of graduate school. However, no one could prepare me for the backlash, retaliation, and pitfalls that immediately challenged my constitution, fortitude, and drive for academic success.

This time I was called to attend an impromptu meeting in the dean's office, which resulted from my challenging the two professors about my grades during my first semester. To my surprise, when I entered the dean's office, the field coordinator was present, along with my academic advisor and two other professors. Everyone in the room was White European American with the exception of one of my former instructors, an African American female. They had met to discuss having me terminated from the graduate program. All conversations were tape-recorded without informing me before the meeting.

I was told that my field instructor would not attend the meeting because she was out for the week on sick leave as a result of almost having a stroke. According to the field liaison, the field instructor's blood pressure had soared as a result of my asking that my grade be reviewed. I was also informed that I had changed my own grade from a "B" to an "A." My calm response to this group was, "This meeting to present false allegations in the absence of my field instructor is retaliation as a result of my appeal during the end of my first semester. I have already informed the affirmative-action officer of these proceedings, and an investigation for discrimination, racism, and retaliation will follow." The affirmative-action officer was an African American male who had informed me that the graduate school of social work had several pending discrimination complaints.

Indeed, the faculty were joining forces to have me terminated or to pressure me into withdrawing voluntarily from graduate school. Instructors from my other classes also chose to give me "B" grades just to see whether I would challenge them. If I questioned any score or grade, I was asked if I thought I was intimidating them. At this point, my goal was just to get out of the program. Another of my African American classmates who challenged the graduate school's clinical-track instructors was labeled as "passive/aggressive" and was terminated after failing to win an academic appeal and grievance. Actually, of the five African American students originally accepted into the graduate program, only three of us graduated.

In spite of the challenges and pitfalls I encountered in graduate school, opportunity came knocking. During a Council on Social Work Education (CSWE) conference, I met Dr. Jay Chun and Dr. Moses Newsome, who encouraged me to apply to the doctoral program. I applied and was accepted into the doctoral program at Howard University in Washington, DC. I was 24; my divine destiny was now being realized. At this same conference, I also met the field coordinator of the Social Work Program at the University of Arkansas at Pine Bluff (UAPB), who invited me to assist UAPB with obtaining accreditation for its social work program once I completed my master's in social work. In response to her sincere plea, I committed to assisting the program in obtaining accreditation, but only after I completed my doctoral education.

In the master's program, my area of concentration was administration. My decision to pursue the administration track was not a choice; it was my *only* option if I wanted to complete my degree requirements. The clinical track courses were taught primarily by instructors whom I challenged through academic appeals. Ultimately, I believe this forced decision to pursue administration was part of my destiny and helped to prepare me for my present position as director of the social work program at the University of Arkansas at Pine Bluff (UAPB).

Doctoral Education

I had never lived outside Arkansas. When I arrived in Washington, DC, I was elated yet ambivalent. Fearing the unknown and realizing that I was separated from my family, friends, church members, and other support systems, I felt overwhelmed. Because I did not have support systems in Washington, I chose to leave my son, who was then three, in the care of my oldest sister in Arkansas for nine months. In spite of my emotional and psychological turmoil, my future success as a woman of color obtaining a doctorate in social work cheered me. My fears were overcome by an inner peace, and I was certain that my educational accomplishments and life experiences thus far had prepared me to

rely on resilience, inner strength, faith in God, and tenacity.

Thirteen students were enrolled in my doctoral social work class. During our first class session, I was informed that I skewed the class's average age. Many of my classmates were college instructors, licensed social workers, independent practitioners, and business owners. There was some debate among some of the instructors and students about whether students should be allowed to pursue a doctoral degree without a significant number of years of social work practice experience. I felt intimidated initially with regard to my social work practice experience; however, I welcomed the academic requirements and challenges.

For the first time in my pursuit of higher education, I had an opportunity to attend a historically Black university, and all of my 13 classmates were people of color. Throughout my matriculation in the doctoral social work program, I had only two instructors who were White European American males. One of them became my mentor, and the other was my reminder of racism, sexism, ageism, oppression, and discrimination. The latter instructor had a hidden agenda and camouflaged realities.

While attending a historically Black university, I did not expect to be subjected to the blatant discrimination, biases, and prejudice demonstrated by a White European American male instructor. Having taken social work courses that included content on historical aspects and events relevant to women of color, their families, and self-help mechanisms critical for their well-being, I was utterly amazed when this instructor questioned the concept of "self-help." He did not have a clue about African American women's history and the significant impact economic and social policies had on their lives. Yet, he managed to accumulate enough doctoral students' papers to include much of the content in a book he published focusing on social welfare policy. Instead of providing class lectures, this instructor required field trips to various legislators, community agencies, and government offices. During one of our field trips, he informed one of my classmates and me that he was only at our university to gain knowledge and information to write a book. Of course, I shared this information with the doctoral program's dean, who immediately explored the merits of my statements. Later, I learned this instructor had several complaints filed against him regarding his teaching strategies, biased statements presented in class, and grading patterns. The students protested by boycotting his class and refusing to take his final examinations. At this time, I was hospitalized, however, I supported the boycott. Needless to say, this instructor's contract was not renewed for the following academic year.

PURSUING EXCELLENCE: LIFE AS A PROFESSIONAL

The role shift from student to professional educator can be a traumatic experience for some. Having to seek employment, selecting the right position, anticipating relocating to another state, and maintaining equilibrium are certainly real challenges for professionals in the world of work. Several of my colleagues who were professional social work educators and mentors instructed me not to accept a position at a university or college whose social work program was not accredited. I was informed that my

opportunities to engage in research, scholarship, and writing for publications would be stifled, if not nonexistent. Knowing I would be sacrificing my research and writing for publications, I chose to fulfill my commitment to work at a university whose social work program was not accredited. A few months after receiving my doctorate, I decided to accept a position at a historically Black university, the University of Arkansas at Pine Bluff, the very institution I promised to assist in obtaining initial accreditation of its social work program while I was still a graduate student.

I recall my interview for the position of assistant professor of social work in the late 1980s, when every professor and instructor had an opportunity to review my curriculum vitae and doctoral transcript and to question me. I was somewhat amazed at the fact that my transcript was made available. Where my practice experience seemed limited to some, my intellectual ability was obvious. During the interview, one of the instructors asked me, "What are your weaknesses?" As I pondered an appropriate response, the very instructor who asked me to come to this social work program to assist with accreditation blurted out, "She does not have any experience." Taken aback, I humbly replied, "My weaknesses will become my strengths as I pursue excellence and a guarantee to gain accreditation of the social work program as committed."

Looking around the interview room, I realized I was the youngest individual present. Nevertheless, my commitment to advance in the academy and to make a significant difference in the lives of students, particularly students who were single parents, was at the forefront. I realized the need for an attitude adjustment; instead of having a negative attitude coming into this academic culture, I had to maintain a positive attitude and display self-confidence, as well as a spirit of excellence.

Mentoring: Myths and Realities

In the world of academe, mentoring and networking are critical, particularly for women of color (Turner, 2002). Although UAPB's social work program operated as an autonomous unit, it was housed within the Department of Social and Behavioral Sciences and was considered a part of the School of Liberal and Fine Arts. Both the department chairperson and dean of the school were African American males who were quite supportive and instrumental in my professional development, as well as advancement within the academy. Within one month of employment, I was appointed coordinator of the social work program. The former coordinator, an African American female, overtly opposed to my leadership. At this time, the social work program consisted of three full-time African American female faculty including me. Therefore, I expected to be embraced and mentored by my colleagues who were mature, experienced women of color educators. My colleagues were slow to accept my leadership and establish camaraderie. However, through working together on the program's accreditation self-study, I managed to demonstrate leadership qualities and skills that were critical in changing my colleagues' mind-set.

Amazingly, the males at my institution, including my supervisors, have served as mentors, supporters, and confidants more than have my female counterparts. However, I established a professional relationship with a former chairperson and dean, an African American with over 40 years of experience at our institution. She was also the first female who served as president of the university's Faculty and Staff Senate; I was the second female president. As a result of my involving this professor in completing the social work program's self-study for initial accreditation, she became an ally and advocated for the program.

As a social work educator in such a visible leadership position, I relied heavily on my mentors, who graciously provided support. All aspects of the institution were exposed, and I began to appreciate and understand the various roles and functions of administrators, faculty, staff, and students, as well as the political, economic, and social climate of the university. A specific case in point involved an assistant professor who was denied tenure and requested an appeal. As faculty, and Staff Senate president, my responsibilities to review the complaint, make a decision regarding its merit, and follow through with the resolution were quite challenging. To my knowledge, an appeal for tenure had never been favorable for a faculty member, so I had to consider the outcomes and possible retaliation if I pursued this appeal and the faculty member was granted tenure. Also, I had to ponder whether my leadership of this process would have a negative impact on our social work program in the future. In the end, the appeals policies and procedures were followed, and the faculty member was granted tenure.

Unfortunately, this faculty member resigned a few months later, and I experienced a backlash of negative comments from some faculty and staff, such as, "You should have never gone over the decision of administration at any level. Now the faculty member is no longer employed on campus, and you stuck your neck out." Of course I was frustrated; however, it was more important to accept the faculty member's complaint as being worthy of appeal regardless of the political climate on campus.

Factors Affecting Advancement

I am a firm believer that a person's abilities, skills, and talents are instrumental to professional advancement and will open doors. I also believe that the individual who comes in early and works late will undoubtedly be recognized and rewarded in some capacity. However, social work educators must be visible; involved with students and other faculty members; engaged in campus activities, including serving on university committees; and made aware of the "shakers" and "movers" on their campuses. Collaborative projects and research activities, as well as interdisciplinary team teaching, allows women of color opportunities to share their interests and to establish professional relationships across campus.

Social work educators cannot afford to isolate themselves from other faculty, students, administrators, staff, and other personnel, all of whom are necessary to the overall success of their institutions. Even the institutions' custodial and grounds workers are valuable and should be included in our networks. Often these individuals are more resourceful and informed about the institution's practices, activities, and forthcoming changes than are faculty, staff, and students.

Regardless of age, race, or gender, demonstrating one's abilities, skills, and knowledge is necessary to become a "key player" and advance within the academy. It is well-known that the majority of colleges and universities' missions reflect an expectation of faculties' commitment to engage in research, scholarship, teaching, and service to obtain tenure and promotion. However, recommendations have been made to transform tenure and promotion criteria by exploring and expanding the definition of scholarly activity to include curriculum development activities (Gregory, 1995) and race-based service to validate rather than "to discourage faculty of color from engaging in it" (Baez, 2000).

While serving as Senate president at my university, I was appointed to a university committee to review and evaluate tenure and promotion criteria. The criteria reflected higher ratings for research and publications in refereed journals and books. Faculty who engaged in services or creative work (e.g., innovative teaching strategies, interdisciplinary team teaching, and including community partners) would be rated lower. It has been my experience that when women of color are employed at universities with limited resources (financial and physical), they are forced to write grants for external funding or collaborate with university and community partners to meet basic needs. Often, they have to improvise and "make do." When faculty are engaged in activities such as leadership development, university and community service, research projects, grant writing, writing self-study documents for accreditation, and conducting graduate and employer outcome studies and assessments, they have invested significantly in the academy in lieu of producing scholarly writings and publications. Some faculty were denied tenure and promotion as a result of this system.

Another factor confronting women of color as social work educators is the continuous demand to serve as a representative of people of color or to satisfy an institution, agency, program, or project's requirement to include women of color. It is not uncommon for women of color to feel they are overused by departments and institutions to "handle minority and gender affairs, representing two constituencies" (Turner, 2002, pp. 81–82). They are also "compelled to serve simultaneously as a role model for their profession, race, and gender" (Mitchell, 1994, p. 387). However, working at a historically Black university limits this practice, and other racial and ethnic groups often are encouraged to participate. Black and Magnuson (2005) found that "female leaders of color identified numerous oppressive experiences that were related to gender and racial stereotyping and that they experienced as isolating. These interactions further devalued or dismissed the subjective quality of their performance" (p. 341).

Research studies demonstrate that, even when women of color hold the same level of administrative positions and academic ranks as their male counterparts, they receive significantly lower salaries (Hogue & Yoder, 2003). For example, I was appointed interim chairperson of the Department of Social and Behavioral Sciences while also serving as director of the social work program. Even after having served in both of these positions for more than one year, my salary did not increase significantly. Once I relinquished the chairperson's position, my base salary decreased. In lieu of an increase to my base salary, I received a supplemental salary that was not commensurate with my job responsibilities and duties. However, the interim chairperson, an African American male who replaced me, received a significantly higher salary increase to his base salary with fewer job responsibilities and

duties. At this juncture, several questions came to mind such as: Is age a factor? Are salaries for male administrators set at a higher pay scale than they are for female administrators? Are gender differences an issue? Is my position as director of the social work program validated comparable to a chairperson's position since our job duties and responsibilities are comparable? Despite the inequitable salaries, I valued the confidence the university administrators obviously had in my leadership abilities, as well as the opportunity to gain firsthand experience in and knowledge of the world of administration within the academy.

Commitment to Stay in Social Work Education

One of the major benefits of my staying in social work education is the belief that I have made significant differences in the lives of students through service, teaching, and sharing my skills, talents and knowledge. The opportunity to serve as a role model for both traditional and nontraditional students, including single parents, has been worthwhile. I concur with other faculty women of color regarding the internal rewards and satisfactions that attract them to and keep them in academia, as presented by Turner (2002), including "satisfaction with teaching, supportive working relationships, sense of accomplishment, and contributing to reshaping the academy" (p. 87). Some of the students enrolled in our university and social work program are often first-generation students; some are single parents from single-parent homes, and have low ACT scores requiring remedial courses; and some are high achievers who represent the "ideal" student.

CONCLUSION

Women of color in academia and those who are social work educators must be empowered and engaged in continuing education to further enhance their skills and knowledge as a means to combat oppressive systems. There is clearly a need to change the societal institutions that contribute to the oppression of women. Understanding empowerment and its tools is critical to the success of faculty women of color in the academic workplace. Pigg (2002) argues that there are three dimensions of empowerment: self-empowerment through individual action, mutual empowerment that is interpersonal, and social empowerment in the outcomes of social action.

The adage, "experience is the best teacher," reflects my response to personal experiences as a woman of color and a social work educator. No individual, class, or practicum can prepare women of color for the unexpected challenges, pitfalls, oppression, discrimination, and social injustices that confront them at some stage of their lives. The political, societal, and personal agendas within the academy, whether hidden or visible, affect faculty women of color and those who are social work educators. Thus, it is imperative to participate actively in college and university committees, engage in interdisciplinary projects and research activities, and include students, as well as community partners.

Faculty women of color must establish collaborative relationships, network, choose mentors, and rely on support systems (e.g., family, friends, spiritual leaders, and colleagues) to maintain their equilibrium. As social work educators, we must continue to promote and make others aware of social and economic justice, equality, and equity for all, regardless of one's race, ethnic group, age, gender, class, sexual orientation, or political affiliation. Being aware of the structural inequalities (Prosper, 2004; Russo & Vaz, 2001) that affect women of color is a first step toward eradicating discriminatory practices. With certainty, women of color share common experiences with all women (Koonce, 2004). However, their unique, individual, and personal experiences can truly be understood if and when we walk in their shoes, see the world through their eyes, and steer their course. Women are often viewed as "better leaders than men" (Pounder & Coleman, 2002). As Banerji (2005) points out, "[W]omen make, often times, better managers because there are certain qualities that they bring to the table, a collaborative, more holistic view, the ability to put themselves in other people's shoes" (p. 29).

As faculty women of color, we should take every opportunity to serve as mentors (Sowers-Hoag & Harrison, 1991) and role models for new faculty women of color within our social work programs and within our institutions. Holley and Young (2005) recommend providing workload release and structured mentoring programs for all junior faculty. It is my practice to insure workload release for social work faculty to pursue research and other academic advancements. Generally, our university administrators encourage and support this practice. These changes within the academic workplace would affect the retention rates of faculty women of color on university campuses where they may experience feelings of isolation, triple jeopardy, and a lack of respect for the work and services they perform. Adams and Hambright (2004) supported the recommendation of "mentoring and sponsoring women so they can become the great leaders they have potential to be" (p. 211). Yet, the stereotype of leadership as a male trait persists (Gutek, 2001). If women exhibit leadership characteristics such as competitiveness, dominance, and decisiveness, they are "typically at odds with the cultural expectations of women (e.g., cooperation, submissiveness, and hesitancy)" (Black & Magnuson, 2005, p. 337).

I personally believe that my competitiveness, truthfulness, and quest for perfection in my work led to others' perception that I am a difficult person to work with. My philosophy is "Do it right the first time." I understand the consequences of taking a stand and promoting a standard of excellence. The academy should demonstrate efforts to accept the changing and emerging roles of women and women of color and foster a campus climate that supports individual and cultural differences.

REFERENCES

Adams, K. L., & Hambright, W. G. (2004). Encouraged or discouraged? Women teacher leaders becoming principals. *The Clearing House, 77,* 209–211.

Baez, B. (2000). Race-related service and faculty of color: Conceptualizing critical agency in academe. *Higher Education, 39,* 363–391.

Banerji, S. (2005). Exceeding expectations. *Black Issues in Higher Education, 22*(9), 28–32.

Black, L. L., & Magnuson, S. (2005). Women of spirit: Leaders in the counseling profession. *Journal of Counseling and Development, 83,* 337–342.

Franklin, D. L. (1992). Feminization of poverty and African-American families: Illusion and realities. *Affilia, 7,* 142–155.

Freeman, E. M., Logan, S. L., & Gowdy, E. A. (1992). Empowering single mothers. *Affilia, 7,* 123–141.

Gregory, S. T. (1995). *Black women in the academy: The secrets to success and achievement.* New York: University Press of America.

Gutek, B. A. (2001). Women and paid work. *Psychology of Women Quarterly, 25,* 379–393.

Hogue, M., & Yoder, J. (2003). The role of status in producing depressed entitlement in women's and men's pay allocations. *Psychology of Women Quarterly, 27,* 330–337.

Holley, L. C., & Young, D. S. (2005). Career decisions and experiences of social work faculty: A gender comparison. *Journal of Social Work Education, 41,* 297–313.

Hyde, J. S., & Kling, K. (2001). Women, motivation, and achievement. *Psychology of Women Quarterly, 25,* 364–378.

Julia, M. (2000). Ethnicity and gender: Introduction of concepts and theoretical framework. In M. Julia (Ed.), *Constructing gender: Multicultural perspectives in working with women* (pp. 1–10). Belmont, CA: Wadsworth.

Koonce, R. (2004). Women-only executive development. *Training and Development, 58*(10), 78–84.

Mitchell, J. (1994). Visible, vulnerable, and viable: Emerging perspective of a minority professor. In K. A. Feldman & M. B. Paulsen (Eds.), *Teaching and learning in the college classroom* (pp. 383–390). Needham Heights, MA: Ginn Press.

Pandey, S., Zhan, M., Neely-Barnes, S., & Menon, N. (2002). The higher education option for poor women with chidren. *Journal of Sociology and Social Welfare, 27*(4), 109–170.

Pigg, K. E. (2002). Three faces of empowerment: Expanding the theory of empowerment in community development. *Journal of the Community Development Society, 33*(1), 107–117.

Pounder, J. S., & Coleman, M. (2002). Women–better leaders than men? In general and educational management it still 'all depends'. *Leadership and Organization Development Journal, 23*(3), 122–133.

Prosper, T. (2004). African American women and the pursuit of higher education. *Encounter, 17*(3), 16–18.

Russo, N. F., & Vaz, K. (2001). Addressing diversity in the decade of behavior: Focus on women of color. *Psychology of Women Quarterly, 35*, 280–294.

Sowers-Hoag, K. M., & Harrison, D. F. (1991). Women in social work education: Progress or promise? *Journal of Social Work Education, 27*, 320–329.

Tebb, S. S., & Schmitz, C. L. (1999). Successful interventions with single-parent families. In C. L. Schmitz & S. S. Tebb (Eds.), *Diversity in single-parent families: Working from strength* (pp. 253–260). Milwaukee, WI: Families International.

Turner, C. S. V. (2002). Women of color in academe. *Journal of Higher Education, 73*, 74–93.

Zhan, M., & Pandey, S. (2004). Economic well-being of single mothers: Work first or postsecondary education? *Journal of Sociology and Social Welfare, 31*(3), 87–112.

Part II: The Voices of Women of Color as Social Work Educators

Chapter 19: The Metaphoric Field Journey of an Asian American Woman: From Farm to Academe

Rita Takahashi

Dedicated to ancestors who worked for a more just world, paved the way, and left an honorable legacy for all of us.

I grew up during the 1950s and 1960s in an area predominantly populated by White European Americans. Before entering the first grade, I already knew what it meant to be perceived as "different." During primary and secondary education, I was the only Japanese American in my class and one of a few persons of color in the whole school. Another factor that set me apart from my baby boomer peers was that I was expected to work in the agricultural fields from an early age.

I lived on a small family farm in Parma, located in Southwest Idaho, near the eastern Oregon border.

From elementary school through high school graduation, I toiled in the fields, pulling and hoeing weeds from the row crops to prevent them from overtaking our food source—and my family's livelihood. With childhood wonderment, I watched as fragile and tender little sprouts turned into monster weeds taller than I within a short period. Some, like the puncture vines, evolved from immature and tender ground cover into mature and hard-spiked puncture needles. Others, like morning glory, started as small shoots, but soon spread out all over the ground, strangling row crops.

I learned then that to prevent weeds from overpowering the crops, they had to be removed in a timely fashion. It was imperative to pull out the roots completely, lest they sprout again, even stronger and tougher. Once weeds matured, it became difficult to eradicate them because their roots were firmly and deeply entrenched in the soil. The roots and stems became fibrous and thick—what I used to call "woody." As a small child, I futilely chopped away at them with my hoe, but it was often impossible for me to uproot them. Some were, after all, bigger than I. The problem was magnified many times over when the weeds dropped seeds and reproduced. I knew that, in a short time, the whole cycle would start all over again once the seedlings sprouted into tender shoots and ultimately grew into giant forests of overpowering weeds.

My experience with the problematic weeds is metaphorically similar to what I encountered when I became a social-service provider and social work educator. Instead of working with weeds, however, I was interacting with human beings. I learned that, just as one must check or eradicate destructive and toxic weeds before they get out of control, so too must one take action to prevent the growth and spread of improper actions of people within organizations, institutions, and communities. Lipman-Blumen[1] (2005) discusses the negative outcomes of taking insufficient action to remove the "toxic leaders" who thrive in our midst:

> Toxic leaders do indeed have poisonous effects that cause serious harm to their organizations and their followers, but the multiple toxins they can dispense create varying degrees of impairment. (p. 17)

> Followers suffer poisonous effects when leaders place their own well being and power above their supporters' needs. Followers and the organizations they inhabit also endure great harm when leaders act without integrity by dissembling and engaging in various other dishonorable behaviors. Corruption, hypocrisy, sabotage, and manipulation, as well as other assorted unethical, illegal, and criminal acts, are part of the poisonous repertoire of toxic leaders. And, of course, in admittedly rare instances, toxic leaders move to the furthest point of the toxic spectrum and perpetrate downright evil. (p. 18)

Throughout my career, I have found it necessary to keep my senses sharpened at all times. It was

---

[1] Lipman-Blumen (2005) uses "toxic leaders as a global label for leaders who engage in numerous *destructive behaviors* and who exhibit certain *dysfunctional personal characteristics*. To count as toxic, these behaviors and qualities of character must inflict some reasonably serious and enduring harm on their followers and their organizations. The intent to harm others or to enhance the self at the expense of others distinguishes seriously toxic leaders from the careless or unintentional toxic leaders, who also cause negative effects" (p. 18).

imperative to speak out when any wrong occurred, lest unchecked injustices take root and harden into ingrained patterns and improper practices evolve into standardized modes of operation. Once this happens, it is difficult—if not impossible—to eradicate the problem without potent outside intervention, just as it was next to impossible for me to remove mature toxic weeds without assistance.

FAMILY BACKGROUND

I was born in Nampa, Idaho, on March 18, 1949. My parents were born in the state of Washington, but ended up spending most of their lives in Idaho because the U.S. government restricted and banished persons of Japanese ancestry from the West Coast, namely, California, Alaska, the western half of Washington and Oregon, and the southern portion of Arizona. Since my parents were of Japanese ancestry, they joined the 125,000 others of the same descent in being restricted and excluded from the West Coast during World War II. They were not allowed to be in the exclusion zones from 1942 until 1945. [2]

When the United States entered World War II, my mother, Ayako "Joyce" Sakauye, and her family were living on Terminal Island, which is located in Southern California, not far from Long Beach and San Pedro. In 1942, she and others living at Terminal Island were given a mere 48 hours to move out of the area permanently. [3] She ultimately had to move four times in less than a year, as she shuffled from Terminal Island to Los Angeles and then to Santa Anita Race Track, where the U.S. government incarcerated her and others in horse stalls. After being held in the U.S. Army's Wartime Civil Control Administration assembly center, she was sent to the Rohwer, Arkansas camp, where she was under the custody of a federal civilian agency, the War Relocation Authority. Months later, she received permission to leave the concentration camp [4] and take a train to Ogden, Utah, where she married my father, Yoshio Takahashi. Thereafter, they made Idaho their permanent home.

My father's family was forced to leave Seattle when President Franklin Delano Roosevelt signed Executive Order 9066, which ushered in restrictions

---

[2] President Franklin Delano Roosevelt signed Executive Order No. 9066 on February 19, 1942, which led to the en-masse restriction, exclusion, and incarceration of Japanese Americans. His order forbade persons of Japanese ancestry to remain in or enter West Coast restricted zones between 1942 and 1945. The majority languished in U.S. concentration camps between 1942 and 1946 (when the last camp closed). In her book, Lipman-Bluman (2005) labeled President Roosevelt's action "toxic" (p. 205) and indicated that he "clearly exhibited serious toxic characteristics" (p. 227).

[3] After Japanese Americans were removed from Terminal Island in 1942, they never returned. The Japanese American community was permanently decimated. The U.S. government's exclusion and incarceration were designed to disperse persons of Japanese ancestry throughout the United States. Specifics about how the U.S. government used "military necessity" as a "rhetorical tool" to justify such infringements on civil and constitutional rights can be read in Takahashi's 1978 paper.

[4] U.S. government officials, including President Franklin D. Roosevelt, used the term "concentration camps" when referring to the War Relocation Authority camps, which were established to incarcerate persons of Japanese ancestry during World War II. Euphemistic term, such as "relocation camps" and "evacuation centers" were used as a substitute to make the camps sound less harsh. In recent years, the most common name used for the camps has been "internment camps." Use of this label is erroneous because, during World War II, "internment camps" were for non-U.S. citizens who were picked up and detained by the U.S. Department of Justice. By authority and definition, "internment camps" were not used to detain U.S. citizens (about two thirds of all excluded and incarcerated Japanese Americans were U.S. citizens).

and exclusion orders leading to the establishment of U.S. concentration camps. He and his family moved to Caldwell, Idaho, where they struggled to make ends meet as newcomers to an area hostile to persons of Japanese ancestry.[5] Initially, he and the family worked as farmhands and helpers, but he eventually bought his own farm in Canyon County, located in southwestern Idaho, where I lived the first 18 years of my life.

SOCIAL WORK CAREER

I began my social work career 33 years ago. In February 1973, after receiving my master of social work (MSW) degree from the University of Michigan (UM), I became a social-service supervisor for the state of Oregon's Children's Services Division (CSD). I quickly learned that, to be effective in delivering social services in sparsely populated, rural environments, one must be adept at micro-, mezzo-, and macropractice. The two MSW concentrations I completed in administration and social treatment helped prepare me for supervision in these one-social-service worker counties.

During my stint at CSD, I was privileged to have worked with an exceptionally competent branch manager who practiced and modeled crosscultural sensitivity, administrative savvy, and interpersonal astuteness. It has been almost 30 years since I left that agency, but, through the years, as student, professor, researcher, writer, activist, and community

volunteer, I have continuously recalled and used the lessons I learned from her. Virginia F. Rose taught me the importance of open, honest, respectful, and consultative communications and the value of shared decision making and governance. She certainly planted many seeds of ideas and principles in my early career, and they have sprouted and matured in many arenas through the years.

My career path was not always toward social work. When I was an undergraduate, I completed a double major in psychology and sociology. Then I worked as a temporary office worker and hairdresser for three months, and, from 1970 to 1971, I traveled solo around the world.

After my world travels, I got married and moved to Ann Arbor, Michigan, where my first and only child was born in 1972, about three months before I entered the MSW program. After graduating from UM in December 1973 with an MSW degree and after my divorce, I decided to move back to the Pacific Northwest. While visiting my parents in Parma, Idaho, I also visited a few social-service agencies directly. I interviewed with the Pendleton, Oregon office, and I was hired to begin work in February 1974. I worked as a social-services supervisor in Umatilla, Morrow, Gilliam, and Wheeler counties for two and a half years before returning to school to pursue a doctorate in social work.

A Social Work Educator

I entered Columbia University's doctoral program in Fall 1976. I received a minority fellowship from the Council on Social Work Education (CSWE), which paid for tuition and provided a small monthly living stipend. Within weeks of my arrival in New

---

[5] The Idaho governor at that time, Chase Clark, said he did not welcome persons of Japanese ancestry to the state. He was vehemently and publicly opposed to their relocating to Idaho. During World War II, some businesses in the Caldwell area posted signs outside their establishments announcing that persons of Japanese ancestry would not be served.

York City, I realized I could not support myself and my preschool-aged son on the stipend and my meager savings. Further, I found I was spending too much time dealing with parking and sanitation problems. I had to study and eat in my car to be ready when a parking space became available. In addition, I had to contend with my roach-and bug-infested Columbia University apartment. During my first semester at Columbia University, I arranged to transfer to the University of Pittsburgh School of Social Work. I was able to transfer midyear because the University of Pittsburgh had granted my admission into the doctoral social work program the year before.

I completed all doctoral social work courses and met all requirements for a master of public and international affairs degree with a concentration in economic and social development by the end of 1978. I then moved, along with my son, to Silver Spring, Maryland, to be close to the National Archives and Records Administration in Washington, DC. For almost a year, I conducted archival research for my doctoral dissertation. The following summer and fall, I completed and successfully defended my doctoral dissertation[6], and I was awarded the PhD in December 1980.

I began my first full-time social work faculty position in Fall 1979—an assistant-professor position at Eastern Washington University (EWU), located in Cheney and Spokane, Washington. I was granted tenure, and I was promoted to associate professor in

1983. For a couple of years, I held a joint faculty position with the Graduate Program in Public Administration, where I taught policy analysis. I remained on the EWU faculty, teaching social work courses in the master's degree program until 1987.

Teaching at EWU was a positive experience. It was an environment where newly appointed faculty could spread their wings, fly, and thrive. I was thankful that the faculty and administration had little or no tendency to use rank and seniority in decisions about what a faculty person could or could not do. I was never labeled a "junior" faculty, and distinctions about privileges of "senior" faculty were never raised. I felt as if I could serve equitably on committees and that my ideas and work were respected and honored. Rites of passage were based on one's work, accomplishments, and track record.

Before my arrival at EWU, Professor Robert Neubauer invited me to give a presentation at the state social work conference about the subject of my dissertation research—the Japanese American exclusion and incarceration. His encouragement not only sent a message of inclusion, it also bestowed value on my civil rights-related research on populations of color. Similarly, other faculty expressed interest in and validated my work. Such actions are important, especially to colleagues new to the institution and profession. I am thankful that I began my social work education career at EWU because colleagues promoted faculty rights, freedoms, and liberties. I felt empowered to speak my mind, use diverse pedagogical methods, pursue research in whatever area I chose, and become involved in university and community work as I deemed important.

---

[6] The PhD dissertation, completed in September 1980, was titled *Comparative Administration and Management of Five War Relocation Authority Camps: America's Incarceration of Persons of Japanese Ancestry During World War II.*

A Civil Rights Lobbyist and Administrator

In 1987, the drive for Japanese American redress was in full swing. For over 10 years, proponents had been pressing the U.S. government to acknowledge wrongs it committed when it restricted the movement of Japanese Americans, excluded them from the West Coast, and incarcerated them in concentration camps during World War II. After more than 10 years of concentrated efforts and almost half a century after the constitutional infringements occurred, many felt that justice was long overdue.[7] The Japanese American community and a strong coalition of diverse organizations and institutions pressed for the passage of the Civil Liberties Act, which called for an official U.S. government apology and $20,000 monetary payment to all eligible persons directly affected by the World War II exclusion and incarceration.

To help in the final drive for passage of the redress legislation, I was asked to go to Washington, DC, to serve as lobbyist and associate director of the Japanese American Citizens League–Legislative Education Committee (JACL–LEC). I took a leave of absence from EWU, moved to Arlington, Virginia, and worked in Washington, DC, from 1987 to 1989. As an employee of JACL–LEC and the Washington Representative for JACL, I also lobbied for other civil rights legislation and I worked with other civil rights organizations and coalitions such as the Leadership Conference on Civil Rights, the American Civil Liberties Union, the Organization of Chinese Americans, and the Anti-Defamation League of the B'nai B'rith.

In the fall of 1987, the Civil Liberties Act passed in the U.S. House of Representatives, and it subsequently passed the U.S. Senate in 1988. Ultimately, after concerted lobbying efforts, President Ronald Reagan signed the Civil Liberties Act into law on August 10, 1988. This act authorized monetary payments, but it did not appropriate the funds needed for implementation. Therefore, after the bill became law, I continued to work for JACL–LEC, concentrating on getting an appropriations bill passed and taking on actions directed at achieving a fair, just, and appropriate implementation of the Civil Liberties Act. I became JACL–LEC's acting executive director, and, during that time, I communicated with and provided information and recommendations to the U.S. Department of Justice's Office of Redress Administration, which was established to implement the Civil Liberties Act. One of the first orders of business was to convince the Justice Department that its newly established office should not be called the Office of Reparations Administration because the word, "reparations," suggests making amends to people of other nations—not persons who were wronged by their own government, as was the case with Japanese Americans.

While in Washington, DC, I continued to be an educator. In June 1989, I cotaught "Human Diversity and Cultural Pluralism" for the Washington Center. While teaching in this program, I worked with students from across the nation and from diverse

---

[7] Individual stories reveal the wide-ranging impact of federal policies. For examples, read the personal stories of women as conveyed to me during interviews. They may be found in Kirk & Okazawa-Rey (2007, pp. 457–463).

institutions of higher education, all of whom came to the nation's capital for internship experiences.

Return to Academia

As originally planned, after redress legislations for Japanese Americans passed, I returned to academia full-time. I wanted to live and work in a culturally diverse environment and to have new and different pedagogical experiences. In the fall of 1989, I was hired as an associate professor of social work at San Francisco State University (SFSU), where I currently continue full-time employment. I was granted tenure in 1991 and was promoted to full professor in 1998. I could—and perhaps should—have gone for promotion much earlier, but I did not because it was not important to me. I figured that the salary would not change much with the promotion, and I was not concerned about titles. Through the years, I have taught baccalaureate and master's degree courses, predominantly policy, planning, and program development; administration and management; innovation and change in organizations, institutions, communities, and systems; human diversity; and civil and human rights.

A WOMAN OF COLOR IN ACADEMIA

As of this writing in 2005, I have been a social work educator for 27 years. Clearly, throughout the entire period, gender, race, ethnicity, and culture were important factors impinging on my work and career. Often the influences were more covert than overt. I encountered colleagues who were critics or opponents of multiculturalism, but they revealed their positions more through actions than words. For some, the "thorns" of multiculturalism include

precisely what Parillo (2005) identifies: immigration, language, culture, and race. While higher education has been a rewarding and deeply satisfying career, challenges have demanded my attention and follow-up action.

Faulty Assumptions

Consistently throughout my career, I was challenged to fend off faulty assumptions that faculty, staff, and students made about me based on my ethnic and cultural background, ancestral heritage, size, and gender. The tyranny of erroneous assumptions was exemplified in one of the experiences I had while seeking a tenure-track faculty position. Typical of what faculty candidates must do during the job interview process, I met with the university's top-level administrators. The school scheduled another candidate and me to meet the administrator at the same time. Within minutes of our joint interview, it was apparent that the administrator focused only on the other candidate, an African American male. He maintained eye contact with the other candidate, asked him questions, and failed even to acknowledge my existence in the room. I was rendered completely invisible as a faculty candidate.

After being ignored for some time, I began to ask typical candidate questions about such topics as faculty benefits, workload, and development opportunities. The administrator responded, but the answers were directed to the other candidate, with whom the administrator continued to maintain eye contact. Lack of eye contact with me lasted for the entire interview. Puzzled by the administrator's behavior, the other candidate and I related the incident to a member of the social work search committee. The social work faculty member investigated and reported back that the administrator ignored me because he *assumed* that I was not a faculty candidate but rather the other faculty candidate's "wife."

The fallacy of faulty assumptions is further exemplified in my interactions with a former dean. When I chaired a faculty-personnel committee, I carefully attended to policies, procedures, and timelines established by the university and ensured that they were applied consistently with rules applicable to all faculty candidates. This is mandated by the university. Regardless, the dean insisted that special concessions be given to one candidate and that written university policies, procedures, and timelines would not apply to this person. He demanded that our personnel committee comply with his edicts. I consulted with the personnel committee, and we were unanimous in our decision to abide by university policy. When I conveyed this decision, the dean literally yelled at me on the telephone and said he "ordered" me to do what he said. The decibel level of his ranting was so loud that I had to ask him to tone it down because he was hurting my ears.

In refusing his order to violate policy, I told him the committee would do what was fair: apply university policy consistently and equitably to all candidates. As such, I indicated that the committee would not infringe university policy unless we received written instructions from the appropriate university administrator(s) to do so. In the end, the dean was forced to retreat and withdraw his demands after the university administration advised him that he was out of line and that our committee's stand was correct.[8]

In processing what transpired, it was clear to me that the treatment I received had much to do with my gender and ethnic and cultural background. Assumptions are often not at the forefront of one's conscious awareness, but they clearly rear their heads in interpersonal interactions.[9] Females are frequently assumed to be submissive and are expected to be compliant. Power and power differentials (real or assumed) are used as a tool for control. Add the dimension of being an Asian American woman and the effects of faulty assumptions are significantly magnified by additional beliefs that Asian Americans are "model minorities" who keep quiet, remain invisible, and are accommodating.

The challenges I faced because of faulty assumptions on the part of others also came from students. Based on my ethnicity and gender, students frequently expressed assumptions they had before taking my classes—from my being demanding to being docile and submissive. A few times, the fact that I might be a professor was too far beyond their domain of possibilities. Even if the evidence pointed to my being the professor, the students may have experienced cognitive dissonance and assumed this could not be the case because of stereotyped images

---

[8]Subsequently, the dean made many decisions that affected me. When another faculty candidate and I tied in an election for the school's director position, the school forwarded both of our names and recommended appointing either of us. The dean selected the other candidate. Years later, when the chair election came up again, the then-associate dean of the college said that the dean advised him that regardless of the election results, he would not appoint me (or, for that matter, any of the other senior faculty members of our school).

[9]Okihiro (2001) addresses "normative assumptions" people make and "the binaries [in such areas as: male/female; black/white; and homosexual/heterosexual] that comprise and sustain them" (p. xii).

of what a professor looks like. Assumptions are based on stereotypes, as the examples below reveal.

Stereotypes

Throughout my life, I have been the subject of many stereotypes. In academia, I experienced the same stereotypes I encountered elsewhere, including ones related to my gender, ethnicity, culture, and background. When I first started teaching in a predominantly White European American institution, for example, it was beyond some students' imaginations that I could possibly be their professor. On the first day of class, I arrived early, and I sat at the desk in front, facing all the students, which was typical of a professor's placement in class. In front of me were stacks of handouts, including the course outline for the class, which I was reviewing. Despite the obvious, that I was the professor waiting for the designated time to begin class, a student came up to me asking for Professor Takahashi. When I told him I was that person, he looked shocked and acted as if he did not believe me.

In another example, I was sitting at my desk in my office, which was clearly marked outside the door with my name. A student came through my open door and asked whether Professor Takahashi "is around." I told him who I was, and he said he was surprised because he thought I was "the secretary." He made this assumption, perhaps based on his stereotype of what a professor looks like, despite the

---

[10]Assumptions based on stereotypes such as this may seem innocent and insignificant, but, as Mink and Solinger (2003) point out, faulty assumptions may lead to very adverse consequences in terms of policies and programs. See their book for a history of how faulty assumptions affected women in terms of welfare policy in the United States.

fact that there was only one desk in that office, I was sitting at it, and the name professor Takahashi was posted on the door.[10]

Many other stereotypes affected me in academia, particularly ones related to my ancestral heritage. As a doctoral student, I had my first pedagogical experience coteaching a baccalaureate social work class with another professor. At our first meeting, she admitted she was still anxious and somewhat uncomfortable around persons of Japanese ancestry because of fears that were drilled into her when she was a child. During World War II, she watched movies that depicted persons of Japanese ancestry as treacherous demons who conducted sneak attacks on unsuspecting victims. As a result, she was very fearful as a child that an evil Japanese person might be hiding under her bed. Despite the passage of time, she had been struggling to dispel this stereotype of persons of Japanese ancestry.

While teaching, I became keenly aware of the prevalence of stereotyped images based on ethnicity and ancestral background. Some students told me that they and others are afraid of taking classes from any Japanese or Asian American professors because they are "rigorous," "demanding," and "difficult."

Erroneous Linkages

Many people of color face being viewed as one and the same as all persons from the country of their ancestry. Through the years, for example, I am often seen as a Japanese immigrant from Japan, not as the U.S. American of Japanese ancestry that I am. Numerous times, I am asked questions like, "How do you like my country [the United States]?" or "Where did you learn to speak such good English?" Frequently, I am asked, "What are you?" or "What's your nationality?" All of these experiences, however, did not prepare me for the jolt I received from another social work faculty member.

To help us come together interpersonally, the faculty in one of the schools in which I taught decided to engage in an exercise designed to help us get to know each other on a more personal level. We broke into groups of three to share personal stories related to our backgrounds and the development of professional values and career choices. I began my personal story by talking about my family's residence in Idaho. I explained the U.S. government's policy of excluding Japanese Americans from the West Coast during World War II, and I described the restrictions, forced removals, and incarcerations imposed by governments. I was setting the stage to explain the beginnings of my social-justice focus and perspective on standing up and speaking out. I was never able to complete the story, however, because one of the professors in my group literally interrupted me and interjected her "anti-story." According to Denning (2005), "an anti-story is a story that arises in opposition to another. . . Anti-stories aim at undermining the original story" (p. 4).

To begin her antistory[II], the professor said that, if we talk of injustices meted out to Japanese Americans, we must talk about the injustices done by the Japanese to the Chinese. She described how Japanese people occupied her parents' homeland before World War II and how her parents and others were forced to vacate their homes in China, fleeing for their lives. It was apparent from her story that she made no distinction between Japanese Americans in the United States, who were supposed to be protected by the U.S. Constitution, and Japanese nationals from Japan. The antistory she presented was reminiscent of what happened to a Japanese American secondary school student who was born in the United States, half a century after World War II: his teacher suggested that he was responsible for the Japanese bombing of Pearl Harbor.[12]

Disconnections and Disparities

When one has connections and associations with people and groups in power, that individual is given advantages and privileges that are often not realized by those who do not have the same associations.[13] I am mindful of opportunities, appointments, and privileges some enjoy simply because they are of the same reference group or because they are a

---

[II] Denning (2004) emphasizes the power of storytelling, which can affect emotions and move people to change beliefs and behaviors.

[12] Werhane (1999) provides a partial explanation for such responses by discussing the mental models we construct and citing the work of Gentner and Whitley (1997, 210–211): a "mental model connotes the idea that human beings have mental representations, cognitive frames, or mental pictures of their experiences—models of stimuli or date with which they are interacting—and these are frameworks that set up parameters [through] which experiences, or a certain set of experiences, are organized or filtered" (p. 53).

Commonly, a mental model that people construct about persons of Japanese ancestry is one whereby there is no distinction between or among persons of Japanese ancestry, whether they were born in the United States or Japan.

[13] Disparate power and privilege are reflected in all areas of policy. For immigration policy, for example, Ngai (2004) reveals how those in power were able to define who should be included or excluded in immigration. In her words, "Immigration policy is constitutive of Americans' understanding of national membership and citizenship, drawing lines of inclusion and exclusion that articulate a desired composition—imagined if not necessarily realized—of the nation" (p. 5).

friend, or associate, or friend of a friend.[14] Many get special breaks, land appointments, receive important awards, or are selected for publication and presentation based on connections and networks. Often, these special perks are covert, rather than open. The potential implications are addressed by Johnson (2001): "[T]rouble is produced by a world organized in ways that encourage people to use difference to include or exclude, reward or punish, credit or discredit, elevate or oppress, value or devalue, leave alone or harass" (p. 19). Feagin (2000) submits that, while "removing discrimination and inequalities. . . are important. . . the eradication of racism will eventually require the uprooting and replacement of the existing hierarchy of racialized power" (p. 270).

Also applicable is Frederickson's (2002) "theory or conception of racism," which is comprised of two components: difference and power. His thesis is:

> It [difference and power] originates from a mindset that regards "them" as different from "us" in ways that are permanent and unbridgeable. This sense of difference provides a motive or rationale for using our power advantage to treat the ethnoracial Other in ways that we would regard as cruel or unjust if applied to members of our own group. (p. 9)

While in-group and out-group disconnections exist, they are difficult to prove. One may not be able to explain processes and dynamics fully and completely, but one can feel and document the disparate results.[15]

Fence-Sitting Colleagues

To create change in academia or to rectify and eliminate wrongs takes collective action. One of the biggest challenges I faced is that many faculty opt to take the easy way out by not standing up, speaking out, and blowing the whistle on wrongs. It has been my experience that many may complain and state the need for change, but when the time comes to actually move, many take the path of least resistance and do nothing.

One example of this was a case some years ago of clear-cut forgery about which the faculty, as a collective, failed to move or take action. The director of the social work program forged two faculty signatures on an MSW student's culminating master's degree paper. He forged mine—I was the sponsoring faculty—and that of the second faculty reader. I filed a complaint, and, in the process of investigation and with solid evidence, the faculty member admitted he forged the signatures. Further, he lied (several times) to cover up what he did. When the case came before the faculty, they decided as a collective not to recommend censure or disciplinary action. All recognized the wrong, but they failed to take corrective action. One faculty member surmised that, if I were not a faculty of color and

---

[14] Pierson (2004) says, "Understanding how institutional arrangements become deeply embedded over time suggests the need to reframe the topic as one of institutional development rather than institutional choice" (p. 16). This same propensity to become embedded can be applied to individuals if they do not engage in ongoing mindful critical analyses.

[15] See Gutmann (2003) for a discussion of the significance of identity politics.

the forger not a White European American male, the vote would have been very different.

Despite this director's behaviors, which fit the definition of "toxic leader" (Lipman-Blumen, 2005), the faculty promoted such behaviors by failing to send the message that such illegal activities would not be tolerated. This is not unusual, Lipman-Blumen says, because "[s]ometimes we ignore toxic leaders' obvious faults because their charisma blinds us" (p. 11). Further:

> Toxic leaders cast their spell broadly. Most of us claim we abhor them. Yet we frequently follow—or at least tolerate—them. When toxic leaders don't appear on their own, we often seek them out. On occasion, we even create them by pushing good leaders over the toxic line. (p. ix)

> Followers of toxic leaders often do much more than simply tolerate them. They commonly adulate, abet, and actually prefer toxic leaders to their nontoxic counterparts. (pp. 3–4)

Beyond this case example, I have found again and again in academia that seldom do faculty take a stand and act. Privately, they frequently talk as if they find a situation intolerable, unethical, and even illegal, but they still prefer not to rock the boat, especially if they are trying to protect an interest. It has been a challenge dealing with faculty who profess one thing, but fail to act on their convictions, particularly when it does not affect them directly.

Illegalities and Unethical Wrongs

Another distasteful challenge I faced through the years involves being asked (and sometimes ordered) to commit unethical actions and wrongs, some of which were illegal. As a lobbyist, I was ordered by a board member of the organization I worked for to forge a signature. As the legislative strategist for the organization, the board member was in a position of power and frequently tried to order me around. I doubt whether he would have done the same to a male in my position. He demanded that I sign a letter he wrote that was supposed to be from the sister of a Japanese American soldier who was killed in action. During World War II, Ronald Reagan was at the posthumous award ceremony, as were the deceased soldier's mother and sister. Years later, to convince then-President Reagan to sign the Japanese American redress bill into law, the legislative strategist planned to send a letter supposedly from the sister to the president, reflecting on the day they were together at the ceremony. Of course, I refused to forge the signature, which angered him and further contributed to his subsequent retaliation.

In academia, I have been shocked when asked or told to either engage in unethical practices or to look the other way. One example involves being asked to change the name of the first director of an institute so that someone else would be credited. When I refused, the person (who wanted credit for being the first director) then called the real first director and asked whether he would be willing to give up the distinction as first director. Rightly, he refused and instead produced proof that he was the first director.

Another case example of questionable behaviors involved an article I cowrote with two other faculty members. Clearly, I was the primary lead author as

I was the person who was invited to write the guest article for a journal and I conceptualized and wrote most of the text. Further, I assembled, organized, coordinated, and edited the final manuscript and worked with the journal editor before publication. In the spirit of collegiality, I invited two colleagues to contribute portions, and I included their names as coauthors. After the article was published, one of the listed coauthors—and, ironically, the one who contributed the least to the article—listed her name first when citing the published article in her resume.[16] This was done despite the fact that her name appears last on the journal publication.

Each of these situations was unfortunate and unpleasant. I felt degraded and disrespected when asked (or ordered) to engage in unethical and improper behaviors or illegal actions. Such behaviors were disturbing, and I was insulted that anyone would expect me to be a participant.

Other Challenges

The challenges I have faced in academia are countless and too numerous to cover sufficiently in this short chapter. Therefore, I simply list a few additional examples.

1. *Talkers, Not Doers:* Talk is easy, but action is what counts. Countless times, people did not deliver what they said they would. This became especially problematic when there was a plan to change something, but, when the critical time came, people did not deliver.

For example, instead of supporting something as they said they would, they opposed or sabotaged it. In other instances, it was critical that people follow through on their share of a task in order for a change effort to occur, but they simply did not deliver, and the efforts were lost. Many who do not follow up spend more time presenting themselves in a way they want others to perceive them and building their image than following up and delivering the promised goods.

2. *Dividers and Conquerors:* I have experienced a range of actions that were set up to pit one faculty member against another. It was sad to witness two women of color pitted against each other, with both coming out on the losing end. The goal of dividing and rendering them powerless was achieved.

3. *Turf Builders and Preservers:* Some faculty members have established their own niche or turf, and they fight to preserve it—often at the expense of newly appointed faculty, many of whom are women or persons of color. It is a sad state of affairs when one sees people so entrenched in preserving their own self-interest and to the expense of the greater good of others and the institution.

4. *Closeted Resenters:* I am mindful of some faculty members who deeply resent alteration of the privilege structure. In the past, they may have had the advantage, but, with diversity initiatives, legal changes, structural modifications, and other edicts, the academic climate may have changed, at least slightly. I have seen, heard, and experienced the resentment, both covert and overt.

---

[16]With regard to "the pursuit of attention," Derber (2000) says, "people hunger for it and suffer terribly from its deprivation; many compete subtly but fiercely to get it; and it is one of the social badges of prestige and success" (p. xii).

5. *Underminers:* Countless times, I have seen how women or persons of color are undermined in various ways. In some instances, their ideas are taken, stolen, or otherwise not attributed, while, at other times, their ideas and contributions are not even heard or acknowledged. I have seen many dynamics with regard to rank and privilege, all the way from club-like exclusion to plantation-like paternalism.

SURVIVAL STRATEGIES

I have found that it is important to stay focused on who I am, what I represent, what foundation principles must be preserved and honored, and what purposes and missions must be achieved. Through it all, I viewed all challenges from the perspective that they are events from which I could learn and develop. I do not allow setbacks or unpleasant events to consume or immobilize me. Instead, they become interesting and stimulating sources of introspection and thought. Most important, I find it imperative to enjoy what I am doing, to feel that I am accomplishing goals, and to have fun.

My top 10 list of survival strategies (not in any order of significance) for academia are:

1. Before taking action, think critically and ask questions[17]. Conduct the "Does it make sense" test. If it does not make sense to carry out an illegal or improper order, for example, then consider all angles and decide how to proceed. Further, bring together and apply all levels of knowledge in Bloom's taxonomy of learning, including knowledge, comprehension, application, analysis, synthesis, and evaluation (Atherton, 2005).

2. Plan and map out an action plan. Think of the implications and consequences of every possible direction.

3. Speak up, protest, and take action, especially when a wrong infringes on ethical standards and principles of social justice[18], human rights, civil liberties[19], and civil rights[20].

4. Work hard and do the job well. Honor commitments and ensure that others will not feel compelled to do your job.

5. Be a genuine team member who carries out an equitable share of the work and responsibilities.

6. Do not do other peoples' jobs. Everyone should be responsible for his or her own work.

7. Adjust your expectations so you will not be disappointed. When people do a lot of talking and little producing and following up,

[17] See Leeds (2000) for a discussion about the powers of asking questions.

[18] See Folger and Cropanzano (1998) for a discussion of different types of justice: distributive, procedural, and interactional.

[19] Leone and Anrig (2003) address the implications the war on terrorism has for civil liberties.

[20] Actions have been taken to weaken or undermine the advances in civil rights, so one must be vigilant. Affirmative-action, for example, has been under attack. See Takahashi (2005) for historical and current issues with regard to advances and erosions to affirmative-action policies, programs, and practices.

you should expect that this is a strong possibility, not an aberration.

8. Be respectful, fair, just, ethical[21], and consistent. Be mindful of the inter- and intracultural factors that are always involved.

9. Stay focused and do not allow extraneous "flurries" (e.g., tantrums and posturing) to derail or throw you off track.

10. Collaborate, communicate, network, and support. Practice "cultural competency"[22] and what Ting-Toomey (1999) calls "transcultural communication competence" (TCC), which is "a transformation process connecting intercultural knowledge with competent practice. To be a competent transcultural communicator, we need to transform our knowledge of intercultural theories into appropriate and effective performance" (p. 261). Further, "a dynamic transcultural communicator is one who creates and

---

[21]Follow NASW (1999) and International Federation of Social Workers (1994). The latter has been updated, but, as of publication, was not posted online.

NASW Code of Ethics Preamble says, in part:
Social workers promote social justice and social change with and on behalf of clients. "Clients" is used inclusively to refer to individuals, families, groups, organizations, and communities. Social workers are sensitive to cultural and ethnic diversity and strive to end discrimination, oppression, poverty, and other forms of social injustice. These activities may be in the form of direct practice, community organizing, supervision, consultation, administration, advocacy, social and political action, policy development and implementation, education, and research and evaluation. Social workers seek to enhance the capacity of people to address their own needs. Social workers also seek to promote the responsiveness of organizations, communities, and other social institutions to individuals' needs and social problems.

Section 6.04 Social and Political Action says:
Social workers should act to expand choice and opportunity for all people, with special regard for vulnerable, disadvantaged, oppressed, and exploited people and groups.

Social workers should promote conditions that encourage respect for cultural and social diversity within the United States and globally. Social workers should promote policies and practices that demonstrate respect for difference, support the expansion of cultural knowledge and resources, advocate for programs and institutions that demonstrate cultural competence, and promote policies that safeguard the rights of and confirm equity and social justice for all people.

Social workers should act to prevent and eliminate domination of, exploitation of, and discrimination against any person, group, or class on the basis of race, ethnicity, national origin, color, sex, sexual orientation, age, marital status, political belief, religion, or mental or physical disability.

Also see Reamer (2001) for an "ethics audit."

[22]Apply NASW's Standards of Cultural Competence in Social Work Practice (2001). In part, it says:
Cultural competence is never fully realized, achieved, or completed, but rather cultural competence is a lifelong process for social workers who will always encounter diverse clients and new situations in their practice. Supervisors and workers should have the expectation that cultural competence is an ongoing learning process integral and central to daily supervision.

Cultural competence refers to the process by which individuals and systems respond respectfully and effectively to people of all cultures, languages, classes, races, ethnic backgrounds, religions, and other diversity factors in a manner that recognizes, affirms, and values the worth of individuals, families, and communities and protects and preserves the dignity of each.

Cultural competence is a set of congruent behaviors, attitudes, and policies that come together in a system or agency or among professionals and enable the system, agency, or professionals to work effectively in crosscultural situations.

Operationally defined, cultural competence is the integration and transformation of knowledge about individuals and groups of people into specific standards, policies, practices, and attitudes used in appropriate cultural settings to increase the quality of services, thereby producing better outcomes (Pope-Davis & Coleman, 1997). Competence in crosscultural functioning means learning new patterns of behavior and effectively applying them in appropriate settings.

Also refer to Lum's (2003) discussion of culturally competent practice and Takahashi's (2004) chapter in Gutierrez, Zuniga, and Lum calling for diversity-focused teaching in all areas of social policy. Takahashi (2003) also pinpoints areas of crosscultural discussion in social policy courses.

manages meanings appropriately, effectively, and satisfactorily in a diverse range of cultural situations" (p. 265).

CONCLUSION

In this chapter, I present reflections on my experience in academia for the past 27 years. In the spirit of learning (and there are many lessons to be learned), I directly and honestly identified specific events, activities, and phenomena that I experienced. I especially pinpointed ones that posed thorny challenges, but that were, at the same time, most important to deal with. As my opening metaphoric story conveys, it is crucial to deal with problems and issues at the onset, before they become overpowering, overwhelming, and all-consuming, similar to the weeds in my story.

My childhood experience in the agricultural fields of Idaho gave me many insights that are critical to my work as an activist, educator, researcher, scholar, and advocate. Once I identified the problem (whether the plant was a weed or planted crop), I learned that I needed to take timely action before the problem (weeds) grew, multiplied, or got out of control. Similarly, with each challenge I faced in academia, I knew I had to pinpoint the problem or issue and take timely action to stop its further growth and development into deeper, stronger, and more powerful injustices and wrongs.

REFERENCES

Atherton, J. S. (2005). *Teaching and learning: Bloom's taxonomy*. Retrieved June 1, 2005, from http://www.learningandteaching.info/learning/bloomtax.htm

Denning, S. (2004). *Squirrel Inc.: A fable of leadership through storytelling*. San Francisco: Jossey-Bass.

Denning, S. (2005). *What are the main types of stories and narratives?* Retrieved May 31, 2005, from http://stevedenning.com/Main_types_story.html

Derber, C. (2000). *The pursuit of attention: Power and ego in every day life* (2nd ed.). Oxford, United Kingdom: Oxford University Press.

Feagin, J. R. (2000). *Racist America: Roots, current realities, and future reparations*. New York: Routledge.

Folger, R., & Cropanzano, R. (1998). *Organizational justice and human resource management*. Thousand Oaks, CA: Sage Publications.

Frederickson, G. M. (2002). *Racism: A short history*. Princeton, NJ: Princeton University Press.

Gentner, D., & Whitley, E. W. (1997). Mental models of population growth: A preliminary investigation. In M. H. Bazerman, D. M. Messick, A. E. Tenebrunsel, & K. A. Wade-Benzoni (Eds.), *Environment, ethics, and behavior: The psychology of environmental valuation and degradation* (pp. 209–233). San Francisco: New Lexington Press.

Gutmann, A. (2003). *Identity in democracy*. Princeton, NJ: Princeton University Press.

International Federation of Social Workers. (2005). *Ethics in social work: Statement of principles*. Retrieved September 27, 2006, from http://www.ifsw.org/en/p38000324.html

Johnson, A. G. (2001). *Privilege, power, and difference*. Mountain View, CA: Mayfield Publishing.

Kirk, G., & Okazawa-Rey, M. (2007). *Women's lives: Multicultural perspectives* (4th ed.). Boston: McGraw-Hill.

Leeds, D. (2000). *The 7 powers of questions: Secrets to successful communication in life and at work*. New York: Berkley.

Leone, R. C., & Anrig, G., Jr. (Eds.). (2003). *The war on our free doms: Civil liberties in an age of terrorism*. New York: BBS Public Affairs.

Lipman-Blumen, J. (2005). *The allure of toxic leaders: Why we follow destructive bosses and corrupt politicians—and how we can survive them*. Oxford, United Kingdom: Oxford University Press.

Lum, D. (2003). *Culturally competent practice: A framework for understanding diverse groups and justice issues*. Pacific Grove, CA: Brooks/Cole–Thomson Learning.

Mink, G., & Solinger, R. (Eds.). (2003). *Welfare: A documentary history of U.S. policy and politics*. New York: New York University Press.

National Association of Social Workers. (1999). *Code of ethics of the National Association of Social Workers*. Washington, DC: Author. Retrieved May 31, 2005, from http://www.socialworkers.org/pubs/code/code.asp

National Association of Social Workers. (2001). *NASW standards of cultural competence in social work practice*. Washington, DC: Author. Retrieved May 31, 2005, from http://www.social workers.org/practice/standards/naswculturalstandards.pdf

Ngai, M. M. (2004). *Impossible subjects: Illegal aliens and the making of modern America*. Princeton, NJ: Princeton University Press.

Okihiro, G. Y. (2001). *Common ground: Reimagining American history*. Princeton, NJ: Princeton University Press.

Pierson, P. (2004). *Politics in time: History, institutions, and social analysis*. Princeton, NJ: Princeton University Press.

Pope-Davis, D. B., & Coleman, H. L. K. (1997). *Multicultural counseling competencies: Assessment, education and training, and supervision*. Thousand Oaks, CA: Sage Publications.

Reamer, F. G. (2001). *The social work ethics audit: A risk man agement tool*. Washington, DC: NASW Press.

Takahashi, R. (1978). *'Military necessity:' An effective rhetorical tool for policy implementation and social change. The plight of Japanese Americans during World War II*. Doctoral competency paper, University of Pittsburgh, Pennsylvania.

Takahashi, R. (1980). Comparative administration and man agement of five War Relocation Authority camps: America's incarceration of persons of Japanese ancestry during World War II. *Dissertation Abstracts International, 42*(09), 4141 (UMI No. AAT 8202328).

Takahashi, R. (2003). What's going on? An experiential simulation for culturally appropriate social policy analysis. In B. S. Jansson (Ed.), *Innovative ways to teach policy practice and policy advocacy: To be used in conjunction with becoming an effective policy advocate: From policy practice to social justice* (4th ed., pp. 76–87). Pacific Grove, CA: Brooks/Cole Thomson–Learning.

Takahashi, R. (2004). Infusion of multicultural diversity content in social policy courses. In L. Gutierrez, M. Zuniga, & D. Lum (Eds.), *Education for multicultural social work practice: Critical viewpoints and future directions* (pp. 55–75). Alexandria, VA: Council on Social Work Education.

Takahashi, R. (2007). U.S. concentration camps and exclusion policies: Impact on Japanese American women. In G. Kirk & M. Okazawa-Rey, *Women's lives: Multicultural perspectives* (4th ed., pp. 457–463). Boston: McGraw-Hill.

Takahashi, R. (2005). Affirmative action policies: To be continued. In R. Takahashi (Ed.), *Diversity: Value, promote, and achieve* (pp. 99–144). San Francisco: Institute for Multicultural Research and Social Work Practice.

Ting-Toomey, S. (1999). *Communicating across cultures*. New York: Guilford Press.

Werhane, P. H. (1999). *Moral imagination and management decision-making*. New York: Oxford University Press.

Part II: The Voices of Women of Color as Social Work Educators

Chapter 20: Epiphany: My Pacific Islander Voice

Halaevalu F. Ofahengaue Vakalahi

To the phenomenal women who have been the creators of my voice—my mom Faleola, mom Vika; sisters Lucy and Lavinia; Grandmas Meleane Fakalata, Mafi Ofahengaue, Sela Tui, Latu Vimahi; and Dr. Katharine Briar–Lawson.

Epiphany is defined by James Joyce (1994) as "a sudden spiritual manifestation, whether in the vulgarity of speech or of gesture or in a memorable phase of the mind itself" (p. 1). He believed that it was for "the man [or woman] of letters to record these epiphanies with extreme care, seeing that they themselves are the most delicate and evanescent of moments" (p. 1). He suggested that all things, human or object, can experience epiphany. Evidently, there is beauty in all things, and requisites for beauty are characteristics of integrity, wholeness, symmetry and radiance. When an object reaches radiance, that object has experienced epiphany, and when we discover the beauty in that object, we have experienced epiphany.

Writing this chapter was one of the most "epiphanized" experiences of my life. As difficult as it was at times, I ultimately saw beauty in all my experiences as I processed and perhaps relived my life as a person and professional. As I wrote this chapter, indeed, I thank God for the epiphanies I received that came every Sunday unfailingly during church. Somehow, I am not surprised at the place of inspiration because of my spiritual upbringing. I come from a family, community, and culture in which spirituality, as practiced often through organized religion, is an integral part of our lives. That spiritual upbringing has literally saved my life as a social work educator.

PERSONAL BIOGRAPHY

My name is Halaevalu Fonongavainga Ofahengaue Vakalahi. In my 30s, I am a Pacific Islander American woman of Tongan descent (Polynesian group). I am the daughter of Moana and Faleola Ofahengaue, bold and audacious immigrants from the islands of Tonga, who lived by their belief that, with God, nothing is impossible. I have two sisters, Lucy and Lavinia, who have been extraordinary exemplars in my life, and three brothers, Likalio, Kelepi, and Tevita, who have taught me how to live and love life to the fullest. I grew up in a very spiritually grounded family and culture, which contributes to my seemingly complex worldview.

I am currently a tenure-track associate professor and director of the MSW program at George Mason University Department of Social Work. In June 2005, I chose to engage in a new academic adventure, essentially an one that stems from my interest in social policies as possible methods of leveling the playing field: I joined the Council on Social Work Education (CSWE) as an accreditation specialist. Before joining CSWE and in the infancy stages of this writing, I was a faculty member at San Francisco State University School of Social Work for two years as a lecturer, one of which I served as Baccalaureate Program Coordinator. Previous to that appointment, I was a tenure-track assistant professor and department chairwoman at Brigham Young University–Hawaii Department of Social Work; and, earlier, I was a tenure-track assistant professor at New Mexico State University School of Social Work, where the support of the faculty made a difference in my first experience as a social work educator. I have been involved in academia, post-PhD, for over six years, all in the social work program at the baccalaureate or master's level. Family circumstances and, perhaps, the endless opportunities that come with a PhD contributed to my four shifts in universities within the past seven years.

PERSONAL JOURNEY

Strengths and Ambitions

Although it would be irresponsible to ignore the realities of injustice in the daily lives of women of color in social work education, it is perhaps a greater commission to celebrate their strengths, ambitions, and phenomenal lives. Because I am a Pacific Islander woman, the strengths and ambitions passed down from those who have gone before me have served as my roots and wings in my personal and professional lives. Who I am as a social work educator is strongly linked to my family and Pacific Islander cultural backgrounds. As I discuss below, certain parts of my family and culture, particularly spirituality, have great bearing on my professional social work self and, perhaps, often explain my way of thinking, speaking, and doing.

Spiritual Grounding

In spite of the impact of colonization and immigration, Pacific Island cultures and identities for the most part have survived (Kenney, 1976; Narokobi, 1983; Ritchie & Ritchie, 1979). There are many reasons for a culture to survive; however, for Pacific Islanders, there is an underlying belief that all matters with a spiritual purpose, foundation, and connection will last forever. For instance, in my Tongan culture, it is an enduring belief that the people of the tiny island kingdom has survived total annihilation and remained free because the people are spiritually grounded and connected to God, each other, and their ancestors. The politics of social work education and dealing with realities of oppression, racism, sexism, and other isms required tapping into these sources of strength.

I have also relied heavily on my religion, another vehicle for my spirituality, particularly in relation to the power of faith and prayer. I have indeed relied on the tender mercies of God as my spiritual grounding to carry me through tough personal and political times in the academy. I have never said so many prayers in my life as I did as a social work student and, especially, as an educator. With much faith, in times when I fail, I get up and get over it.

Intergenerational Living

A Pacific Island child enters a world of abundant love and attention from a wide circle of people of all ages and genders (i.e., aunts, uncles, cousins, and grandparents). Because the Pacific Island child has many parents, the social world of affection and attachments spreads wide; the voices that reprimand are collective; and the hands that discipline are considered loving and caring (Kenney, 1976; Narokobi, 1983; Ritchie & Ritchie, 1979). In intergenerational living, trust is not dependent on one person, but is invested in many (McDermott, Tseng, & Maretzki, 1980).

Growing up with multiple parents and living in an intergenerational setting have served as a source of protection from the harsh realities of the American educational system. Encouragement and expectation to reach the highest level of education came from my many mothers and fathers, aunts and uncles, cousins, and grandparents. Because a lot of dialogue about encouragement, expectations, dreams, and aspirations commonly took place during mealtimes, while growing up, I seldom remember eating alone. As a result of being constantly surrounded by family during mealtimes, I had unlimited access to the teachings, strengths, and ambitions of my aunts, uncles, cousins, and grandparents, which ultimately served as a source of strength in my adult years as a social work educator.

I thank God for the many phenomenal women in my life, my many mothers who influenced me during my early years of life, those named herein, and many others: my elementary school Title I teachers, Ms. Alofipo, Ms. Moea'i, and Ms. Ah You;

my high school teachers, Ms. Vanisi and Ms. Long; my young women teachers, Lanae, Laura, Kapua, Lilian, and Marina; my *fanga mehekitanga* (father's sisters) and *fanga fa'e* (mother's sisters); my many mothers and grandmothers from Hauula, Laie, and Kahuku; and my other mothers, Elisa and Leutogi, and, of course, my sisters, Cathy, Trina, Jorie, Jolene, Tiare, Fredda, and Deloma. I am also extremely blessed to have had Drs. Marge Edwards, Joanne Yaffe, Rowena Fong, and Meripa Godinet in my life as I struggled through academia as a social work student and now an educator.

Value of Womanhood

Another great value of Pacific Island cultures that contributed to my identity is reverence for women and womanhood. Although there are variations within Pacific Island cultures pertaining to the traditional role and status of women, reverence for women and womanhood is a constant. For example, in my native Tongan culture, the eldest sister of one's father occupies the role of a *fahu*, meaning symbolic matriarch (Ervin, 1985). By virtue of being a woman, a *fahu* has unconditional inherent social status and material and political powers that supersede those of men and others in the family—powers that must be acknowledged whether or not she is present. In addition, the value of women and womanhood is a fundamental part of the doctrines of my religion. According to Cannon and Mulvay-Derr (1992), "Women of the Church [of Jesus Christ of Latter-day Saints (LDS)] are given some measure of divine authority particularly in the direction of government and instruction in behalf of the women

of the church." Despite differences in opinions and experiences regarding this issue, particularly in relation to women of color, the value of women and womanhood continues to be taught and embraced in the church and extended to me as an equal to men.

The idea of reverence for the inherent authority and power of women in my Tongan culture and the value of womanhood in my religion are often foreign and conflicting values in the academy, the "White man's castle." As a Tongan woman, I find being highly valued is an unconditional and inherent right that does not require a verbal reminder or demand. With colleagues and administrators in the academy, respect often is not extended; instead, it always occurred in a quid pro quo and conditional format (I will respect you if you first respect me). Sometimes, the alternative paradigm of my race and gender generated disrespect and disregard from students and faculty. Nonetheless, drawing on my spirituality and my worth as a Tongan LDS woman, I continue to work hard upholding my standards as a woman of color and focusing on the fact that I, too, have a right to be in the academy as an educator.

Challenges and Barriers

Although the celebration of strengths and ambitions is critical, the realities of the challenges and barriers I have encountered as a Pacific Islander American woman are not forgotten. The select personal challenges discussed below have built my character and served as a source of motivation to achieve as a social work educator.

Immigration

As a middle school principal in Tonga, my father received the opportunity to attend Church College of Hawaii (currently BYU–Hawaii) located in Laie. Thus, in April 1977, when I was nine, my family migrated from Tonga to Hawaii. As a recent immigrant family into the United States, we found the economic demands especially high, and my parents' moderate educational achievements resulted in extensive sacrifice of time and energy for the family to survive. Upon arrival in Hawaii, both of my parents started working at the Polynesian Cultural Center, which provided a decent living. But it was quite an adjustment from living a very comfortable life in Tonga, where my mother was a nurse and my father a middle school principal. Nonetheless, these challenges strengthened and reinforced my parents' dreams and aspirations for their young family.

Forgetting their personal needs and interests, they focused on assuring that each one of their six children earned a university degree (secretly praying that at least one would earn a PhD). Grounded in the idea that education is the great equalizer and that nothing is impossible with God, they worked harder, making available every tool and mechanism for their children to excel in education. All six of us have earned our bachelor's degree, with careers ranging from teachers and counselors to engineers and entrepreneurs; one earned a PhD; and one is currently working on completing a graduate degree. My parents' educational dreams and aspirations also extended to the spouses of their children (three have earned graduate degrees) and their grandchildren, the current generation of the Ofahengaue

family entering universities. I truly echo my parents' belief that, with God, nothing is impossible.

Although immigration was an enormous personal challenge, I learned to appreciate sacrifice and hard work, especially as a social work educator. I have a deep appreciation for my parents' sacrifices, and I extend the same appreciation and respect to my students through always expecting and demanding their best work in and out of the classroom.

Language

When my family arrived in Hawaii, I was immediately placed in the Title I program, where I learned English as a second language. It was through this program that I became extremely motivated to master the English language in order to alleviate the negative consequences of the language barrier. Ultimately, I developed a passion for written communication that has benefited me as a social work educator. In hindsight, the difference in my experiences with the language barrier was the selfless support of my Title I teachers and my mother, who woke up tirelessly at 4:30 each morning to help me with my spelling and vocabulary. Essentially, the Title I program cultivated my character and love of writing, which made me a stronger and more capable social work educator, particularly in relation to understanding the struggles of students speaking English as a second language, yet expecting nothing less of language mastery.

Perceptions

I cannot honestly say that I have met anyone who had 100% unquestioning confidence in my abilities as a human being, student, and educator, except my parents and brothers and sisters. There always seem to be reservations at some unspoken level, often in relation to my Pacific Islander background as a barrier. On several occasions, after a seemingly positive meeting with me, social work program hiring committees have asked bystanders, "Is she a typical Pacific Islander—not too academic, lazy, too laid back?" Regardless, I continue to do my best to combat the oppressive nature of misperceptions, and I hope, in the process, I will recognize when I am the oppressor and take the proper action against it.

PROFESSIONAL JOURNEY

As a Student

As immigrants to this country, my parents encouraged my siblings and me to dream big, especially in pursuing a fine education. In addition to the encouragement to dream, my parents taught us that fulfillment of dreams is not an investment in or the contribution of one person, but an investment in and the contribution of many. In other words, any success I ultimately enjoy is a result of the contribution of others.

The PhD was in a league of its own, but it was an accomplishment that broke many barriers for young Pacific Islander women. It was a long, hard fight to be accepted into the PhD program. One of the most influential conversations I had during this time was with an administrator who told me bluntly, "I don't know if you'll ever get into the PhD program." It was "someone's" reality check, but it was also a defining moment in my life in relation to

pursuing a PhD. I walked out of the office with the determination to prove her wrong. With the grace of God and contributions of many, I received my chance to pursue and complete the PhD. Again, to my good fortune, I met a few Good Samaritans, students and faculty, who nurtured and mentored me through the program. It is noteworthy that many of my mentors were White European American men and women. As a social work educator, I have done my best to give my students the same courtesy offered to me by these mentors.

Earning the PhD was definitely making a statement that barriers ought to be broken. Having the gift of the PhD is a liberating experience on many levels. It has given me access to privileges unavailable to many, the means to travel and live where I so desire, and some authority in mentoring students, especially students of color.

As A Social Work Educator

Sociocultural Justice

The most significant reason for my interest in the academy relates to my desire to give voice to my Pacific Islander culture, particularly in a setting where the predominant voice is male and White European American. Sharing my culture, particularly in terms of my Pacific Islander community orientation, collectivity, reciprocity, and respect for the elderly, contributes to social justice and diversity in social work education. Being a part of the academy offers a unique opportunity to change the system from within.

Teaching

Christa McAuliffe, an exemplary teacher and NASA's first teacher in space, said, "I touch the future, I teach" (Hohler, 1986). I believe that social work education makes a difference in the future of people, communities, cultures, and the world. Making a positive difference in a person's life has been my goal as a social work educator, and I hope I have contributed positively to changing one person's life for the better. As a social work educator, I find that, among my joyous moments in teaching, is when students begin "to think outside the box" and embrace paradigms alternative to their own. Venturing beyond your own imagination and worldview into understanding and accepting the existence of others is the beginning of building the future.

Research and Publication

My enjoyment of writing has been an escape and a coping mechanism for survival in the academy. Social work education has afforded me the opportunity to engage in research and publication, and I have taken advantage of such opportunities to begin contributing to the literature on Pacific Islander issues. Although my achievement in this area is moderate, I do value contribution to the literature as a possible vehicle through which Pacific Islander voices are heard.

Service

Seeing Pacific Islander parents give all they have to support their children through school; engaging in dialogue with a young woman who knows her destiny; seeing a young man excel in school out of respect for his mother and grandmother; and hearing youths describe the PhD as a possible dream make my time spent in community service worthwhile. The opportunities to serve on boards and committees in my Pacific Islander community and the social work profession have truly enriched my life.

The Wage Gap

My worth as a person is not measured by how much money I make. However, how much I am paid in social work education is determined by how much an administrator thinks I am worth. Throughout my years in the academy, I have learned that monetary compensation is a tangible measurement of my worth to the workplace, so it has become an important issue.

Since the beginning of my social work education career, salary has been the most delicate, disheartening, and distressing issue I have faced. In one school, a White European American male with limited teaching and service experience and no research or publications was paid $15,000 more than I, a PhD with more teaching, research, publication, and service experience. When I inquired about it, I was told that salary was based on a formula, obviously one that excluded me. Time and time again, individuals administering salary would explain their way out of a situation with common statements such as, "According to our formula," "You have less experience," "You are too sensitive," and "It is all in your head." Although I learned in graduate school that salaries are negotiable, my experiences thus far have been, "You take it or we'll offer it to someone else." I commonly hear my White European American colleagues saying they negotiated their salary, but that has not been my experience.

Divide and Conquer

How do you conquer a people? Divide them. How do you divide them? Cause mistrust, bickering, backbiting, backstabbing, and so forth. Practice wisdom suggests that a divided faculty and student body is commonplace in the academy, and social work programs are not exempt; sometimes they are at the heart of such issues. Such bickering and backstabbing have divided an entire social work program of faculty and students in terms of overall mission, goals, objectives, and interests. Survival of the fittest in the system is often at the root of this conflict.

Despite so many negative experiences, in the beginning of my career, I was very fortunate to be hired by a school that valued my needs and respected my ethics. In this school, the cliques and camps were apparent; however, each group contributed positively to my success. I was not forced to pick sides, but was nurtured by both and given the autonomy to work with whomever I wanted. They respected my unspoken preference to be my own person and do my own things. In fact, the faculty and staff nurtured me so well that it manifested itself in my excellent teaching evaluations, research and publication agenda, and service to social work and the local community. My later experiences were not very fortunate, but, as a social work educator, I look back and draw hope and energy from this social work program.

Some Learned Lessons

I learned that my true reason for getting the PhD was to be mobile, to have "wings," to have the freedom and choice to venture, and to be able to engage in a variety of activities in and out of academia whenever and wherever I desire. I learned from my family that I can accomplish anything with hard work. In contrast, I learned in the academy that, if you are not politically connected, you are the odd girl out. I learned that a person is hired if there is a "fit" between the person and the social work program. However, the stunning variation in the definition of "fit" could stretch from one's ability to join a clique to one's having similar philosophies. I do not want to "fit" in; I just want to do my job well, influence a few lives for the better, and share my culture. I learned that sometimes the price of institutional support is "losing your voice" and not being able to speak your mind because you have to be quiet to be seen as a team member.

I learned that student evaluations sometimes can be a popularity contest. Even with my PhD, teaching, research, publication, and service experience, many students continue to question my ability and whether, as a woman of color, I belong in social work education. An area of constant questioning, most often by White European American students, is my feedback on student papers and examinations. Although my expectations and demands for excellence in student performance are honestly without malice, often they have been interpreted as such, and a woman of color who is not afraid to provide honest feedback is sometimes perceived as intimidating and aggressive.

In essence, I have had many positive spiritual connections, and I have been mentored and supported by many individuals of color, as well as by White European American individuals. Their willingness and dedication to mentoring give me hope of the possibility of parity and a level playing field. In carrying on the legacy of these mentors, I have strived to encourage the same hope in my students.

Sometimes social justice is difficult to achieve because people, time, and space are not conducive or receptive to it. As social workers, we are responsible for preparing ourselves to make time, space, and opportunities for social justice. The inclusion of the Standards for Cultural Competence in Social Work Practice (NASW, 2001) in social work curriculum, in faculty and student dialogue and activities, gender, and ethnic and racial diversity in *Educational Policies and Accreditation Standards* for all CSWE-accredited social work programs (CSWE, 2003), and even the very act of publishing this book contributes to social justice, equity, and fairness, particularly for women of color.

CONCLUSION

Implications for Social Work Education

1. Social work education needs to make an effort to visibly infuse the experiences of women of color into the social work curriculum (institutionalization).
2. Social work administrators need to foster an environment that helps maintain the spiritual and ethnic cultural strengths of women of color. New mentoring opportunities should be created.
3. Social work education needs to create opportunities for the voices of women of color to be heard and to find ways to protect women of color in social work education in terms of tenure, promotion, and advancement to leadership positions.
4. Social work administrators need to combat the wage gap and develop a plan to level the playing field in terms of salaries and other resources.
5. Often a chance is all that it takes for a woman of color to excel. Active recruitment of women of color, particularly Pacific Islanders, into PhD programs is imperative.

Implications for Policy, Practice, and Research

1. Underrepresentation of women of color in social work education prompts the absolute need for their visibility. For their voices to be heard, underrepresented women of color need to occupy the most visible position in social work education.
2. In working with ethnic minority students, social work educators must be considerate of their cultural responsibilities and the impact of spirituality and intergenerational living patterns on their lives. For example, certain family responsibilities take precedence over educational and other obligations.
3. Expansion of the existing literature is desperately needed. Studies of the impact of spirituality on women of color and intergenerational supports as protective factors must be conducted.

4. Studies of other protective and risk factors for women of color in social work education in terms of tenure and promotion are urgently needed.

Implications for Future Generations of Pacific Islander Women

1. Pursue and obtain the PhD: make no excuses.
2. Do not waste precious time and pick your battles carefully.
3. If you have "wings," use them.
4. Remember the basics. Respect for God and fellow beings can be your greatest source of energy for survival and success in the academy and social work education.

REFERENCES

Cannon, J. R., & Mulvay-Derr, J. (1992). Relief society. In D. H. Ludlow (Ed.), *Encyclopedia of Mormonism* (Vol. 3). New York: Macmillan.

Council on Social Work Education. (2003). *Handbook of accreditation standards and procedures.* Alexandria, VA: Author.

Ervin, A. M. (1985). Culture and agriculture in the North American context. *Culture, 5*(2), 35–52.

Hohler, R. T. (1986). *I touch the future: The story of Christa McAuliffe.* New York: Random House.

Joyce, J. (1994). *James Joyce: Definition of epiphany.* Retrieved September 8, 2006, from http://theliterarylink.com/joyce.html

Kenney, M. (1976). *Youth in Micronesia in the 1970's: The Impact of changing family, employment, and justice systems.* Report on youth development research conducted under Law Enforcement Assistance Administration, U.S. Department of Justice. Saipan, Marianas Islands: Trust Territory Printing Office.

McDermott, J. F., Jr., Tseng, W., & Maretzki, T. W. (1980). *People and cultures of Hawaii: A psychocultural profile.* Honolulu, HI: The University Press of Hawaii.

Narokobi, B. (1983). *The Melanesian way.* Suva, Fiji: Institute of Pacific Island Studies, University of the South Pacific.

National Association of Social Workers. (2001). *Standards for cultural competence in social work practice.* Washington, DC: Author.

Ritchie, J., & Ritchie, J. (1979). *Growing up in Polynesia.* North Sydney, Australia: National Library of Australia.

Part II: The Voices of Women of Color as Social Work Educators

Chapter 21: Seeking a Balance: Perspectives of a Lakota Woman in Social Work Academia

Hilary N. Weaver

This chapter is dedicated to my children, Iris and Wanblee, my husband, Joseph, my family and supporters, all those who have gone before me, and those who will follow. —Mitakuye oyasin.

My name is Hilary Weaver. I am a Lakota woman in my mid-40s. While not everyone recognizes the term Lakota as referring to one of the First Nations of the Great Plains region, for me it is a more accurate reflection of my identity than broader terms like Native American and American Indian. While I will always remain Lakota, I have also been adopted into the Beaver Clan of the Seneca Nation. This is also an integral part of my identity.

I am currently an associate professor at the School of Social Work at the University at Buffalo (State University of New York). While clearly this is far from my traditional home on the Great Plains (or colonized home of Rosebud Reservation in South Dakota), I believe there is something quite fitting about a Lakota woman in a place called "Buffalo." After all, we Lakota see ourselves as relatives of the Buffalo Nation or *Pte Oyate*.

I have been teaching in Buffalo since 1993 and am now one of the "old timers" in my school. I've been an associate professor since 1999, and now it's time to think about applying for the rank of "full professor." In many ways, it is unusual for a Lakota (or other Native American) even to complete college, much less aspire to the rank of full professor, yet my path has been set by those who have gone before me. While, in many ways, our relationship is strained, I am proud of the fact that my mother was the first woman of color to attain the rank of full professor at Washington State University. At the time of her retirement in the 1990s, she was still the only woman of color at her university to attain that rank.

Currently, I teach in an MSW program and also have some involvement with doctoral students. All in all, I have been in social work academia since I inadvertently stumbled into a teaching job in 1988. Before coming to UB, I taught for five years at the University of Idaho as a one-person social work undergraduate program. That program was dismantled shortly after I left Idaho to come to Buffalo.

Ironically, one of the most devastating policies for indigenous people in what is now the United States contributed to my individual success. After the U.S. Civil War, it became federal policy to remove Native children from their families and communities as a way to destroy their cultures and ways of life. These children were sent to boarding schools, often hundreds of miles away from home, and allowed limited, if any, contact with their families. My grandparents were taken from the Great Plains to be assimilated into U.S. society through a school in Virginia known as Hampton Institute. While now known primarily as a historically Black college (HBCU), Hampton was also a residential training school for Native Americans from 1878 to 1923.

My grandparents were born shortly after the massacre of Lakota people at Wounded Knee in 1890, often cited as the last major stand for independence by indigenous people (or uprising, depending on your perspective). They were born into a time of hopelessness, when they and many others saw no way to survive but to educate themselves in the ways of White European American people. My grandfather believed in education as a survival mechanism to the extent that he went on to earn a master's degree at Harvard and to pursue a doctorate at Yale. In fact, he completed his dissertation, but, at the last minute, was denied his PhD. He attributed this to racism, and, in a rage, he tore up the only copy of his dissertation. As some sort of "consolation prize," Yale awarded him a second master's degree.

Like her father before her, my mother also went on to earn multiple degrees. She was told that the university where she attained her master's degree would not consider granting a PhD to "someone like her," so she went to another university. She ultimately went on to earn her doctorate and teach at the university level for another two decades.

With this family background, my path into academia was relatively smooth. The racism and bigotry I encountered, while painful, were not sufficient to deter me from a career in academia. However, I have always felt emptiness from the destruction of culture that took place in order for my family to find its way into careers defined as successful by dominant society standards. As far as I am concerned, the price of our heritage and culture is far too expensive for an admission ticket to academia. I have benefited greatly from the pain and suffering of others. I do not forsake what they have given me, but I do seek to reclaim what was taken from them. I wish to reclaim our rightful heritage and culture and contribute from these treasures to reshaping academia in a way that makes it more welcoming to diverse cultures.

PROFESSIONAL JOURNEY

A Student and Social Worker

I remember vividly my first day in the MSW program at a prominent New York university. I was excited as I listened to the dean welcome the incoming students as part of the orientation program. He described the composition of our class in detail: the number of men and women; the number of part-time and full-time students; the number of international students; and the number of African American, Latino, and Asian American students. He then paused and joked that we even had one student who did not know what she was since she had checked the box "other" on the registration materials. The dean elicited the laughter he sought from the audience while I wanted to sink under my chair, or, better yet, become invisible. The problem was, however, that I was already invisible. Apparently, whoever created the form did not think that Native Americans or American Indians was a category worth listing on the materials. Not finding a box on the form that represented me, I checked "other" and thus became the butt of a joke on the first day of my eagerly anticipated MSW program. The invisibility continued as I did not see Native people reflected in either the faculty or the curriculum. During my time in the MSW program, I only found one other Native student, who identified herself as being mostly estranged from her indigenous heritage. I found myself largely without role models or peers.

After graduation I worked for a large agency. For the most part, the work was interesting, but even after being there for almost two years, various people in the agency kept referring Spanish-speaking clients to me. I do not speak Spanish and made this clear time and time again. I can only assume that most of my colleagues failed to look past my skin color to see who I really was culturally to accurately perceive my skills and abilities.

A Social Work Educator

I have a great appreciation for how academic freedom allows me considerable flexibility to shape what I do in the classroom. I have been able to draw from the gaps and stereotypes in my own educational experiences and try to do something better for those whom I teach. There is very little oversight of what goes on in the classroom, so I have felt few constraints on what I teach.

Things are a bit different when it comes to publications since they are essentially more "public" than a classroom. What is put into print stays there indefinitely and can be reviewed by others who have the authority to judge "merit." I have had to think twice about whether I feel safe putting some of my thoughts and beliefs in press. This has led to some self-censorship to enhance my chances of surviving in academia. In particular, as I was preparing my materials for tenure review, I was working on two manuscripts in which I used a fair amount of self-disclosure. The first was for the journal, *Reflections* (Weaver, 1997). I responded to a call for papers on what it was like to be a foreigner in social work academia. The issue was targeting primarily authors who came to the United States from other countries, but the theme rang true for me since, through colonization, a foreign nation had taken over my homeland. Writing this article was very meaningful for me, but I was apprehensive about having it as part of my dossier for tenure. My feelings about alienation and not fitting in were not things I felt comfortable sharing with the gatekeepers reviewing my application to the "academia club."

Likewise, about this time, there were violent confrontations between the state of New York and local indigenous nations over taxation issues. I wrote an article on how social workers can be activists on indigenous issues that fit nicely in the *Journal of Progressive Human Services* (Weaver, 2000b). The article took a strong position on the inherent sovereignty of indigenous nations. I clearly believe the New York State government (my employer) was acting unethically in its bullying of First Nations people, yet strong statements to this effect would not win me many friends among powerful people in my university or region. My fears continue to lead me to be cautious in expressing my views on sovereignty and other indigenous issues, even though I have tenure and, supposedly, academic freedom.

PROFESSIONAL CHALLENGES

I face a variety of professional challenges—some overt and some covert. Some might seem rather small to others, but have significant ramifications for me. For example, I was well aware that I had taken a job in a "publish or perish" setting and spent considerable time working on publications. One of my first tasks was to see what publications I could pull out of my dissertation. I was quite excited when I had an article accepted in a well respected journal. After making a few minor changes, I thought I was all set with my first data-based publication. Sometime later, the "proofs" came back, and I was shocked to see how my words had been changed to fit the standard format of the journal. I was informed that the journal did not use the term Native American, so every time I had used that term it had been changed to American Indian. Likewise, the editor changed the term "indigenous" to "aboriginal" throughout the manuscript. It was clear that the editor saw these as purely stylistic changes; I, however, felt they were taking away my right to define myself. If I have no power to define my own identity, I have nothing. I anguished over whether I should confront the editor or pull my manuscript from publication altogether. In the end, I was afraid to compromise a publication that would help pave my way to success in academia and, instead, compromised my integrity. I did not feel I had the strength or power at that point in my career to do anything other than go along with "the system." What may have seemed trivial to others became a tremendous challenge for me: one that I remember more than a decade later.

Another challenge I face is being able to meet the demands of students while also meeting the other demands of an academic career. In particular, Native students have often sought me out for extensive guidance and assistance. I believe this is an important part of my job and an opportunity to give support I wish had been available to me. On the other hand, it is clear that student contact is not the most valued way to spend time in a "Research I" university.

Additionally, my emphasis on serving the community does not reflect the priorities of academia. Native American cultures place a strong emphasis on the well-being of the group. I do not come from an individualistic culture. I believe the skills that I have developed throughout my career have positioned me well to give back to indigenous communities. I can use my writing skills to bring attention to important indigenous issues. I can seek funding to support Native communities. I can try to shape social work academia so there is recognition that indigenous people still exist. Indeed, my sense of giving back to my community fits well with social work notions of community service. Again, however, these are not priorities at a Research I university. Rather, they are seen as detracting from the more valued tasks of obtaining external research funding and publishing.

At times, I have been rather oblivious to some of the challenges awaiting me. For example, at one conference on cultural diversity, two of my lunch companions commended me on my bravery in daring to focus my research and writing in an area where faculty of color are often marginalized. They confided that they would also like to do research on cultural issues, but feared they would never be able to attain tenure with this focus since this area was often devalued. I assured my colleagues that I was not brave, but, in fact, rather naïve. It was not until I was well into my research agenda that I recognized the possibility that the focus of my work and, by association I, would be marginalized and not valued as legitimate scholarship. In this case, I am thankful that I was oblivious to this barrier and naïvely forged ahead. As a person of color, I always felt I needed to have more publications, presentations, and visibility than my colleagues, but I did not think I might have to compromise my area of interest to succeed in academia.

Perhaps my biggest challenge is trying to balance my commitment to being a mother with surviving in academia. In many ways, I think I am fortunate that I earned the protection of tenure before having children. In my publications and presentations, I describe the great value ascribed to the family (including extended-family networks) in indigenous cultures. It would be hypocritical of me to speak of the importance of family and not actively include and value my children. I work to blend professional and family responsibilities as much as possible, but I recognize that some of my colleagues think this devalues work. My family always travels with me to professional meetings and conferences.

My daughter was born when I was serving on the National Association of Social Workers (NASW) board, and she came with me to every meeting until the end of my term. Likewise, both my daughter and son have come to Council on Social Work Education (CSWE) conferences since they were two months old. Fortunately, I now feel secure enough that I will not accept a new service commitment that is not "family friendly." This is a luxury many women of color do not have if they wish to attain professional advancement.

Although challenging, the commitment to balancing family and academia can pay off. A couple of years ago, I delivered a keynote address at a child welfare conference. My daughter, who was then 14 months old, crawled around in the back of the room as I spoke, occasionally making remarks of her own. Afterward, one of the participants commended me and said how refreshing it was to actually have a child present at a child welfare conference. It was an important reminder of why we do this work in the first place.

Last year, I had a similar, but even more visible challenge. As the keynote speaker at Michigan Indian Day, I was asked to address issues of intergenerational healing. As usual, I acknowledged my husband, preschooler, and toddler in the back of the room. Only this time, they did not stay in the back of the room. The children kept running up on stage during my speech, grabbing at microphones, and demanding to be held. I struggled with how I could continue to speak under these conditions. I also believed that I could not turn my children away and be true to what I was trying to communicate about generational issues among First Nations people.

What was the audience thinking? Would I be perceived as not scholarly or a bad choice of a keynote presenter since I was allowing my kids to climb all over me? For me, this incident graphically represents the dilemma I feel in trying to be whom I need to be as a First Nations person and who I need to be as a successful scholar. I had many doubts and no real resolution. I will say that, after my presentation, my arms were exceedingly tired from holding my oldest child for most of my talk.

Although I choose to have my children as an active and visible part of my life, I often receive messages that this is not perceived in a positive manner. My daughter attends preschool in the same building that houses the School of Social Work where I teach. She is particularly visible around the school when I pick her up at the end of her class, and she accompanies me as I wrap up things at my office. Likewise, I nursed my son for an additional year after I returned to teaching. On days when I needed to be on campus my husband would bring my son to me for his "lunch." With both my children highly visible at work, I received many "looks" or less-than-subtle remarks that indicated some of my colleagues perceived me as no longer invested in my work. In other words, since I already had tenure, now I could be a mother and become a "slacker," no longer making a meaningful contribution to the school.

Recruitment and Mentoring

I have mixed feelings about the recruitment of minorities. In many ways, it is a double-edged sword. I would like to believe that I have my position because I have earned and maintain it through hard work. Indeed, I think my credentials are quite good.

I did not realize until I reviewed the materials compiled in my tenure dossier that I had actually been hired on an additional line, and my original salary did not come out of the budget of the School of Social Work. Was I somehow not as good as my colleagues hired at the same time? I know that my credentials are good, but what might other people think? Do they see me as the "token Indian" or an affirmative-action hire? These are very troubling thoughts.

Equally troubling are some of the practices regarding students of color. As a case in point, several years ago, I reviewed an admissions application for a Native American applicant. The application was weak and contained indications of trouble at the undergraduate level. As much as I would like to have more Native students in my program, I did not think it appropriate to admit this particular applicant. Another reviewer, however, made a different decision, which I attribute to wanting to boost the number of minority students without regard for their potential for academic success. In short, I believe the student was used. After numerous years in the program and multiple probations and expulsions, the student ultimately was terminated without a degree. Recruiting must be done in a thoughtful rather than exploitive manner.

Mentoring can be an important method of retaining both faculty and students. Indeed, in a study I did of Native people in professional education programs, the respondents repeatedly mentioned their desire for mentoring and role models and how meaningful it had been to those who received them (Weaver, 2000a). During my early years at the university, my administrator took a strong stance against mentoring. He believed that it was not pro-

ductive to artificially match a junior and senior faculty member and assume that this would result in a productive relationship. Either it would happen naturally or it would not happen at all. I would have welcomed the opportunity to collaborate with a senior faculty person, but the reality was that there were few people either in my department or in the university with similar research interests, with the exception of a colleague at the rank of an instructor with whom I did some writing.

I did not, however, "go it alone;" in fact, my success is largely connected with the support I have received from others. I have never had a mentor per se, but if we look beyond an individualistic model of mentoring, I have had many sources of support, both locally and nationally. One of my biggest sources of support was a women's research group founded by another junior faculty person. It was a nonhierarchical group of women (primarily assistant professors and doctoral students) throughout the university who were focused on writing for publication. We met regularly to critique manuscripts and to support each other in our efforts to navigate academia successfully. Another important source of support is the American Indian Alaska Native Social Work Educators' Association, a national group that provides networking and support. Members of this group intimately understand the struggles of being indigenous in social work education. Indeed, we look out for each other. At a time when another junior colleague and I were moving along toward tenure, two senior colleagues from this association created an opportunity for us to coedit a special edition of a nationally known journal, thus bolstering our academic credentials at a key moment. While not privy to one-on-one models of mentoring, my academic career has blossomed with the extensive assistance of these key groups.

Culturally Based Alternative Pedagogical Strategies

While I do not explicitly use culturally based alternative pedagogical paradigms, who I am as a cultural being is a decisive factor in my teaching style, the way I conduct research, and my service commitments. I believe in inclusiveness and the value of what various participants can bring to a discussion or project. I arrange my classrooms so the students and I sit in a circle to facilitate discussions. I do not lecture at them, speak from behind a podium, or use PowerPoint presentations. While there are different roles for teachers and students, I prefer to facilitate learning through a group process and minimize, rather than reinforce, distances and hierarchies. I use a similar inclusive approach to research in which I value the voices of many participants rather than reinforcing one way of knowing or doing. These beliefs are grounded in my sense of self as a Lakota person and how I am taught to interact with others.

Functioning in a Dual Culture

Functioning in a dual culture means trying to be responsive to multiple demands that are at times mutually exclusive. As a middle-aged Lakota woman, I am expected to take on more responsibility for the well-being of my community. I need to assume a greater role in ceremonial activities and learn traditional knowledge that I can later transmit to future generations. I am positioned as the caretaker of both children and elders. My focus should be increasingly on family, community, and culture; a focus on my individual needs must be supplanted with serving others.

The responsibilities of an associate professor are somewhat different. I am expected to be highly productive as a scholar and to bring in substantial external funding for research. I am expected to maintain a high rate of publication, while taking on increasing responsibilities for the internal workings of the school and university through tasks such as committee service. Likewise, I am expected to nurture and guide junior faculty members.

Both academia and my culture have increasing expectations for me at this stage of my career and life. These expectations pull me in different directions. I try to balance both types of responsibilities, but I frequently find that trying to do both leads to success in neither. I often find that I need to be in two places at once—an expectation that dooms me to failure. For a while, I was semisuccessful at meeting some of my cultural needs and expectations through traveling to South Dakota to participate in Sun Dance ceremonies, an integral part of the Lakota belief system and ceremonial life. Sun Dance conveniently falls in the summer, when I am relatively free from competing academic responsibilities. I have not been as fortunate with Haudenosaunee ceremonies, which are generally set by the phases of the moon, and it is difficult to know in advance what specific dates they will take place. Early in the semester, my calendar fills up with meetings and teaching responsibilities, making it difficult to fulfill my spiritual obligation for nine days of mid-winter ceremonies in January or February.

Fulfilling my cultural requirements necessitates a choice between competing obligations and somehow seeking "special accommodation" that those of other faiths never have to worry about. Christian holidays are institutionalized in the academic calendar. For instance, we never have classes on Sundays, Christmas, or Easter. Additionally, my university is closed on Jewish holidays. I typically do not feel comfortable disclosing my spiritual needs as I am afraid of being labeled as someone requesting special treatment. This could be a dangerous position to put myself in since some already see me as the "slacker mom" who no longer puts energy into academic commitments. I have some job security because I have tenure, but I am still afraid that people in power could make my job unbearable for me if I were to speak up. I have found there are inherent conflicts between the different requirements for success as a Lakota woman and success as an academic. Managing this dualism is a source of significant stress rather than an area in balance.

In some ways, being away from my cultural context is difficult. Indigenous people are inherently tied to their lands of origin. The Great Plains, the sacred Black Hills, and the *Pte Oyate* are shaping influences for Lakota identity, but these are not things I can draw on for daily sustenance, living as I do in western New York rather than western South Dakota. Being away from my cultural context is difficult, but I am also aware that living in the Great Plains would also present challenges. A significant fear that I have is that, in the eyes of some Lakota people, by virtue of my position in academia, I might never measure up as Lakota. Indeed, because of the way education was forcibly used against

Native people as a tool of cultural destruction, there is a lingering suspicion of educated people among many Native Americans. People with a college education are often perceived as "them," not "us." This is particularly true if they continue to work in academia. Nevertheless, I do what I can to maintain and enhance my sense of self as a Lakota woman. My cultural context shapes who I am as a social work educator. It influences what and how I teach, how I conduct my scholarship, and my choices around community and professional service.

Paying the Price for Institutional Support

To achieve institutional support and success in academia, I have made and alluded to many compromises throughout this chapter. These compromises come at a price of dignity, respect, and sense of self. To reiterate three major areas: (1) the type of scholarship I value and feel is appropriate and most beneficial to indigenous communities is not valued as much as some other types of scholarship; (2) my commitment to being an active member of my cultural community takes me out of the office and may lead colleagues and administrators to perceive me as absent or a "slacker;" and (3) because I am a woman of color, some people will always question whether my scholarship is really meritorious or whether I am an "affirmative-action hire." To survive in academia I have made some compromises, such as missing ceremonies and having some quantitative research projects mixed in with qualitative and conceptual work. Ultimately, I can only influence so much of how others perceive me. I am unwilling to totally sacrifice my cultural needs, beliefs, and priorities.

STAYING IN SOCIAL WORK EDUCATION

I stay in social work education because I still believe, on some level, that I can make a difference. What some students experience in my classroom and others learn through my writing may ultimately make a difference in how social workers approach their work with First Nations clients. This is a wonderful opportunity and a significant responsibility. Also, I hope the research I conduct will provide tangible and meaningful benefits to Native people and communities. In a way, I can be a shock absorber or buffer between academia and indigenous people. If I can absorb the negative parts of academia, I can filter the positive aspects through to the benefit of Native people.

Also, I am well aware from both my research and personal experience how difficult it can be for indigenous students not to have role models. I can share my struggles and experiences with others. Native people can see that there is a social worker and an academic who highly values culture and traditions while functioning within a dominant societal institution. In fact, while this is a rather daunting task, I still hold out hope that I may be able to work to transform academia rather than completely being transformed by it.

In spite of all the struggles and challenges I have mentioned, ultimately, I enjoy what I do. I am proud to be a social worker. I enjoy teaching. I even enjoy the challenges of shaping research to make it culturally appropriate. I get positive feedback from my students, which affirms my desire to continue in this line of work.

There are also concrete reasons to stay in academia. I have a family to support. I earn a good salary and have reasonable benefits. Many people in my community do not have this level of stability. While I'm certainly not rich, in many ways, I feel very privileged to have this job. Additionally, the academic calendar does afford me more flexibility than most jobs to try to fulfill my cultural and community responsibilities. Although my schedule is often challenging and stressful, I am able to manage it so I do not have to use daycare for my young children, and I can provide respite for family members caring for elderly and disabled relatives.

RESPONSIBILITIES OF SOCIAL WORK PROFESSION

I believe the social work profession has a responsibility to be open to differences. Being open to differences requires recognition of and respect for the fact that people may have different values, beliefs, and worldviews. I am reminded of a meeting at my school a number of years ago. At that time, there were several people of color and people who identified as gay or bisexual on our faculty. This group of "minorities" was expressing a strong opinion about leadership in the school, while the "nonminority" faculty held a very different viewpoint. In exasperation, a White European American tenured male faculty member stated that, of course, the White European American faculty supported diversity because of whom they hired (meaning the rest of us "minorities"). For me, that interaction was a clear reflection of misunderstanding what it means to embrace diversity. The senior White European American faculty had been open to hiring "minorities," but it was clear that they expected us to think, feel, and see the world the same way they did. They welcomed diversity, but were unprepared for any significant differences. They frantically tried to stuff the parts of diversity that they were unprepared for back inside. Social work education must *truly* embrace diversity.

In addition to being inclusive, it is imperative that social work education draw on its social justice foundation. We need to embrace social justice and model it in the way we govern our schools, the way we teach our students, the way we treat faculty and staff, and the way we interact with the communities around us. We need to critically examine the structures in academia and choose to use those that maximize success for our students and provide a comfortable fit for faculty and staff. If we expect to be truly responsive, we need to be open to change and "think out of the academic box."

THE POLITICAL, ECONOMIC, AND SOCIAL NATURE OF MY ACADEMIC SYSTEM

Sometimes it seems that my school and university are completely oblivious, while at other times they seem blatantly hostile to Native American issues. In fact, I do not remember my school or university ever taking a positive stance on any of the indigenous issues prominent in the news in western New York in recent years. Indeed, only occasionally have individual faculty or students made efforts to connect social work's commitment to social justice and underserved populations with the many contemporary issues of local First Nations communities.

The state (my employer) is often active on Native issues, but in destructive and divisive ways. A few years ago, when local First Nations communities were involved in heated internal debates about whether it would be appropriate to open casinos, the governor of New York issued a long and detailed statement about how no employee of the state university system would be allowed to speak to any Native American. This was an attempt by the governor to prevent any state employee outside his or her office from participating in preliminary conversations that might later lead to negotiations around opening casinos. This bizarre edict made it illegal for any of my colleagues (state employees) to talk to me (a Native American) about anything. If only this had been an adequate excuse to get me out of faculty meetings or committee service. To the best of my knowledge, this edict is still in force, although few people remember its existence.

To say that it is awkward being an indigenous person and an employee of the State University of New York is an understatement. The state is hostile, the school is oblivious, and, for the most part, I feel compelled to be "discreet" about my beliefs, priorities, and culture to remain safe and avoid being targeted. While these reflections on the political, economic, and social nature of the system within which I work are, in part, brief because of space considerations, other considerations limit further reflections as well.

CONCLUSION

In reflecting on the status of women in American society, it is clear that we are devalued. The evidence is irrefutable as a quick glance at salary structures, occupational breakdowns, or the number of women in leadership positions makes clear. The picture is even bleaker for women of color. I know, however, that it does not need to be this way. I come from a culture where women are central to spirituality, governing structures, and the perpetuation of ways of life. My culture teaches me that women are sacred. I draw strength from my cultural teachings to survive as a woman of color in social work academia and in American society.

Living in two worlds is challenging and stressful. It is particularly difficult since the dominant society and its institutions (like academia) show little understanding of, respect, or even tolerance for my culture and belief system. I survive because my culture sustains me. Throughout this essay, I have openly shared some of my experiences, thoughts, and feelings. Perhaps these reflections will be of use to some readers. There may be a Native social worker beginning in academia who feels less alone. There may be a non-Native colleague who becomes less oblivious. There may even be a powerful official who thinks twice before acting in a heavy-handed way with First Nations peoples. Perhaps things will be better for future generations of women of color in academia. I know that I am able to benefit from the struggles of those who have gone before me. Perhaps I can play some small part in making things better for those who will come after me.

REFERENCES

Weaver, H. N. (1997). Which canoe are you in? A view from a First Nations person. *Reflections: Narratives of Professional Helping, 4*(3), 12–17.

Weaver, H. N. (2000a). Balancing culture and professional education: American Indians/Alaska Natives and the helping professions. *Journal of American Indian Education, 39*(3), 1–18.

Weaver, H. N. (2000b). Activism and American Indian issues: Opportunities and roles for social workers. *Journal of Progressive Human Services, 11*(1), 3–22.

A woman who writes has power. A woman with power is feared. In the eyes of the world this makes us dangerous beasts.

(Moraga & Anzaldua, 1983)

Discussion and Conclusions

Carmen Ortiz Hendricks
Halaevalu F. Ofahengaue Vakalahi
Saundra Hardin Starks

Ironically, the process of creating this book engendered the many realities of women of color as social work educators, including being overworked and underpaid. While attempting to make a contribution to this work, the authors whose voices are heard here were also dealing with the realities of balancing the demands of their families, friends, community, and the university; consistently not having a summer break to recuperate; and attempting to complete a rather heavy semester of academic work. Some authors were transitioning to new jobs, new geographical locations, or being considered for tenure and promotion. Several authors were dealing with the hospitalization and death of family members, whereas others were dealing with the aftermath of natural disasters, including the tsunami in East Asia and Hurricane Katrina in New Orleans. For some authors, writing about their personal experiences in the academy was different from any other work in which they have been engaged and, therefore, was extremely difficult. Nonetheless, all of the authors persisted and completed their chapters for this book. In terms of the editors, the time, resources, meeting personally, communicating via e-mail and telephone, and even the deprivation of sleep needed to create this book were all worth it.

As stated in the purpose of this work, the authors hoped that this book would answer questions pertaining to the experiences of women of color in social work education and, thus, inspire self-assessment and advocacy for change in both the person and institutional systems. Indeed, this book honored and brought to life the voices of women of color as scholar change agents; enlightened and inspired all to work toward collective equality and justice; provided a spirit of support among all women; expanded the existing literature on issues of diversity and crosscultural contents; informed future research, policy, and practice; and recognized the value of culturally based alternative pedagogical paradigms.

Using grounded theory (Denzin & Lincoln, 1994), the voices of the women of color as social work educators are critically analyzed for recurring categories, themes, and patterns and their meanings for social work education, practice, policy, and research.

EMERGING CATEGORIES

Three major categories emerged from the analysis of the voices of the women of color in this book: (a) the culture of women of color; (b) the culture of educational institutions and social work education; and (c) the culture of students in social work education.

The Culture of Women of Color

The women of color, in general, expressed a positive perspective of self and womanhood. The callings of womanhood and motherhood were honored by these women of color as they spoke of their mothers, grandmothers, and their own roles as mothers. These women describe themselves, their mothers, grandmothers, and all women in their lives as powerful women or *mana wahine*, sacred women and the house of humanity. Such a perspective is contrary to the dominant culture's idea of Eurocentric, paternalistic less-than-one-down position of women. In the family, community, and university settings, the absolute resilience and perseverance of these women of color shifted them from adversity to challenge to strength. Moreover, these women of color affirmed that they have "earned" every degree, reward, promotion, and tenure. Indeed, these women of color expressed a strong sense of justice and equality, and, regardless of the behavior of the academic system and individuals within that system against these women of color, it has not and will not break their spirits!

Spirituality was consistently identified as the backbone of the success and survival of women of color in academia and the anchor to one's soul. Some of these women of color defined spirituality explicitly as connection to a higher power or God; others defined it as connection to family, culture, and community. Regardless of the definition, connection is the core of their spirituality.

A majority of the women of color in this book are experiencing midlife transitions in ways unique to each woman's family, community, and university contexts. These experiences and transitions speak to age and ultimately link to wisdom that comes with age. Even with some intergenerational differences, these women of color are concerned about those who follow behind them. As a result, mentorship was identified as a crucial part of educational achievements, including the pursuit of the PhD, tenure, and promotion, as well as holding leadership and administrative positions. The women of color expressed that their successes and accomplishments were a result of the contributions of many people from cultures similar to and different from their own. These women of color discussed the strength that comes from being nourished by others, as well as from the act of nourishing others. Moreover, many of these women expressed ethnic and cultural pride, as well as the joy and pain that comes with language preserved or language lost and sacrificed.

The family, including children, parents, ancestors, the community, and those who have gone before, were honored in the stories of these women of color. True to their cultural value of reciprocity, these women of color recognized the expectation to achieve and have given back to those who have paved the way.

The Culture of Educational Institutions and Social Work Education

The women of color affirm the power of formal education to change a person on an individual and communal level, but not necessarily for the better. On a personal level, some of these women of color became hard-core and intolerant toward injustices, yet they remain in the academy to advocate for changes in the system. On a communal level, although education is seen as a survival mechanism by these women of color and a mechanism for making a better life for oneself and one's family, with that same education, a woman of color is seen as suspect by her own community. Some of these communities see a formally educated woman of color as an asset, particularly for younger generations; other communities perceive a formally educated woman of color as an outsider and, perhaps, a traitor. A majority of these women produced doctoral dissertations on issues related to their ethnic culture; however, their work and research is often suspect and not always considered credible or valid by the academy.

In the academy, women of color educators are promised academic freedom, but such academic freedom is defined tightly by the system of administrators, colleagues, and students. These women of color often find themselves trapped or pigeonholed in a box. In other words, administrators, colleagues, and students commonly question the expertise of women of color and seek to approve their selection of classroom discussion topics and research subjects, which are often outside of the White European American box.

For women of color, academic freedom can be a painful reality. Furthermore, these women have to deal with the public nature of publications and legitimizing culturally unique scholarship. In the academy, the demand for publications is seen as a means of publicly legitimizing one's abilities and scholarship. However, culturally unique research, publication, and scholarship, which are the predominant focus of these women of color, are often discounted or devalued in academic and public environments. For women of color, the unequal workload and negative reactions of students contribute to self-censorship and the adoption of the "workhorse syndrome." In other words, a woman of color will work twice as hard and neglect her personal life to prove that she is as capable as or more capable than the next person. Pay inequities are especially prevalent when women of color are asked to administer a program, but offered no additional compensation. Regardless of the situation, however, women of color have and will step up to the challenge and deal with inequitable opportunities for recruitment, retention, promotion, and tenure not only to prove that they are a "qualified person of color," but also to pave the way for the next generation because, ultimately, the academy expects them to represent all women of color.

The Culture of Students in Social Work Education

The women of color involved in this work shared their experiences with students in social work education—predominantly White European American students—demonstrating resistance and opposition in in-depth discussions of diversity issues. Students, predominantly White European Americans, render less respect for the expertise and achievements of women of color, which is reflected not only in classroom discussions, but in poorer student evaluations. It may be valuable for White European American students to recognize the benefits they gain from the expertise of faculty of color, which are as much if not more than do students of color. Although academic freedom is within the purview of an educator, self-censorship often results from student resistance and criticism from colleagues.

The manifestation of the interaction among the culture of women of color, the culture of the academy, and the culture of students in academia and social work education all speak to the themes of marginalization, racism, and duality, as discussed below. Although these themes are amplified in academia as the larger system, for these women of color, the wounds are deeper in relation to social work education because of the possible violation and breach of professional values and ethics that all social workers supposedly vowed to observe. Nonetheless, these experiences also force these women of color to begin transforming the academy and their communities.

EMERGING THEMES

Three major themes emerged from the combined voices of women of color: (a) marginalization; (b) racism; and (c) duality—classic themes in the literature on cultural diversity and oppression.

Marginalization

The women of color in this book say, "Nobody like me has ever been in academia!" Although the professoriate is supposed to be open to all, it still remains mostly White European American, middle-class, Christian, and male. Women of color enter the academy already marginalized. Then the very structure of the academy further marginalizes them with its hierarchical and patriarchal system. There are students, graduate assistants, lab technicians, management information staff, administrative assistants, lecturers, tenure lines, clinical lines, presidents, provosts, and deans, to name a few staff and academic appointments. It is hard to overlook the "pecking order" and degrees of separation. Add the politics of the academy and its mission or research agenda and out emerges the culture of the academy—a maze of inscrutable power and powerless positions or a transformative bastion of scholarship and new ideas. It is easy to be marginalized within this culture if one does not understand how to negotiate the politics of the classroom and the politics of promotion and tenure. The lack of good mentors and collegial support are the biggest contributors to marginalization.

Marginalization is reflected in invisibility and color-blind policies that fail to see the unique position of women of color within the academy. As women of color, we are token representatives of our cultural groups, and it is a sad feeling to be the only one of a racial or ethnic group within a faculty or PhD program dominated by White European Americans. We confront our differences every day.

If we happen to teach in a predominantly diverse or historically Black college, we experience the prejudice and bias toward the school and the inadequacies of students and faculty, and, although not directly pointed at ourselves, it still hurts. Marginalization is most painful when discrimination comes from our own racial and ethnic or gender groups in the form of horizontal violence. When colleagues who look like us and talk like us turn on us, we feel violated in very profound ways. As women of color, we have a right to define ourselves without injuring ourselves in the process. We do not need the stamp of approval by the academy if we can provide our own stamp of approval that says we are true to ourselves and our profession. As women of color, we have just as much right to be in the academy, even if we are learning to walk the walk and talk the talk in new and distinctly different ways.

Racism

In the worst of circumstances, academia promotes a "culture of racism" that further oppresses and dehumanizes women of color. Through prejudice, discrimination, exclusion, tokenism, sexual harassment, internalized oppression, and horizontal violence, we become each other's worst enemy in a microcosm of society. Each woman of color in this book spoke eloquently about how women of color oppress each other and are oppressed by others. As a result, we run the risk of becoming disconnected, oppositional, and angry members of faculty groups. This can lead to bitter tenured faculty intent on revenge. Other faculty will not challenge the status quo and use covert language to address these individuals such as, "You know how she can be when race is mentioned," or "He does not collaborate on any of our projects." It is the fear of confronting racist behaviors on both sides that perpetuates this status quo and furthers the idea that women of color cannot be trusted or are not on a par with other faculty members. Racism has to be attacked on all levels and at all times. The good ole boys' and good ole girls' networks are very much alive, but White European Americans have to fight racism in the academy as much as women and men of color have to fight it. Administration, faculty, staff, and students cannot permit racism to exist in the academy any more than they can allow sexism, homophobia, xenophobia, religious intolerance, ageism, ableism, and classism to exist. These forms of discrimination stifle learning and perpetuate the worst examples of education possible.

Duality

One of the hardest things to deal with as a woman of color is the duality of conscience and experience. As women of color, we have to negotiate the expectations of our own culture and gender with the dominant, mainstream expectations of the academy. Those of us who have adopted mainstream cultural values have struggled to reconcile them with our own homegrown cultural values. We do not want to be seen as "selling out to the bosses," but being equally true to two cultures is a daunting task. Many of us believe that we must help our own, and we share an onus of responsibility for reaching

out and helping our fellow sisters and brothers that White European American colleagues do not always share. We cannot get away nor do we wish to get away from representing our own groups. Sometimes the academy wants us to represent a certain constituency when it is advantageous to the academy, and sometimes it is dangerous to be too identified with a particular constituency. This is a delicate balancing act we play each day.

There are so many stereotypes and misconceptions associated with different groups that permeate the academy. Asians are viewed as high achievers and a model minority group that should be tracked into math and science programs rather than the helping professions. Latino social workers are assigned every Latino client in the agency, and Latino faculty are expected to be good mentors to all Latino students in a social work program. African Americans are perceived to have made strides in the academy and therefore are no longer in need of affirmative-action protections. Beliefs like these sometimes push us to be overachievers and to prove that we are as capable as other faculty. And the duality extends beyond the academy. It involves a commitment to serve our families, the community, the university, and our professions, often putting ourselves last. In this book, the reader has met many overachieving women of color. We have not only succeeded for ourselves, but we have leveled the playing field and demonstrated that we are equal and respected members of the academy. So why do the marginalization, racism, and duality continue to exist?

STRATEGIES FOR PRESENT AND FUTURE SCHOLARS

Balance

The women of color in this book constantly talk about the importance of finding the proper balance between personal and professional lives, emphasizing the importance of both and the need to not sacrifice for either. Role strains and competing demands produce enormous stress in women of color, especially if we are ambitious, dedicated, and scholarly. We want to be true to ourselves while competing in the academy as equals with our colleagues. Most of us learned this balancing act by observing our hardworking and career- and family-oriented "super" mothers. In other words, we were trained from a very early age to put family first, but to keep our eyes on the prize: higher education and all the privileges it brings. We also recognized from the beginning how hard and how rewarding this balancing act would be if we succeeded.

Fight, Flee, Flow

An important aspect of maintaining our balance in academia is to know when to fight, when to flee, and when to go with the flow. Each woman of color shared stories and detailed descriptions of the battles she fought to remain in the academy, and when she would "go with the flow" in the academy. Each of us has spoken passionately about not giving up and running away from racism, sexism, homophobia, sexual harassment, and character assaults. We also spoke eloquently about not selling out while doing what was necessary to achieve the PhD, a tenure-track position, promotion and tenure, and

job satisfaction. Being true to our culture and ethnicity is like breathing and eating and is as important as being a prominent scholar, even when these two worlds would collide. Most of us clearly felt that there was a line in the sand we would not cross when it came to our sense of self and identity as women of color.

Transform the Academy

Transformation of the academy and social work programs is needed on and across multiple levels. As women of color, we transform the academy every day in the way we teach, administer, and pursue scholarship and research. Many of us spoke about how we teach to make a difference, courageously confronting the tough diversity issues that arise in every U.S. class discussion today. We continue to share alternative paradigms in the classroom despite the possibility of being discounted or devalued. We are willing role models for all students, especially students of color. Although role modeling is fraught with all kinds of rewards and dangers, we have a deep appreciation for the needs of students of color and a real commitment to their success.

Transformation is urgently needed in terms of recruiting and retaining more women of color as faculty and administrators. Faculty of color are needed in the academy to reshape or transform it into a more humane and culturally friendly environment for us and future women of color in social work education. We cannot transform the academy if we are not in it. However, to be in the academy, we have to go through the rite of passage in achieving the PhD. Specific to retention, institutions and social work programs must ensure equity in workload and salary; provide genuine support for tenure and promotion; and create a safe system that considers the duality of the lives of women of color. Moreover, we must also transform and control our research. We need to continue our research on issues affecting our communities of color through positive endeavors and not solely deficit models, even if they are not lucrative research topics. Similarly, transformation is needed in terms of recruiting and retaining more diverse students into all levels of social work education—BSW, MSW, and PhD. Likewise, there is a need to infuse social work curricula with more content on diversity and culturally competent social work practice.

This multilevel approach would, indeed, reshape and transform social work education and reduce the stress and isolation that women of color describe in their stories. A diverse faculty, student body, and curriculum would significantly improve the quality of social work services that diverse clients need and deserve. It would go a long way toward changing the discourse and converting scholarship into life-affirming and life-validating practice and research.

Mentorship

Over and above having the support of family, every single women of color credited her success to the efforts of caring and supportive mentors every step of the way in her academic career. In a certain way, this book is a form of mentorship for women of color in the academy and those soon to be in the academy. Some mentors reached out to us, and we sought others. Some mentors helped us with conceptualizing dissertation proposals and understanding the challenges of research, and some helped us traverse the troubled waters of promotion and tenure reviews. Some mentors could be wolves in sheep's clothing who further infantilize and disempower us, but we overcame them as well. Those of us who experienced positive mentorship are "giving it back" in the form of mentoring other women of color or students of color who doubt they can succeed in the academy or who are getting negative messages about their skills and abilities from others. And not all of their mentors were people of color. Mentorship comes in all shapes and sizes. It is about being inclusive and not exclusive. It is about collaboration and connection and not about competition and divisiveness. It is about being secure enough about one's knowledge and expertise that one can comfortably share it with others in the academy. Mentorship is not about weakness, but about strength.

COLLEGIALITY

In addition to mentorship, collegiality was identified as the lifesaving force of the academy. Many of us formed support groups to study for oral exams, wrote articles with colleagues, received teaching tips from fellow faculty, and, above all, felt the support of a community of colleagues. Collegiality, perhaps even more than mentorship, led to our successes in the academy. The academy cannot be transformed unless there is a sense of community—we are all in this together with everyone working toward the mission of the social work program. When social work programs experienced difficulties —directors and staff leaving, budget crises, death, and illness—women of color in administrative positions relied on committed colleagues to work through these difficult periods. We cannot do it alone. We need men of color and White European American female and male colleagues to work together to change the social arrangements that prevent the transformation of the academy into a more inclusive and friendly environment for all students and faculty.

Furthermore, we became very active in our professional associations and relied on equity committees for collegial nourishment. The three editors of this book met while serving on the National Association of Social Workers (NASW) National Committee on Racial and Ethnic Diversity, a committee that connected people of color in a national and international arena. Becoming active in a professional association is a form of mentorship and collegiality that leads to more opportunities for success and recognition in the academy and allows us to exercise leadership within the profession. These professional associations can be more proactive in attracting and nurturing women of color in social work education. For example, when acting as an accrediting body to social work programs, the Council on Social Work Education (CSWE) can ask more incisive questions about the kind of culturally friendly environments women of color experience and if mentorship and collegiality exist and in what form.

Troubleshooting

Sometimes it is easy to find oneself in a verbal altercation when insensitive racist or sexist remarks are flung. However, it is best if we avoid such duels of words and, instead, ask the person, "What did you say?" and "What do you mean by that?" Continue to quiz the person about what he or she is saying to you and why. This clearly puts the speaker, instead of you, on the defensive. Make certain to carefully document such incidents, including names, dates, times, places, and the actual comments. Keep these notes at home, not in the office. If the opportunity arises, audiotape the remarks. Know the affirmative action and sexual harassment policies and procedures of the institution. If the administration is supportive, do not hesitate to tell the chair of the department, as well as other colleagues about the incident(s). Keep others informed about what is going on, share the notes about the incidents, and do not keep quiet! We need to protect ourselves by decreasing our isolation and marginalization. Be confident that you deserve better treatment by administration, faculty, and students.

In summary, the women of color in this book urge us to use the following strategies to succeed in the academy: (a) balance the demands of the academy on both our personal and professional development; (b) pick our battles and choose wisely whether and when to fight, flee, or go with the flow; (c) work to transform the academy from within; (d) seek out mentorship opportunities and work to build collegiality; and last, (e) become active in professional associations that give us opportunities to collaborate with other women of color around the country and around the world. Barriers can be broken, but it takes work and commitment. No one will do it for us. But we can do it together!

RECOMMENDATIONS FOR BUILDING CULTURALLY COMPETENT INSTITUTIONS AND SOCIAL WORK PROGRAMS

To build culturally competent institutions and social work programs, the academy, social work programs, faculty, and students must all be held accountable. Unfortunately, the reality is that most of the women of color in this book created their own culturally competent workplace environments. As they progress through the academy, they have become experts at building strong networks of educators, scholars, and administrators that can transform the academy into culturally competent organizations. However, the academy has a responsibility and obligation as well to transform itself into a culturally competent academy of scholars.

The NASW (2001) National Committee on Racial and Ethnic Diversity recently proposed indicators for levels of achievement of the *NASW Standards on Cultural Competence in Social Work Practice.* Under Standard 5, Service Delivery, are several indicators on building culturally competent organizations, which are appropriate and beneficial for this discussion. Recommendations are as follows:

1. "Effective recruitment of multilingual and multicultural staff." It goes without saying that there is a need to actively recruit and retain diverse faculty to teach diverse students. Women of color should not be token members in social work programs when their demographic representation in the general population is more of a majority than a minority. The academy is responsible for seeking diverse faculty and students and should have specific strategies in place for active recruitment, retention, and graduation of women of color at the BSW, MSW, and PhD levels.

2. "Staff composition reflecting the diversity of the client population." When a social work program is embedded in a diverse community, the staff, faculty, and administration at all levels should reflect the diversity surrounding the institution.

3. "Service planning strategy that includes an assessment of the demographics and demographic trends of the service community." The academy must attend to its surrounding environment, which is ever changing due to the mobility of the population and the influx of new members. Such environmental information and resources also need to inform the curriculum that prepares students to work in these environments.

4. "Expanded service capacity to improve the breadth and depth of services to a greater variety of cultural groups." Social work practice must change as it struggles to respond to increasingly diverse clients through developing more culturally competent practice approaches and methodologies. In turn, such developments must inform the curriculum of social work programs.

5. "Meaningful inclusion of clients representing relevant cultural groups and/or community members representing relevant cultural groups in decision-making and advisory governance entities, program planning, pro-

gram evaluation, and research endeavors." This is probably one of the most controversial indicators of cultural competence—meaningful involvement of community representatives in real decision-making roles in the academy. However, it would be a major breakthrough for the academy to actually listen to its constituencies' opinions and recommendations regarding practice, research, and curriculum development. Likewise, it would be empowering for women of color to see other women of color in decision-making roles in the academy.

6. "Physical plant designed and decorated in a manner that is welcoming to the diverse cultural groups served." In general, the academy should reflect the diversity of all those who work, study, and teach there.

7. "Engagement in advocacy to improve social issues relevant to client groups." The academy should not be silent when human rights are challenged and oppressive policies are imposed on diverse client groups in the community. It should practice what it teaches.

8. "A work climate, through formal and informal means, that addresses workforce diversity challenges and promotes respect for clients and colleagues of different backgrounds." Dealing effectively and sensitively with the issues that arise from having a diverse faculty and student body is the most important challenge for the academy. Confronting biases, insensitivity, and outright racism are the moments that truly test the culturally competent organization's strength and survival.

9. "Documented advocacy for culturally competent policies and procedures of accrediting, licensing, certification bodies, contracting agencies, etc." The academy can be a very active player in, rather than a passive member of, these constituencies. For example, field placement agencies that do not demonstrate cultural competence in service delivery should be assisted in developing cultural competence, or risk disaffiliation with the academy.

10. "Inclusion of cultural competency as a component of human resource management, job descriptions, performance evaluations, promotions and training, etc." Many of the women of color in this book commented on not knowing what was expected of them as new faculty in the academy. However, if women of color are expected to be experts on their particular racial and ethnic group, then this expertise should be valued and considered in promotion and tenure matters.

OUTCOMES: STRENGTHS AND SURVIVAL

Culture, language, spirituality, and family have sustained us through our professional journeys in academia, while marginalization, racism, sexism, and duality have challenged us every step of the way. The culture of women of color in the academy is one of strength and survival. If we survive the challenges, then we gain the respect and recognition we have earned for our scholarship, leadership, and hard work. Women of color in professional roles demonstrate enormous strength in the face of adversity. Comas-Diaz and Greene (1994) write, "Endurance, resilience, self-reliance, and tenacity have been characteristics of many women of color in the U.S." (p. 350). And yet we can never be comfortable that we have truly been accepted by the academy, and we continue to watch our backs for the next assault or challenge. It is impressive that the women of color in this book appear to be resilient, optimistic, healthy, and hopeful considering the struggles they describe. One would think that their self-image and mental health would have suffered from the daily challenges they faced. Comas-Diaz and Greene (1994) studied women of color with professional status and concluded, "The stress of adapting increases their vulnerability to health and mental health problems. Their professional status may make them more vulnerable to depression, anxiety, and other stress-related reactions, psychosomatic disorders, and addictive behaviors" (p. 348). The real question is why we stay in the academy and risk so much of ourselves. We stay in the academy to emphasize the point that we have something unique to offer to social work education. The academy will not break or take our spirits, and our voices will be heard. We believe that barriers can be broken, slowly and gradually, and we hope that those women of color who follow us will complete the circle by benefiting from our struggles and continuing to transform the academy as a place for equality and social justice for all.

My voice is the voice of the town.
My voice is the voice of my generation.
My voice will echo through generation after generation.
What makes you call my speech madness!
Why do you presume to pronounce
The advancing tempest to be an illusion?
(Kishwar Naheed, 1995, p. 83)

REFERENCES

Comas-Diaz, L., & Greene, B. (Eds). (1994). *Women of color: Integrating ethnic and gender identities in psychotherapy.* New York: Guilford Press.

Denzin, N. K., & Lincoln, Y. S. (1994). (Eds). *Handbook of qualitative research.* Thousand Oaks, CA: Sage Publications.

Moraga, C., & Anzaldúa, G. (Eds.). (1983). *This bridge called my back: Writings by radical women of color.* New York: Kitchen Table, Women of Color Press.

Naheed, K. (1995). Speech #27. In F. Rafiqu (Ed.), *Aurat durbar, The court of women: Writings by women of South Asian origin.* Toronto, Canada: Second Story Press.

National Association of Social Workers. (2001). *NASW standards on cultural competence in social work practice.* Washington, DC: Author.

Sooknanan, R. (1995). Heroine. In F. Rafiqu (Ed.), *Aurat durbar, The court of women: Writings by women of South Asian origin.* Toronto, Canada: Second Story Press.

Appendix:
Guiding Questions

The research questions guiding this book are:

1. What are the experiences of women of color in social work education?

2. What personal, social, cultural, and systemic-based factors contribute to success or failure among women of color in academia and social work education?

Additional questions the authors explored include: How does "functioning" in a dual culture, gender and ethnic or race-based, affect women of color who are social work educators? What is the "grow your own" phenomenon in academia as it relates to women of color who are social work educators? What is the price paid for institutional support in terms of dignity and respect for women of color educators? Is parity possible in this arena? Why do women of color stay in social work education? What are the patterns of underrepresentation of women of color in social work education? Does social work education practice what it preaches? To what overt and covert roles, rules, and rituals must women of color adhere? What is the responsibility of the profession to women of color?

Photo Credits

Women of Color as Social Work Educators

Index

C

Candales, Andres, 62

Candales, Arturo, 62, 71

Candales, Barbara A., 61–72
  academic career, 63, 67–72
  biography, 62–63
  education, 63–64, 66–67, 68–69, 70
  Puerto Rican Studies Project, 65–66
  social work practice, 64–65
  tenure and promotion experience, 70–71

Candales, Candelaria Hernandez, 62

Candales, Elba, 62

Carmichael, Stokely (Kwame Ture), 116

Celebrating Social Work (Dumez and Sardella), 110

Central Connecticut State University BSW program, 68, 69–70

Chan, Diana Wei Ming, 35

Charles, Millie, 35, 132

chemistry departments, diversity in, 15–16

Child Welfare League of America, 104

Chun, Jay, 222

Civil Liberties Act, 236

Civil Rights Act, 7, 92

Civil Rights movement, 77, 92–93, 110–11

Clarke, Helen, 105

class differences, 185–86

Cleveland, Ohio, 93–94

closeted resenters, 243

collective unconscious, 137

Columbia University School of Social Work, 104, 106

comadres, 179–80

Comer, M. Jenise, 75–88
  academic career, 80–88
  biography, 76
  education of, 77–79
  personal journey, 76–79, 87
  professional journey, 79–87
  response of majority students to, 83–85
  social work practice, 79–80

  spirituality, 85–86
  tenure and promotion experience, 86–87

Comprehensive Education and Training Act (CETA), 65

confianza (mutual trust), 67

Connecticut Association of Latin Americans in Higher Education (CALAHE), 68

connection, 67

constellated archetype, 137

contrasexual elements, 137, 140–42

Council on Social Work Education (CSWE)
  accreditation of baccalaureate programs, 35
  diversity issues in, 4, 50, 51
  Educational Innovation Exchanges, 54
  learning context and environment standards (Accreditation Standard 6.0), 36
  Minority Fellowship Program (MFP), 36, 50
  Office of Social Work Education and Research, 50
  racial and cultural diversity standard, 35–36

Counter-Affirmative Action demon, 176, 177

cultural competence
  and, notion of, 75–76
  culturally competent organizations, 37, 280–81
  definition, 102
  NASW standards on, 53, 245, 280–81

culture and history
  of African Americans, 113
  of American Indians, 263–64, 266–67, 269–70
  of Asian Pacific Americans, 166–67, 168–69
  dominance of White European Americans, 166–67
  of Hispanic Americans, 67, 179, 215
  Jungian psychology on, 138–39
  of Latinas, 181–84, 185–86, 188–89
  of Pacific Islanders, 251–52
  poverty, culture of, 184
  recognition of value of, 177–78
  responsibility toward, 179
  reverence for women, 9, 140–41, 252, 269–70
  special accommodation requests, 267
  of women of color, 272–73, 281–82

F

faculty of color. *See also* women of color
- affirmative action and faculty appointments, 4, 20–21, 22, 80–81, 213, 264–65
- barriers to advancement, 42–43
- challenges and rewards for, 20–29, 40–43, 87–88, 96–98, 129–32, 197–99
- CSWE racial and cultural diversity standard, 35–36
- culture in academia and, 37–38, 83, 273–76
- data on, 38–40
- educational attainment, 39–40
- by ethnicity, 42–43
- evaluations and reviews of, 27–29, 56, 128–29, 151, 156, 197, 214, 256, 274
- experiences in context, 37–38
- female faculty by rank, 39, 42–43, 91
- historical overview, 33, 34–36
- overachievement response, 22, 51, 117, 177, 197–98, 199–200, 274
- response of majority students to, 83–85, 239
- satisfaction of in academia, 19–20, 227, 268
- service expectations, 26–27, 40–41, 99, 129, 177, 226–27
- strength and survival culture, 272–73, 281–82
- success and survival strategies, 190–91, 202, 244–46, 277–79
- use of term, xviii

faculty women's organizations, 25, 26

fahu, 9, 252

female faculty by rank, 39, 42–43, 91

feminine principle, 137, 140

feminism, 4–5

feminist theory, xvii–xviii, 2, 4–5, 102

fight, flee, flow, 277

First Nations, xviii. *See also* American Indians

Fong, Rowena, 49–50, 252

"For Mereana a Metaphor" (Wineera), 59

Francis, E. Aracelis, 50–51

Friere, Paulo, 157

Furuto, Sharlene, 132

G

gender arrangement, 94–95

gender gap. *See also* wage gap by gender
- in academia, 15–20, 98, 201–2
- employment, 6
- higher education, 6, 14
- political participation, 6

Giddings, Paula, 91

Gil, Rosa, 35

Glasgow, Douglas, 111, 112

glass ceiling, 97–98

Godinet, Meripa, 252

Gourdine, Ruby M., 109–19
- academic career, 110, 113–19
- education of, 112–13
- mentors of, 113
- personal journey, 110–12
- professional journey, 112–19
- social work pioneers of influence, 111

Granbois, Herb, 157

Great Mother archetype, 144–46

grounded theory, xix, 272

"grow your own" programs, 36, 126–27

Gutierrez, Lorraine, 55–56

H

Hall, Gladys, 132

Hammock, Marjorie B., 111, 132

Hampton Institute, 260

Harris, Fred, 106

Harris, Ladonna, 106

hattitude, 124

Heart Mountain, Wyoming, 163, 165

hedgehogs, 177, 178, 180

Height, Dorothy, 132

Hendricks, Carmen Ortiz, 181–91
- academic career, 182
- education of, 182, 183–84

cultural values, 181–84, 185–86, 188–89

double marginalities, 189

mentors for, 188

political participation, 7

promotion and advancement of, 43

publication rates, 42

as representatives of race, 187

stereotypes, cultural, 8, 175–76

success strategies of, 190–91

use of term, xviii, 182–83

wage gap, 7–8

Latinos, 182. *See also* Hispanic Americans

Latino Social Work Task Force (NASW), 53

leaders and legends, 34–35, 47–56, 101–8, 111

leadership

toxic leaders, 232, 242

women as leaders, 228–29

Lee, Serge, 153

lesbian journeys, 179–80

Lewis, Oscar, 184

liberation, 38

life model of social work practice. *See* systems theory (ecological theory)

Lindsay, Inabel Burns, 34

literacy rates, 5–6

literature, academic and popular, 1–2

Lockett, Patricia, 132

Longres, John, 54

Lowery, Christine, 149–59

academic career, 149, 151, 154–58

education of, 149–50, 152–53

evaluations and reviews of, 151

mentors of, 154–55

personal journey, 150–51, 158–59

professional journey, 152–58

social work practice experiences, 150, 155

tenure and promotion, 157

M

mana wahine, 140, 141

Maori culture

Great Mother archetype, 144–46

mana wahine, 140, 141–42

reverence for women, 140–41

stereotypes, cultural, 143–44

marginalization, 2, 189, 275

masculine principle, 137

math departments, diversity of, 16

Mayden, Ruth, 132

Mayes, Clifford, 135–46

McAdoo, Harriette, 112

McAdoo, John, 112

Me Book, 206

Menominee Termination Act, 106

mental models, 240

mentorship and collegiality

benefits of, 51, 132, 179–80, 214, 228–29, 278–79

challenges and rewards of, 23–25, 41, 225–26

characteristics of, 170

glass ceilings and, 97–98

importance of, 48–49, 50–51, 52, 97, 98–99, 132, 273

interdependence of, 25

for Latinas, 188

pipeline for women of color, 98–99

productivity increase with, 24, 25

research efforts and, 22

retention of faculty and, 228–29, 265

tenure and promotion assistance, 98–99, 113–15, 180, 201

methodology, xviii–xx

midlife transition, 139–40

military service, 8

minority

as category, xviii

power position of, xviii

A woman who writes has power.
A Woman with power is feared.
In the eyes of the world this makes us
     dangerous beasts.

(Moraga & Anzaldúa, 1983)